FOSTERING CRITICAL REFLECTION IN ADULTHOOD

Jack Mezirow
and Associates

FOSTERING CRITICAL REFLECTION IN ADULTHOOD

A Guide to Transformative and Emancipatory Learning

Jossey-Bass Publishers • San Francisco

FOSTERING CRITICAL REFLECTION IN ADULTHOOD
A Guide to Transformative and Emancipatory Learning
by Jack Mezirow and Associates

Copyright © 1990 by: Jossey-Bass Inc., Publishers
350 Sansome Street
San Francisco, California 94104

Jossey-Bass Web address: http://www.josseybass.com

Library of Congress Cataloging-in-Publication Data

Mezirow, Jack, date.
    Fostering critical reflection in adulthood : a guide to
transformative and emancipatory learning / Jack Mezirow and
associates.
        p.   cm. — (Jossey-Bass higher education series) (Jossey-Bass
social and behavioral science series) (Jossey-Bass management
series)
    Includes bibliographical references.
    ISBN 1-55542-207-1
    1. Adult education—United States. 2. Learning. I. Title.
II. Series. III. Series: Jossey-Bass social and behavioral science
series. IV. Series: Jossey-Bass management series.
LC5251.M45   1990
374'.973—dc20

89-39667
CIP

Manufactured in the United States of America on Lyons Falls Turin Book. This paper is acid-free and 100 percent totally chlorine-free.

JACKET DESIGN BY WILLI BAUM
The cover illustration is the *ofamfa (hwendua)*,
the traditional Ghanaian symbol for critical examination.

FIRST EDITION

HB Printing   10 9 8 7

A joint publication in

The Jossey-Bass
Higher Education Series

The Jossey-Bass
Social and Behavioral Science Series

and

The Jossey-Bass Management Series

Consulting Editor
Adult and Continuing Education

Alan B. Knox
University of Wisconsin, Madison

Contents

ix

Contents

Preface

In traditional societies learning focuses on acquiring the outlook and the skills necessary to perform according to well-established rituals and customs. Learning in adulthood is confined to preserving these ways of knowing by interpreting them in different practical contexts and perpetuating them by socializing the young. Traditional sources of authority are unchallenged. Old ways of seeing the world and one's life in it become cherished sources of solace and security.

With modernization, old sources of authority, taken-for-granted norms of thought and behavior, and cultural codes that distribute privilege and power are subject to validity testing through rational dialogue. Changing social norms reinforce our need to critically examine the very paradigms through which we have been taught by our culture to understand our experience. This process of critical self-reflection has the potential for profoundly changing the way we make sense of our experience of the world, other people, and ourselves. Such transformative learning, in turn, leads to action that can significantly affect the character of our interpersonal relationships, the organizations in which we work and socialize, and the socioeconomic system itself.

The pervasiveness and significance of change in modern society have become axiomatic. Freed from the inevitable dependency imposed by the socialization process, adult learners can make dramatic gains in self-direction. Understandably, one may find transformative learning threatening, exhilarating, and empowering. Such learning requires interaction with others to iden-

tify alternative perspectives, to provide emotional support during
the process of transformation, to analyze one's own interpretation of one's situation from different points of view, to identify
one's dilemma as a shared and negotiable experience (in the sense
that it is a dilemma by interpretation), and to provide models
for functioning within the new perspective. Clearly, these are
functions for which all kinds of educators, as well as counselors
and therapists, can provide assistance to facilitate learning. It
is the kind of innovative learning that the Club of Rome called
indispensable for dealing with the problems of a modern world,
"the type of learning that can bring change, renewal, restruc-
turing, and problem reformulation . . . a type of learning that
emphasizes value-creating more than value-conserving" (Botkin,
1979, pp. 10–11). Transformative learning can take place without professional interventions, within an educational context,
or within the context of psychoanalytic treatment.

Who Should Read This Book

This book is meant to be a resource for educators, counselors, advisers, psychologists, and trainers who are interested
in helping adults identify the frames of reference and structures
of assumptions that influence the way they perceive, think,
decide, feel, and act on their experience. These perspectives,
which define how we construe meaning, are factors often neglected
in attempts to understand and facilitate adult learning. It is our
conviction that the transformation of these uncritically assimilated habits of perceiving, thinking, remembering, problem solving, and feeling affords the most significant opportunities for
learning, creativity, self-realization, and social action in adulthood. These habits determine what, where, how, and when we
learn, as well as the nature of our perceptions and thoughts about
the world, other people, and ourselves. For the most part, these
frames of reference, which serve as the context for construing
meaning, are culturally assimilated rather than intentionally
learned. Yet we can and do become aware of these *meaning
perspectives,* their sources and their consequences; and, by critically analyzing them as they influence adult learning, we can

transform them. This is a generic process of adult learning, usually undertaken without the help of a professional educator. If an educator assists the learner, whole new dimensions of adult development and action are opened up.

Major contemporary learning theories in psychology have given surprisingly limited attention to the habitual ways in which we symbolically categorize and interpret reality, focusing instead on the more limited subject of how we learn to perform. A transformation theory of adult learning would have as its central focus understanding the nature of these meaning perspectives and how they can be changed to allow exciting new possibilities for realizing meaning and values. It is with such an orientation that this book challenges prevailing adult learning theory and mainstream approaches to adult education.

Fostering Critical Reflection in Adulthood suggests methods and program approaches for precipitating and fostering transformative learning in the context of the classroom, in special workshops, in informal group settings, in collective social action, in counseling sessions, and in the workplace. Each contributing author has identified and analyzed a useful method of analysis or approach to program development to help adults learn about the validity and authenticity of both the assumptions on which their understandings, values, beliefs, opinions, and feelings are predicated and the norms and cultural codes that inform them. The authors draw on insights from adult education, psychology, psychiatry, sociology, and philosophy. Many chapters include approaches and methods of critical self-study that we think will be of direct interest to adult learners who want to gain greater insight into themselves.

Key Terms Used in This Book

Our common concern is *emancipatory education*, which fosters such critical self-reflection. Because the focus and central concepts of critical reflection and transformative learning as used here may be unfamiliar to some readers, we have agreed to use the following definitions in discussing key ideas:

Meaning perspective: The structure of assumptions that constitutes a frame of reference for interpreting the meaning of an experience.

Reflection: Examination of the justification for one's beliefs,
primarily to guide action and to reassess the efficacy of
the strategies and procedures used in problem solving.

Critical reflection: Assessment of the validity of the *presup-*
positions of one's meaning perspectives, and examination of their sources and consequences.

Critical self-reflection: Assessment of the way one has posed
problems and of one's own meaning perspectives.

Transformative learning: The process of learning through
critical self-reflection, which results in the reformulation of a meaning perspective to allow a more inclusive,
discriminating, and integrative understanding of one's
experience. Learning includes acting on these insights.

Emancipatory education: An organized effort to precipitate
or to facilitate transformative learning in others.

Educators are currently interested in *critical thinking,* a term
that can mean many things. Often it has been associated with
logical or academic reasoning, with problem solving, or with
learning the specific language and expectations of a dialogic community. There have been lively exchanges between academics
about critical thinking issues, including the question of whether
critical thinking is an unnatural way of knowing for women (see
"Scholars Debate How to Encourage 'Critical Thinking,'" 1987).
National conferences have been convened, several universities
have created centers for the study of critical thinking, and a
number of books have been written on the subject.

Despite this burgeoning scholarly interest, the concept of
critical thinking continues to suffer from great ambiguity of meaning. In this book, greater precision is made possible by the analysis
of the concept of reflection (in Chapter One), and its three functions: to guide action, to give coherence to the unfamiliar, and
to reassess the justification for what is already known. It is the
last function that is central to critical reflection; all three functions may be involved in critical thinking. The same emphasis

on the critically self-reflective and validity-testing functions of critical thinking that we adopt in *Fostering Critical Reflection in Adulthood* was expressed by Stephen Brookfield in an earlier work (1987, p. 13):

> Being a critical thinker involves more than cognitive activities such as logical reasoning or scrutinizing arguments for assertions unsupported by empirical evidence. Thinking critically involves our recognizing the assumptions underlying our beliefs and behaviors. It means we can give justifications for our ideas and actions. Most important, perhaps, it means we try to judge the rationality of these justifications.

Leonore Langsdorf's definition of critical thinking (1988) comes closest to the view we present in this volume. She writes that critical thinking "is concerned with developing the ability to assess both explicit and implicit claims, so as to determine what I ought to do, or which claim I ought to accept, on the basis of good reasons for that decision — rather than on the basis of force, chance or custom" (p. 45).

Critical thinking is informed by reflection; in the language of this book, it is the same thing as reflective learning. Although it is possible to think without either reflecting or learning, thought that involves critical reflection involves learning.

Overview of the Contents

Chapter One provides a theoretical framework for understanding the nature and functions of reflection — and particularly how critical reflection makes possible the process of transformative learning. In this chapter I identify three kinds of limitations or distorting presuppositions that can hobble learners: epistemic limitations (addressed in Chapters Six and Eight); sociocultural distortions (discussed in Chapters Three, Four, Five, Nine, Thirteen, and elsewhere); and psychic distortions (elaborated on in Chapter Seven). In Part One, we describe six promising program approaches for identifying and transforming frames of reference, which can be used by any professional within either formal or informal learning contexts and may provide provocative insights into anyone's habits of expectation and interpretation. When, where, in what sequence (if any), and for whom these approaches are used will depend on the context and circumstances in which the educator, counselor, or trainer is working and on the characteristics of the learners being served.

Chapter Two describes how meaning perspectives are transformed in workplace learning. Chapter Three thoughtfully reviews how consciousness raising occurred in the women's movement, and the relevance of this legacy for adult educators. In Chapter Four, the context for perspective transformation is collective social action as inspired by the Highlander Folk School and the work of Paulo Freire. Chapter Five describes how critical reflection on racism, sexism, and classism can be fostered through an analysis of meaning perspectives in formal educational settings. In Chapter Six, an informal workshop is the context for transformative learning about how our perceptual filters influence the way we think and feel. Chapter Seven describes an innovation in counseling technology: a computer program embodying many of the benefits of short-term psychotherapy, which can be used by counselors and educators to foster critical reflection on psychic presuppositions that impede learning and adult development.

In Part Two we describe six different procedures for helping learners to become aware of and critically reflect upon their own meaning perspectives. (The distinction between Parts Two and Three is potentially deceptive, in that any approach that helps learners identify meaning perspectives can initiate the process of critical self-reflection that may result in transformative learning.) Chapter Eight presents a provocative, empirically researched model from developmental psychology. It delineates stages in the development of reflective judgment and suggests educational approaches for moving learners toward higher stages. Chapter Nine describes an approach to fostering critical reflection in which the assumptions implicit in the critical incidents of a person's life are systematically examined. Chapter Ten describes the use of *learning biographies* as a basis for analysis and for opening us to the realization that the way we interpret our own life histories (a meaning perspective) is only one among many possible interpretations, some of which may be more insightful than our own. Chapter Eleven details how personal journals can be used to foster critical reflection in the context of transformative learning. Chapter Twelve closely examines the assumptions and presuppositions behind what we see on television and explains how learners can be assisted to become critically reflective viewers. Chapter Thirteen helps us see how we can use literature to help learners question their established frames of reference, by involving them with familiar existential dilemmas of adulthood as presented through works of fiction.

Part Three details four specific approaches for identifying and mapping meaning perspectives. Chapter Fourteen explores the use of repertory grids, an innovation derived from George Kelly's theory of personal constructs. Using these grids, learners can literally and figuratively sort out the assumptions they make in differentiating similarities and differences in objects and events. Chapter Fifteen introduces educators to an analysis of metaphors, which we use not only to describe and explain but also to *construe* our experience. It is often crucial that we become aware of how we have unwittingly permitted the metaphors we use to create meaning for us. Chapter Sixteen describes a systematic approach for transforming reasons given for actions into argument themes that reflect meaning perspectives. Chapter Seventeen introduces conceptual mapping, a procedure that helps learners delineate their meaning perspectives from the way they group concepts in a specific learning situation. Emerging themes and common ground among contributors are identified in the concluding chapter (Chapter Eighteen), which also provides a brief review of instructional methods by other educators for fostering critical reflection. Not every contributor would necessarily agree with the way I attempt to delineate the process of emancipatory education in this final chapter.

Many of the educational approaches described in this book are also adaptable as research methods for studying the nature, significance, and changes in meaning schemes and perspectives. In transformative learning, the line between learning, education, and research often becomes mercifully blurred. The educator becomes a co-learner, helping the learner explore alternative ways of interpreting his or her experience. In the reflection-decision-action-reflection cycle, reflection often comes to mean reflection on the consequences of disciplined inquiry, so that learning and *action research* become moments in the same process.

Each contributor presents a description of a method or approach with illustrations of its use, a brief explanation of its theoretical context and of the process of learning and facilitating involved, and an in-depth explanation of how adult educators can use it to foster critically reflective learning and action.

We have attempted to identify methods and program approaches that can be used by a wide variety of adult educators. Many others that might have been included were not because their practice has hitherto been limited to clinically trained psychologists. Still others, like T groups, were not included simply because they have become so widely known over the past forty years. This is not a cookbook with step-by-step instructions for the educator, but it does present a collection of practical and useful approaches for helping adults to become aware and critically analytical of their own meaning perspectives.

We hope that our book will provide a wide range of educational practitioners with a fresh and provocative perspective concerning the possibilities and approaches for fostering the most significant kind of adult learning, that which opens the way for personal and social transformations.

I want to acknowledge the special contributions made by three persons associated with the publisher, Jossey-Bass. Lynn Luckow's initial encouragement of the concept made the book possible, and he contributed imaginative chapter titles for it. Alan Knox contributed an insightful critique of the manuscript and was instrumental in the reorganization of topics. Candace Demeduc transcended the role of copyeditor to help authors clarify, see discrepancies, and identify oversights. All functioned with consummate professionalism in guiding the production of this volume.

New York, New York   Jack Mezirow
December 1989

References

Botkin, J. W. *No Limits to Learning: Bridging the Human Gap. A Report to the Club of Rome.* Elmsford, N.Y.: Pergamon Press, 1979.

Brookfield, S. D. *Developing Critical Thinkers: Challenging Adults to Explore Alternative Ways of Thinking and Acting.* San Francisco: Jossey-Bass, 1987.

Langsdorf, L. "Ethical and Logical Analysis as Human Science." *Human Studies,* 1988, *11,* 45.

"Scholars Debate How to Encourage 'Critical Thinking.'" *Chronicle of Higher Education,* Dec. 2, 1987, p. 14.

The Authors

Stephen Brookfield is professor of adult and continuing education at Teachers College, Columbia University. He is author
of articles and several books, including *Understanding and Facilitating Adult Learning: A Comprehensive Analysis of Principles and Effective Practices* (1986, winner of the 1986 Cyril O. Houle World
Award for Literature in Adult Education and the 1986 Imogene
Okes award for Outstanding Research in Adult Education) and
*Developing Critical Thinkers: Challenging Adults to Explore Alternative
Ways of Thinking and Acting* (1987, winner of the 1989 Cyril O.
Houle World Award for Literature in Adult Education). He is
currently working on a new book on the adult teaching/learn-
ing process in higher education. Brookfield received his Ph.D.
degree (1980) from the University of Leicester in England in
adult education.

Philip C. Candy is a faculty member in the Department
of Administrative and Higher Education Studies at the University of New England in Armidale, Australia. He has published
articles, papers, and a monograph on personal construct theory
in adult learning, *Mirrors of the Mind: Personal Construct Theory
in the Training of Adult Educators* (1981). He received his Ed.D.
degree from the University of British Columbia in adult education.

David Deshler is associate professor of extension, continuing, and adult education at the New York State College of
Agriculture and Life Sciences, Cornell University. He is author
of several research reports and publications, among them a

recent module for the National Cooperative Extension system, *Techniques for Futures Perspectives* (1989). Deshler is currently working in the field of public policy education for solid waste management. He received his Ed.D. degree from the University of California, Los Angeles (UCLA), in adult education.

Pierre F. Dominicé is professor of adult education at the University of Geneva, Switzerland. He has published studies in the field of evaluation and adult learning and has recently completed a new book on educational biography (to be published in French). He received his Ph.D. degree from the University of Geneva in education.

Roger L. Gould is a psychoanalyst, associate clinical professor of psychiatry at UCLA, and president of Interactive Health Systems. He has written many articles on adult development, the chapter on adulthood in the current edition of the *Comprehensive Textbook on Psychiatry* (1989), and the book *Transformations: Growth and Change in Adult Life* (1978). He received his M.D. degree from Northwestern University and an M.S. degree from the School of Public Health at UCLA, and he is a diplomate of the American Board of Psychiatry and Neurology.

Maxine Greene is William F. Russell Professor in the Foundations of Education (emerita) at Teachers College, Columbia University. She is a past president of the American Educational Research Association and of the Philosophy of Education Society. Among her books are *Teacher as Stranger* (1973), *Landscapes of Learning* (1978), and, most recently, *The Dialectic of Freedom* (1988). She received her Ph.D. degree from New York University and holds honorary degrees from Lehigh University, Hofstra University, and Bank Street College.

Mechthild U. Hart is assistant professor at the School for New Learning, De Paul University. She has published articles on adult learning and is currently working on a book, *Education, Work, and Everyday Experience*. She received her Ph.D. degree from Indiana University in adult education.

Thomas W. Heaney is director and co-founder of the Lindeman Center for Community Empowerment through Education, Northern Illinois University. He has been the recipient of the Mina Shaughnessy Scholars' Award from the Fund for the Improvement of Post-Secondary Education and has published several articles on education for social action. He received his Ph.D. degree from the Union Graduate School, Union for Experimenting Colleges and Universities.

Aimee I. Horton is associate director and co-founder of the Lindeman Center for Community Empowerment through Education, Northern Illinois University. She was a recipient of the Mina Shaughnessy Scholars' Award from the Fund for the Improvement of Post-Secondary Education. Her book *The Highlander Folk School: A History of Its Major Programs, 1932–1961* was published in 1989. Horton received her Ph.D. degree from the University of Chicago in adult education.

William Bean Kennedy is Skinner and McAlpin Professor of Practical Theology at the Union Theological Seminary and professor of religion and education at Teachers College, Columbia University, and the Jewish Theological Seminary of America. He has published articles and book chapters and is coauthor of *Pedagogy for the Non-Poor* (1987, with A. F. Evans and R. A. Evans). His research interests focus on the relationship of ideology to education. Kennedy received his Ph.D. degree from Yale University in religion and an LL.D. degree from Wofford College.

Patricia M. King is associate professor of education at Bowling Green State University. She has conducted research and published articles on adult development and the reflective judgment model, which she developed with Karen S. Kitchener. King received her Ph.D. degree from the University of Minnesota in educational psychology.

Karen S. Kitchener is professor of education at the University of Denver, where she is also training director of the counseling psychology program. She has written many papers, articles, and book chapters on reflective judgment and on ego and moral development in young adults, and she developed the reflective judgment model with Patricia M. King. She is coeditor of *Adult Cognitive Development: Methods and Models* (1986, with R. A. Mines). Kitchener received her Ph.D. degree from the University of Minnesota in counseling psychology.

Joseph Lukinsky is professor of education at Jewish Theological Seminary and professor of religion and education at Teachers College, Columbia University, and the Union Theological Seminary. He has published several articles on education, Jewish education, and legal studies. He has studied psychodrama at the New York Center for Psychodrama and journal writing with Ira Progoff. Lukinsky received his Ed.D. degree from Harvard University.

Victoria J. Marsick is assistant professor of adult and continuing education at Teachers College, Columbia University. She has written several articles and book chapters on learning and education in the workplace and is editor of *Learning in the Workplace* (1987) and coauthor of a new book, *Informal and Incidental Learning: A Challenge to HRD* (forthcoming). Marsick has twice received an award for outstanding research from the Management Institute of Lund (Sweden). She received her Ph.D. degree from the University of California, Berkeley, in adult education.

Jack Mezirow is professor and coordinator of graduate studies in adult and continuing education and director of the Center for Adult Education, Teachers College, Columbia University. He has written articles, chapters, and books on transformative adult learning, adult education, and community development. He coauthored *Last Gamble on Education* (1975, with G. Darkenwald and A. Knox), which received the 1980 Imogene Okes Award for Outstanding Research in Adult Education. He is currently working on a book on transformative learning. He received his Ed.D. degree from UCLA in adult education.

John Peters is professor and coordinator of the graduate program in adult education at University of Tennessee. He has written articles and scholarly papers on adult learning, interviewing, and adult problem solving and is the editor of *Building an Effective Adult Education Enterprise* (1980). Peters is a former secretary of the Adult Education Association of the USA. He received his Ph.D. degree from North Carolina State University in adult education.

Irvin Roth is a psychotherapist in Chicago and an adjunct faculty member of the School for New Learning, De Paul University. He is particularly interested in the areas of communications and reasoning, with specific emphasis on the ways people make meaning of their experience. Roth received his Ph.D. degree from the University of Chicago in psychology.

One

How Critical Reflection Triggers Transformative Learning

Jack Mezirow

To make meaning means to make sense of an experience; we make an interpretation of it. When we subsequently use this interpretation to guide decision making or action, then making meaning becomes learning. We learn differently when we are learning to perform than when we are learning to understand what is being communicated to us. Reflection enables us to correct distortions in our beliefs and errors in problem solving. Critical reflection involves a critique of the presuppositions on which our beliefs have been built.

This chapter elaborates on these ideas to attempt to develop a theoretical foundation for explaining how transformations occur in adult learning. The remainder of this volume addresses the ways educators can foster such learning.

Learning may be defined as the process of making a new or revised interpretation of the meaning of an experience, which guides subsequent understanding, appreciation, and action. What we perceive and fail to perceive and what we think and fail to think are powerfully influenced by habits of expectation that constitute our frame of reference, that is, a set of assumptions that structure the way we interpret our experiences. It is not possible to understand the nature of adult learning or education without taking into account the cardinal role played by these habits in making meaning.

Structuring Meaning

It is helpful to differentiate two dimensions of making meaning. Meaning *schemes* are sets of related and habitual expectations governing if-then, cause-effect, and category relationships as well as event sequences. We expect food to satisfy our hunger; walking to reduce the distance from one point to another; turning the knob and pushing on a door to open it. We expect that it will take less time to get somewhere if we run rather than walk; that the sun will rise in the east and set in the west. When we open the front door, we expect to see our front lawn, not a tidal wave or a charging rhino. Meaning schemes are habitual, implicit *rules* for interpreting.

Meaning *perspectives* are made up of higher-order schemata, theories, propositions, beliefs, prototypes, goal orientations and evaluations, and what linguists call "networks of arguments." Lover-beloved, teacher-student, employer-employee, priest-parishoner, and other familiar role relationships are predicated on established meaning perspectives involving habitual expectations familiar to everyone. Meaning perspectives refer to the structure of assumptions within which new experience is assimilated and transformed by one's past experience during the process of interpretation. They involve the application of habits of expectation to objects or events to form an interpretation. These habits of expectation are analyzed by the writers in other chapters of this book as personal constructs, perceptual filters, conceptual maps, metaphors, personal ideologies, repressed functions, and developmental stages. Learning styles such as "field dependent" and "field independent" are also habits of expectation that become meaning perspectives when used to interpret an event. All these habits of expectation and many other predispositions provide the presuppositions on which we make interpretations and take action.

Meaning perspectives are also the distinctive ways an individual interprets experience at what developmental psychologists describe as different stages of moral, ethical, and ego development and different stages of reflective judgment. Meaning perspectives involve criteria for making value judgments and for belief systems. We are familiar with conservative, liberal, and radical viewpoints and believe we can differentiate an Irishman from a Frenchman or a painting that is ugly from one that is beautiful. Most meaning perspectives are acquired through cultural assimilation, but others, like positivist, behaviorist, Freudian, or Marxist perspectives, may be intentionally learned. Others are stereotypes we have unintentionally learned regarding what it means to be a woman, a parent, a manager, a patriot, a member of a particular racial group, or an older person. In addition to such sociocultural concepts, meaning perspectives may also involve ways of understanding and using knowledge and ways of dealing with feelings about oneself.

The most familiar examples of a meaning perspective and of transformative learning come from the women's movement (see Chapter Three). Within a very few years, hundreds of thousands of women whose personal identity, self-concept, and values had been derived principally from prescribed social norms and from acting out sex-stereotypical roles came to challenge these assumptions and to redefine their lives in their own terms. The women's movement provided a support climate for this kind of personal reappraisal by publicizing the constraints on personal development, autonomy, and self-determination imposed by such stereotypes and by providing support groups and role models.

Perspectives provide *principles* for interpreting. They involve symbol systems that represent "ideal types," the qualities of which we project onto objects or events in our experience. What we then perceive is often seen as an instance of our symbolic categories. Both schemes and perspectives selectively order and delimit what we learn. They define our "horizons of expectation," which, as Karl Popper emphasized, significantly affect the activities of perceiving, comprehending, and remembering meaning within the context of communication (Berkson and Wettersten, 1984, p. 7).

Meaning perspectives are, for the most part, uncritically acquired in childhood through the process of socialization, often in the context of an emotionally charged relationship with parents, teachers, or other mentors. The more intense the emotional context of learning and the more it is reinforced, the more deeply embedded and intractable to change are the habits of expectation that constitute our meaning perspectives. Experience strengthens, extends, and refines our structures of meaning by reinforcing our expectations about how things are supposed to be.

Our habits of expectation are not merely taken-for-granted actions or reactions that tend to repeat themselves. They are dispositions and capabilities that make up our everyday involvement within situations that "make sense." John Dewey saw habit as a structure of experience that enables one to make sense of a situation and consciousness itself as a possibility occasioned by our acquired habits of involvement. "Phenomenologically, the meaningfulness of present experience is an activity of habit, a 'tension' between habitual grooves of sensitivity and the world, through which self and environment are simultaneously transformed" (Ostrow, 1987, p. 214–216). Believing, valuing, perceiving, thinking, and feeling are all affected by these patterns of sensibility and stylistic preference with which we interpret the meaning of objects and events.

To describe meaning schemes and perspectives as powered by habits of expectation that construe and hence structure meaning is not to suggest that they exist as structures of the brain or storage bins for memory. Nor does it imply that experience automatically follows the "habitual grooves" of sensitivity and thus can only confirm our assumptions. This confirmation often happens, but it happens only as the result of the dynamic interaction between habit and the event being interpreted. The process is often mediated by reflection.

Nonetheless, what we do and do not perceive, comprehend, and remember is profoundly influenced by our meaning schemes and perspectives. We trade off perception and cognition for relief from the anxiety generated when the experience does not comfortably fit these meaning structures (Goleman, 1985). When experience is too strange or threatening to the way we think or learn, we tend to block it out or resort to psychological defense mechanisms to provide a more compatible interpretation.

Reflection and Making Meaning

Much of what we learn involves making new interpretations that enable us to elaborate, further differentiate, and reinforce our long-established frames of reference or to create new meaning schemes. Perhaps even more central to adult learning than elaborating established meaning schemes is the process of reflecting back on prior learning to determine whether what we have learned is justified under present circumstances. This is a crucial learning process egregiously ignored by learning theorists.

Reflection is generally used as a synonym for higher-order mental processes. Boud, Keogh, and Walker (1985, p. 3) refer to reflection as "a generic term for those intellectual and affective activities in which individuals engage to explore their experiences in order to lead to new understandings and appreciation." By this definition, reflection would include making inferences, generalizations, analogies, discriminations, and evaluations, as well as feeling, remembering, and solving problems. It also seems to refer to using beliefs to make an interpretation, to analyze, perform, discuss, or judge — however unaware one may be of doing so. Although such a broad definition faithfully reflects common usage, the term needs additional analysis to differentiate reflection from thinking or learning, of which it is a part.

For Dewey (1933, p. 9), reflection referred to "assessing the grounds [justification] of one's beliefs," the process of rationally examining the assumptions by which we have been justifying our convictions. The critical dimension in Dewey's definition is echoed in *Webster's International Dictionary* (1950) as the "mental consideration of some subject matter, idea or purpose, often with a view to understanding or accepting it, or seeing it in its right relations." Dewey's definition provides us with a useful point of departure for understanding some fundamental distinctions regarding adult learning.

Because we must accommodate to a life of continual and rapid change, most of what we learn is the result of our efforts to solve problems, from the infant's problem of how to get fed to the adult's problem of how to understand the meaning of life.

Dewey and William James helped us understand that the process by which we define and solve problems becomes the context for most learning. What is important here is to make explicit the differences involved in reflecting on the content, process, or premises of problem solving.

If reflection is understood as an assessment of *how* or *why* we have perceived, thought, felt, or acted, it must be differentiated from an assessment of *how best* to perform these functions when each phase of an action is guided by what we have learned before. Simply reflexively drawing on what one already knows in order to act is not the same thing as reflection. Instead, this is the way one often takes *thoughtful action* in playing chess or making an argument or otherwise using one's wits while actively engaged. All human action, other than that which is purely habitual or thoughtless, is thoughtful action, which involves consciously drawing on what one knows to guide one's action.

Reflective action, understood as action predicated on a critical assessment of assumptions, may also be an integral part of decision making. Thoughtful action is reflexive but is not the same thing as acting reflectively to critically examine the justification for one's beliefs. Reflection in thoughtful action involves a pause to reassess by asking, What am I doing wrong? The pause may be only a split second in the decision-making process. Reflection may thus be integral to deciding how best to perform or may involve an ex post facto reassessment. When applied to deciding how best to perform immediately, reflection becomes an integral element of thoughtful action. Consequently, although reflection and action are dialectic in their relationship, they should not be polarized as in Kolb (1984).

Ex post facto reflection, which looks back on prior learning, may focus on assumptions about the content of the problem, the process or procedures followed in problem solving, or the presupposition on the basis of which the problem has been posed. Reflection on presuppositions is what we mean by *critical reflection.* These distinctions are graphically depicted in Figure 1.1.

Edward Cell (1984) makes a helpful distinction between active and reflective interpretation. The former can be a creative process but one involving our prejudices, distortions, and pro-

Figure 1.1. Reflection.

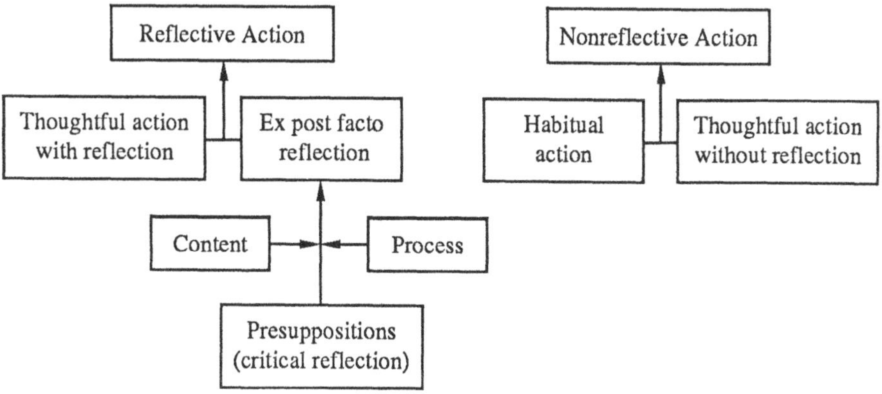

vincialisms. Reflective interpretation is the process of correcting distortions in our reasoning and attitudes. Active interpretation is what is involved in thoughtful action; reflective interpretation, in reflective action.

Instrumental Learning. When we engage in task-oriented problem solving—how to do something or how to perform—we are engaged in instrumental learning; reflection is significantly involved when we look back on content or *procedural* assumptions guiding the problem-solving process to reassess the efficacy of the strategies and tactics used. We look back to check on whether we have identified all the relevant options for action, correctly assessed the consequences of alternative hunches or hypotheses, controlled the right variables, used the best methods of problem solving and used them correctly and carefully, made inferences warranted from the evidence and as free from bias as possible, generalized from a dependably representative sample, and correctly interpreted the feedback on actions taken.

We may also look to make sure that our actions have been consistent with our values, to see how well we are doing in relation to our goals, whether our attitude has been objective and our interpretations of the results convincing. This is how we reflect on the process by which we have learned meaning through instrumental problem solving. *Metacognition* is the term psychologists use to refer to this process of knowing about cognitive states and their operations. The function of metacognition is seen as that of informing and regulating cognitive routines and strategies.

Instrumental learning involves the process of learning to control and manipulate the environment or other people. Results can be empirically demonstrated. The criteria for judging the validity of our beliefs concerning prior instrumental learning reside in (1) an informed consensus regarding the logic of analysis and inference inherent in the paradigm of the problem-solving process we have used and (2) empirical evidence about whether our efforts have succeeded in solving the problem. We can measure changes resulting from our learning to solve problems in terms of productivity, performance, or behavior. The problem-solving process for instrumental learning is a familiar one. Essentially, it is the method of problem solving, canonized by the natural sciences, that we all use or misuse in learning how to *do* things.

Communicative Learning. Not all learning involves learning to do. Of even greater significance to most adult learning is *understanding the meaning* of what others communicate concerning values, ideals, feelings, moral decisions, and such concepts as freedom, justice, love, labor, autonomy, commitment, and democracy. When what is asserted or implied pertains to these norm-governed concepts, judgments, propositions, beliefs, opinions, or feelings, then determining the conditions under which such an assertion is valid requires a two-dimensional assessment. This includes a critique of the assertion itself. It also requires a critique of the relevant social norms and of cultural codes that determine the allocation of influence and power over whose interpretations are acceptable.

Communicative learning focuses on achieving coherence rather than on exercising more effective control over the cause-effect relationship to improve performance, as in instrumental learning. The problem-solving process involved in instrumental learning is the hypothetico-deductive approach. In communicative learning, the approach is one in which the learner attempts to understand what is meant by another through speech, writing, drama, art, or dance. Communicative learning is less a matter of testing hypotheses than of searching, often intuitively, for themes and metaphors by which to fit the unfamiliar into a meaning perspective, so that an interpretation in context becomes possible.

In our encounters with the unfamiliar, we begin with partial insights to direct the way we collect additional data; compare incidents, key concepts, or words; and relate emergent patterns metaphorically to our meaning perspectives. When the properties of the event do not fit our existing schema, we create new meaning schemes to integrate them. Each item of relevant information becomes a building block of understanding, which is transformed by further insight. We continually move back and forth between the parts and the whole of that which we seek to understand and between the event and our habits of expectation, following the process described as the "hermeneutic circle" (Bernstein, 1985, pp. 131–139). Over time, the resulting understanding can be further transformed as we come to discover its metaphoric significance in other experiential, theoretical, literary, or esthetic contexts.

Reflection in communicative learning is a critical assessment of this distinctive process of problem solving, checking to make sure that we have accurately identified the distinguishing patterns of similarity and have found metaphoric labels that give them coherence in relation to a meaning perspective. Interpreting the unfamiliar is one major way meaning is construed. Another has to do with establishing the validity of an expressed idea.

Validating Meaning

Because instrumental learning involves learning to control and manipulate the environment or other people, results are amenable to empirical demonstration. Validating a belief in the realm of communicative learning involves making a judgment regarding the situation and its circumstances in which what is asserted is justified. To understand the meaning of a sentence or any expressed idea, one must understand under what conditions it is true (in accord with what is) or valid (justifiable) (Habermas, 1984, p. 276). We can turn to an authority, tradition, or force to establish the validity of an assertion, or we can turn to a decision by rational discourse, that is, a consensus regarding its justification. In communicative learning there are no empirical tests of truth; we rely on consensual validation of what is asserted.

In everyday situations, we challenge the validity of what is being communicated when we have doubts about the truth, comprehensibility, appropriateness (in relation to social norms), or authenticity (in relation to feelings) of what is said or about the truthfulness of the speaker or writer. Further dialogue is interrupted until we can satisfy ourselves that the problematic assertion is justifiable. We engage in reflective learning through the kind of discourse in which we bracket our prior judgments, attempt to hold our biases in abeyance, and, through a critical review of the evidence and arguments, make a determination about the justifiability of the expressed idea whose meaning is contested. This very special form of discourse is also distinguished by its objective, which is to arrive at an agreement about the justification of an expressed idea as an end in itself.

Because we are all trapped by our own meaning perspectives, we can never really make interpretations of our experience free of bias. Consequently, our greatest assurance of objectivity comes from exposing an expressed idea to rational and reflective discourse. Nonreflective learning is defined by Habermas (1976, p. 16) as learning that "takes place in action contexts in which implicitly raised theoretical and practical validity claims are naively taken for granted and accepted or rejected without discursive consideration."

To seek a consensus, we turn to those we feel are best informed, least biased, and most rational to critically assess the evidence and arguments and arrive consensually at the best judgment. As new evidence and new ways of seeing emerge, this provisional judgment about the validity of a disputed belief is subject to change. Because each situation in which an assertion is true is significantly shaped by social norms and cultural codes, validity testing also implies a critical assessment of how appropriate they are at this time. As situations change, social norms change, and the validity of what is asserted is subject to change as well. The informed consensus we seek is provisional; it is the best we have at the moment. It may be changed with the addition of new evidence or new arguments based on a more inclusive paradigm or meaning perspective.

Ideally, the consensus would be such that any informed, objective, and rational person who examined the evidence and heard the arguments would agree, much as it is assumed in a court case that one juror may be replaced with another, but the jury's decision would be the same.

In reality, the consensus on which we depend to validate expressed ideas almost never approximates the ideal. We never have complete information, are seldom entirely free from external or psychic coercion of some sort, are not always open to unfamiliar and divergent perspectives, may lack the ability to engage in rational and critically reflective argumentation, seldom insist that each participant have the freedom and equality to assume the same roles in the dialogue (to speak, challenge, critique, defend), and only sometimes let our conclusions rest on the evidence and on the cogency of the arguments alone.

Nevertheless, Habermas argues that these standards are implicit in the very nature of human communication. One would not participate in a discourse without implicitly accepting the supposition that genuine consensus is possible and that it can be distinguished from false consensus (McCarthy, 1978, pp. 307–308). As such, these standards can serve as a philosophical foundation and as criteria for judging both education and the social conditions prerequisite to free and full participation in reflective discourse. No need is more fundamentally human than our need to understand the meaning of our experience. *Free, full participation in critical and reflective discourse* may be interpreted as a basic human right. This concept suggests an epistemological foundation for understanding such constructs as rationality, freedom, objectivity, adult development, democratic participation, social responsibility, self-directedness, and adult education.

Critical Reflection

Whereas reflection involves the assessment of the assumptions implicit in beliefs, including beliefs about how to solve problems, there is a special class of assumptions with which reflection has to deal that are quite different from these procedural considerations. While all reflection implies an element of critique, the term *critical reflection* will here be reserved to refer to challenging the validity of *presuppositions* in prior learning. (Although it would be more exact to speak of *premise reflection,* so many of us have used *critical reflection* to mean the same thing that it seems better to continue this practice.) Critical reflection addresses the question of the justification for the very premises on which problems are posed or defined in the first place. We very commonly check our prior learning to confirm that we have correctly proceeded to solve problems, but becoming critically aware of our own presuppositions involves challenging our established and habitual patterns of expectation, the meaning perspectives with which we have made sense out of our encounters with the world, others, and ourselves. To question the validity of a long-taken-for-granted meaning perspective predicated on a presupposition about oneself can involve the negation of values that have been very close to the center of one's self-concept. An example is the time-honored definition of what it means to be a "good" woman, which was questioned through the consciousness raising of the women's movement. Challenges and negations of our conventional criteria of self-assessment are always fraught with threat and strong emotion. Transformation of perspective has cognitive, affective, and conative dimensions. Taking action on a new transformative insight can be blocked by external or internal constraints (or both), by situational and psychic factors, or simply by inadequate information or lack of skill to proceed.

We become critically reflective by challenging the established definition of a problem being addressed, perhaps by finding a new metaphor that reorients problem-solving efforts in a more effective way. This crucially important personal learning dynamic is analogous to the process of paradigm shift that Thomas Kuhn (1970) characterized as the way revolutions occur in science; which, after all, is only a more formal mode of inquiry for construing the meaning of experience. As we encounter new meaning perspectives that help us account for disturbing anomalies in the way we understand our reality, personal as well as scientific paradigm shifts can redirect the way we engage the world.

By far the most significant learning experiences in adulthood involve critical self-reflection — reassessing the way we have posed problems and reassessing our own orientation to perceiving, knowing, believing, feeling, and acting. Arlin (1975) has found problem posing to be the most significant characteristic of adult development beyond the acquisition of formal operations in adolescence.

Although reflection may be an integral part of making action decisions as well as an ex post facto critique of the process, critical reflection cannot become an integral element in the immediate action process. It requires a hiatus in which to reassess one's meaning perspectives and, if necessary, to transform them. Critical reflection is not concerned with the how or the how-to of action but with the why, the reasons for and consequences of what we do.

Perspective Transformation

Adulthood is the time for reassessing the assumptions of our formative years that have often resulted in distorted views of reality. Our meaning schemes may be transformed through reflection upon anomalies. For example, a housewife goes to secretarial school in the evening and finds to her amazement that the other women do not have to rush home to cook dinner for their husbands as she does. Perspective transformations may occur through an accretion of such transformed meaning schemes. As a result of the transformation of several specific meaning schemes connected with her role as the traditional housewife, she comes to question her own identity as predicated upon previously assumed sex stereotypes.

In addition, and more predictably, perspective transformation occurs in response to an externally imposed disorienting dilemma — a divorce, death of a loved one, change in job status, retirement, or other. The disorienting dilemma may be evoked by an eye-opening discussion, book, poem, or painting or by one's efforts to understand a different culture that challenges one's presuppositions. Anomalies and dilemmas of which old ways of knowing cannot make sense become catalysts or "trigger events" that precipitate critical reflection and transformations. Changing social norms can make it much easier to encounter, entertain, and sustain changes in alternative perspectives.

Perspective transformation may be individual, as in psychotherapy; group, as in Freire's (1970) learning circles or in "popular education" in Latin America; or collective, as in the civil rights, anti–Vietnam War, and women's movements. Perspective transformation is the process of becoming critically aware of how and why our presuppositions have come to constrain the way we perceive, understand, and feel about our world; of reformulating these assumptions to permit a more inclusive, discriminating, permeable, and integrative perspective; and of making decisions or otherwise acting upon these new understandings. *More inclusive, discriminating, permeable, and integrative perspectives are superior perspectives* that adults choose if they can because they are motivated to better understand the meaning of their experience. Meaning perspectives that permit us to deal with a broader range of experience, to be more discriminating, to be more open to other perspectives, and to better integrate our experiences are superior perspectives. There are three areas of common distortion in perspective.

Distortions in Meaning Perspective

Meaning perspectives are transformed through a critically reflective assessment of *epistemic, sociocultural,* and *psychic* distortions acquired through the process of introjection, the uncritical acceptance of another's values. While it is desirable for learners to understand how ideology in the wider sense affects distorted epistemic and psychic beliefs, for purposes of making educational interventions these perspectives need to be differentiated from distorted, normative social beliefs, here designated as ideological.

Epistemic Distortions. Epistemic distortions have to do with the nature and use of knowledge. The chapter in this volume by Kitchener and King elaborates on their extensive empirical investigation of reflective judgment, which has identified the developmental stages by which we move away from the distorted presupposition that every problem has a correct solution if we could only find the right expert, and toward a provisional consensual judgment based upon critical discourse. Individuals at each stage have a distinctive meaning perspective about problem solving. It might be more accurate to refer to such earlier ways of knowing as less developed rather than distorted, although any way of construing meaning in adulthood other than one involving reflective judgment — which is developmentally more inclusive, differentiating, permeable, and integrative — could be seen as a distortion of the ideal.

Another epistemic distortion is reification, seeing a phenomenon produced by social interaction as immutable, beyond human control, like the law, the government, atomic warfare, environmental destruction, homelessness, famine, or the military-industrial complex. A third distortion is using as prescriptive knowledge that is based on description; for example, using what psychologists describe as life stages as standards for judging a particular individual's development. Yet another distortion is regarding an abstraction as though it were an existing object, objectifying it (Whitehead's "fallacy of misplaced concreteness"). Interpreting reality concretely when what is required is interpreting it abstractly is a familiar epistemic distortion. Still another is the early positivist supposition that only those propositions are meaningful that are empirically verifiable.

Sociocultural Distortions. Sociocultural distortions involve taking for granted belief systems that pertain to power and social relationships, especially those currently prevailing and legitimized and enforced by institutions. A common sociocultural distortion is mistaking self-fulfilling and self-validating beliefs for beliefs that are not self-fulfilling or self-validating. If we believe that members of a subgroup are lazy, unintelligent, and unreliable and treat them accordingly, they may become lazy, unin-

telligent, and unreliable. We have created a self-fulfilling proph-
ecy. When based on mistaken premises in the first place, such
a belief becomes a distorted meaning perspective. Another distortion of this type is assuming that the particular interest of a
subgroup is the general interest of the group as a whole (Geuss,
1981, p. 14). When people refer to ideology as a distorted belief
system, they usually refer to what here is understood as sociocultural distortion.

As critical social theorists have emphasized, ideology can
become a form of false consciousness in that it supports, stab-
ilizes, or legitimates dependency-producing social institutions,
unjust social practices, and relations of exploitation, exclusion,
and domination. It reflects the hegemony of the collective, mainstream meaning perspective and existing power relationships that
actively support the status quo. Ideology is a form of prereflective
consciousness, which does not question the validity of existing
social norms and resists critique of presuppositions. Such social
amnesia is manifested in every facet of our lives—in the economic,
political, social, health, religious, educational, occupational, and
familial. Television has become a major force in perpetuating
and extending the hegemony of mainstream ideology.

The work of Paulo Freire (1970) in traditional village
cultures has demonstrated how an adult educator can precipitate
as well as facilitate learning that is critically reflective of long-
established and oppressive social norms.

Psychic Distortions. Psychological distortions have to do
with presuppositions generating unwarranted anxiety that im-
pedes taking action. Psychiatrist Roger Gould's "epigenetic"
theory of adult development (1978, 1988) suggests that traumatic events in childhood can result in parental prohibitions
that though submerged from consciousness continue to inhibit adult action by generating anxiety feelings when there is
a risk of breaching them. This dynamic results in a lost function—such as the ability to confront, to feel sexual, or take
risks—that must be regained if one is to become a fully functioning adult.

Adulthood is a time of regaining such lost functions. The learner must be helped to identify both the particular action that he or she feels blocked about taking and the source and nature of stress in making a decision to act. The learner is assisted in identifying the source of this inhibition and differentiating between the anxiety that is a function of childhood trauma and the anxiety that is warranted by his or her immediate adult life situation. With guidance, the adult can learn to distingish between past and present pressures and between irrational and rational feelings and to challenge distorting assumptions (such as "If I confront, I may lose all control and violently assault") that inhibit taking the needed action and regaining the lost function.

The psychoeducational process of helping adults learn to overcome such ordinary existential psychological distortions can be facilitated by skilled adult counselors and educators as well as by therapists. It is crucially important that they do so, inasmuch as the most significant adult learning occurs in connection with life transitions. While psychotherapists make transference inferences in a treatment modality, educators do not — but they can provide skillful emotional support and collaborate as co-learners in an educational context. Recent advances in counseling technology greatly enhance their potential for providing this kind of help. For example, Roger Gould's therapeutic learning program in Chapter Seven represents an extraordinary resource for counselors and educators working with adults who are having trouble dealing with such stressful existential life transitions as divorce, retirement, returning to school or the work force, or a change in job status. This interactive, computerized program of guided self-study provides the learner with the clinical insights and many of the benefits associated with short-term psychotherapy. The counselor or educator provides emotional support, helps the learner think through choices posed by the program, explains its theoretical context, provides supplementary information relevant to the life transition, makes referrals, and leads group discussion as required.

Summary

This chapter briefly adumbrates an emerging transformation theory of adult learning in which the construing of meaning is of central importance. Following Habermas (1984), I make a fundamental distinction between instrumental and communicative learning. I have identified the central function of reflection as that of validating what is known. Reflection, in the context of problem solving, commonly focuses on procedures or methods. It may also focus on premises. Reflection on premises involves a critical review of distorted presuppositions that may be epistemic, sociocultural, or psychic. Meaning schemes and perspectives that are not viable are transformed through reflection. Uncritically assimilated meaning perspectives, which determine what, how, and why we learn, may be transformed through critical reflection. *Reflection on one's own premises can lead to transformative learning.*

In communicative learning, meaning is validated through critical discourse. The nature of discourse suggests ideal conditions for participation in a consensual assessment of the justification for an expressed or implied idea when its validity is in doubt. These ideal conditions of human communication provide a firm philosophical foundation for adult education.

Transformative learning involves a particular function of reflection: reassessing the presuppositions on which our beliefs are based and acting on insights derived from the transformed meaning perspective that results from such reassessments. This learning may occur in the domains of either instrumental or communicative learning. It may involve correcting distorted assumptions — epistemic, sociocultural, or psychic — from prior learning. This introductory chapter constitutes the framework in adult learning theory for understanding the efforts of the other chapter authors, who suggest specific approaches to emancipatory adult education.

Emancipatory education is an organized effort to help the learner challenge presuppositions, explore alternative perspectives, transform old ways of understanding, and act on new perspectives. In the final chapter, I will discuss themes, issues, and methods common to experienced educators who have attempted to encourage emancipatory education.

References

Arlin, P. K. "Cognitive Development in Adulthood: A Fifth Stage?" *Developmental Psychology,* 1975, *11,* 602–606.

Berkson, W., and Wettersten, J. *Learning from Error: Karl Popper's Psychology of Learning.* La Salle, Ill.: Open Court, 1984.

Bernstein, R. J. *Beyond Objectivism and Relativism: Science, Hermeneutics and Praxis.* Philadelphia: University of Pennsylvania Press, 1985.

Boud, D., Keogh, R., and Walker, D., (eds.). *Reflection: Turning Experience into Learning.* London: Routledge & Kegan Paul, 1985.

Cell, E. *Learning to Learn from Experience.* Albany: State University of New York, 1984.

Dewey, J. *Experience and Nature.* (2nd ed.) Chicago: Open Court, 1925.

Dewey, J. *How We Think.* Chicago: Regnery, 1933.

Freire, P. *Pedagogy of the Oppressed.* New York: Herter and Herter, 1970.

Geuss, R. *The Idea of a Critical Theory: Habermas and the Frankfurt School.* Cambridge; England: Cambridge University Press, 1981.

Goleman, D. *Vital Lies, Simple Truths: The Psychology of Self-Deception.* New York: Simon & Schuster, 1985.

Gould, R. *Transformations: Growth and Change in Adult Life.* Simon & Schuster, 1978.

Gould, R. "Adulthood." In H. I. Kaplan and B. J. Sadock (eds.), *Comprehensive Textbook on Psychiatry.* (5th ed.) Baltimore, Md.: Williams & Wilkins, 1988.

Habermas, J. *Legitimation Crisis.* London: Heinemann, 1976.

Habermas, J. *The Theory of Communicative Action.* Vol. I: *Reason and Rationalization of Society.* (T. McCarthy, trans.) Boston: Beacon Press, 1984.

Kolb, D. A. *Experiential Learning.* Englewood Cliffs, N.J.: Prentice-Hall, 1984.

Kuhn, T. S. *The Structure of Scientific Revolutions.* Chicago: University of Chicago Press, 1970.

McCarthy, T. *The Critical Theory of Jurgen Habermas.* Cambridge, Mass.: MIT Press, 1978.

Ostrow, J. "Habit and Inhabitance: An Analysis of Experience in the Classroom." *Human Studies,* 1987, *10,* 213–224.

Parsons, A. S. "The Conventions of the Senses: The Linguistic and Phenomological Contributions to a Theory of Culture." *Human Studies,* 1988, *11,* 3–41.

Schön, D. A. *The Reflective Practitioner: How Professionals Think in Action.* New York: Basic Books, 1983.

Shor, I. *Critical Teaching and Everyday Life.* Boston: South End Press, 1980.

Webster's International Dictionary. (2nd ed.) Baltimore, Md.: Merriam-Webster, 1950.

Part One

Precipitating Critical Self-Reflection: Six Exemplary Programs

Two

Action Learning
and Reflection
in the Workplace

Victoria J. Marsick

Workplaces are not typically associated with reflection or critical self-reflection, ideas that are often considered "soft" and somewhat irrelevant to the hard-nosed, bottom-line, and results-oriented world of business. In the workplace, reflection of any type has been considered a luxury, something that takes place only in the ivory towers of academe, and by its very nature somewhat unrelated to "real life." Yet, paradoxically, reflection is becoming more part of the lifeblood of organizations in today's turbulent economic environment. It used to be that businesses thrived on the unexamined, almost mindless repetition of a proven formula. Today, workers at all levels are called upon to think differently and more deeply about themselves, their work, and their relationship to the organization. This is nowhere more evident than in the ranks of managers, whose very survival is threatened by mergers and acquisitions, downsizing, and flattening of the organizational pyramid. Frequently trained to implement policies rationally, managers are being called upon to make subjective judgments, take risks, and question the assumptions on which they have operated (Mitroff, 1987).

In the preface and introductory chapter to this book, Mezirow draws attention to several concepts further explored in this chapter that are relevant to new demands for learning in the workplace: (1) reflection on experience, (2) the linkage between personal meaning and the socially created consensual meanings embodied in the organization's culture, and (3) the transformation of personal frames of reference. These concepts parallel the three types of learning described by Mezirow.

The first concept pertains to instrumental learning, which will always be a primary focus in the workplace because of the nature of the social contract in organizations. Rapid change has forced workers at many levels to call into question time-honored prescriptive solutions. For instrumental learning to be meaningful, employees must rely increasingly on learning from their own experience. While this has long been true on the shop floor for a variety of reasons, good and bad, it is only recently that more attention has been paid to managers and professionals who learn in this way. Unfortunately, learning from experience can lead to repetition of mistakes. This chapter looks at a program strategy known as action learning, which reduces error by coupling experience with reflection.

The second concept refers to communicative learning, because of the interrelationship between individually held, personally constructed meanings and the body of socially constructed meanings that operate in the workplace. The meaning that people attach to their work and learning is, indeed, influenced by their own personal histories, which are constructed from past interaction with the cultures of families, schools, religions, and communities. However, individual meanings are further influenced at work by the collective meanings and agreements that often remain implicit in the organization's culture. This chapter looks at program strategies that acknowledge the key role played by the examination of these personally interpreted organizational meanings.

Finally, learning as discussed in this chapter reflects a concern for the transformation of personal frames of reference. It is impossible to separate one's professional, work-related knowledge and skills from the rest of oneself. Many people would call this "holistic," although people using that word often fall into the same trap as those whom they criticize because they focus solely on the opposite end of the same continuum, that is, personal development to the exclusion of work-related knowledge and skills. This chapter describes the potential transformation of personal frames of reference that are central to the way in which people see themselves both inside and outside the workplace. Moreover, this transformation is not solely psychological or personal, since workplace learning inevitably involves other people and a common culture.

These three related concepts are examined in this chapter as they relate to action-learning programs, which provide a framework for learning from experience that necessarily involves reflection, that typically also involves critical reflection, and that can — when well designed — involve critical self-reflection. An example from the Management Institute, Lund, Sweden (MiL), is used to define and illustrate action learning. Action-learning programs are much more common in Europe than in the United States. Quality circles, which have some currency in the United States, are based on principles similar to action learning, but they do not always incorporate aspects of critical reflection and critical self-reflection. Action-learning programs can help workplace learners become more reflective and critically reflective. After describing action learning, I will briefly discuss the theory behind it, when it should be used, and some of its potential shortcomings. The next sections will deal with the learning/facilitation process and strategies that can be used through this program approach to foster critically reflective learning.

The Practice of Action Learning

Program Design. Action learning has been implemented in many different ways, but at the heart of it is some combination of action — through project work on real-life problems — and reflection seminars — where participants draw out the lessons learned from their project work. An action-learning program run by MiL is used to illustrate one of many ways action learning can be designed. I believe that MiL's program illustrates reflection, critical reflection, and critical self-reflection (Marsick and Watkins, forthcoming) and that this kind of action learning is highly suited to helping employees learn in today's rapidly changing organizational environment (Marsick and Cederholm, 1989).

MiL often describes its programs as using three parallel tracks: projects (experience and reflection seminars); workshops and seminars around issues that arise from the project work, scheduled as appropriate; and discussion of back-home concerns that arise as participants reexamine concerns from their daily work in light of new learning. The art of action learning rests, in part, on the weaving together of these three strands into an integrated whole. A central theme often helps unify these components. MiL programs, for example, have emphasized themes such as a corporate culture change or a service orientation.

Each of MiL's programs is typically designed for fifteen to twenty people. Programs are sometimes designed for many companies, sometimes for one company, and sometimes for a group of companies that choose to work together as learning partners. MiL runs the collaborative multicompany program every year. Companies are actively involved in selecting themes, deciding on topics relevant to their specific needs, and nominating projects. Companies familiar with the program may invite MiL to run internal programs for their own employees from different divisions, or a group of companies may invite MiL to design a partnership program solely for their employees.

In a multicompany program, each company nominates one or two projects on which it would like to have participants work. Participants are invited to select the project of their choice. This same process is followed with internal and partnership programs except that in an internal program projects are nominated by different divisions of the company, and in a partnership program they are nominated by the partner companies. The project hosts are the people who are responsible for solving the selected problems. They are willing to serve in this capacity because they know they will benefit from the advice of a team of experienced managers. Most companies are highly satisfied with the help they receive in solving difficult problems even though the primary purpose of the project work is learning, not expert advice.

The participants benefit more in a multicompany program because they usually feel freer to ask questions outside the constraints of their own corporate culture and the expectations imposed on them by others because of their status or relationships within the company. On the other hand, the company may benefit more when a program is run internally because the participants form a critical mass who have been helped to think critically and who can be instrumental in carrying out company-wide changes.

MiL holds many of its seminar activities in one of several of its own facilities located in a quiet rural location in southern Sweden. However, some seminars may be hosted by participating companies; or the participants in a program group can decide to hold a seminar at a resort hotel, other public accommodations, or while they are traveling on a study tour to another country. Teams working on a particular project may choose to meet near the site of the company that is hosting their project.

These programs take more time than most training activities because participants must work on real-life problems that do not get solved overnight. For example, in MiL, programs require twenty to forty person-days, but these are spread out over a period of six to nine months in a "sandwich" format, that is, short activities (one-half day to five days each) scheduled in between the regular events of work life. Time is divided evenly between project work, including reflection seminars for small teams, and activities with the entire group. Project teams plan their work flexibly to suit their own schedules. All team members may not be involved in every stage of the project.

MiL staff members design programs to help people learn how to learn — to understand problems, to work with other people in this process, to challenge one another's thinking about related topics, and to gain self-insight. In the opening seminar, participants are introduced to one another, the program, key themes, the companies, and the projects, spending much of the time in small groups, both to begin planning for project work and to gain insight into themselves and the dynamics of the group. About halfway through the program, all project groups gather for a midcourse revision in which the teams critique one another's efforts. The final seminar is oriented primarily toward a discussion of project results, usually in dialogue with project hosts and other contact people from the companies.

In addition to these three project-oriented seminars, several MiL seminars focus on theme-related topics selected in collaboration with participating companies. These seminars are often informal and experientially based, involving simulations, case examples, exercises, and discussion. The tone is one of challenge and mutual inquiry. Finally, at least one seminar, or its equivalent in shorter-term activities, is devoted to in-depth personal insight. This seminar, which at MiL is based on transactional analysis, takes place approximately halfway into the program. That the seminar is duplicated on a voluntary, shorter-term basis for participants and their spouses demonstrates a belief that work cannot be separated from personal life.

Learning from Project Experience. The project experience, and reflection on it, form the centerpiece of action learning around which the other seminars are arranged. With the exception of its senior-executive program, where managers often work on their own problems, MiL generally organizes participants into project teams of three or four in order to multiply the different viewpoints people bring to the situation. People select the projects on which they work but are advised not to choose those in which they are experts, because everyone, including the facilitator, gains most when he or she can ask what might otherwise be considered "stupid" questions. For similar reasons, it is preferable that people work outside their own work units so they can get beyond their assumptions and biases about "how things work around here." A project host, someone in the host company who "owns" the problem, acts as a guide to the team on the culture of the organization, a sounding board, and a link with others in the organization with whom the team wants to interact. Each team also has its own facilitator, someone who both guides the process and catalyzes critical reflection, as will be discussed later. In addition, each team can call upon others for information and advice, much as managers would in real life, and can avail itself of a contact person in the host company, usually in personnel, who serves as a liaison with the MiL staff.

Projects vary, but they share some common characteristics. The problems addressed are not simply puzzles awaiting discovery of a predetermined right answer. They are real dilemmas with real consequences, or problems of the type that often require outside consulting assistance. They are usually complex and touch on different parts of the entire organization as a system. For example, projects involve decentralization, reorganization, corporate identity, relationships among different operating units of a company, new markets, the impact of technology, or strategic issues, such as the unification of European markets planned for 1992.

The project provides a microcosm of experience that is used as a laboratory for learning—about the task itself, about the way in which people work together in groups to solve problems, and about one's own self as a problem solver. The reflection seminars are the vehicle for such learning. There is no recipe for facilitating these seminars, and while they are oriented toward reflection, the seminars are a mix of thought and action. They are task oriented in that they center around a problem, but they are also person oriented in that people are helped to gain insight into themselves as individuals and group members.

The Theory of Action Learning

Revans, originally a physicist, is the best-known spokesman for action learning (see, for example, Revans, 1971, 1980, and 1982), although MiL developed its approach independently of Revans. At the heart of Revans's thinking is his distinction between "P" and "Q" learning, that is, between the programmed knowledge of the past and the questioning insight needed for the future. Revans's work is as applicable today as it was when he began his work during the nationalization of the British coal industry; during a turbulent period when, as today, habitual responses and attempted solutions were often ineffective. Now, as then, it is clear that old answers from the past are not adequate to help people deal with complex problems that change almost as fast as they are formulated.

Revans was considered "unacademic" because of his attempts to blend theory and practice. He noted that managers needed to develop their own "frame of reference for describing, communicating and evaluating the subjective consciousness of personal action." He found academic language "a code of depersonalized abstractions. . . . But the manager who personally challenges reality must first ask 'What view of the me-here-and-now is appropriate in using any of my knowledge?'" (1971, pp. 20–21).

Revans incorporated polarities into his learning design. Prime among these was a then-current dichotomy between religion and science. Revans's work is peppered with phrases and lessons from the Bible; yet the original syllabus he developed for a university-based, action-learning, management-development program was based on the scientific method. It consisted of three interactive system: system *alpha,* or the use of information for designing objectives; system *beta,* or the use of information for achieving objectives; and system *gamma,* or the use of information for adapting to experience and change. Revans noted that there is an objective reality to a problem but that it is filtered through the manager's unique personality, previous practical experience, and predisposing mental set. Errors in interpretation become compounded because this same filtering takes place among those with whom the manager interacts in making a decision. Revans became a strong believer in a continuous learning/change process to counteract this filtering process. At its heart is a dialectic between acting and reflecting on the consequences of action.

Reflection, as described in Chapter One, is central to action learning: The focus is on both finding the right problem and working together with others to solve it. Action learning is also concerned with critical reflection, as seen in Revans's concern for learning, by which a person digs more deeply into the premises that guide the basic formulation of the problem. Action learning can also be concerned with critical self-reflection, although programs do not always take that direction. However, MiL's programs do encourage critical self-reflection. Staff help managers to probe more deeply into the way they view themselves and the way these self-perceptions shape norms that, in turn, influence their interactions with others in the workplace.

Pedler (1983) provides an edited collection of practical advice about how programs are designed and run, not only for managers in business but in other settings, such as communities, social services, and universities. In an appendix, David Pearce discusses guidelines for getting action-learning programs started. He notes that action learning is not the right strategy for problems that are highly technical in nature, where the answer is known by experts, where there is little ambiguity, where there is only one stakeholder, or where the decision maker has decided what he or she is going to do, disregarding other possible options. Action learning is an appropriate strategy, however, when a program designer is looking for a way to help people reflect on, experiment with, and learn from their experience in conditions of ambiguity. Under these conditions, it is often valuable to foster reflection on the problems, critical reflection on organizational norms that govern conditions for identifying and solving the problems, and critical self-reflection vis-à-vis the situation.

Argyris and Schön separately and together write about a process called action science that shares some similarities with action learning (for example, see Argyris and Schön, 1974, 1978; Argyris, Putnam, and Smith, 1985). They distinguish between single- and double-loop learning, using a thermostat to explain this concept. Single-loop learning occurs when simple problem solving takes place—the temperature is simply adjusted to a preset norm. Double-loop learning takes place when one digs below surface expectations and asks why the temperature should be set at that level. There are many differences between action science and action learning. At their best, both involve reflection, critical reflection, and critical self-reflection. Essential to both is dialogue about undiscussable norms, typically achieved through group examination of dilemmas, values, beliefs, and assumptions. However, action science involves a highly defined, rigorous method (discussed in the last chapter of this book), while the methods used by the facilitator in action learning are not codified and are, essentially, left to the skill of each individual. Action learning is thus more flexible and, as such, is more appealing to many workplace educators. However, its impact may be less predictable. It is this author's opinion that action learning can be strengthened by incorporating some of the tools of action science.

The Learning/Facilitation Process

There are three key, integrated components of the action learning/facilitation process: action, reflection, and the building of one's own theories.

Action. The action component is developed in two ways: through appropriate experience, provided by the project work, and through an action-oriented approach to the way in which people learn from experience. The action-oriented approach is a proactive stance taken by teams in solving project problems. Action learning emphasizes finding the right problem, as discussed in the next section. To find the problem, people engage in an active investigation that produces information, upon which they reflect. This leads to a reexamination of the problem, in a cycle that often recurs three or four or five times before the project group can agree on a redefined problem.

One typical intervention in MiL, for example, took place around an electric company's desire to change from selling electricity to providing energy service. The company thought these changes would have to take place primarily at the periphery of the organization, so the project team started interviewing the appropriate people. However, the team members found they then needed to interview the supervisors, and so on up through many layers of the organization. Through this process they involved the company in an organization-development intervention.

Another project team confronted the headquarters (HQ) of a consumer cooperative with the reality that it was not giving full authority to storekeepers to make the kinds of changes HQ said it wanted. HQ blamed the storekeepers, saying that they had no courage and that there was no limitation but the law to actions storekeepers could take. To test these attitudes, the team helped storekeepers do some experiments. For example, at one of the stores, which sold the cooperative's own brand of beer as well as that of a competitor, the storekeeper was posed with the competing beer company's horse and wagon and took a photograph for the company's newsletter. This met with an unfavorable response from the owners of the cooperative, revealing the existence of unspoken rules for making decisions that they expected the storekeepers to follow. Through ths experiment, these rules were made visible, and HQ staff were forced to examine the way in which their actions contradicted their stated beliefs.

As mentioned earlier, each project team is led by a facilitator, who plays a key role in helping the project team do things to find out about a problem — for example, by interviewing people, taking a field trip to try to understand the nature of the problem, asking staff to draw pictures of their understanding of it, or experimenting with new policies and procedures.

Reflection. The reflection component of the learning/facilitation process in MiL's programs ranges from the simple to the critical. This author's research on MiL programs indicates that reflection, which at times is critical reflection, takes place in many interrelated ways. Managers are helped to take off blinders, challenge assumptions, benefit from differences in perspective, and reformulate problems.

Taking off the blinders implies broadening the participants' perspective. As one manager put it, "the problem is that when you are sitting in a company, you are so involved in the process that it's very hard to get a helicopter view of the process by itself." The program removes blinders, in part, by forcing managers to question what they have taken for granted. A good example is a service management program in which participants and staff took over the service at a local hotel for a weekend. Participants questioned their understanding of the service role when, for example, they found themselves waiting on friends at tables in the dining room who did not even recognize or acknowledge them.

Central to taking off blinders is the creation of an unfamiliar environment in which managers can ask what otherwise might seem to be stupid questions and the facilitator can play the role of Socratic gadfly. Facilitators report prodding groups to move into uncharted territory, continually asking their project teams, "What the heck does this matter to you, dear friend?" and drawing a contrast against which reflection can occur.

By asking such questions, the facilitator helps team members to stop and think about things that they ordinarily say and do without reflection.

Challenge is related to this broadening of perspective and occurs at different levels, as does reflection. In some cases, managers challenge their own thinking and behavior and that of people around them in project groups or back on the job. Deeper levels of challenge have to do with fundamental questions, such as those reported by one manager who often asks himself, Why am I working like this today? Why is my organization like this today? Not everyone can understand fully what it is that enables people to challenge themselves and others both during the program and later, during regular work. This was especially true of some employees who had almost literally grown up in their firm, preceded as employees by generations of their forefathers. Before the MiL program, they never questioned the thinking and behavior that was considered appropriate for them as employees.

Action learning is designed to incorporate differences, a practice that helps participants see things from multiple perspectives. As one MiL facilitator indicated, many managers are so involved in their businesses that they are not open to talking with people who have "another viewpoint, another language, another way to see." The program designs differences into the composition of the project teams and into the type of educational experiences offered. For example, artists will be brought in to discuss their understanding of leadership, or participants will be asked to interview people with very different perspectives and then role play that point of view for others.

Finally, reflection is encouraged through what Schön (1983, 1987) calls problem setting or what might be called problem reformulation by the MiL staff. As project teams gather data, they revisit what they thought was the problem, continually questioning whether or not they are dealing with the right problem. Managers generally indicate that their understanding of the problem changes, in most cases, as one manager put it, by "180 degrees." In the electricity project discussed earlier, for example, the problem was gradually redefined, from a need to train local-level staff to be customer-oriented to a need to resolve a conflict at the highest level of the organization between the marketing and distribution divisions. Frequently, the problem starts out with a somewhat narrow definition, but is subsequently understood in terms of the misperceptions and inappropriate actions of people in the company. In many cases, the problem *is* the project host, who "owns" the problem and who must be helped to become reflective or critically self-reflective before the problem can be solved.

Building Your Own Theory. The third component of the process is theory building, which can be interpreted in two ways. First, managers cannot rely on experts to make decisions. They must learn to trust their gut reactions and then to integrate intuition with both rationality and the advice of others. That does not mean that managers should ignore, or be unaware of, the best theory available, nor does it mean that everyone should shoot from the hip. Managers should have the opportunity to test pieces of theory out in a safe laboratory, to combine others' thinking with their own, and to develop the habit of continually testing out their assumptions publicly and getting feedback on which they can reflect. Revans's concept of Q learning fits in well here. In other words, managers cannot be prescriptive in their actions; they must constantly experiment, keep themselves fully open to results, discuss the undiscussable, open their eyes to the deniable, and experiment. Theory building is thus a living, growing activity.

A second interpretation may not be common to all action-learning programs. In MiL, building your own theory also means the development of critically self-reflective insight into onself as both a person and a manager. Unlike many schools of thought in the United States that separate personal and professional development, MiL staff believe that the manager's life outside the workplace is as important to effectiveness as is the learning of specific skills. If a person is not well rounded and balanced in personal relationships, he or she will bring imbalance and tunnel vision into workplace decisions and human interactions. This component involves self-analysis tied to issues, problems, and concerns that come up through interaction with others in the program, particularly project teams.

Facilitation of Critically Reflective Learning

If people could easily learn from one another, as they do in action-learning groups, there would be no need for special programs such as these. However, for a variety of reasons, people do not learn from their experience, or if they learn, they may simply reinforce errors. I will now look at the way workplace educators can facilitate reflection, critical reflection, and critical self-reflection in action learning that helps people learn more effectively from their experience.

Modeling the Process. Facilitators model critical reflection to help people think critically both in and outside of formally arranged activities. For example, at a recent dinner celebrating MiL's tenth anniversary, a participant began speaking in a rather dull, pedantic manner about the programs. Suddenly, what seemed to be a totally irrelevant discussion about the dinner began excitedly at one table. Instantly, the room was in the middle of a full-blown, action-learning drama (of which the speaker was a part) in which staff members joined with their somewhat irreverent skits that commented tangentially on leadership, management, and the "MiL way." A visitor from a well-known training group commented that his organization would never be able to do this kind of thing, but he and everyone else was surprised and delighted—and able to see things from another point of view—as the drama unfolded.

In many U.S. programs it may not be possible for adult educators to take on roles so dramatically different from what is expected. Even in Sweden, such behavior runs counter to mainstream adult learning activities. However, this example is typical of one way in which MiL staff model critical reflection. Without losing the respect of those involved, staff will engage learners round-the-clock in surprising activities that may at first seem irrelevant and that often involve playacting, caricature, and humor. This puts the spotlight on taken-for-granted norms of behavior or thinking and forces participants to reexamine their beliefs about themselves and these norms. The lightness provides an atmosphere in which this critical examination is less personally painful, and where the threat of social castigation for talking about what is usually undiscussable is alleviated.

Modeling the process cannot be reduced to a prescription. Action-learning facilitators can and do trade "what worked for me" stories with one another but never lose sight of the fact that they must rely on themselves and their own best judgment when they are facilitating groups. At their best, they live critical self-reflection, each in his or her manner and style, and hence do not fit an exact profile. Facilitators at MiL come from many different personal and professional backgrounds, and they bring these resources to the process: business, personnel and human resources, psychology, organizational behavior, law, medicine, and the arts.

Facilitators are not simply process consultants, although they must definitely be skilled in group dynamics. Neither are they solely oriented to solving problems, since their primary concern is that people learn even if the projects fail; but they do play a role in helping team members to collect data on the problem, to interview people in companies around the problem design, to carry out surveys, and to engage in a host of other problem-solving strategies. Key words in MiL's own description of this process include "holds back and helps the group grow by letting *them* produce good answers" and "allows the group to make its own mistakes" (Söderholm, 1988). As important as *what* facilitators do are the personal qualities that make them role models. Thus, Söderholm continues, they must be self-confident, insightful about themselves as managers, curious, and persistent in their search for knowledge.

Integrating Personal and Job-Related Development. Among other things, facilitators model the belief that personal development is central to one's behavior on the job. Thus, when designing and implementing action learning, the adult educator must confront the barrier erected in many U.S. competency-based programs that separates the "objective," job-related knowledge or skills "out there" and the "subjective" understanding of "who I am as a person." The starting and ending points for learning can still be competencies needed for the most successful identification and resolution of problems. However, the facilitator recognizes that becoming more competent at tasks often touches on deep personal questions and requires an examination of the "way things are done around here." To put it in Mezirow's terms, instrumental learning often touches on communicative or self-reflective learning needs, although in many competency-based programs, these needs are left to be worked out by the individual. For example, instrumental tasks as technical as learning to use a computer or run new machine-shop equipment may bring to light questions that are not discussed in class, about one's self-confidence or about organizational norms regarding rewards. In action learning, the problems addressed are even more complex and ill defined, and hence can raise many questions about group norms or one's own self-esteem.

This does not mean that education should be psychotherapy or sensitivity training, but it does mean that facilitators should be aware of the territory into which they are moving. When working with issues and concerns that touch on people's self-perception, powerful feelings and long-held distortions are bound to come to the surface. Most of the time, it is just these sensitive, difficult-to-explore issues that hold a person back from being as effective as possible—that are open secrets to co-workers and that often are responsible for poor performance reviews or plateaued careers because no one is prepared to give or receive the feedback necessary.

Perhaps because separation of job and personal life has become such a sacred norm in most workplaces, there may very well be resistance to delving into difficult issues unless the right conditions are created. Ideally, these conditions include a climate of trust, strict confidentiality, respect, active listening, equality of participation, and an ability to help people to examine their behavior as separate from who they are and to understand their capability to change. While the facilitator may not be able to control all of these conditions, he or she can set ground rules similar to those advocated by many self-help and peer counseling groups. For example, all comments must be kept within the classroom and never brought up outside unless the person so requests; when someone speaks, everyone else should give them full attention.

The focus should be on examining and challenging beliefs and behaviors and, as discussed below, trying out new behaviors through role play and critique. However, in the process, strong feelings often emerge linked to personal insights that affect one's work. For example, a woman in an action-science session taught by this author examined a recurring difficulty she had in setting realistic limits on workload, agreeing to take on more than she could manage and not getting appropriate help from co-workers. In working this through with the class, she realized that her professional concerns were often linked to personal concerns — nonassertiveness, difficulty in challenging authority, and hesitancy to ask for what she needed — and with norms in the workplace. She was able to turn this situation around the next time she faced it.

In working through such cases, each person retains the right to either disclose personal information or refrain from disclosing it when queried by others. However, everyone should agree to participate. If anyone is uncomfortable about delving into difficult issues and wishes to abstain completely from the discussion, he or she should be allowed to leave, since complete nonparticipation would seem voyeuristic and might make those who do disclose personal information feel vulnerable. When feelings arise around difficult issues, people should be allowed to vent them, within reasonable limits, without being made to feel uncomfortable. The drawback to this latter qualification is that the culture frequently does not support venting of feelings.

The facilitator can model a willingness to let feelings emerge but simultaneously can challenge self-blinding beliefs or behavior, such as "acting out" as a cover for facing issues. Once feelings have been vented, the facilitator helps people relate insights into themselves to internalized norms defined by the culture (for example, nonassertiveness for women, or over-responsibility patterns for men) and to job-related problems. The facilitator should shift the attention of the person and the group to the dysfunctional actions they have been stuck in rather than to personality issues — and brainstorm about alternative ways of acting in the situation. In action learning, these conditions can usually be met because group members become very close, committed to one another's success, challenged to uncover and discuss the undiscussables, and catalyzed to take new action.

Starting with the Learners' Experience. Adult educators believe in starting with the learners' experience. However, many workplace training programs are expert based, not learner based. Including experience often means holding a practice session in which learners try out prescribed skills. Action learning simulates reality, and reality cannot be designed in advance. Hence, facilitators must both provide a certain amount of structure to enable group members to focus on a task and begin their work, while remaining flexible and open to dealing with group issues that arise spontaneously. In fact, the facilitator must be sensitive to issues the group may not even recognize, bringing them to people's attention and helping everyone make sense of them.

In learning from experience, facilitators help people identify and reevaluate the frames of reference according to which they understand an experience. This is the heart of problem reformulation, sometimes called reframing. To use an example provided by a MiL staff member, the head of a small company that provides technical educational seminars to engineers wanted to reorganize his company to make it more rational in its operations. He felt the central problem was a lack of planning; by contrast, his staff saw the problem as too much planning and not enough action. In many such situations, as in a study by Kaplan, Drath, and Kofodimos (1985), those surrounding a chief executive officer do not dare to confront him or her with what are often open secrets. But the project team in this case "had to give him the message, that you're working too much with words, in writing papers to your group, organizing everything. You have to be more of a leader, taking positions, making your will more flesh and blood." The feedback urged reframing the problem, from one couched in procedural terms for rationalizing operations to a personal statement concerning the CEO's dysfunctional management style. The feedback helped the team and the CEO to reframe the problem. Originally defined as procedures for reorganization and rationalization through better planning, the problem was eventually reformulated in terms of the CEO's ineffective style of leadership. Reframing almost always demands that people understand and examine the context in which actions take place. In reframing, one highlights and questions the backdrop against which problems are understood. In this way, a person sees that a problem can be formulated in many different ways, depending on which aspects of the entire context are selected for attention.

A useful tool for reframing, as well as for helping people become aware of their own practical reasoning and theory building, is a learning journal that can be discussed in groups. It need not be sophisticated; its format will depend on the individual keeping it. To encourage keeping a journal, for example, MiL provides its managers with a blank book entitled "Management" and inscribed with the person's name. Journals help managers keep track of reflections, feelings, reactions, responses, and personal beliefs. Journals also enable a group to build a documentary trail of how the group's understanding of a problem has changed and to track influences on this shift in understanding.

Experience does not just take place in the projects or seminars. To be maximally effective, bridges must be built between insights gained through the program and problems faced back on the job. In some action-learning programs these links are left to the skill of the facilitator, the openness of the participants, and the degree to which the problem commands attention. However, in many situations, leaving this component to chance means that it will not get addressed. Time can be built into the seminars to reflect on back-home concerns, preferably in small groups of three or four. This could be done in project teams if trust is still being built, but people would also benefit from others' points of view to stretch their thinking. Ideally, linking learning in the program and learning back on the job should not be limited to the project groups. Once they get to know each other well, team members' familiarity may itself blind them to alternative ways of seeing or may prevent them from confronting each other with feedback that they anticipate may not be well received.

When people are analyzing a recurring, difficult problem, they often remain blind to the thinking of others because they strongly believe their own points of view; they address one another from their own preformed opinions rather than taking a critical look at what is actually happening. Action-science tools, which are discussed further in the last chapter of this book, could be used to strengthen action learning. Action science is a highly sophisticated method for helping people change their behavior that takes time and coaching to learn, but even minimal levels of mastery help people dig below their surface beliefs and presumptions.

Building Theory Through Action. Projects are central to this learning design because they invite action, but people must be encouraged to take a proactive stance toward them. It is not enough to talk about action; it is in the doing that insights are gained that would otherwise be drowned in speculation. Action confronts people with the consequences of their beliefs. Reflection on action takes place in various ways: as people act and try to make sense of what they do, and subsequently in seminars where they have an opportunity to reconstruct and dig deeper into the meaning of what took place.

Facilitators should help their groups design experiments to gather information about a problem and to try out different solutions to it. They must also help people identify and examine what Scribner (1984, p. 9) calls "practical thinking" in their theories: "all thinking embedded in larger activities and that functions to carry out the goals of those activities." Usher (1988) contrasts this practical thinking, which he relates to informal theory, with more formally constructed theories. Informal theory is an integrated blend of "personal experience, values and transmitted knowledge" (p. 434) and is thus linked to formal theory through transmitted knowledge. However, much informal theory is based on unexamined, habitual, routine responses and thinking. Usher suggests that practitioners can build their own theories more effectively (and critique formal theory) when they "review" their informal theories by contrasting them with formal theory: "The term 'review,' given its connotation of 'looking back' and 're-considering,' aptly characterizes the process" (p. 435).

To combine action with review, facilitators must help people make explicit what often remains implicit, that is, what Polanyi (1967) calls "tacit knowing." Since people are frequently unaware of their informal theories, facilitators and participants alike in action learning must give feedback to others about what they perceive them as doing. As one MiL staff member put it, the facilitator acts as a mirror to show people what they are saying and doing, and to explore with them the possible links between their action and their beliefs about this action.

Review goes one step further. Once a person is aware of his or her informal theories, he or she must contrast these with other people's theories and with theories in the literature about the same phenomena. As this critique is carried out, people can begin to explore the way in which their impressions of reality have been shaped by the sociocultural context in which they form and sustain their beliefs. Journals are helpful here, since people can keep an ongoing record of their actions, feedback, beliefs, and assumptions and then compare their own theories with those of others: the ways in which their theories are similar or different and how they are contradicted or reinforced by experience.

Summary and Conclusion

Action learning combines individual responsibility and reflection on personal experience with comprehensive attention to the multiple perspectives of various stakeholders within a social unit — in this case, the organization. It is thus oriented to problem solving, but with a twist, since the emphasis is on helping people better understand and formulate problems through continual cycles of action (implementation of some sort) and reflection on, and in, action (to use terminology developed by Schön, 1983, 1987). In this way, people identify their practical reasoning and begin to build personal theories of action, a concept on which Mezirow expands in the last chapter of this book.

Action learning is uniquely suited to critical reflection in the workplace because it helps people, both individually and collectively, make explicit and then question the social norms that govern their action; people begin to be attuned to the way they help create and maintain meanings, often without questioning them, and the way their untested assumptions, beliefs, and expectations influence their perception of factors that influence and sometimes limit their thinking and decision making.

Action learning is highly compatible with many of the premises on which adult education is built. It is driven by peers, focused on immediate problems, based on learner experience, and highly participatory. Because action learning is built around real-life problems with real consequences, learners are usually motivated to deal with issues that arise that block understanding and solution of the problem, even though many of these issues stem from misperceptions, beliefs, and dysfunctional habits that raise powerful feelings and often have not been examined before. Unlike in many situations where the stimulus for learning is artificial, in action learning learners are not inclined to evade issues, because they see how relevant they are to effective action. This is particularly true when participants work in teams, because colleagues who are peers give feedback that participants find difficult to dismiss under pressurized, but relatively safe, conditions.

For action learning to be effective, a climate must be fostered that allows participants to examine beliefs, practices, and norms. The facilitator is central to this process. He or she ensures that people look at a problem from many perspectives, challenge one another and themselves, ask "stupid" questions, draw contrasts, probe connections, try out new behaviors, see and confront their own dysfunctional behavior, act when they would rather talk, and reflect some more when they are ready to act prematurely to solve a problem that has not been thoroughly considered. There is no prescription for this kind of facilitation, although much can be learned from watching those who do it well.

Action-learning practitioners advocate reflection because of their interest in learning instrumentally from experience with pressing work-related problems. They advocate critical reflection because of their central concern with Q learning, which leads to questioning of premises on which problems are defined, over P learning. And, in programs, such as those at MiL, action-learning practitioners advocate critically self-reflective learning because it is clear that the transformation of personally held meaning schemes affects socially constructed meaning schemes in the organization.

References

Argyris, C., Putnam, R., and Smith, D. M. *Action Science: Concepts, Methods, and Skills for Research and Intervention.* San Francisco: Jossey-Bass, 1985.

Argyris, C., and Schön, D. A. *Theory in Practice: Increasing Professional Effectiveness.* San Francisco: Jossey-Bass, 1974.

Argyris, C., and Schön, D. A. *Organizational Learning: A Theory of Action Perspective.* Reading, Mass.: Addison-Wesley, 1978.

Kaplan, R. E., Drath, W. H., and Kofodimos, J. R. *High Hurdles: The Challenge of Executive Self-Development.* Technical Report no. 25. Greensboro, N.C.: Center for Creative Leadership, 1985.

Marsick, V. J., and Cederholm, L. "Developing Leadership in International Managers — An Urgent Challenge." *Columbia Journal of World Business,* 1989, *23* (4), 3–11.

Marsick, V. J., and Watkins, K. E. *Informal and Incidental Learning: A Challenge to HRD.* London, England: Routledge & Kegan Paul, forthcoming.

Mitroff, I. I. *Business Not as Usual: Rethinking Our Individual, Corporate, and Industrial Strategies for Global Competition.* San Francisco: Jossey-Bass, 1987.

Pedler, M. (ed.). *Action Learning in Practice.* Aldershot, England: Gower, 1983.

Polanyi, M. *The Tacit Dimension.* New York: Doubleday, 1967.

Revans, R. W. *Developing Effective Managers: A New Approach to Business Education.* New York: Praeger, 1971.

Revans, R. W. *Action Learning.* London: Blond & Briggs, 1980.

Revans, R. W. *The Origin and Growth of Action Learning.* Bickley, England: Chartwell-Bratt, 1982.

Schön, D. A. *The Reflective Practitioner: How Professionals Think in Action.* New York: Basic Books, 1983.

Schön, D. A. *Educating the Reflective Practitioner: Toward a New Design for Teaching and Learning in the Professions.* San Francisco: Jossey-Bass, 1987.

Scribner, S. "Studying Working Intelligence." In B. Rogoff and J. Lave (eds.), *Everyday Cognition: Its Development in Social Context.* Cambridge, Mass.: Harvard University Press, 1984.

Söderholm, J. "The Role of the Facilitator in Action Learning Management Training Programs." Unpublished paper, Management Institute, Lund, Sweden, 1988.

Usher, R. "The Practical and the Critical in the Study of Adult Education." In M. Zukas (ed.), *Papers from the Transatlantic Dialogue.* Papers from the combined meeting of the Standing Conference on University Teaching and Research in the Education of Adults, Adult Education Research Conference, and Canadian Association for the Study of Adult Education, University of Leeds, July 11–13, 1988. Leeds, England: School of Continuing Education, University of Leeds, 1988.

Three

Liberation Through Consciousness Raising

Mechthild U. Hart

To write about consciousness raising is to write about an experience of personal and social transformation that pulsates with the joy and pain of subversive power. Twenty years later it is difficult to recapture the spontaneity and scandalousness of women coming together, deliberately excluding men, talking in a way that named what had not been named and revealed what had been silenced, ridiculed, or denied. Twenty years later the explosiveness of women trying to to find their own voice has been transformed into a formidable body of feminist theory based on a continued and ever-widening examination of those early ideas and practices and of new and different ones as well. We can look back on the consciousness raising of twenty years ago from our present, more knowledgeable vantage point—more sober and disillusioned than in those heady years, and more critical of past mistakes and shortcomings in our analysis and practice. Many of the themes discussed in the early consciousness-raising groups have been co-opted by the media, taking away their critical sting; consciousness raising has been sucked into the whirlpool of the conformist therapeutic self-help and self-improvement movement of the seventies and eighties. A strong social and political conservatism today directly fosters antifeminist ideas and policies.

When I accepted the task to evaluate consciousness raising as a "tool for transformative learning," I asked myself the question: Is it possible to take consciousness raising out of its original context—which fueled its very existence—and to place it into a general, broadly defined, and therefore necessarily vague adult education context? At first glance, the answer is a qualified no. Qualified, because consciousness raising reckons with the internal and external effect of power, which precisely makes it a form of emancipatory learning, entailing the processes of critical reflection and self-reflection and involving a transformation of meaning perspectives. No, because it remains bound to threefold, interwoven dimensions of its content, methods, and epistemological presuppositions: an analysis of sexual oppression, a grounding of this analysis in everyday experience, and a structure of analysis that calls for a reciprocal, interactive relationship among knowers who are linked by common experiences, as well as between the knowers and their object of knowing. In other words, consciousness raising is part and parcel of a *feminist education.*

If, however, the concerns that influence feminist theory and practice are considered to be universally valid, because they examine, criticize, and act upon power relations that are fundamental and that permeate every single aspect of social and individual life, at second glance the answer to my question becomes an unqualified yes.

In the following, I want to broadly outline the historical context that produced consciousness-raising groups in order to clarify the impetus behind these groups as well as the major elements of an incipient feminist theory that was to emerge, expand, and diversify in the decades to come.

The women's liberation groups, among which consciousness-raising groups have to be counted, have their origin in the various movements of the New Left. They were formed by women who had become exasperated with their male comrades' sexist expectations and treatment and who realized that their attempts to publicly discuss their complaints and concerns were bound to fail precisely for the same reasons that lay behind their oppression in the first place: Their experiences, as *women's* experiences, were considered irrelevant, trivial, and of no political or general importance (Hole and Levine, 1971; Evans, 1980; Mitchell, 1973; Carden, 1974). Furthermore, to assert their own independent voice threatened women's sexual availability, and their attempt to speak about "the woman question" was not only drowned in laughter but also met with the shouting of obscenities that reminded women in rather precise terms of their "proper place": "The most appropriate position of woman is prone," "take her off the stage and fuck her," and "she just needs a good screw" (Mitchell, 1973, pp. 85, 86; Hole and Levine, 1971, pp. 112, 135).

Women quickly saw that they could not change the order of things from within because they did not have a place in that order except as defined and assigned by men, and they drew the consequences. The new feminist movement was begun by a group of women forming their own autonomous, all-women's group in the summer of 1967.

Women made themselves visible and broke "the culture of silence" (Freire, 1970) by coming together and talking. This was different from the time-honored feminine tradition of gossiping. What was happening in these women's groups was a ritual of verbal unveiling of women's reality — a ritual that was perceived as scandalous by men (Hole and Levine, 1971). Women tried to reappropriate, indeed to create, their own unique experience by trying to find their authentic voice.

Women recognized and denounced their oppression by thoroughly reevaluating and reinterpreting their own existence. Problems, sufferings, and difficulties were no longer seen as individual or personal failures and shortcomings but as being rooted in structures affecting the life of every woman alike: "They were slowly and hesitantly beginning to conclude that what seemed to be a woman's idiosyncratic pattern of behavior was in fact a predescribed role, and . . . that what was thought to be a personal problem 'has a social cause and probably a political solution'" (Hole and Levine, 1971, p. 125). Gradually, the rigid separation of the personal from the political — which had given rise to women's discontent — became blurred the more the personal accounts of individual women were recognized as testimonies for the workings of general structures. The slogan "The Personal Is Political" conveyed the gradual destruction of these false opposites.

The Theory

Consciousness raising was not derived from an identifiable, coherent body of theory, but from the experience of oppression. It was a practical answer to this experience that, by
its very method, generated the core of an explicit albeit continuously diversifying body of feminist theory (MacKinnon,
1982). My attempt to summarize some of the major theoretical
premises of the women's movement is therefore informed by the
history of the early themes, issues, and concerns voiced by the
participants of consciousness-raising groups as well as by feminist
theories that have developed since the sixties.

The critique contained in the slogan "The Personal Is
Political" inscribed on the banner of the women's liberation
movement addressed two levels simultaneously: First, it challenged an understanding of politics, or of what could genuinely
be called political, as standing in clear and rigid contradistinc-
tion to its counterpart, the personal (Rowbotham, 1974); second, the slogan signified a different value placed on the personal
altogether. In political as in legal or scientific discourse, the personal is trivialized or viewed with suspicion because it threatens
the validity of the ideal of the "rational actor." These actors must
detach themselves from their subjectivity, including the world
of affection, hopes, and aspirations, in order to be truly objective and to arrive at generally valid knowledge. They must first
travel into the outer space of a purely formal and presumably
neutral "Archimedean point," which is given by the preexisting
conceptual framework of their science or discipline (Smith,
1977). Since the slogan "The Personal Is Political" was originally
voiced, an impressive body of literature has evolved criticizing
the "metaphysics of neutrality" (Horkheimer and Adorno, 1972,
p. 23) of academic and public discourse as generalizing the experience of a very specific social group occupying a particular
point in the structure of social relations (Bleier, 1988; Bowles
and Duelli Klein, 1983; Fox Keller, 1985; Langland and Cove,
1983; Spender, 1981). In the case of women, but also of members
of other oppressed groups, the expert knowledge produced from

this decidedly partial position has consistently missed or falsified the true nature of their particular reality.

Rather than investigating social reality from an (illusory) Archimedean point, the participants of consciousness-raising groups sought the source of knowledge and information and of political relevant concerns elsewhere:

> The distinctive and deep significance of consciousness-raising at an earlier period of the women's movement was precisely this process of opening up what was personal, idiosyncratic, and inchoate and discovering with others how this was shared, was objectively part of women's oppression, finding ways of speaking *of* it and ways of speaking it politically. It is this essential return to the experience we ourselves have directly in our everyday worlds that has been the distinctive mode of working in the women's movement — the repudiation of the professional, the expert, the already authoritative tones of the discipline . . . the science, the formal tradition, and the return to the seriously engaged and very difficult enterprise of how to begin from ourselves [Smith, 1977, p. 144].

The need to begin "from ourselves" directly arose out of the nature of female oppression itself, which keeps the content of specifically female experience strangely suspended as "nonexperiences." This is true in a twofold sense. First of all, as "women's issues" they are conventionally trivialized into nonissues when measured against the really important matters. Second, the descriptive power of this vocabulary is at the same time prescriptive because it expresses what women are expected to do, think, feel, and want. The mirror image is sometimes used to illustrate this problem: A woman looks into the mirror but instead of her own reflection she sees the phantasmagoric reality of male projections (Figes, 1971). In that sense, woman's existence is close to the abyss of meaninglessness. Consciousness raising directly satisfied the need for naming and interpreting a life lived at the brink of a meaningful social world. In the terminology proposed for this anthology, we can speak of the problem of a *colonized meaning perspective,* whose assumptions are derived from an experiential context that has usurped the context of women's experiences. Thus, these assumptions not only distort the possibilities for learning but are entirely inauthentic.

To give meaning to one's reality requires, among other things, to be aware of one's true interests and intentions. Women could not recognize their own intentions in the available systems of explanations and interpretations that give social expression to individual experience. Those interpretations had nevertheless settled into women's consciousness as "pseudo-objective determinants" of their identity (Habermas, 1974).

The power of the normative systems governing proper feminine and masculine conduct is therefore twofold. First, women may be effectively kept from expressing and pursuing their interests because these interests are considered illegitimate in view of established standards or norms of true femininity. A variety of mechanisms can support or uphold the power of these norms, ranging from benign ridicule to stigmatization as "deviant." Ultimately, however, the threat of violence, open or latent, lies at the bottom of these mechanisms. The different and manifold forms of violence done to women, sanctioned by a conspiracy of silence and trivialization by the powerful alliance of interest between individual men and social, political, medical, and legal institutions, was consequently one of the most important early themes to be voiced by the women's movement. But these forms of violence were only the most immediately felt pains of female oppression. A more indirect but by no means less powerful mechanism of repression is secured by norms that have been internalized through the process of socialization. They inconspicuously censor and silence certain interests, thus keeping women not only from *pursuing* but also from *perceiving* them. Thus, a woman may not *know* what she wants, correspondingly lacking the initiative and the ability to act that could arise from the recognition of her interests. Here, power has produced "effects on the level of desire" (Foucault, 1980, p. 59). In consciousness-raising groups, when women spoke about what they really felt rather than what they were supposed to feel, they collectively tried to discover what they *could* want and also what they *should* want. To find out what they could want was a process of resurrecting and reconstructing the past. To find out what they should want was a process of discovering and shaping common interests (Hart, 1985).

The Process

At the First National Women's Liberation Conference outside Chicago, in November 1968, Sarachild (1978) reported how a woman in her New York radical women's group mentioned that the more she learned about women's oppression, the "higher" her consciousness got. She told the group that she had begun to see the reality of "being attractive" in terms of a whole system of coercion, entailing "all the false ways women have to act: playing dumb, always being agreeable, always being nice, not to mention what we had to do to our bodies with the clothes and shoes we wore, the diet we had to go through, going blind not wearing glasses, all because men did not find our real selves, our human freedom, our basic humanity 'attractive'" (p. 144). The group was moved and decided to "raise its consciousness by studying women's lives by topics like childhood, jobs, motherhood, etc." (p. 145). Housework, childcare, and sexuality became other "key areas" to be addressed in consciousness-raising groups. Although these were the "areas of deepest humiliation for women" (p. 146), any topic could potentially serve the purpose to raise consciousness. Two major principles governed the methods and procedures of consciousness raising and determined its content: Concrete, lived experience was the primary or "original" source to be "checked out" (Sarachild, 1978), and the experiences that were shared and discussed had to be essential in the sense of contributing to an illumination of the nature of female oppression. In general, these principles were upheld by staying within the realm of the personal or the private—it was there that women experienced their oppression most acutely, and there that experience contained a particularly dense matrix of themes and questions directly relating to female oppression. For example, a seemingly trivial theme like color coding the nursery could fan out into an entire "thematic universe" containing all the major philosophical, sociological, or psychological aspects of sexual difference (Freire, 1970).

In general, whether a theme or topic that was suggested for discussion could be "generative" (Freire, 1970) or not could not be decided beforehand, as this would have violated the principle of "checking out the original source" (Sarachild, 1978); that is, each individual woman's experience. In practice, however, some themes or topics turned out to be more generative than others, and this gave rise to the appearance of a number of consciousness-raising manuals with suggestions for topics as well as structures or procedures. As Sarachild (1978, p. 148) pointed out, these "paraphernalia of rules and methodology" posed the danger of "creating vested interests for the methodology experts, both professional (for example, psychiatrists) and amateur." Based on my own experience, however, I want to claim that as long as an issue was suggested because a group member felt strongly and urgently about its importance, it had the potential to become a primary cognitive cell for consciousness raising. The real danger lay in getting stuck in the personal by focusing on the individual woman herself instead of moving on and outward to a collective analysis of the situation of women (Sarachild, 1978, p. 148; Mitchell, 1973, p. 62; Hanisch, 1971, p. 76; Hart, 1984, pp. 119–137). The danger therefore did not reside in the topic itself, but in the group members' inability or unwillingness to see an experience or problem as testimony for a general state of affairs rather than as an individual problem calling for individual solutions.

During consciousness raising, individual experiences are most frequently recalled by remembering certain scenes. For instance, a question like "Were you treated differently from your brother or friends who were boys when you were a child?" recalled a number of individual situations that were in fact common to many women. Those scenes are recalled — and in the process of remembering and understanding them, they become concrete as their true meaning emerges. In the past, the scene was not perceived or experienced in its real meaning. The woman who participated in it acted out her prescribed role. She may have felt frustration, disappointment, or even rage at her brother's or father's differential treatment but may not have known what to do with those feelings or how to explain their existence. The importance of expressing these feelings, of "speaking bitterness" (Hinton, 1966), is stressed during consciousness raising because the ultimate meaning of the situation — the denial of a woman's self-determination and autonomy — is encapsulated in the mute symptom of misery or unease. The previously idiosyncratic or private experience of misery is now de-privatized by being recognized as a symptom of oppression. It is recognized as symptomatic of something that *caused* it. This is the same as saying that the scene is understood.

In a way, consciousness raising "skips" the process of simple reflection (in the sense suggested by Mezirow). Because the muteness of women's experiences has not (yet) allowed them to reach a level of belief that can be examined and validated, the simultaneity of remembering and understanding that occurs in consciousness raising always constitutes *critical (self-)reflection.*

Understanding is both a process of completion and of opening up the view on the terrain of unexplored interpretations of experience and of possibilities for action. The woman who remembers the scene and understands its arrangement participates in it once more but on a higher and more mature level. The meaning of the scene unfolds because "the normative contents and values embodied by the norms of everyday life institutions [have become] thematized and rendered accessible to communication" (Habermas, 1974, p. 100). Consciousness raising is therefore a process of transformative learning because it changes the structure and the frame of experience in general and thus the entire frame of reference within whose parameters the individual woman has been acting so far:

> If in the course of consciousness-raising . . . a woman responds strongly, it is not because she has found something new to bitch about, but rather she has found something old to bitch about, because she perceives something old in a new way. "Yes," she cries, "I remember. . . . " "Ah," she says, "I understand. . . . " And the "Ah" arises not merely from her lips and mind, but from her entire being [Ruth, 1975, p. 299].

At the very moment at which a woman *understands* what she remembers (and those are inseparable acts), she looks at her entire life in a new way. The "Ah" arising from her "entire being" shows that the perceptual shift occurring at the moment of remembrance and understanding, both crucial elements in the process of critical self-reflection, is itself an experience. Within the medium of this experience, speaking takes on the form of action because it has immediate practical consequences. The object of cognition, the woman's view of herself and of the world — that is, her consciousness — is structurally transformed at the moment of understanding her life or the true meaning of her life.

Such a process of understanding is secured through the medium of the group because only by sharing their previously simply idiosyncratic feelings could women validate those feelings as subjective experience — as something that really and truly happened to them and was therefore not a hallucination or a figment of the brain. Through a process of *mutual self-reflection,* women's experiences became de-privatized; each individual woman's life became meaningful *for herself* because it became meaningful within the larger context of women's oppression.

Furthermore, women's experiences became de-privatized in a more comprehensive sense. In the light of larger social and political structures, they ceased to be "simply women's issues" and could be recognized as a matter of common and therefore public concern. The battered-women's movement shows how the issue of wife beating was taken out of the realm of private affairs and proclaimed a public issue, of concern to all members of society (Schechter, 1982).

To recognize the similarities of common experiences also served to set a distance to what could be considered an individual woman's problem. Such a distance to personal experience needs to be gained and sustained if previously isolated, personal reality is to be recognized as consisting of specific instances of a general state of oppression and if this general state is to be examined and understood. In other words, a *theoretical* distance to personal experience needs to be acquired. Women started from personal experience because existing theoretical knowledge, the truth of established facts, was criticized as inadequate for grasping and explaining not only women's reality, but the true nature of social reality as a whole. These theories need to be scrutinized, and new ones developed and created: "The idea of consciousness-raising was never to end generalizations. It was to produce truer ones. The idea was to take our own feelings and experience more seriously than any theories which did not satisfactorily clarify them, and to devise new theories which did reflect the actual experiences and feelings and necessities of women" (Sarachild, 1978, p. 148).

The move to producing new and truer generalizations was not an easy one to make (for reasons I will discuss below), and rarely did it occur as a systematic, ongoing process, least of all as a phase or stage, as some consciousness-raising manuals would suggest (which were written by feminists with a decidedly conceptual-analytical bend). In my own experience, theorizing occurred spontaneously and sporadically. In its most successful moments, theorizing was a collective effort that started with the telling of a seemingly minor incident, sparking critical comments, interpretations, and explanations that eventually evolved into a complex analysis of female oppression. Theorizing therefore was a continuous process of cognitively "opening up one cell of reality" and of entering with ease the next (Adorno, 1974, p. 87). It did not mean to subsume individual experiences under the general categories of preexisting theoretical frameworks. In contrast with the painful phase of "speaking bitterness," collective theorizing is a joyful event as it offers fresh interpretations that unfreeze numerous possibilities for individual and collective action within a better-understood social reality.

Implications for Educational Practice

One of the early founders of consciousness-raising groups, Sarachild (1978, p. 147) writes, "There has been no one method of raising consciousness. What really counts in consciousness-raising are not methods, but results. The only 'methods' of consciousness-raising are essentially principles." What I have described above are precisely those principles. In the following,

I want to illustrate the point I made at the beginning of this chapter: That content (analysis of women's oppression), interactive structure (reciprocity and equality), and epistemological premise (to start from subjective experience) all mutually determine each other as well as give consciousness raising its unique power. I want to discuss the possibilities as well as the limits and problems associated with attempts to incorporate major principles of consciousness raising into educational practice in general. Instead of talking about methods or strategies per se, I will therefore talk about *enabling conditions* for such educational practice, as well as about some major caveats that adult educators interested in using the main ideas of consciousness raising should be aware of. As much as possible, I will give more specific suggestions on whether or how consciousness raising can be incorporated into certain settings or environments. I want to stress, however, that educators ultimately have to judge for themselves whether their particular setting is conducive to the method as well as to the particular purposes of consciousness raising. I am quite reluctant to translate a complex program and process that is dependent on specific historical and social circumstances into a straightforward set of techniques. Rather, I consider it to be the responsibility and task of individual educators to carefully translate their understanding and interpretation of consciousness raising into their own practical modifications and adaptations that make sense in their particular setting. As the contributions in this volume show, consciousness raising is not the only form of transformative learning, and adaptations or modifications may turn it into another form or process that is nevertheless emancipatory. Obviously, the process and the concerns out of which consciousness raising arose have to first be thoroughly understood in their uniqueness before the necessary adaptations to other (unique) contexts can be made.

In the following, I will list and discuss the main principles and characteristics of consciousness raising. In the light of these, educators must decide whether their particular setting is conducive to an enactment of consciousness raising and whether the main principles can be realized.

The Acknowledgment of Oppression. Whatever the consistency of a particular learning group, the entire enterprise of consciousness raising rests on an acknowledgement of the concrete, objectively given existence of power, which also provides for a basic commonality of experience irrespective of individual differences. Thus, the first principle quite simply means that the educator has to work with a group whose members are representative of an oppressed or marginalized group. This principle obviously depends on the educator's theoretical-analytical understanding of what constitutes oppression. In other words, it depends on the educator's sociopolitical analysis of society. Based on my own understanding, let me give a few suggestions: Oppressed and marginalized groups may include undocumented workers, illiterate people, women, racial or sexual minorities, the poor, and so on (acknowledging crossovers among those categories). Consciousness raising could therefore be an empowering process for neighborhood self-help groups, antipoverty groups, support groups of various kinds (for instance, for the unemployed, for immigrants, for poor women who are heads of households, for victims of racial or sexual violence, for women in patriarchal religious organizations, or for racial or sexual minorities in organizations such as churches, colleges, and corporations).

An objection to this emphasis on oppressed or marginalized groups is sometimes heard in the form of "the oppressors need to change or raise their consciousness, too." While this is true, they are faced with different tasks and difficulties, and they have to find their own methods and procedures. Consciousness raising is a version of "speaking bitterness," of denouncing injustice and violence done to the body and soul either directly by individual members of a dominating group or indirectly by the social and institutional arrangements that support it. To give an example: In her review article on the growing literature of the new men's movement, Banner (1989) illustrates the problem of simply taking over approaches and methods shaped by the women's movement. In men's groups, for instance, to speak bitterness harbors the danger of "explicating patriarchy's victimization of men" or of "plumbing male sensitivity" (p. 705), thus bypassing the task to first examine and indict individual men's complicity in women's oppression. Clearly, a process that first of all has to move through an acknowledgment of one's own role in perpetuating oppression has to look quite different.

The Importance of Personal Experience. The second principle concerns the importance of using personal experience as the original source to be critically reflected upon. This has to make sense in the light of a group's particular purposes. Group members not only have to be motivated to do so, but they also have to have the time, that is, they should not be under the pressure to act or to make decisions. An educator working with a task-oriented group will have to set aside special meetings where no decisions have to be made and critical reflection can take place. In that sense, academic settings, which already constitute some "time out" from the everyday pressures of having to act, provide a better environment. However, the academic setting is also generally strongly associated with the impersonal mode of objectively and detachedly addressing issues and has a tendency to invalidate the importance and usefulness of personal experience in the learning process. A teacher may have to spend time undoing these particular "ways of knowing" before consciousness raising can become a possibility (see, for instance, Belenky, Clinchy, Goldberger, and Tarule, 1986).

The Homogeneity of the Learning Group. The third principle, for reasons outlined above, requires the educator to examine the makeup of her or his group in terms of the homogeneity of experience and the assumptions of its members. Only a learning group that is relatively homogeneous with respect to major social differences like gender, race, or class would share a vital interest in liberation, as well as a fund of vital experiences. Gender, race, or class do not simply represent "differences." In our society, a complex and dynamic system of hierarchies and inequalities directly feeds on an interpretation of differences like skin color, age, or sex as signifying inferiority or superiority. Our very identities are shaped by the differential social valuations associated with these differences. The possibility of establishing relations of trust, one of the key issues with which the participants of consciousness-raising groups wrestle, is thereby severely curtailed if not entirely denied. In these groups, intimate self-disclosure — itself prone to producing fear, anxiety, and pain — could only take place within the relative safety of a group where the members were not distinguished by major differences signifying major power differentials. Such a condition of mutuality and reciprocity of experience goes beyond formal democratic rules and procedures. For instance, a participatory structure of shared leadership, rotation of roles or tasks, equal say in decision-making procedures, and the like, could be created without in the least challenging any deeper-lying inequalities represented by the differences between ages, sexes, races, and classes. Because the relations of power that exist between these groups signify not only inequality but also major differences in experience, the prerequisites of mutual trust as well as of *shared* experiences is directly contradicted by the deep-seated divisions that these different "life-worlds" represent. This may be true even in the case of an all-women's group, and to categorically talk about "women" — as I have done in the preceding discussion — obscures the profound differences and inequalities that exist between women of different races, classes, ethnic identities, or sexual-affectional preferences. Because the early participants of consciousness-raising groups were mostly white, college-educated, and married, a certain homogeneity of background assumptions was guaranteed. In contrast, Geiger and Zita (1985) give an example of the prevalence of self-protection rather than self-disclosure, as well as (well-founded and historically rooted) distrust toward open sharing of personal experiences in a class composed of black and white women. In cases like these, the content of speech will be highly circumscribed and severely censored by the presence of larger social inequalities brought into the classroom, thus seriously undermining the very purpose of consciousness raising: to give a voice to those experiences that have been suppressed or silenced precisely because of existing structures of inequality. In the following quote, Maria Lugones addresses the relationship between Anglo-

Saxon and Hispanic women, but her vivid description of the self-constraint and humility required of the more privileged group has validity for all situations where heterogeneity signifies larger social power differentials:

> You will need to learn to become unintrusive, unimportant, patient to the point of tears, while at the same time open to learning any possible lessons. You will also have to come to terms with the sense of alienation, of not belonging, of having your world thoroughly disrupted, having it criticized and scrutinized from the point of view of those who have been harmed by it, having important concepts central to it dismissed, being viewed with mistrust, being seen as of no consequence except as an object of mistrust [quoted in Grimshaw, 1986, pp. 102–103].

However, to work with a mixed group of, for instance, black and white participants, or of men and women, does not necessarily call for abandoning the use of consciousness raising but calls for realistically assessing the limitations and constraints that are produced by such a situation. The process will probably not be a pure or smooth one, and special attention must be paid to keeping a check on the inequalities represented by nonhomogeneity and on the pressures that will be exerted on those members who represent the weaker or oppressed groups. The particulars of the mix may make a difference. For instance, in a group composed of men and women, men must definitely be in the minority (as a way to redress at least minimally the existing power imbalance). However, since it takes only one vocal and resisting man to destroy the process, a further stipulation has to be that the men not only should be aware of their socially guaranteed privileges qua men but should also be willing to listen rather than to speak — no easy task for someone who is socialized into thinking that women have nothing important to say. Judging from my own experience of attempting some elements of the process in my (mixed) undergraduate classes, consciousness raising works only in a rudimentary form and is directly dependent on the level of awareness and the willingness of the privileged members of the group to be actively and supportively silent. I experienced situations such as the following, where a group of women spent an entire evening to raise the consciousness of the only male student, who had consistently questioned the validity of their experiences because they were not his own. While the male student greatly benefited from this collective effort, the women members of the group had their energies diverted from their own learning and left frustrated and exhausted. Furthermore, the presence of even the most humble and willing "oppressor" will act as a censor on the content as well as on the degree of candidness of individual contributions. In another of my classes, the women took great pains not to offend a male student especially because he was so nice (and, as everyone pointed out, "exceptional"), thus putting considerable constraints on their accounts of their personal experiences of oppression.

Equality. The critique of mechanisms of power has to be directly reflected in a structure of equality among all the participants of these groups. This constitutes a problem in cases of institutionalized differences between a teacher or facilitator and a learning group. In educational settings where there is a designated teacher, facilitator, or leader, this principle can therefore be fulfilled only partially. I do not think that the conventional emphasis of the andragogical model on adults' self-directedness (accompanied by considerable squeamishness about using the word *teacher* rather than *facilitator*) in any way escapes this problem. Whether teacher or facilitator, it is the intentions of this person, and of the institution or program he or she represents, that govern and control the overall learning process and that structure each individual learning situation. The privilege to be able to surrender special authority is not shared equally by all participants but remains a privilege of the leader. However, as Freire (1970) discusses in great detail, a situation of genuine equality can possibly be established on the motivational level. The teacher or facilitator would have to find ways to tie her or his special authority or expertise to a common or shared context of intentions and interests. He or she would have to be

able to assume and identify with the perspective of all the participants of the learning situation. However, Freire maintains
that this must go beyond the merely cognitive ability of "taking
perspective" as it is usually understood. The teacher must be able
to link her or his motivations to those of the other participants
as an oppressed group and share with them their interest in
liberation. Clearly, in an institutional setting, such an identification has to remain partial as well as temporary. It may be severely
limited by or come in conflict with institutional boundaries, particularly in the case of established, mainstream institutions that
have historically been built on certain class, race, and sexual
privileges and therefore represent precisely those forces that are
to be critiqued in consciousness-raising groups.

Furthermore, not only must the educator be able to identify with the concerns of the group, but he or she must also
deserve the trust of the group. The members of the learning
group must be able to feel entirely safe in expressing their personal
concerns. Although building trust is primarily a psychological
process, it is nevertheless dependent on material or structural
requirements. Once more, this relates to the above-mentioned
requirement that the group leader or facilitator cannot be an
official delegate or representative of a group or institution that
signifies oppression for the learners. Also, time constraints,
especially in the form of a set period during which the members
of the group meet (as is the case in academic settings), may cause
problems for building trust, which usually occurs at its own rate
of development. Academic time constraints present obstacles
or problems in another way as well. I personally struggled with
the fact that opening up, sharing experiences, and facing the
reality of oppression calls for continued, mutual group support,
which is unfortunately abruptly withdrawn at the end of the
school term.

A related issue has to be discussed: In a world where individual and social power is distributed unequally, all forms of
interaction are permeated with the spirit of competitiveness. This
is a problem all groups — homogeneous or heterogeneous — have
to face. In consciousness-raising groups, this issue was considered
particularly devastating for women because it isolated them even

further from each other, making them even weaker in the face of the powerful tradition of male bonding. The issue of competition therefore became an explicit content of discussion, laying the foundation for alternative forms of practice and interaction that were characterized by reciprocity and equality (Hart, 1984). There was another layer of division, however, that became explicitly thematized in consciousness-raising groups, giving rise to the concept of "woman-identified woman." Woman's identity was seen as essentially male derived, her whole sense of self as dependent on the approval and legitimation of men. Relations among women tended to reflect a deep-seated sense of worthlessness and "an enormous reservoir of self-hate" (Radical lesbians, quoted in Eisenstein, 1983, p. 52). To find ways to validate each other as women and to shape different forms of interaction and relations among women became other primary themes of consciousness raising.

Gaining and Sustaining Theoretical Distance. The previous points highlight how subjective experience shaped by the reality of power is fully intertwined with an equally distorted, intersubjective structure. Both were *thematized* in consciousness-raising groups in the form of analysis of current reality and of expressed concern for future practice, leading to attempts to build nonoppressive, egalitarian forms of *interaction.* Thus, a critique of power shaped the content as well as the structure of consciousness-raising groups.

As I stated in the beginning, the analysis of oppression is a fundamental aspect of consciousness raising. Absence of designated leaders, the ordering of speech in a way that guarantees that everybody's voice is heard, an emphasis on support by simultaneously abstaining from criticism — all these structural and procedural guidelines were meaningful only in relation to the underlying understanding of female oppression. Conceivably, any of these principles could be instituted without this critical content. We would, however, no longer speak about consciousness raising but about something else. Based on my own and on others' experience, in many instances consciousness raising did indeed become something else, usually marked by a subtle perceptual shift from "meaningful themes" (Freire, 1970) opened up through the contributions of individual women to the women themselves (Hart, 1984). Whenever this shift occurred, content and structure of interaction were immediately affected. I believe this is the crucial point where consciousness-raising as a *radical* method to examine and overcome the articulation of power in subjective experience and individual consciousness is transformed into the *liberal* (and essentially individualistic) enterprise of validating feelings or personal experience.

To get stuck in the personal is a danger that is nourished by a whole barrage of cultural and ideological forces, above all a prevailing concept of the individual and of the self as an isolated, self-sufficient monad, thus placing a fetish "on the uniqueness of the individual and the authenticity of personal experience" (Geiger and Zita, 1985, p. 114). This ideology, supported by the conformist psychotherapy movement of the seventies, locates authenticity in the *immediately* felt and experienced. But, as discussed in detail above, it is precisely this experience that is permeated through and through with social and political power and that is therefore to a large degree shaped by external forces. As one social critic expressed it: "The subjectivity that parades its authenticity covers for a social reality that commands. For subjectivity to attain itself, to become subjective, it must achieve self-consciousness: insight into the objective reality that falsifies the subject. Without this consciousness, the subject is ideological, a tool of a repressive society" (Jacoby, 1975, p. 128).

The tendency toward "an unreflective glorification of immediate life" (Cocks, 1985, p. 178) is complemented by a culturally deeply engrained anti-intellectualism that considers theory as too abstract in the sense of abstracting from immediate experience. Cocks, criticizing the antitheoretical attitude of large parts of the women's movement as collaborating with a general cultural anti-intellectualism, describes the "special powers of theory" as the power to unravel the complexities of the human world. She emphasizes that theory "does *not* follow the contours of immediate experience" but rather sets a distance and sustains "a distance to fathom aspects of the world hidden from the eyes of its own authors and actors." In words that are similar to

Jacoby's she writes that "becoming theoretical and becoming self-conscious belong to precisely the same genre of mental activity" (pp. 175–176).

The difficulty in gaining and sustaining a theoretical distance was present in consciousness-raising groups from the start, giving rise to numerous early warnings against turning the process into a form of group therapy (Sarachild, 1978; Mitchell, 1973; Hanisch, 1970). Eastman (1973), who extensively studied the development and life of a consciousness-raising group in the Greater Hartford area, reports that the "examination of issues from a political perspective" hardly took place. Rather, a tendency prevailed to "value personal expression of emotional material . . . with a resultant deemphasis or at times outright sanction against more intellectual and cognitive formulations" (p. 175).

If consciousness raising is to remain a radical program for transformative education, a theoretical distance to personal experience has to be gained. Theoretical knowledge must at some point become an explicit concern because it supplies the general tools that can make transparent the relations that obtain among isolated and fragmented incidents of personal experience. This also means to acknowledge the limits of individual experience as well as the limits of the collective experience of the participants of consciousness raising. Personal experience can only be the necessary *point of departure* for gaining socially valid knowledge; it cannot itself constitute the whole universe of such knowledge. Its "inner determinations are not discoverable within it" (Smith, 1977, p. 176) because it is organized by forces and structures that are located outside individual experience (for a detailed discussion of this issue, see Smith). However, it is precisely the power of theory that can explain why "social participants may not have a grasp of certain levels of, or constraints on, their thought and action" (Cocks, 1985, p. 176). Therefore, relevant questions originate in the world of individual experience, but neither individual experience nor society as a whole can be understood by remaining within its scope. Both can only be understood in their determinate relationship to each other.

Phases and Stages. We are now in a better position to look at the specific phases with which consciousness raising is often identified. It may help to envision the overall pattern of the process as one of moving from surface phenomena related to the immediate present; then to the depths of pain, anger, or bitterness related to past experiences; and outward again toward utopian outlooks for the future.

Allen (1973) suggests four phases: opening up (fostering "a feeling of intimacy and trust"; p. 273), sharing ("building a collage of similar experiences"; p. 275), analyzing ("the period when questions can be asked about how the entire society functions"; p. 277), and abstracting ("take the concepts and analysis we have devleoped and discuss abstract theory"; pp. 277–278). Allen emphasizes, however, that these are not necessarily successive stages, but that all elements typical for each phase are always present, although the relative emphasis may shift over time. In general, I would warn against attempts to procedurally regulate the development of a learning group along the lines of these phases but instead would consider them essential moments in the overall process. The possibility for them to emerge and to actually take place has to be guaranteed by the enabling conditions described above.

Furthermore, the actual pattern of affective and cognitive group development may depend to a large extent on the concrete circumstances of a learning group as well as on the specific cultural context. Bonder (1985), for instance, proposes a different framework for analyzing stages in the educational process of a women's studies class in Argentina that enacted the major principles of consciousness raising.

If we look at the phases Allen discusses, "opening up" refers to those moments in the overall process where feelings are expressed and experiences are recounted, remembered, or relived. "Sharing" refers to those phases where similarities of experience are discovered and articulated, and the nonindividual, testimonial character of these experiences moves to the center of attention. This is also the point where deliberate attempts to overcome competitive habits of speech and interaction are made or have to be made.

Although the special training, knowledge, and greater access to information and knowledge that educators usually enjoy all have the potential of creating a power imbalance, these privileges can be used positively. For instance, educators may stimulate and facilitate the phase of sharing experiences by proposing certain topics or issues that they — after some studying of their own — consider relevant for the lives of the group members as oppressed people. At the same time, whether these themes are indeed relevant will have to be proven in the ensuing process itself. Once this phase has begun, it is a simple but highly effective procedure to go around the circle and let everybody talk before comments are made. Other rules may be established. For instance, the group members may decide that they only talk about their own experience and do not refer to what others have said before. The latter can be done in a second round where people consciously reflect on their previous contribution in the light of what others have said, pointing out how their experience is different or how hearing others speak has illuminated their own understanding.

Obviously, this phase continues the work of disclosure, as well as containing elements of "analysis" and "abstraction." As mentioned above, the movement to explicit analysis or conceptualization is a difficult one to achieve, and no single method can enable the simultaneous work of criticizing old and shaping new concepts, as well as of developing new analytical-conceptual competences. Only an ongoing process of learning and unlearning could accomplish this. However, I believe that an explicitly shared definition as an oppressed group, hence a shared interest in individual and social liberation, is a major enabling condition for this process. By its very nature of being shared — that is, nonpersonal — and by being utopian — that is, oriented toward a better future — such an emancipatory interest directly fosters theoretical self-consciousness and provides a stimulus to conceptualize and generalize because it constitutes an interest in understanding and changing the whole dynamic complexity of reality.

I believe that a particular responsibility of the facilitator lies in making sure that the tension between the personal and the general is kept, and that the process does not turn into a therapy session (although at times this may be what is needed). In academic settings, readings can be assigned that propose theoretical explanations relevant to the experiences shared. In nonacademic settings, reports on such studies and accumulated knowledge and information may be offered to the group members for discussion.

Finally, the phase of creating new and original solutions based on a new and shared theoretical understanding of the group members' situation may come in different forms. The group may work on strategies or suggestions for policies (in the case of an antipoverty group, for instance). In a more academic environment, the group members may engage in utopian thinking, making proposals for a society not yet realized but reflecting their hopes and their newly discovered possibilities for living and acting.

In conclusion, I want to stress that the power of consciousness raising derives in large measure from its spontaneity and from its roots in a sociopolitical movement of liberation. It ignites around the theme of oppression, presupposes a certain view about knowledge and knowing that empowers rather than extinguishes the individual knower, and calls for a relationship between theory and practice that begins with a however vaguely felt or articulated acknowledgment of power and finishes with a systematic understanding of the nature and complexity of the entire power-bound social reality. To "raise consciousness" means to arrive at such an awareness and to anchor the process of becoming aware in individual reality rather than in analyses and theories that were produced elsewhere. Consciousness raising is therefore a program for social groups that have been considered marginal, that have been denied full social membership, and whose reality and experience is not reflected in mainstream analyses and theories. Consciousness raising is a process of reclaiming social membership — not in the sense of adjusting to the normative view that produced a situation of marginality in the first place but in terms that tend to abolish all special claims and privileges for any identifiable social group. The full cycle of consciousness raising therefore includes the actual experience of power on the individual level, a theoretical grasp of power as a larger social reality, and a practical orientation toward emancipatory action.

References

Adorno, T. W. *Minima Moralia.* London: NLB, 1974.

Allen, P. "Free Space." In A. Koedt, E. Levine, and E. Rapone (eds.), *Radical Feminism.* New York: Quadrangle/New York Times, 1973.

Banner, L. Book review. *Signs,* 1989, *14* (3), 703–708.

Belenky, M. F., Clinchy, B. M., Goldberger, N. R., and Tarule, J. M. *Women's Ways of Knowing.* New York: Basic Books, 1986.

Bleier, R. (ed.). *Feminist Approaches to Science.* New York: Pergamon Press, 1988.

Bonder, G. "The Educational Process of Women's Studies in Argentina: Reflections on Theory and Technique." In M. Culley and C. Portuges (eds.), *Gendered Subjects.* London: Routledge & Kegan Paul, 1985.

Bowles, G., and Duelli Klein, R. *Theories of Women's Studies.* London: Routledge & Kegan Paul, 1983.

Carden, M. L. *The New Feminist Movement.* New York: Russell Sage Foundation, 1974.

Cocks, J. "Suspicious Pleasures: On Teaching Feminist Theory." In M. Culley and C. Portuges (eds.), *Gendered Subjects.* London: Routledge & Kegan Paul, 1985.

Eastman, P. C. "Consciousness-Raising as a Resocialization Process for Women." *Smith College Studies in Social Work,* 1973, *18* (3), 53–83.

Eisenstein, H. *Contemporary Feminist Thought.* Boston: Hall, 1983.

Evans, S. *Personal Politics.* New York: Vintage Books, 1980.

Figes, E. *Patriarchal Attitudes.* New York: Random House, 1971.

Foucault, M. *The History of Sexuality.* Vol. 1: *An Introduction.* New York: Vintage Books, 1980.

Fox Keller, E. *Reflections on Gender and Science.* New Haven, Conn.: Yale University Press, 1985.

Freire, P. *Pedagogy of the Oppressed.* New York: Seabury Press, 1970.

Geiger, S., and Zita, J. N. "White Traders: The Caveat Emptor of Women's Studies." In B. Hillyer Davis (ed.), *Feminist Education.* Special issue of *Journal of Thought,* no. 20. Norman: University of Oklahoma, 1985.

Grimshaw, J. *Philosophy and Feminist Thinking.* Minneapolis: University of Minnesota Press, 1986.

Habermas, J. "On Social Identity." *Telos,* 1974, *19,* 91–103.

Hanisch, C. "The Personal Is Political." In S. Firestone and A. Koedt (eds.), *Notes From the Second Year: Women's Liberation.* New York: Radical Feminism, 1970.

Hart, M. "Towards a Theory of Collective Learning." Unpublished doctoral dissertation, Department of Adult Education, Indiana University, Bloomington, 1984.

Hart, M. "Thematization of Power, the Search for Common Interests, and Self-Reflection: Towards a Comprehensive Concept of Emancipatory Education." *International Journal of Lifelong Education,* 1985, *4* (2), 119–134.

Hinton, W. *Fanshen.* New York: Vintage books, 1966.

Hole, J., and Levine, E. *Rebirth of Feminism.* New York: Quadrangle Books, 1971.

Horkheimer, M., and Adorno, T. W. *Dialectic of Enlightenment.* New York: Seabury Press, 1972.

Jacoby, R. *Social Amnesia.* Boston: Beacon Press, 1975.

Langland, E., and Cove, W. *A Feminist Perspective in the Academy.* Chicago: University of Chicago Press, 1983.

MacKinnon, C. "Feminism, Marxism, Method and the State: An Agenda for Theory." *Signs,* 1982, *7* (3), 515–544.

Mitchell, J. *Woman's Estate.* New York: Vintage Books, 1973.

Rowbotham, S. *Woman's Consciousness, Man's World.* Baltimore, Md.: Penguin Books, 1974.

Ruth, S. "A Serious Look at Consciousness-Raising." *Social Theory and Practice,* 1975, *2* (3), 289–300.

Sarachild, K. "Consciousness-Raising: A Radical Weapon." In Redstockings (eds.), *Feminist Revolution.* New York: Random House, 1978.

Schechter, S. *Women and Male Violence.* Boston: South End Press, 1983.

Smith, D. "A Sociology for Women." In J. A. Sherman and E. T. Beck (eds.), *The Prism of Sex: Essays in the Sociology of Knowledge.* Madison: University of Wisconsin Press, 1977.

Spender, D. *Men's Studies Modified.* Oxford: Pergamon Press, 1981.

Stacey, M., and Price, M. *Women, Power, Politics.* New York: Tavistock Publications, 1981.

Four

Reflective Engagement for Social Change

Thomas W. Heaney
Aimee I. Horton

"Conscientization" is one moment in the larger drama of social change. New ways of thinking about the world become possible, when the promise of those "ways of thinking" can be realized in action — when there is a political apparatus at hand into which the energy of a transformed learner can flow.

The Potentials of Transformative Learning

From Sit-In to a Southwide Movement. On April 1–3, 1960, a workshop was held at Highlander Folk School near Monteagle, Tennessee, that had a major transformative effect on participants and, in turn, on the Southwide civil rights movement. The workshop was planned with student sit-in leaders on the action theme "The New Generation Fights for Equality." At the opening session, Myles Horton, founder and educational director of the movement-related adult education center, observed: "As far as I know this is the first time since this protest started that a group of people from various places has gotten together. Something may come of it that would help further the things you believe in. And I just want to emphasize that we are here to help you do what you decide to do" (Horton, 1971, p. 299–300).

74

Something did "come of it." In a three-day period, the seventy-five black and some white college students from the forefront of early demonstrations in Greensboro, North Carolina, Orangeburg, South Carolina, Nashville, Tennessee, Atlanta, Georgia, and elsewhere in the South became, as one young sit-in leader expressed it, "one movement instead of many."

Beginning with enthusiastic accounts of their local actions, inspired by the first spontaneous sit-in by four freshmen at a lunch counter in Greensboro, Highlander challenged the independent protest leaders to begin thinking as a movement and to address some of the problems involved in building it. They were asked questions about their basic philosophy, about the method of nonviolence, about the dilemma of law and morality and their presumed right to defy an "unjust law," as well as about their future plans and relationship to the larger community.

In the rigorous day and night sessions that followed, the students divided into working groups on philosophy, methods, community relations, and communications to think through some of the problems and issues raised and to decide on next steps. Out of these sessions, they projected the broad outlines of a southern student movement, which in the years that followed was to profoundly affect the South and the nation. Their brief workshop report on the "Philosophy of the Movement" was to continue to be their essential philosophy: "We believe in democracy. We are Americans seeking our rights. We want to do something. We are using non-violence as a method, but not necessarily as a total way of life. We believe it is practical" (Horton, 1971, p. 303).

Their report and recommendations on direct-action methods to achieve change became the actions and methods of their emerging Southwide movement. These included "better planned sit-in demonstrations as long as they are useful; participation in economic boycott when it is practical and picketing where it will be effective." Their report stressed, too, the importance of major registration drives, which, as they correctly predicted, "would give the Negro community more political power . . . especially in areas where Negroes outnumber the white population" (Horton, 1971, p. 304).

Finally the local student sit-in leaders declared that "a Southwide organization for promoting the student movement" should be formed, emphasizing that its function should be "not to direct activities but to coordinate them" (Horton, 1971, p. 304). Two weeks later in Raleigh, North Carolina, student leaders from across the South formed the organization envisioned at the Highlander workshop. They named it the Student Non-violent Coordinating Committee (SNCC).

Participants in the April 1960 college workshop at Highlander went on to play leading roles in SNCC and, later, in the wider political arena. One of the college workshop participants, Marion Barry, was elected first president of SNCC; another, John Lewis, was subsequently elected president. They and others from the workshop went on in the sixties to assume leadership for the jail-no-bail movement, for the Freedom Rides that desegregated interstate transportation, and for the voter registration drives in Mississippi and other Deep South states that were to open up the electoral process to hundreds of thousands of blacks and produce a number of black officeholders in the South for the first time since Reconstruction. Among the officerholders were some of the former college sit-in leaders who had come together at Highlander: Julian Bond, the first black elected to the Georgia state legislature, and, later, nominated for vice-president of the United States; Marion Barry, elected mayor of Washington, D.C.; and John Lewis, recently elected to serve in Congress as a representative from Georgia.

In the Beginning, Nothing Happened. For six years prior to the sit-in, students from the same primarily black and a few white southern colleges had come to Highlander for weekend workshops. Beginning in 1954, they had come together from their segregated campuses to discuss the problems that concerned them. Each year, in spite of Highlander's free and challenging learning environment, they chose to have conventional lecture-discussion sessions on human relations, interpersonal relations, and race relations.

The traditional, socially and educationally controlled and sheltered environment of their several colleges was a world apart from Highlander and from the separate and unequal southern society that Highlander was determined to change. The southern black college was typically dominated by a patriarchal president who ruled over a student body of well-mannered, upwardly mobile young people who would become the successful preachers, teachers, and other professionals within their segregated communities.

In 1959, during the Sixth Annual Workshop, the students evidenced an inclination to move from theory and analysis to dealing with actual problems when they selected as their topic "Campus Leadership for Integration." That inclination was reinforced by opening speaker Dr. Herman Long of the Race Relations Institute, Fisk University, who traced the history of earlier generations of activists and asked the group, "Why have you been so silent?" He concluded by raising a series of questions to rouse them: How can we stimulate college students to think of issues of today? What types of action can we address ourselves to? What is effective protest? What are the limits? (Horton, 1971, p. 299).

A student report indicates that even the inspired oratory of Dr. Long failed. For the remainder of the weekend, discussions centered almost solely on campus questions. In their final session, students drew up a list of so-called action projects. These included "a well-written newspaper for exchange," the promotion of "inter-collegiate activities," and a conference for representatives of eight private colleges on "The Role of Private Colleges in Criticizing the Social Order." Since they had not yet been involved in struggle to change the society, they could only envision changing campus relationships.

Gaining Control in Public Housing

Self-Development Without Social Change. In the early 1970s in the last of the machine-dominated big cities and the most segregated city in the North, a center for adult education was established within the City Colleges of Chicago to support and encourage the social change and self-help efforts of black and other poor communities and groups. Its staff shared a commitment to adult learning as a means of not only empowering individuals, but also changing the conditions of day-to-day life.

The poorest and most segregated of groups served by the center were the "people in the projects" — the thousands of black families, most of them headed by women on welfare, living in the massive Chicago Housing Authority (CHA) developments. "The projects," as viewed by the political machine, were useful in two important ways. They were a sure source of votes in exchange for promises, small favors, and transportation to the polls at election time. Equally important, they provided a lucrative source of jobs, from managers to janitors and clerks, to reward the machines' vast patronage army.

For residents, who put up with deteriorating buildings, broken elevators, uncollected trash, and gangs operating unchallenged, it was the housing of last resort. Their only means for redressing their many grievances were the local advisory councils (LACs) at each development. The LACs were supposed to represent the residents and serve as their voice. Instead, since their privileged members were paid for their services by the Housing Authority and rewarded in other ways by a patronage system, they generally ignored or diverted resident complaints rather than responding to them. It was among oppressed residents in these developments that the new center at the City Colleges sought to begin emancipatory education.

The program was called simply "Peer Group" by participants and "Peer Group Education and Counseling" when a grant was requested from the Illinois Community College Board. The peer group concept was inspired by the Woodlawn Sisterhood. Organized in 1970 by a small, determined band of welfare mothers in a poor, black neighborhood on Chicago's south side, the Sisterhood set up a storefront center to help one another survive the system. Its founders were women who had somehow managed to stretch their meager dollars, care for their children and themselves, and take part in community struggles against mounting housing, gang, and other problems. In the spirit of a local movement, they decided to reach out to their "low-surviving sisters" who were being overwhelmed by their problems and withdrawing into themselves or into drugs and alcohol.

Although the center run by the Sisterhood ceased to exist when modest funds from a local church were no longer available, it served as the basis for the program developed with CHA residents.

The idea as it evolved was to organize small groups of women from a building or a development who, with a peer group leader, would decide on an agenda of problems and, assisted by whatever resource persons they needed (from the college, the community, or the development), begin to act together to deal with them. As they proved able to deal effectively with day-to-day problems affecting their children and themselves, it was assumed they would gain in confidence and members and begin to address their underlying problem: the CHA landlord who controlled their unhappy living environment.

To initiate the program, a strong and wise black woman, Ona Banks, was selected who had grown up poor but self-confident in Mississippi and had spent most of her adult life in Chicago. She was known to the center through her work in CHA housing, where she had been able to bring isolated, older people together in supportive social groups, encouraging them to function on their own and reach out to others.

In spite of her prior experience working with groups in several developments, she encountered widespread skepticism among potential Peer Group members. A number of women whom she contacted could not believe that the program would be "theirs," that they would be free to decide the problems and issues to be discussed. Others wondered why the group meetings were being held — who was behind the program? Why was this woman involved? After several weeks, a small group of women gathered at the fortresslike Robert Taylor development in the apartment of one of the less skeptical participants. But, again, there were questions about the program. Concern was expressed that if CHA or their LAC "spies" heard about the program, they might decide to screen out troublemakers. Gradually, as confidence grew among participants in the unlikely group-defined program and in the facilitator, the women began to speak out on their problems. Other women began to join.

At one level, the Peer Group program, which spread to five public housing developments over the next several years, was a success. For its members, the experience was a strengthening one. "We all lived separately," one woman, who later became a Peer Group leader, explained. "We were able to share some ideas and goals for ourselves that we needed to work on." Most women worked on their personal goals. Thus, for example, a school dropout who, as she expressed it, "spent most of my life trying to get my children reared" finished high school at an alternative high school for adults and went on to take community college courses in child development in preparation for working with a day-care center. A young woman, who dreamed of moving her five children out of public housing, attended real estate school, obtained a license, and managed to find a job and acquire a house for her family. Some women pooled their ideas and efforts to improve life for their families. One group devoted considerable time to developing after-school and summer programs for their children in a gang-ridden area.

But from the perspective of social transformation, the program that fostered a degree of critical reflection among increasing groups of women failed nonetheless to significantly alter the conditions of their day-to-day lives. They never attempted to challenge the arbitrary and dehumanizing control that CHA exercised over their lives and their living conditions nor even to demand that their grievances be heard. Living in a city where even Martin Luther King and his veteran staff of protest leaders and negotiators finally gave up, defeated in their efforts to achieve a more open city by a callously indifferent political machine, the Peer Group members had no expectation of being heard.

Finally, a Movement Begins. In 1983, what would have been unimaginable a decade earlier happened: Harold Washington, a reform candidate, was elected the first black mayor of Chicago. The triumphant groups who supported him included a huge turnout of black voters together with white liberals and Latino newcomers to Chicago politics. When black leadership approached Congressman Washington to be their mayoral candidate, the seasoned, articulate politician, who had "grown up" in Chicago politics, responded that he would be willing to run if they were able to register fifty thousand black voters. A zealous voter registration drive followed. Ward by ward, blacks from throughout the city's segregated south- and west-side neighborhoods, including residents in the nineteen CHA developments, became involved in the drive to register their neighbors. By the end of the summer, they had registered one hundred thousand new black voters. The Washington campaign that followed was aptly described by its manager, Al Raby, a longtime civil rights leader: "This is not a campaign; it's a movement."

The dedicated movement spirit that carried Washington into office by a narrow margin prevailed over the next years in the face of bitter opposition by racist leaders of the aging machine. Although living conditions in the poorly managed Housing Authority evidenced little change, residents who had been part of the movement that elected the first black mayor began to believe in the possibility of change. Several former Peer Group members from Cabrini Green, reputedly the most dangerous gang-dominated development, heard about resident management in St. Louis and had traveled there to see for themselves. They returned convinced that under the new mayor resident management could become a reality in Chicago, "starting in Cabrini Green," one of the group predicted.

To support this promising new spirit, Lindeman Center of Northern Illinois University sponsored a weekend workshop, "Toward a New Partnership," which was planned with residents. The weekend session brought together small groups of residents from three developments and administrators from CHA, including the executive director, with leaders of successful resident management corporations in St. Louis and Jersey City. The CHA residents participating in the weekend were inspired by hearing, firsthand, about the successful struggles against intolerable living conditions that caused protesting residents to organize resident management corporations and negotiate with local authorities to run their own developments.

The weekend workshop, although it generated excitement and a vision of what might be, failed to produce a group of residents committed to action. Returning to their several developments, they met with active opposition on the part of the manager and local advisory council (who viewed resident management as a threat to their jobs and power base); they also faced a vast majority of residents whose years in public housing left them resigned, apathetic, or, at best, skeptical and a Chicago Housing Authority, in spite of the apparent interest expressed by its director in "the new partnership," that continued to be an aloof, bureaucratic, and top-down structure.

In the course of follow-up workshops offered by Lindeman Center to help participants examine and deal with the resistances they were encountering, local leaders from other developments, who had heard about the resident management weekend, asked to join. Three of these local leaders, from Dearborn Homes, asked Lindeman Center to work with them to achieve resident management in their development. In response to their invitation, Lindeman Center and a core group of enthusiastic residents embarked on what they have since called "our journey."

The journey has been a learning experience for residents, for the Lindeman Center, and, ultimately, for the Chicago Housing Authority. The residents who formed the Dearborn Homes Resident Management Steering Committee, primarily women heads-of-household who had never served on a board or steering committee before, had to learn how to manage their own meetings as well as to learn about management. In the course of their early meetings, the Lindeman Center served both as a resource and a prod to action, introducing the idea of group agenda building, simplified Robert's Rules, and raising questions that forced members to reflect on proposed solutions before acting. They had to engage in considerable reflection, for example, before they decided how to deal constructively with a threatened and negative local advisory council: They decided to invite its president and others to serve on their steering committee and assume joint leadership in working to achieve resident management. They had to learn about the intricacies of developing a board structure and bylaws before they could apply to the State of Illinois for incorporation to become the Dearborn Homes Resident Management Corporation (DHRMC). Far more difficult, they had to think through the development of ways to organize their neighbors so that most of the twenty-five hundred residents of Dearborn would support resident management. Their initial idea was to tell them about resident management through public meetings. When this effort failed to attract significant support or even understanding of the idea, Lindeman Center worked with them to develop a six-week workshop, "Introduction to Resident Management." In the workshop, groups of twenty to thirty residents at a time learned about and discussed aspects of resident management and how, as in other cities, they could join together to improve living conditions in their development.

Beyond merely introducing a growing number of residents to resident management, the DHRMC, working with Lindeman Center and others, learned how to develop and carry out programs that involved and directly benefited participants and the community. Among these have been handyman workshops, where residents gained skills for doing long-neglected repairs in their apartments, a youth-in-action project to give youth a voice and role in the community as well as providing them with an alternative to gang membership, and a young parents association to respond to the needs of young mothers as inexperienced parents and as young adults needing social and educational opportunities. To carry out these programs, the DHRMC had to learn how to develop grant proposals so that it could obtain funds and hire residents to staff them. This, in turn, led to learning how to keep books and prepare financial records.

Perhaps most difficult, they had to learn, along with Lindeman Center, how to deal with the bureaucracy and changing politics of the Chicago Housing Authority. In preparing themselves to manage their development, they have met with four successive CHA executive directors in two years to attempt to learn the criteria for contracting management services to tenant groups. They have also sought training funds available under recent federal housing legislation. After submitting a lengthy proposal and documentation to CHA and learning that their proposal had received a federal appropriation, they have sought for many months to actually receive the funds. Each time, they have been given new requirements to fulfill and new reasons why the funds have been held up.

If the Dearborn Homes Resident Management Corporation and growing numbers of residents were not so totally committed to their goal, they would have given up the journey long

ago. Instead, the president of the corporation, a thirty-year resident of Dearborn Homes and a "full-time volunteer," said quietly
but firmly to the most recent CHA executive director when they
met recently, "We are going to achieve resident management."
Lindeman Center had learned, above all, how powerful a tool
emancipatory education can be when the learners are committed to completing the journey, to achieving their vision no matter
what the obstacles.

Reflective Engagement

Paulo Freire became known to American adult educators
in the early 1970s when, for the first time, several of his works
were published in English (Freire, 1970a, 1970b, 1973). His
literacy efforts in Brazil and later in Chile quickly became
models for numerous grass roots educational efforts throughout
the United States. As with the student leaders at Highlander
or the CHA residents in Chicago, Freire organized emancipatory
education as a component of a larger revolutionary movement.
The outcome of literacy classes was not individual skills, but
full participation in land reform, the democratic organization
of villages and communities, and economic development. The
aim was not *individual* empowerment, but *social* empowerment.
Freire recently wrote: "Even when you individually feel yourself
most free, if this feeling is not a *social* feeling, if you are not
able to use your recent freedom to help others to be free by
transforming the totality of society, then you are exercising only
an individualist attitude toward empowerment or freedom" (Shor
and Freire, 1987, p. 109).

Freire began with a critical analysis of traditional forms
of schooling — what he called "banking education" (Freire, 1970b,
p. 58) wherein educators *deposit* knowledge in the empty vaults
of students' minds. Education is never politically neutral. It either
offers *reasonable* explanations for oppression — thus serving to
maintain the existing social order — or it offers possibilities for
critical self-reflection to challenge assumptions underlying those
explanations. The latter is possible only within a praxis of
liberation — critical self-reflection in the context of transformative
action to change the social order. The term that Freire uses to

describe this process is *conscientization.* Conscientization is not simply bringing what is hidden into consciousness through the revelation of a teacher who "knows." This would, after all, be merely another instance of "banking education." Conscientization is a breaking into consciousness of hidden dimensions of our reality through our *reflective engagement* in resisting the oppressions of day-to-day life. Both critical reflection and transformative action are essential to conscientization.

Educators frequently promote their work as *the* remedy for pervasive social problems, from inequality to teen pregnancy. Individuals, equipped with new knowledge and skills dispensed in schools, are expected not only to transform themselves but to be simultaneously empowered to transform the world. That schooling has consistently failed to make a significant difference in the social and economic situation of most learners seems not to dampen educators' confidence in the singular importance of education to social change.

Adult education, as a movement with historical roots in voluntarism, reflection, and democratic action, might seem exempt from such school-based pretensions. But even those progressive adult educators who have resisted the security and prestige of formal institutions can and frequently do hold an exaggerated view of their role in the transformation of society. Professionalization and the detailed division of labor within specialized organizations have combined to separate educational enterprises from other activities — most notably, organizing and direct action — leaving the transmission of knowledge and skill disembodied from day-to-day conflict and its resolution. While many emancipatory education efforts encourage critical reflection and transformative learning, little attention is given to the political apparatus into which the newly released energy of "transformed" learners must flow. This latter task is, after all, not the responsibility of a professionalized and specialized adult educator. The problem still remains that, even in a Freirean model of education, people can change their theories without having improved their capacity to change their situation.

At issue is the relationship between education and the transformation of society. What is the influence of *mind* in situations of oppression? To what extent does the way we *think about* our reality affect our ability to change it? Clearly our *meaning perspective* can be both a defense against oppression and an obstacle to liberation. The mind adjusts to the body's chains, develops a rationale that makes sense of injustice and order out of chaos. A cartoon shows a man pressed in the grips of an enormous vise and carries the caption, "What I lose in freedom, I gain in security." The security of dependency *is* a pervasive trade-off for freedom, substituting a welfare system (which preserves inequality) for transformative action (which challenges the economic system's disproportionate allocation of resources). Fatalism — an adjustment of the mind to the inevitability of poverty and disenfranchisement — is an antibody, attacking occasional virulent strains of discontent and rebellion. As Mannoni (1956) noted in his studies of colonized peoples, the oppressed only feel inferior when their dependency is threatened. As the welfare system becomes less and less dependable and as a gap between media images and actual life in America widens, so do discontent and rebellion attain epidemic proportions, occasionally breaking out in a movement for liberation and change (Piven and Cloward, 1977).

The potential for adult education to play a critical role in the development of a counterhegemonic perspective at such times is beyond dispute. In fact, in the absence of adult education and the critical reflection that it can foster, vision is likely to be limited and its outcomes short-lived. Many of the noted "victories" of community groups organized by Saul Alinsky in the 1950s were destined to reinstitute the oppression they initially overcame, because people drawn to these organizations were never developed. They understood the immediate objective of their struggle, but not the principles upon which it was based.

Developing vision, exploring the range of the possible, and strengthening the capacity and resolve for change are tasks for which adult educators should be well suited. However, vision is not rooted in education but in the social world itself. Education interprets and transmits but does not cause the conditions, the concrete tasks and limits, that shape social and historical change. Education is a road with successive destinations. It cannot of itself build a new society but can only accompany and strengthen each newly identified act of social reconstruction. In the dialectic of liberation, both new and old coexist, the new being born even before the old has ended. By investing in education without social or political organization to effect change, learners meet with frustration and failure. Even the remarkable achievements of Freire in Chile quickly disappeared with the assassination of President Salvador Allende; the political context for newly literate peasants to have a voice succumbed to a military dictatorship. Doomed to failure from the start are the efforts of those who attempt to create emancipatory education with no vision of the future grounded in present or emerging events and organizations. They are like purchasers of land parcels in retirement villages who later find they own a desolate patch of desert. This desert is no more habitable than the futureless world proposed by adult educators without vision.

Even with vision, the substitution of new theories for the old, fatalistic ones is simply not enough. At the same time, there must be structures at hand through which action can be undertaken — a reform government, political party, community organization, or a social movement — or the potential for developing such structures. It is not merely the mind, dulled into acquiescence by an atrophied imagination, that blocks liberating, transformative action. It is concrete situations, structures, and organizations that maintain oppression. Only in creating equally concrete alternatives to these does liberation occur. The task is never simply educational. While education is critical to social transformation, it is not decisive. The celebrated "National Literacy Initiative" of the Reagan administration was unable to accomplish in four years what Nicaragua accomplished in three months. Why? Because only in Nicaragua had education been linked with the mechanisms by which newly literate adults could have a voice and effect political change.

Developing emancipatory education *in the absence* of concrete political options raises serious and wide-ranging ethical questions for the adult educator. Freire faced this in Brazil and Chile, when military coups interrupted progressive reforms, as well as in his last major literacy campaign in Guinea-Bissau

(Freire, 1978). Emancipatory education always requires political judgment concerning the configuration of a just society, for justice is always concrete and embodied in specific political options. If education is not neutral, as Freire contends, then neither is the educator. Educators can, and do, make errors of judgment that hold terrible consequences for others. Freire was criticized for just such a lapse of judgment in relation to Guinea-Bissau (Harasim, 1983). The responsibility in emancipatory education, as in all education, is awesome because it is ultimately a political act. And all political acts, however well intentioned, involve risks. Nonetheless, for an educator to do nothing or to merely continue the hegemonic practices of state-sponsored education is also to choose and to risk choosing wrongly.

Redefined as *part* of a social change process, emancipatory education is sustained by the same ethical imperative that drives movements for reform or revolution—its value is measured in terms of the social transformation toward which it points. It provides a dialogical process by which learner-activists engage in critical self-reflection, discerning ambiguity and cultural dissonance in day-to-day struggles by which their new consciousness faces squarely the moral demands of their own freedom. Conscientization forces a choice but does not determine the result: One may choose to act or to acquiesce and adapt.

Conscientization—the dynamic and dialectical interplay between critical reflection and transformative action—is not produced by educators. It is the result of reflective engagement in history—of what Freire calls the "praxis" of liberation. Educators can reveal oppressive conditions and the mechanisms, often hidden from consciousness, by which human freedoms are diminished. But, ultimately, conscientization can only occur when learners *experience* and *reflect upon* the boundaries between their own ability to act and the moral demands of their freedom. A picket line, fear of violence in public housing, the degradation of unemployment, or the arbitrary denial of the right to vote can become such a "boundary situation" and a beginning for emancipatory education. Conscientization is not merely speculative or theoretical interpretations of experience. It is not simply a new way of making sense of nonsensical and oppressive conditions. It is critical reflection—looking back on assumptions underyling our experience and redefining our own being not merely as knowers but as reflective doers. The knowledge content of conscientization is embedded in resistance (Merleau-Ponty, 1962).

Therefore, transformative learning accompanies historical struggles for change, such struggles being that toward which critical reflection bends and within which contradictions in the social order become apparent. Transformative learning does not create struggle; it is the gradual and progressive creation of a conceptual framework for participation in a struggle already begun.

The Cycle of Conscientization

Educators who would link critical reflection with struggle for change follow a cycle that begins and ends in action. Critical learners attempt to learn from action—either their own or the action of others. For student leaders meeting at Highlander it was a sit-in, for residents of public housing in Chicago it was the emergence of black political leadership and the example of residents of Cochran Gardens in St. Louis and Kennelworth-Parkside in Washington, D.C.

A Learning Stance. Emancipatory education begins with the invitation of a community or group engaged in a struggle. An educator's first responsibility is to listen, to learn from the community, and experience in a critical way the struggle in which the community is engaged. With the community's consent, an educator begins to seek out others who have faced similar problems in their communities, some of whom might have developed solutions. It is from among these others that peer resources and allies in struggle can be found to assist in subsequent stages.

Collective and Critical Reflection. Before a learning-related solution can be advanced, the question must be clear. Identification of the problem—what Ira Shor (1987, p. 93) calls "extraordinarily reexperiencing the ordinary" — is the first and most important educational task in which peers undertake participatory research, systematically examine their assumptions, and expand their awareness of options. Ever-widening circles of community participation are encouraged. Adult educators can facilitate this process, assisted by the peer resource persons already mentioned. Alternative strategies are developed. The shape and direction of a project emerges that will mobilize participants and engage their knowledge and skill in action.

Transformative Action. The community acts. New organizations may be formed or ongoing organizations strengthened. An educator's role during this phase might include continued support of participatory research, training, preparation of written materials, film or audio documentation, proposal writing, or the legitimation of community-produced knowledge. This, in turn, leads to further learning and critical reflection as the cycle continues.

The student sit-in leaders who gathered at Highlander for their historic workshop came knowing that the agenda was theirs, based not on what educators thought they should learn and do but on their experiences and their goals. The Greensboro sit-in was fresh in their minds as they reassessed their situation and their potential for changing it.

Thus, at the opening season as the students shared their protest experiences, the Highlander staff listened and learned how and what their bold efforts had accomplished from spontaneous, uncontemplated beginnings. In helping the group to move beyond their local actions to conceptualizing a Southwide movement, the educators played a vital role. By asking probing questions, they caused the students to reflect on their implicit beliefs, their methods, and their relationship to the larger community.

As a result, with Highlander as a movement resource, in one short weekend student sit-in leaders were able not only to understand the larger social implications of their actions but to project possible strategies and an organizational structure that were to become the strategies of the southern student movement under the leadership of the Student Nonviolent Coordinating Committee.

We Cannot Inspire Unless First We Conspire

The practice of emancipatory education, as discussed in this book, is marginal to the overall adult education enterprise in the United States for two reasons: First, adult educators have generally failed to link their efforts with movements for change and, second, agents of change have been unable to create a unified and compelling vision of the future.

Reflecting Without Acting. Transformative action is both source and consequence of transformative learning. The new pedagogy to which seminal resistance gives birth heightens consciousness of the contradictions between old and emerging realities and leads to further, more clearly defined strategies for action. "Doing education" might well be a logical beginning for those of us who spend a major portion of our lives in school. But when we *begin* with education — when critical reflection reflects only upon the structures of learning — our focus moves inward, and change, if it occurs at all, is confined to an artificial school world. Some educators build alternatives that avoid many of the more oppressive characteristics of traditional classrooms, but nonetheless mimic schools in recruiting individuals whose only shared activity is the school itself. Such alternatives frequently become ends in themselves, unrelated to social, political, or economic change. They aim to transform minds without transforming action. But for individual learners, with neither peers nor parties to support them, transformative action in relation to oppression outside the classroom is unlikely. They are all dressed up, with no place to go.

A commitment to social change is generally absent in programs that recruit individual competitors for wealth and status, those who believe schooling is the key to personal success and freedom. Not only are such programs disconnected from underlying social issues and struggles that permeate day-to-day life and from which critical reflection emerges, but they lack channels into which the transforming energies of a liberatory praxis can flow.

Learning Without Vision. A second reason for the marginality of emancipatory education has been a lack of vision. Vision implies knowledge of the destination — where the educational path is headed. Designs for social transformation are disparately conceived. Strategies and organizations are not connected to a generalized struggle. Reasons for this abound: the resiliency of the American social system and its ability to absorb dissent and thwart coalitions, as well as the inadequate visions of leaders and participants in social activist groups. The interests of women are effectively played against the interests of minorities, and the needs of blacks are used against Hispanics, so that a shared vision of a new social order is fragmented and contradictory. But even more, in programs unaffiliated with transformative action, no socially transforming goals are presented and the journey is thereby without destination. In place of such goals, the illusory vision of dominant society is offered: jobs, a position in the economic order, and special-interest voice in its political processes.

Clarity of vision is preceded by acts of resistance that bring to consciousness possibilities inherent in an emergent social order. Without commitment to action, emancipatory education lacks the possibility of vision, because transforming action is the ground upon which the future is experienced and known in the present. Action upon the world fills consciousness with the past (the world before we act upon it), the present (the action itself), and the future (the world that is coming into being). Visions of possible futures abound, but unless these visions accompany transforming action they lack political relevance. Education can give words to the vision, but emancipatory education anticipates that vision in its alliance with social movements that give the future its shape. The "word" in which vision is first spoken is transformative action. For Freire, this is true literacy, not the accumulation of words, but the achievement of a voice.

With neither action nor vision, emancipatory education atrophies. Action and vision are the matter and form of liberation and the sine qua non of conscientization. Although many participants in adult education programs across the United States are in the midst of struggle — are, in fact, under siege — their programs do not allow them to be co-participants in transformative action. No vision of the future is offered them, other than Horatio Alger stories of individual accomplishment. Among these programs there are exceptions — alternatives that work better, that give learners room to express themselves and to share in learning rather than compete for knowledge as though it were a prize. But most alternatives remain irreconcilably distinct from the day-to-day world in which the battle for survival rages.

Our Vision and Agenda. Most of what is acknowledged to be adult education now occurs in schools — formal institutions formed specifically and exclusively for instruction, training, and credentialing such as adult education centers, college-related extension and community service offices, and the like. Less likely to be reported in adult education journals and textbooks is the work of community activists who also function as adult educators in unions, coalitions, block clubs, women's rights organizations, welfare groups, day-care centers, and associations of racial or ethnic groups. There is little collaboration between school-based educators and social activists, and in pursuing their separate agendas, it is the activist who is better positioned to facilitate conscientization.

Conscientization is the mind's bending back to reflect upon experienced, collective resistance, to theorize and create a rationale for acting against existing oppression while simultaneously imagining alternatives. It occurs dialogically, that is, in communication with others who are similarly engaged in struggle. For Freire (1970a, p. 17), conscientization occurs in relation to collective action. When adult educators attempt to *do* emancipatory education within a school or other specialized educational agency, they encounter great difficulty in identifying both generative themes — common experiences of oppression and resistance — and the agency through which learners can engage in transformative action. Only in alliance with social activists and in identification with the aims of social justice and equality can adult educators develop a curriculum for *social* empowerment based on critical reflection and transformative action. The meaning perspective that emerges in such a curriculum is both visionary and grounded in day-to-day struggle. Involvement in transformative action cannot be merely tacked onto an already existing program, like an optional field experience. It is the core of emancipatory education.

Numerous factors inhibit the alliance of formal educators and activists. The self-interest of well-endowed and publicly supported institutions — the employers or funders of adult educators — frequently conflict with the interests of community-based organizations representing low-income, disenfranchised groups. Schools and universities adopt narrowly defined missions that serve society's dominant agenda and preserve the status quo. To avoid the wrath of legislators or wealthy alumni, these institutions often separate learning from doing and emphasize a speculative and abstract curriculum, lest learners begin to use their knowledge in political action. Schools and universities are places to get away from day-to-day life, not vehicles for immersion into struggle. They emphasize the development of individuals who, through schooling and the mastery of knowledge and skill, will be "advantaged" in rigged competition for status and fortune. If educational institutions are allies of resistance, it is only in resisting change.

Not only educational institutions inhibit the alliance of formal educators and activists. By training, adult educators themselves are ill disposed to support resistance and transformative action and hence are likely to keep more "respectable" company. Underlying the professionalization of adult educators is a functionalist model in which the preservation and maintenance of the stability and immutability of the social order are highly valued. Any interference in the normal equilibrium of society is assumed to jeopardize not only the social order but, more important, the improving social and economic status of professional educators.

The bottom line for specialized, academically trained educators is that it is difficult for them to engage in emancipatory education — difficult but not impossible. Even within hegemonic institutions, open spaces can be found wherein educators play upon the system's embedded contradictions and align themselves with movements for change. Only in testing the boundaries of sanctioned behavior can we discover our true limits. That so many fail to do this is possibly one more instance of what Jack London once called the "trained incapacities" of academics. The fact remains, despite systemic conservatism, that educational organizations can and do support educators who, through their academic work, pursue a transforming and liberating agenda outside the classroom. Participatory and action research, prison education, technical support of grass-roots initiatives, community-based internships, and direct support for popular education are but a few examples of vehicles through which institution-based educators engage in an emancipatory praxis while at the same time building a constituency and political base for themselves and the institutions that employ them.

Emancipatory projects will be defined in collaboration with activist groups and organizations rather than individuals. Underlying such projects are values consistent with a Freirean pedagogy:

- Emancipatory projects should be initiated at the invitation of the community for whom they are undertaken and in response to its agenda.
- Emphasis should be placed on resources indigenous to the community itself, rather than on institutional resources that are beyond the control of the community and therefore foster dependence.
- From the beginning, steps should be taken to ensure community control of projects involving the educator's institution.
- Emancipatory educational activities should encourage and support full community involvement in the production of knowledge related to local goals and strategies, building on the rich tradition within adult education for participatory research (Hall, 1975).

In its best moments, emancipatory education deprofessionalizes the adult educator. Critical, self-reflective learners become their own teachers and facilitators of critical reflection in others. By building emancipatory education projects within action-oriented groups and organizations, educators provide a base for ongoing educational work independent of their institutions' vested interests. These projects are spun off, often becoming freestanding organizations. Emancipatory educators build no empires but often leave behind them ongoing programs under community control. The success of their work is not measured in test scores or retention rates but in specific improvements in the conditions of life, in the attainment of economic and political power by formerly dispossessed and disenfranchised groups, and most especially in the programmatic independence of the community as it continues training and education on behalf of its goals.

Education will become emancipatory only to the extent that emancipatory acts are pursued within political institutions and social movements. Durkheim stated this in his work on the evolution of educational thought:

> Educational transformations are always the result and the symptom of the social transformations in terms of which they are to be explained. For a people to feel at any given moment the need to change its educational system, it is necessary that new ideas and needs have emerged for which the old system is no longer adequate. But these needs and ideas do not arise spontaneously; if they suddenly come to the forefront of human consciousness after having been ignored for centuries, it is necessarily the case that in the intervening period there has been a change and that it is this change of which they are an expression [Durkheim, 1977, p. 92].

A growing interest in emancipatory education parallels a cultural transformation already begun. Our history provides rich, if infrequent, examples of how adult education can contribute to social movements. That history also suggests that admonitions against the old order and panegyrics in praise of the new both ring false, unless accompanied by political action. Not by what we say but by what we do are we judged. We cannot inspire unless first we conspire. Adult educators must strategize together with the people whose interests they hope to serve and outline the practical consequences of their mutual learning. Emancipatory education is not an academic task or even a specialized one. Its teachers are not prepared in graduate programs of adult education, where a "banking" pedagogy predominates. Instead, both educators and learners become critically reflective in shared struggles for nontechnocratic, nonpatronizing, nonbureaucratic, nongovernmental solutions to real problems. It is here — in these struggles — that conscientization begins.

References

Durkheim, E. "On Education and Society." In J. Karabel and A. H. Halsey (eds.), *Power and Ideology in Education.* New York: Oxford University Press, 1977.

Freire, P. *Cultural Action for Freedom.* Cambridge, Mass.: Harvard Educational Review Press, 1970a.

Freire, P. *Pedagogy of the Oppressed.* New York: Seabury Press, 1970b.

Freire, P. *Education for Critical Consciousness.* New York: Seabury Press, 1973.

Freire, P. *Pedagogy in Process.* New York: Seabury Press, 1978.

Hall, B. "Participatory Research: An Approach for Change." *Convergence,* 1975, *8,* 2.

Harasim, L. M. "Literacy and National Reconstruction in Guinea-Bissau: A Critique of the Freirean Literacy Campaign." Unpublished doctoral dissertation, Ontario Institute for Studies in Education, University of Toronto, 1983.

Horton, A. I. "The Highlander Folk School: A History of the Development of Its Major Programs Related to Social Movements in the South, 1932–1961." Unpublished doctoral dissertation, Department of Adult Education, University of Chicago, 1971.

Mannoni, D. O. *Prospero and Calaban.* New York: Praeger, 1956.

Merleau-Ponty, M. *Phenomenology of Perception.* London: Routledge & Kegan Paul, 1962.

Piven, F. F., and Cloward, R. A. *Poor People's Movements: Why
  They Succeed, How They Fail.* New York: Pantheon Books,
  1977.

Shor, I. *Critical Teaching and Everyday Life.* Chicago: University
  of Chicago Press, 1987.

Shor, I., and Freire, P. *A Pedagogy for Liberation: Dialogues on
  Transforming Education.* South Hadley, Mass.: Bergin & Garvey, 1987.

Five

Integrating
Personal and
Social Ideologies

William Bean Kennedy

Each of us "breathes in" an ideology as we live and grow in our society. Each person takes on or takes in the prevailing set of assumptions about reality—the meaning perspective—of the particular social group that provides the immediate context for his or her socialization. Each such particular social group in turn takes on and passes on the overall hegemonic ideology of the broader society. Through that process of enculturation, a person develops a self-identity and a self-interest, both of which reproduce the reality framing and value assumptions of the social group and the larger society. Each person therefore is located in a matrix of personal and group self-identity and self-interest. The ideology of that matrix shapes the way that person views the world and all social relationships. The ideology is to some degree a false consciousness, since the "filters" through which one perceives are products of the person's and the group's history and favor the vested interests that have sustained and nurtured them. That same self-interest aspect of the group's ideology demands constant negotiation with the larger hegemonic ideology, which is continually shaping and reshaping itself as it tries to maintain control over the society as a whole.

But the process is not simply automatic, nor does the hegemony automatically control. Rather, the negotiations are

99

continual, in a sense constituting the breathing of the body politic as it continues to exist in history. Nor does an individual simply reproduce the prevailing assumptions, either of the hegemonic sphere of influence or of the immediate social group. Instead, cultural and personal characteristics foster resistance in the individual. For various reasons, each person has a reservoir of idiosyncratic characteristics that do not fit neatly the prevailing social perspectives. What happens is a constant negotiating and conflictual process between individual and social group similar to the ideological negotiating and conflictual process under way among the social groups in the larger society.

Most of this negotiating process at the two levels is hidden from our consciousness, going on with the seeming naturalness and inevitability that the ideological process encourages. The inertia of the powerful macrostructure and the momentum of the enculturating process upon each person appear to be givens. These givens are accepted and internalized as are the various assumptions making up the whole. Yet, as persons experience other perspectives or sense contradictions within the accepted framework, they often wonder about and question the givens they receive.

A helpful metaphor is that of the cocoon, within which protective framework the larvae develop. Changes occur inside, but the parameters of reality are formed by the limits of the cocoon. In a more complex way, human beings are formed and form themselves within some limited perspective. The larvae eventually break out of the cocoon and fly away as butterflies. Human beings experience many potential breakthroughs when events in their lives test the perceived parameters or thrust these people "outside," where they can gain some distance on the framework. There, they may question not only the internal contradictions but the limitations themselves.

This chapter attempts to explore those moments in personal histories when such questions and challenges to the ideological context occur and to analyze the forces that nurture those moments into greater critical consciousness. Such probing, employing critical self-reflection and critical reflection and analysis, can contribute substantively to transformative learning.

The method will be, first, to conduct an autobiographical search through one person's history, asking:

1. What events or relationships in my life have awakened in me a consciousness of dissonance, a questioning of the given and the accepted, particularly those intense seminal ones that are remembered because they illumine others?
2. What forces or influences have shaped my experience and perceptions of those events and relationships, and how can I probe into their systemic connections in such a way as to develop a larger, more systematic critique of the "given"?

My purpose in this search is educational, to help us analyze those experiences in order to identify the ideologies at work and to develop supportive or resistant responses to them. From that analysis, we can find clues for strategies by which educators can offer liberating possibilities for human awareness and action.

This ideological probing will be discussed through two approaches. The first describes an exercise that opens up the subject for individuals, introducing them to critical reflection and analysis of the ideological dimensions of their experience. The second is a more analytical organization of the results of personal breakthrough experiences in regard to racism, sexism, and classism — three massive fault lines in the human ecology today.

Ideological Analysis of
Personal Breakthrough Experiences

Many ways of probing into one's experience avoid serious effort to make connections between the individual and the macrostructures that shape the ideological context within which one lives. However, the approach discussed here focuses directly on those ideological dimensions that connect the personal and the political.

In classes and workshops over the years, I have developed a method by which people can reflect critically and then analyze the ways they are influenced by and resist the dominant or hegemonic ideology of their society. Below is an illustration of the process I use to get people in my classes to examine breakthrough experiences in their lives. Each section (to which the class participants would respond) is followed by my response, from events in my own life, to illustrate how this process works. In my workshops, after writing their notes either in advance of the session or during it, participants discuss their breakthroughs with one another in small groups and perhaps in the full group as well. Later they may expand their analysis in a written paper.

Probe back into your life and identify some moment or event when you became aware that you had been living in a particular, closed cultural and ideological cocoon. Describe what happened when you "broke through," had an "ah-hah!" experience, and became conscious that you now saw things in a new way. Briefly describe the event.

I was in high school during World War II. The education director in our large church had encouraged us to invite a young Japanese American who had been interned with her family in California to spend a weekend with our youth group in Spartanburg, South Carolina. The education director asked me if I would take the young woman to the movies on Saturday night. I said, "Sure." Gas was rationed, so that night I walked with the young woman to the theater — a mile up Main Street, then three blocks down Church Street to the Carolina Theater, and the same way back home after the show. Spartanburg was crowded on Saturday with all the folks who came to town, and the sidewalks were full of people most of the way. One-third of the people in our town were black, but with segregated schools and churches, we whites had only occasional interpersonal contact with them. Through a part-time cook in our home and a washerwoman's family, I knew "colored" people but was not seriously aware of "racism." That night I became conscious of it! All the way to the movies, I felt the stares and sensed the disapproval of people as I walked with a young woman with a Japanese face — the "enemy" who had attacked Pearl Harbor! I still remember the emotions that were part of that learning.

Locate yourself at that time in your life, for example, in regard to socioeconomic class, family situation, and educational or work setting.

Our family was not "country club," although most of the young people in our church group were. My father had lost his drugstore a decade earlier during the Depression and since then had worked in other drugstores without much enthusiasm. Times were not easy. My older brother and two older sisters had finished college, and the brother and two brothers-in-law were either in service or soon to be there. My younger brother and I were home with my parents and my father's sister, who taught high school English. New Deal housing legislation had saved our house, and we all worked spare-time jobs to help out. Our church meant a great deal to me, and my brother and brother-in-law-to-be were in theological seminary prior to their becoming chaplains. I guess we could be called poor but cultured middle class.

Analyze the forces that were keeping you in your cocoon, and those that helped the breakthrough occur. Record your notes, using the back pages if necessary.

Toward Breakthrough	*Social Forces*	*Toward Status Quo*
Wartime economic upswing in town	*Global, national, historical events*	Segregated society, schools, churches
Mobility with military service		Textile domination of the economy
Army camp, soldiers from the North		Patriotism intensified

Aunt's resignation over women's rights	*Family*	Dress, haircut code
Intellectual curiosity		General racism from culture
Daddy's uneasiness over "Jim" and "Cap'n" when talking with blacks		Black cook, black washerwoman
Sense of class in "tracks," courses, teachers	*Schooling*	Teacher's pet, conformity expected
Socioeconomic mixtures in music, sports		Racial segregation
		Assumed college in future
Military draft ahead		Military draft ahead
Educational director leadership	*Religion*	Docetic, abstract theology
High school ecumenical group		Nonprophetic preaching; worship
Brother in "liberal" seminary against an elder's advice		Conservative Sunday school teachers
Family memory of courageous preacher-grand-father		Choir and music "Negro mission"

Similar notes are requested for three other basic social forces: *social group, work,* and *media,* completing a rough survey of the major mediating groups between the macrostructures and the individual.

In the discussion that follows, we then ask, "How do we make connections between our own formation and the ideological macrostructural influences?" For instance, how did the church's education director learn about the opportunity to have the Japanese-American young woman? No doubt through a mailing from the Federal Council of Churches (predecessor to the National Council of Churches). Larger religious structures and networks were necessary for her to make the connection. Why did the education director respond to the letter, when the preacher probably would not have done so? In part, because she had been in a campus ministry at Florida State University, where she had been exposed to broader church activities and more prophetic social witness than were customary in local congregations.

My congregation provided a lively youth-group experience under the director's leadership, in a generally conservative religious context. Although my parents belonged to their time and place regarding general racism, it did not occur to me that they would object to my dating the young Japanese-American woman, and they did not.

The war loomed over those high school years, and we all absorbed stereotypes of the "enemy" Japanese, but that did not translate to me personally. In fact, it gave me a kind of kick to take the young woman to the show. I did not foresee the tension and learning but no doubt the education director did. It was a good lesson for me: It set me up to become conscious of the injustices of racism in society, and it stimulated me to begin making the connections between my personal life, my local social relations, and the larger social structures and processes.

These comments suggest how group discussion — with dialogue, questions, and comments from others — can develop the clues in the written notes into fuller and deeper analysis of the ideological and structurally related forces at work, by probing the connections between one's personal experience and the larger structures of society.

This focus on breakthrough experiences counteracts the determinism and sense of futility that can result from studying the immense power of ideological and material forces upon our lives. This approach can sensitize persons to the relative self-autonomy of culture in institutions of education and religion and to the fluidity and continuing negotiation and reconstruction of the ideological matrices within which we live. From this kind of probing, people can open up a host of memories as their antennae become tuned more sharply to the contradictions in and challenges to the dominant ideology. It helps them respond to an offbeat rhythm rather than to the heavy drumbeat of their culture.

Such a pivotal moment points to all the following actions in one's life, both planned and unplanned, when a person builds on the breakthrough. If more adult education experiences focused on critical reflection of these experiences, the cumulative effect would be powerful. Particularly when I became engaged in the civil rights struggle and added risk and involvement to the earlier breakthrough did the critical self-reflection deepen and expand. In the following pages, I trace such a growing process in regard to racism, sexism, and classism.

Ideological Analysis Related to
Racism, Sexism, and Classism

What forces were at work that kept a breakthrough event alive in one's memory and its meaning expanding in scope and depth? What influences prevented it from vanishing again into the vortex of the ongoing hegemonic ideology? The second approach in our analysis focuses on personal breakthrough experiences in terms of three major social-political-economic "fault lines" in today's world: racism, sexism, and classism. Again, I shall illustrate from my own experiences how such focused probing can build a broader and deeper analysis.

Racism. The breakthrough moment described and analyzed above focuses on racism. What preceding events in my life set up the readiness for that experience, and what were the forces at work in those events? What experiences since then have contributed to its cumulative effect? I shall give only a few examples.

One of the earliest came on a family trip to the beach, when my father stopped the car to ask directions of an elderly "colored" man sitting in a chair tilted back against the front of a store. "Is this the road to Charleston, Jim?" my father asked. "Yessir, Cap'n," he replied. As we drove off, I asked my father how he knew the man's name was Jim. My father hesitated, then said, "Well, that's just what we call colored men." But he was embarrassed, and I sensed that. "Why did he call you 'Cap'n'?" I asked. "Well, that's what colored men call white men." Again I got a double message — one spoken, one unspoken. What I learned did not fit neatly together.

It was "natural" to have a cook in our house. The one I remember most was a dignified colored woman named Carrie. She was much like my mother: gentle, caring, poised, and slow and careful in what she did. When I was in college, I once went to her church with her. There, she was called Mrs. Andrews and was evidently a leading pillar of the congregation. I was ashamed that I had not even known her last name. Although she was proud to have me there, I could not avoid sensing the dissonance between her status in our home and her standing in that church community.

When I was drafted in 1945, my life became more diverse. My navy experience began with boot camp in Maryland. Half of our company were from the South, as I was. The other half were Yankees from New York City and other Northeast areas, with strange names like Reggioni, Kienzle, and Rafalowitz. The first week, we trained on a huge drill field under a strong-voiced chief named Kurowski. I had heard he was the brother of Whitey Kurowski of the St. Louis Cardinals, which was my baseball team. Kurowski shouted for all those from south of the Mason-Dixon line to put up their right hands. We all did. "Now," he yelled, "stick 'em up your asses — I hate Rebels!" Suddenly, I was "the other," terribly vulnerable. Studies of the Civil War had not prepared me for that!

One day I drew a work assignment with a Negro sailor. A truck took us to the far reaches of the base and left us to do some stupid busywork. So we sat down in the shade and began to talk. He was from Cowpens, a little mill town ten miles from Spartanburg. We were both excited by the discovery that we were from the same place. So we began to ask each other, "Do you know . . . ?" To our surprise and dismay, we knew nobody in common. Suddenly, the radical separation back home of blacks and whites hit me—and him, too, I think. Again, the incident sharpened my awareness that behind what I had taken for granted there was something wrong.

In 1948, I began three years of teaching history, one in high school and two in college, and began to sense, without being able to articulate it, how the prescribed history books failed to help us become conscious of the realities of racism. The overt curriculum served the ideology of a segregated society and its segregated schools by masking the reality. Ideological distortion dominated my basic education about racism.

Many other such experiences since have continued to raise my consciousness about racism in our society and in me. Why do I remember those incidents? Had subtle counterideological questions and attitudes of protest been communicated to me by family, religious mentors like the church education director, teachers, and others whose words and influence I have now forgotten? Was it because of the uneasiness that informed my puzzlement over the contradictions I experienced? Long before I knew the word *ideology*, I experienced the conflict of different value assumptions in my context—and in my self.

Through these and other educational processes, critical reflection on the ideological forces at work gradually brought together the event with the Japanese-American young woman and my experiences of white-black relationships. As a result, my antennae have become more tuned to racism in U.S. society and in myself.

Social action against racism rounds out the learning circle, as it provides testing of our commitments at that time and forces us to deepen and sharpen our critical reflection.

In similar ways, I have seen such critical self-reflection and critical reflection and analysis open up exciting insights in students and others as they work on transformative learning with this kind of approach. Consistent and repeated educational attention to such critical reflection both refreshes and builds upon an initial breakthrough experience.

Sexism. My many experiences with sexism as an ideological issue make choosing one major breakthrough difficult.

However, for illustrative purposes, I shall select one pivotal moment and show briefly how it and related events contributed to critical self-reflection and analysis.

A breakthrough experience occurred for me in 1964 when I was invited to address a women's conference in a church conference center. During a sabbatical leave in New York, I was introduced to the emerging women's movement and had subsequently read Betty Friedan's (1964) *The Feminine Mystique.* In preparing my lectures, I could not ignore the new questions being asked by that movement.

In one of the lectures, I tried to address the implications of what I was saying from a female point of view. There were perhaps a thousand women and very few men in the audience. Since then, I have reread the transcription of that lecture and the ambivalence fascinates me — I used masculine language throughout! Nevertheless, I tried to suggest that our culture was changing in ways that demanded serious challenges to patterns and practices of patriarchal domination. Women were just beginning to be elected church officers, and ordination of women would soon come in our denomination. Therefore, it was clear that structures in both church and society, as well as personal and familial patterns, were changing. The effort to articulate to a women's audience the whole issue of sexism opened up to me a radical sense of how social structures have operated to oppress women. Only much later have I been able to see the absurdity and irony of my serving as a male authority to affirm the right of those women to fight their oppression!

Other events had prepared me for that experience. An aunt of mine was dean of women in a women's college integrated into a new university. With credentials equal to those of the male faculty, she was not permitted, as a woman, to march in the faculty processions; she protested. When nothing changed, she resigned to show her disapproval. During the 1930s and 1940s she lived with us and taught at Spartanburg High School while I was there as a student. I came to feel her pain and frustration at the patriarchal structures of education.

During my first year of teaching, in my own high school, I gradually began to see that girls and boys tended to respond differently to certain kinds of questions. When I asked questions that called for feedback of textbook material or lectures, the girls tended to do better than the boys. When I asked questions that freed students to make their own connections and refashion creatively their experiential knowledge with the textual material, the boys engaged in the activity more easily. Why? I asked. "Sugar and spice and everything nice" and "snakes and snails and puppy-dog tails" — was there something to cultural expectations of females that made them better repeaters while more dependent on the authority of text or teacher than males? The difference bothered me. Recent critical studies of education, such as Weiler's (1988) *Women Teaching for Change,* are helping us analyze more clearly some of these forces.

In my theological studies, a female professor in an ethics course lectured one day on the issue of sexism and ethical responses to sexist discrimination. One student challenged her on the basis of biblical and traditional male superiority in "nature" and the church. Obviously upset, he kept arguing, until she too became upset, losing her usual cool, dialogical style. The next day she began class by apologizing, saying, "I did not realize how difficult it would be to lead that discussion in a large, all-male class as the first and only woman teacher in this seminary." We were able to learn about the ethical issue from her emotions as well as from her intellectual mastery of the subject. Later, I was present when she became the first woman ordained in the (southern) Presbyterian church.

As I have worked with the breakthrough approach in workshops and classes, women students have shared experiences more dramatic and often more traumatic than my male examples indicate. Their struggles against patriarchy in their families, schools, and workplaces raise questions that both threaten and enrich the understanding of others, especially males.

My actions regarding sexism and my reflections on those actions have continued through many engagements with the issue in my family and my work. A strong wife and three articulate daughters have helped keep me reflecting critically on my often patriarchal behavior! My involvement in church efforts for inclusive language in worship, for instance, has deepened my awareness and changed my actions.

Classism. A third major fault line in U.S. society is that of class, the rich-poor issue. The hegemonic ideology has been able to mask or distort this problem rather successfully, making it difficult for persons both poor and well-off to perceive the issue clearly. Asking people in my workshops to describe their "social location" helps them relate their own socioeconomic background to the connections they will be making later.

A seminal occasion for my introduction to the economic problems of U.S. society came before I began school, when my father lost his drugstore in the Depression. Frustrated earlier because he could not afford medical school, he had worked hard as a young pharmacist to buy the store and develop it. I remember not actual hunger but odd things, like not having a morning newspaper delivered and having my father cut our hair with clippers borrowed from the barber. Always after losing his store, except for one brief attempt to run a small bowling alley, my father had to work for others. In those days, pharmacists worked long and hard hours, including every other Sunday. (My father actively discouraged any of us from working in the drugstore or becoming pharmacists.)

Once, in elementary school, we had to fill out a questionnaire that asked if we owned our house. "Yes," my father told me, "me and uncle!" "Uncle who?" I asked. "Uncle Sam," he said, referring to the homeowners loan program of the New Deal. We were told that had it not been for that government help, we would probably have lost our home, too. We children never worried about it, although we were quite aware of the difficulties of living on a very limited income. Once, when I was in high school, I said to my father, "Money is not everything." To which he replied, "No, but by the time you are as old as I am, you will realize it is 99 percent of it!"

From first through fifth grade, I attended Oakland Avenue School, where the majority of pupils came from families whose parents worked in a nearby cotton mill and lived in company-owned houses. The mill kids were different from us culturally and economically, although we were also poor.

I remember one little girl in second or third grade. She dressed poorly, and on cold days she wore a coat I still remember as too big for her. She had half-sisters and half-brothers, and

I did not know what that was. At Christmas, she said what she most wanted was a permanent wave! Such different values posed early questions for me about what later I would study as the relationship of economics and culture. The mill families presented another world to me, and I did not know how to "read" it. Our little neighborhood gang realized we were different from the mill kids, and they frightened us because they were "tough." I did not know how to understand the differences nor how to relate to them, although my mother tried to teach us to respect the equality of all persons.

Teachers liked me. Why should they not? I was "smart" in school skills. I had been reading before the first grade. I came from a home with books, music, and good talk and from a family who included a teacher (my aunt), and a former teacher (my mother). School learning was easy for me. I was conditioned to think I was smart, intellectual, and therefore, by school standards, better than others. It never occurred to me what a headstart I had, as I did not work as hard as many others and got better grades. Later, and gradually, I began to question the role of schooling in perpetuating both cultural and economic privilege.

The summer after high school graduation, I worked at a nearby mill to make money for college. The experience plunged me into the midst of the culture of mill workers. I learned new words I did not know existed, given my lack of education about sex! I saw how tiring the work was: women would work eight-hour shifts with only short breaks, watching a five-foot roll of cloth wind by as they checked it for bad spots. I learned how they needed interchange, conversation, and games to enable them to stand the boredom. Although I was quite out of place, it was a good education in class differences.

Later, when I was teaching in a junior college, one of my brightest students came from a carpeting factory center in north Georgia. He did not know who his father was and was ashamed of his mother. Fortunately, someone saw his potential and gave him money for that first year—during which he struggled to fit in, to balance his enthusiasm for studying with learning how to get along with other students. At the end of the year and with no money to return, he went home to work in a mill. During the summer, he wrote me a very discouraged letter, to which I replied that with his good mind he could certainly return and do well and finish—and not to worry about taking time out to earn the money to do so. Many years later, as a senior partner in a leading law firm, he told me that he still had my letter and re-read it occasionally just to remember. He helped me see how very difficult it is to overcome class disadvantage in one's background.

Years later, a colleague in the World Council of Churches wrote about how such "confidence mechanisms" spotlight the few people who move up to a higher class by luck and hard work and then use that example to "teach" lower-class people that it is their individual failure if they do not do likewise (Elliott, de Morsier, 1975).

As staff colleagues and I worked to establish the Office of Education in the World Council of Churches, we became aware of how church missionary programs had helped construct elitist structures of higher education around the world. The newly emerging countries all had a strong faith in education as the best instrument for their development, so it was difficult to know how to develop a critical analysis that would be acceptable to them.

We tried. Paulo Freire was a member of our staff, and in a series of conferences around the world, we looked at some of the ways education all too easily conforms to and helps reproduce the ideologies of society and the global political and economic structures. We recognized how our educational credentials set up and maintained the privileges we enjoyed and how the system internalized failure in the majority who left school and continued to live as the underprivileged. Those years did not provide any simple answers, but they brought my questions into a broader context and provided means of interpretation that had been missing in my U.S. educational background.

In the 1980 general assembly of the (southern) Presbyterian church, a major position paper on labor-management relations was seriously weakened by amendments in a committee that I chaired. An amendment, for instance, tied all violence to labor and left management looking quite innocent. In plenary debate, only four persons of the more than 450 present belonged to unions, and three of them were teachers, in the National Education Association! The weakened paper was adopted. For me it was a dramatic example of the class nature of the Presbyterian church, a profile that repeated surveys have supported. What, I asked myself, is the connection between the ideology of the economic system of the United States and a Protestant church known for its commitment to education and a "learned clergy"?

Such probing opens up discussion about the relationships of macroeconomic structures to the various forces and groups in society and to oneself. It raises questions about how power works through ideologies in systems of education and religion. It provides another area for critical self-reflection and critical reflection and analysis.

Conclusion

The method outlined above has proved useful in both workshops and classrooms. For it to work well requires more than one two-hour session. Participants in either setting need a good introduction, with some brief demonstration of how to get into the critical dimension of self-reflection and analysis. As I illustrated earlier, I often use a brief example of my own to begin.

I have tried to use this method to enhance the values of travel seminars, building it into the preparation, the reflection sessions during the experience, and the follow-up. This makes seminar participants conscious of the ideological filters they bring from their culture and allows them, through their various cross-cultural experiences, to analyze critically both their own ideologies and those of people back home with whom they will be sharing the experience. Such travel seminars are often breakthrough experiences for participants. When this method is included, transformative learning is enhanced (Evans, 1987). In semester-long courses on ideology and education, the approach can lead to a much more thorough self-reflection and critical analysis of students' work, family, and other life situations.

For effective long-range use of this approach, there must be carefully planned action that in turn calls forth further critical reflection, to be picked up by other adult educators in the future, in a continuing process.

I hope that readers of this chapter have been stimulated by my experiences to call up memories of their own and to subject them to critical self-reflection and critical reflection and analysis. For many, the method outlined here has contributed to a more sensitive tuning of their antennae to the ideological and structural forces to which they, and we all, are connected.

References

Elliott, C., and de Morsier, F. *Patterns of Poverty in the Third World: A Study of Social and Economic Stratification.* New York: Praeger, 1975.

Evans, A. F., Evans, R. A, and Kennedy, W. B. *Pedagogies for the Non-Poor.* Maryknoll, N.Y.: Orbis Books, 1987.

Friedan, B. *The Feminine Mystique.* New York: Dell, 1964.

Weiler, K. *Women Teaching for Change: Gender, Class and Power.* South Hadley, Mass.: Bergin & Garvey, 1988.

Six

Challenging Habits
of Expectation

Irvin Roth

One of the classic mysteries of human identity revolves around the question of how we come to be what we are. The facilitator of personal development — the teacher, the adviser, the psychotherapist — provides guidance to the student or client who is evolving from one identity to another. The facilitator operates out of an individual set of assumptions about the nature of this process, the learner or client operates out of another set of corresponding assumptions, and the process is somehow channeled by the interaction of their resulting patterned behavior. At least since the time of Plato, scholars have reflected on the true nature of the learning process and the person as a learning system, debating such questions as whether our minds are initially blank slates that record raw experience or whether they contain prior patterns and rules that guide the processing of experience. It is a relatively new approach to shift the emphasis of this enterprise to the study of the individual learner's perceptions of the process of learning, of self as learner, and of the environment as a potential support (or antagonist) to learning. Mezirow (1985) in particular has focused attention on the possibility of helping the learner reflect on his or her assumptions as a tool of taking charge of the learning process. This chapter analyzes the nature of these assumptions, which act as perceptual filters, and describes a workshop for helping learners to become aware of them.

116

One of the strategies for simplifying the understanding and management of the learning experience is to consider that it is a process of building internal representations. Korzybski (1933) spelled out very clearly the distinction between the simplified world maps we create and the infinite complexity of the experiential territory we are mapping. Bandler and Grinder (1975) described the major simplifying operations by which we transform experience into the individualized models that guide us. They identified three categories of transformational process: generalization, deletion, and distortion.

It is through generalization that we detach elements from their original experiences, using these elements to represent entire categories of experience and deriving rules for managing those experiences. For example, we learn that very hot objects cause pain and derive a rule like "stay away from them" or (more usefully) "take certain precautions with them."

Deletion refers to those processes that enable us to selectively attend to some aspects of experience and ignore others. In dealing with hot objects, we may ignore their color or surface texture in guiding our behavior. The ability to delete background noises and minor bodily sensations enables us to concentrate on conversations, tasks, and so on. Deletion that is excessively effective leads us to remain in cramped postures until our limbs fall asleep.

Distortion refers to the process by which we focus, direct, and organize sensory and conceptual information. A very fundamental example of distortion is our organizing of the perceptual world into background and foreground (and reorganizing it to suit our puposes). Distortions of perceptions are regularly used to support current beliefs (right or wrong). For example, someone who believes that men are insensitive may consider that an instance of coolness under pressure shows insensitivity, missing the possibility that the particular instance of coolness might have been a perceptive and caring behavior in the circumstances.

We each have a variety of characteristic mental patterns for organizing experience into our model of the world, specific ways in which the modeling processes are carried out. These processes are our tools for dealing with the world, and they facilitate and limit us as does any set of tools. The more tools we have, and the more flexibility and precision we have in applying those tools, the more effective we are. Human development may be seen as a cyclical movement between developing environmental mastery and refining our internal processes — our methods of organizing experience — into ever more effective tools.

It may be worth noting that the framing of mental development in this chapter differs somewhat from Mezirow's emphasis in Chapter One. Where he highlights the identification and *correction* of distortions, this chapter emphasizes the inescapable nature of distortion (as well as of generalization and deletion) in creating our models of the world. From this perspective, we are here discussing the desirability of identifying and artfully *utilizing* our distortions and other modeling processes, by refining and contextualizing them better. The difference in emphasis does not, in my understanding, reflect a difference in substance but rather one of benign competition for the possession of a common word to refer to somewhat different levels of mental function. I trust the reader will enrich his or her own understanding by noting these differences in emphasis.

A greater variety of characteristic mental patterns (perceptual filters, organizing principles) have been identified. Discussions of them are scattered throughout the literature of education, psychology, and human development. Among these patterns are such categories as leveling and sharpening, inclusive and exclusive styles of thought, introversion and extraversion. In Chapter One, Mezirow refers to processes at this level as "habits of expectation," a usage that will be followed in this chapter. No effort will be made to survey this literature. Instead, this chapter will draw on the most comprehensive listing of habits of expectation I know. I learned about them in a workshop conducted by Leslie Cameron-Bandler around 1982. The only published summary of them now available is in James and Woodsmall (1988), where they follow Cameron-Bandler in calling them "meta programs." Their account is sketchy and incomplete, but a useful orientation; I am solely responsible for the manner in which the habits of expectation are formulated in this chapter. In addition, I've amplified and elaborated James and Woodsmall's descriptions for application to education.

This chapter presents a framework that can be used to design a workshop for teachers and other communicators in identifying, utilizing, and modifying habits of expectation. The workshop has the following aims: (1) sensitizing the participants to their own habits of expectation; (2) providing some guidance and practice in identifying others' habits of expectation; (3) orienting the participants to the relevance of these habits to education; and (4) learning to utilize and modify habits of expectation. The workshop framework and elements may be used as starting points for developing adaptations to various contexts, time frames, and audiences. Simply reading about this material cannot substitute for training and experience with it. Readers may expect to need to read the material more than once and to try out parts of it in appropriate settings to acquire some mastery. Mastery of this material will broaden the participants' understanding of the dimensions of mind, will help them remedy intellectual deficits in their students and clients, and will help them to enlarge the mental dimensions of those who have no significant deficit.

Below is an outline of major categories in the constructed world of the individual and some variables in each category.

1. *Objects, enduring physical structures:* Subject to individual's power (or not); changeability
2. *Persons:* Similar to self; different from self and serving as sources of reward and punishment; similar to nonhuman physical objects (a sociopathic perception); subject to individual's power; understandable through patterned behavior, through attributed attitude
3. *Ways of learning:* Relative priority of reward and punishment in the learning process; favored sensory avenues (seeing, hearing, doing); temporal sequences (how often does something have to happen to be considered a pattern; number of repetitions needed to be considered a pattern); attending to similarities or differences

4. *Microstructure of attentional processes:* Clarity of detail, attention to outlines and boundaries, sharpness of differentiation between figure and ground; narrowness or expansiveness of field of awareness; relative emphasis on larger forms and global percepts versus details and specifics

5. *Temporal structuring:* Tempo, speed of passage, perception of flow, narrowness of temporal focus, time as figure or ground

6. *Organization of behavioral sequences:* Approach versus avoidance; source of outcome specifications and values, external versus internal

This outline is intended as a general orientation to this area; it is neither exhaustive nor precise in its formulations. The variables in each category suggest ways in which the individual's habits of expectation may be organized. For example, under Objects, "Subject to individual's power," passive people may perceive physical structures as relatively permanent and immutable, whereas more assertive, dynamic people may see them as easily subject to change and modification (a desirable stance for architects and experimental scientists); under Ways of Learning, "Relative priority . . . ," some people may organize most of their learning around the attainment of rewards, while others may organize it around avoidance of pain and loss. We will refer to an individual's characteristic position on each variable as his or her *pole* or *value* on that variable. It should also be noted that these characteristic positions usually do not preclude the person's functioning in another position in different contexts or using one position as a supplement to the predominant position.

We will focus on four habits of expectation that are particularly important in education and personal development. Suggestions are presented for identifying the individual's predominant pole or value for each habit. It is important to understand that all poles of all habits are useful. The ideal is for the individual to be capable of functioning at any of the poles, guided by well-developed intuitions about the pole appropriate to the various contexts.

The habits of expectation described below fall into two different categories. The first category—which includes the

Direction, Global/Specific, and Sameness/Difference habits—characterizes different aspects of the individual's cognitive functioning, that is, his or her approach to perceiving and organizing any information. The second category consists of the External/Internal habit and concerns itself with the individual's relative emphasis of external or internal bases for making judgments.

Cognitive Habits of Expectation

The Direction Habit. The Direction emphasis is concerned with whether people organize their thoughts and behavior in an approach or avoidance style. When they scan their experience for a cue to start a sequence of thought or behavior, do they seek something to approach or something to avoid? Do they do homework assignments in order to learn and master material (approach), or to avoid poor grades (avoidance)? Do they entice themselves out of bed in the morning with thoughts of what they will enjoy doing (approach), or do they remind themselves of the undesirable consequences of staying in bed (avoidance)? When they are given an assignment, do they more clearly see the possible approaches to a solution or the difficulties of executing it? Are they more talented in understanding the meaning and possible application of new ideas (approach) or the limitations and shortcomings of the ideas (avoidance)?

An imbalance in Direction can be disastrous. Excessive avoidance leads to pathologies like agoraphobia, to constricted and fearful life-styles, and to an inability to accept or create new ideas. Excessive emphasis on approach strategies leads to incautious behavior. Some people are born without the ability to feel pain and thus do not learn to avoid damaging experiences; their approach tendencies are not adequately counterbalanced by learned avoidance, and they do not live very long. On a less extreme level, I once had a client whose highest priority in life was to buy things for her family and others. The day she found out she would have to declare bankruptcy, she hired a yacht and invited everyone she knew for a big party on Lake Michigan. She then married the financial adviser who helped her with her bankruptcy, and they ended up consulting me because she was in the process of again spending them into bankruptcy.

The avoidance style can sometimes be identified by the many negatives in a person's conversations. People who often say things like "I don't want you to think that I . . . (never get down to work; never take responsibility; don't know how to have fun)" are prime examples. A classic illustration of a triple avoidance is the person who said to me, "I *can't* imagine how anybody could *not* want to *stop* smoking." Avoiders with an inadequate leavening of approach strategies may be obsessively attentive to flaws in others, to ways in which they disagree with others, to ways in which they themselves fall short of their ideals, and so on. Every faculty adviser eventually runs into students who are experts on what is wrong with their instructors, the educational program, the grading system, our corrupt society, and so on. A variation of this stance that may be even more debilitating is found in those students who focus obsessively on their own lack of intelligence, poor personality, lack of ambition, and other traits they want to avoid.

The above illustrations are drawn from various areas of life experience; functioning in the intellectual area will generally be similar to other areas in Direction, but this should not be taken for granted. In the intellectual realm, an approach person will be most strongly oriented toward understanding concepts and finding ways of integrating and accepting them. Too strong an approach style will lead to uncritical acceptance of any idea, research report, or other academic product with a modicum (sometimes barely discernible) of credibility. Such a style will also tend to support a freer flow of self-generated, creative ideas. A strong avoidance style will result in the overdevelopment of criteria for rejecting ideas, research, and so on; to poorly developed criteria for accepting ideas and new information; and to a strong inhibition against generating ideas.

In an adequately balanced Direction style, a person will start with either an approach or an avoidance operation but will switch between the opposing modes in a well-modulated way.

The Global/Specific (G/S) Habit. The Global emphasis has to do with attending to pattern, purpose, and connection. It includes an emphasis on superordinate (rather than subordinate) categories, on the organization of the parts in a system (rather than on the individual parts), and on the purposes or goals of actions or plans (rather than the specifics of the action sequence or plan). A Specific emphasis involves relatively greater attention to subordinate categories, the individual parts of any whole, and the specifics of plans and action sequences. In the realm of the sciences, a theoretician like Albert Einstein is more Global, whereas an experimentalist like Ehrlich (who discovered a cure for syphilis after systematically trying out 666 medications) is more Specific. A good corporate manager must give high priority to goals (Global) and avoid getting bogged down by too great a concern with details (Specific). A troubleshooting mechanic must have a strong Specific orientation.

Good functioning, thinking, and communication require a shuttling between the Global and Specific. This shuttling must be properly organized, so that the shifts occur at useful points in the thought process; so that the Global frame that is accessed is proper to the task at hand; and so that the Specifics accessed are relevant to the Global frame. An excessive emphasis on the Global orientation may lead to a tenuous contact with the real world; an excessive emphasis on the Specific may lead to disorientation, drift, or loss of a sense of purpose.

The learning facilitator can identify rigidities in G/S and design a program of remedial education when alerted to this dimension. It is also useful to notice whether people focus on the Specific first to build their Global frames or focus on the Global first as an orientation to the Specific. Organizing communications in the style of the listener will ease the listener's task of understanding.

The Sameness/Difference (S/D) Habit. The S/D emphasis is concerned with whether people understand their experience by primarily attending to similarities and uniformities or to differences and discrepancies. It operates on the basic ways in which we organize our perceptions and structure our world. When we understand a category or idea, we must know what belongs within its boundaries (Sameness) as well as what does not (Difference). Some people do their initial scanning for boundaries, discrepancies, and exceptions (Differences). Others scan initially for similarities, connections, and uniformities (Sameness). People further vary in the flexibility with which they switch to the other pole in processing an area of experience and the extent to which they are ready to use their preferred pole in different contexts. Illustrations of inflexibility are the extreme gun enthusiast who considers any regulation of guns an unacceptable curtailment of freedom (Sameness, ignoring the difference between a bazooka and a hunting rifle) and the bigot who regards the life of a member of a minority group to have no value (Difference, ignoring the equal rights to life of minorities).

An important function of S/D is in the development of differentiated conceptions and perceptions. When people realize that their present frames do not adequately organize some area of experience, they are stimulated to develop new frames or recontextualize old ones. When a child realizes that being "good," which was a very useful frame within the family, does not get the same results in the larger world, the ground has been laid for a new frame or for adapting an older one. Thus, the child will move from seeing the social worlds within and outside the family as operating by the same rules (Sameness) to noting that they do not (Difference) and will develop an alternate frame, such as the idea that some situations call for persistence and ingenuity rather than "goodness." The inability to give up an old frame (that is, to notice or accept a difference between experience and expectation) is a common block to learning.

The interplay between S/D and Direction can occur in any combination. A person may preferentially notice Sameness and seek it out (approaching the routine) or avoid it (avoiding boredom); or notice Difference and seek it out (approaching stimulation) or avoid it (avoid stimulation).

It should also be noted that Sameness and Difference orientations can operate at the level of fine perceptual processes (for example, someone who is exquisitely sensitive to minor musical disharmonies, or minor imperfections in a paint job) or at a very global level (for example, changing jobs every year or two). James and Woodsmall (1988) claim that S/D patterns on the fine perceptual level are strongly indicative of patterns on the global level.

In communicating with people at the extremes of S/D, the learning facilitator will be alerted to the difficulties a Sameness person has in appreciating differences and the difficulties a Difference person has in appreciating similarities. Understanding this may also suggest corrective education.

The Source-of-Evaluation
Habit of Expectation

Emancipatory education has its focus on helping students reflect on and make choices about their own premises (as Mezirow discussed in Chapter One). The External/Internal framing habit is of special importance for this focus, in that it refers to the location of the individual's standards of evaluation. People with a predominantly External frame depend on the judgments of others as to what is correct or incorrect, good or bad, desirable or undesirable, and so on. In the Internal frame, such judgments are based on internal reference standards. Where students are rigidified at the External pole, there will be no resistance to the internalization of learning, with a conscious focus on the evaluation of the teacher or other authority. Where students are rigidified at the Internal pole, there will be resistance to provisional adoption of alternative frames—a step that is very important for the revision of limited and mistaken sets of assumptions—unless they are perceived as originating with self.

In infancy and early childhood, there is a lack of differentiation between Internal and External reference standards. Children do not make sharp distinctions between their own perceptions and evaluations and those of their parents, especially of their mothers. The distinction between Internal and External evaluation develops as part of the differentiation between self and other and is subject to all the possible deficiencies in this development.

With secure, supportive, and well-informed parenting, children distinguish those situations in which Internal evaluations should be primary (for example, in regard to bodily sensations of hunger and bladder distention) and those in which External evaluations are most useful (for example, when learning something from an expert). From the E/I perspective, it is the task of the emancipatory educator to assist the student in examining her or his own approach to making evaluations and to considering whether some revision would be beneficial. In addition, the educator will be able to communicate more successfully by making use of the individual's current E/I perspective rather than by ignoring it. (For example, emphasizing respected authority with a strongly Internal student will make it harder for that student to use the proferred input.)

A Workshop on Habits of Expectation

Preparing the Participants. Beforehand, provide all participants with a description of the habits of expectation to be covered in the workshop. In addition, ask them to bring five statements or questions that exemplify their subject area. The following list illustrates the kinds of statements and questions that are useful and shows how people with different habits of expectation might start thinking about each of the statements.

Statement I: Explore the relationship between educational experience and student curiosity.
A.   Direction Habit
  1.   Approach pole: What data demonstrate this effect? What else supports education? Education is most effective when the student's curiosity is engaged.
  2.   Avoidance pole: What blocks the development of the trait of curiosity? What blocks the occurrence of an attitude of curiosity in the classroom? What undermines the effectiveness of a class, teacher, educational program?
  3.   Uncertain (more inquiry needed to establish whether the framer is open to both directions or has a single, underlying directional mode): Explore previous experience under x conditions.
B.   Global/Specific Habit
  1.   Global pole: What evidences are there that the students' attitudinal predisposition has a bearing on the outcome of education? What is the purpose of exploring this

question? Are there other developmental experiences channeled or affected by curiosity?
2. Specific pole: What measures of curiosity and of educational experience can we use? What aspect of educational experience are we exploring?
C. Sameness/Difference Habit
1. Sameness pole: What outcome measures should we use (thus mapping out more fully the realm identified in the question)? In what areas of research can we find parallels (for example, personality development)?
2. Difference pole: How can we distinguish educational outcomes from other developmental effects in our subjects? Does the way a teacher thinks about curiosity influence the relationship between curiosity and the outcome of a course? (This reverses the direction of causality suggested by the initial question.)
3. Sameness and Difference: Measure the relation between curiosity of students and their achievement levels in courses where teachers encourage curiosity. Repeat for courses where teachers discourage curiosity. Compare and contrast.

Statement II: What are the factors that influence the effectiveness of a marketing strategy?
A. Direction Habit
1. Approach pole: How do focus groups contribute to a strategy? What other sources of input help in creating a marketing strategy?
2. Avoidance pole: What are the costs of focus groups (emphasis on barriers)? Analyze market resistances.
3. Uncertain (further inquiry needed): What portion of the budget can we put into this? What has been our experience in marketing to x segment of the market?
B. Global/Specific Habit
1. Global pole: Explore your knowledge of advertising and mass hypnosis to get hypotheses (focus is on Global pattern).

    2.   Specific pole: What specific measures of effectiveness will we use? What are the kinds of factors we want to focus on here?

C.   Sameness/Difference Habit
    1.   Sameness pole: What are the types of factors we will be considering? (Asking for the types of factors is a request for criteria of similarity.) Study the common factors in successful campaigns. Study the common factors in unsuccessful campaigns.
    2.   Difference pole: Compare a successful marketing campaign to an unsuccessful one. How can we tease out the effects of temporary political and economic conditions from the effects of the marketing strategy itself?
    3.   Sameness and Difference: Find the common factors in a sample of successful marketing campaigns, the common factors in a sample of unsuccessful marketing campaigns, and compare and contrast the findings in these two categories.

Statement III: Explore the relationship between parenting and self-confidence in children.

A.   Direction Habit
    1.   Approach pole: What parental behaviors support the development of self-confidence in children? What are some biological predispositions to self-confidence?
    2.   Avoidance pole: What are some parental behaviors that block self-confidence? (Unsupportive parenting creates lack of self-confidence in a child.) What are some biological predispositions to low self-confidence?
    3.   Uncertain: What are the findings in the literature?

B.   Global/Specific Habit
    1.   Global pole: What is the evidence that environmental factors influence personality traits? What purpose will this research serve?
    2.   Specific pole: Make separate analyses for single-parent and dual-parent families. Should we focus on parental attitudes or behaviors? In what specific ways will we use our findings?

C.   Sameness/Difference Habit
  1.   Sameness pole: What are the common outcomes of
       directive (or any other single variable) parenting?
  2.   Difference pole: Compare outcomes of permissive and
       directive parenting. How do different courses of child
       development influence parenting approaches? (This
       last creates a different question by reversing rela-
       tionships.)
  3.   Sameness and Difference: Compare the outcome of
       permissive and directive parenting in urban, liberal
       contexts and rural, fundamentalist contexts.

Opening Orientation to the Workshop. Include aims, time
frame, practical details, and a brief theoretical frame (possibly
along the lines of the introduction to this chapter). Elicit and
discuss any concerns about the risks of openness. This is the
time to set a tone of curiosity and appropriate lightness, through
joking and metaphor.

Subgroup Preparation. Ask the participants to form subgroups of three, which will remain together for the exercises on
the cognitive habits of expectation. You may want to group participants by subject matter; however, you might consider mis-
matching subject matter areas as much as possible, to prevent
distraction from the methodological emphasis of the workshop.
Give the following instructions: (1) Members of the subgroup
give copies of their statements to the other members. (2) Subgroups are to go over each other's statements to see if they are
as simple and neutral as the assignment called for. Anyone with
a question about the neutrality of a statement is to mark it for
discussion. (3) After everyone has completed Step Two, members
are to discuss with each other any statements that anyone judged
to reveal a position on the Direction habit. If there is agreement on such a challenge, they are to collaborate in reformulating the statement to be as neutral as possible in regard to the
Direction habit. If not in agreement, save the question for discussion in the entire group. (4) Reassemble the entire group. Share
responses and deal with any questions.

Habits of Expectation Review. Give a brief introduction and review of the habits of expectation, to remind participants of the material they received earlier and how it connects to the introductory remarks and to any questions that have emerged. You may want to confine yourself to the Direction habit at this point and insert some remarks on each of the other habits just before the rounds of exercises concentrating on them.

Exercise: Direction Habit Identification. Members should return to their subgroups. They are to select any three of the five statements they brought in and write down the next step they would take in thinking about or acting on that statement, at the level of specificity and detail illustrated in the preliminary handouts. Remind them that this is not primarily an exercise in rigor but a probe to find out their natural inclinations in thinking about their subject matter. The group is to concentrate on each member in turn, analyzing the responses obtained in Step One from the point of view of the Direction habit and identifying each member's style on that habit. Reassure them that a response may be unrevealing with regard to the habit; in such instances, the subgroup should question the member who made it to get the background of thought that may reveal the Direction pole it represents. Reassemble the larger group, share experiences, and discuss.

Exercise: Flexibility. Members should return to subgroups. They are to generate new responses to the statements they used in the exercise on Direction habit identification, designing them so they will show a different pole of the Direction habit than they showed in the first round. Share responses in subgroups, rotating after a single response from each member and continuing until time runs out. Each time a member reads a new response to a statement, each other member is to generate yet another response to the same statement, representing the same pole as the initiating member is attempting to express. Critique each other and help generate alternative responses for those who have trouble doing so. Recycle through the habit identification exercise and the flexibility exercise, first focusing on the Global/ Specific habit and then on the Sameness/Difference habit.

Exercise: External/Internal Framing. Have the participants form new subgroups of three. Subject matter areas are not important for this exercise. Everyone is to write responses to the following: (1) Rank the top three considerations that led you to take this workshop. (2) How will you know whether it was of value to you? Give specific criteria and indicate how you will determine whether they have been satisfied. (3) Identify contexts or issues in your field of specialization in which you would base your opinion or belief about something on each of the following: (a) foremost authorities; (b) preponderance of opinions of your peers; (c) how the matter in question fits into your preexisting beliefs and experience; and (d) personal, professionally disciplined experience (experiment, controlled observation, systematic review of the literature on the topic, and such). Share reactions and discuss whether it is useful to characterize the reported responses on the External/Internal dimension. Identify the criteria used in the different bases for belief and explore with the subgroup their appropriateness. Assemble in the larger group for reports and discussion, and then return to subgroups. Have people identify those areas where they are more dependent on others' opinions than they want to be and those areas where they are more resistive to others' points of view than they consider desirable. Discuss with your subgroup what each person would prefer as a response in the identified areas and what gets in the way of achieving it. Finally, assemble in the larger group for reports and discussion.

Exercise: Contextualization. Form new subgroups of three to five members. Have a volunteer give a brief characterization of a problem student or a problem encounter. The group discusses whether this problem can be understood to stem from rigidity or from poor contextualization of one or more of the habit expectations. If there is a possible fit with any habit expectation, develop a *general* approach to helping the student (for example, modify a faculty member's communication to fit better;

identify the specific flexibility that the student needs). Make some specific action recommendations to carry out the general approach. If a specific case does not readily fit into a habit of expectation frame, quickly move on to another case. Report to the entire group. Discuss.

Additional Comments

It is possible to adapt this workshop for communicators of any sort. Faculty and students can be replaced by ministers and congregations, lawyers and clients, lawyers and juries, salesmen and customers, administrators and staff, husbands and wives, parents and children, and so on.

This workshop could also be revised to promote self-development. For example, students could discover their own habits of expectation and develop greater flexibility with them.

A workshop with all the above components takes two and one-half to three days and gives the participants a solid grounding in the recognition and utilization of habits of expectation. Awareness of habits of expectation sensitizes the learner to different possibilities of functioning. This gives one guidance in selecting self-development goals, one of the keystones of emancipatory education. For example, a learner who relies almost excessively on others' thinking may be stimulated to develop criteria for recognizing situations where his or her own thinking is the desirable basis for evaluation. Conversely, a learner who never accepts others' judgments may be encouraged to distinguish situations where others' judgments are a better guide than his or her own. Becoming aware of habits of expectation and taking action to change them is at the heart of transformative learning.

References

Bandler, R., and Grinder, J. *The Structure of Magic.* Palo Alto, Calif.: Science and Behavior Books, 1975.

James, T., and Woodsmall, W. *Time Line Therapy and the Basis of Personality*. Cupertino, Calif.: Meta Publications, 1988.

Korzybski, A. *Science and Sanity*. (4th ed.) Lakeville, Conn.: International Non-Aristotelian Library, 1933.

Mezirow, J. "A Critical Theory of Self-Directed Learning." In S. D. Brookfield (ed.), *Self-Directed Learning: From Theory to Practice*. New Directions for Continuing Education, no. 25. San Francisco: Jossey-Bass, 1985.

Seven

The Therapeutic
Learning Program

Roger L. Gould

Early in my career as a psychoanalyst, I was also engaged in community psychiatry. The two realms of my life were not easily put together. At that time, there was much talk about understanding psychotherapy as a learning system and the benefits that would accrue once that translation had occurred, including the possibility of delivering effective psychotherapy services on a large scale through educational methods.

I took that challenge seriously and began to work on a bridging model, which I described in papers and in a book, *Transformation: Growth and Change in Adult Life* (Gould, 1978). From my point of view, the bridge between psychotherapy and adult learning is the structure of concepts of adult development. When adults develop, they have to learn how to adapt to a whole new set of circumstances as they go through life's transitions. But when individuals meet the demands of current, evolving life situations, they have to revise a meaning perspective of the past and change behavior patterns and attitudes that were once adaptive. Even though these patterns are outdated, they continue to make the person feel safe and comfortable. There is an illusion of safety attached to each familiar pattern of behavior, whether or not that pattern of behavior is truly adaptive. The issues of separation-individuation, object relations, anxiety, depression, and self-esteem are all evoked when new adaptive behaviors need to be learned.

134

With a team of other professionals, I developed a computer model that has since become an actual computer intervention program helping people through transitions. This program is used in medical and mental health settings as a computer-assisted, short-term psychotherapy and may be used by counselors in educational and work settings as a powerful method for fostering critical self-reflection. The program will be described in detail in this chapter.

About ten years ago, I was introduced to the concept of perspective transformation by Jack Mezirow and over the years have become conversant with his writing on transformative learning and emancipatory education. The program described in this chapter, called the therapeutic learning program (TLP), is a method whose goal is emancipatory education and whose processes involve transformative learning.

This chapter will start with a synopsis of adult developmental theory and then show how that can be translated into seven steps of therapeutic work that are required to complete one unit of adult development. As I describe the seven steps, the reader will see that they constitute transformative learning as defined in the preface of this book. In the second part of this chapter, I'll describe the method by which this transformative learning is carried into action.

The TLP is an organized effort to facilitate transformative learning in educational, work, and treatment contexts. Throughout the whole TLP process, the participant is centrally engaged in critical self-reflection. The role of the computer in mediating self-reflectivity is the most important observation in this chapter.

Adult Development and a Unit of Psychological Work

There is no clear consensus among researchers in the field of adult development as to what actually constitutes the work of developmental progression. For some, it is the passage through a transition and the learning of new coping skills; for others, particularly psychoanalysts, it is the recognition and mastery of some aspect of the nuclear neurosis of childhood. For Erikson (1950), Gould (1978), and Levinson (1978), it is a new posture or reconfiguring of the self in response to age-related realities of the life cycle. For Valiant, it is the substitution of more mature, reality-attuned ego defenses for the immature defenses that served childhood. There are even some in the field (Musgrove, 1977) who are not sure that there is any adult development. They see changes of behavior that appear to be developmental as merely new responses to changing contexts. These new responses were always ready to be elicited but were never previously called up.

Despite the differences in definition and aspects of behavioral phenomenology that are selected as central for each of the different schools of thought, there is at least one common element: Each definition identifies a specific changing pattern of behavior that is responsive to a new set of facts. An adaptational response is required to meet some demand implicit in a situational context, and that context is frequently catalogued as either a transition, a crisis, a stress situation, or a challenge.

All people change with age because new priorities in the life cycle require new attitudes and new behavior. New attitudes and new behavior can be straightforward responses to new facts when there is no internal conflict among the agencies of the self. The reality of facts (or roles or responsibilities) dominates the response of action or attitude. The participant's change is a conflict-free adaptational response to the changing reality of the present. As people get older, they necessarily go through many such adaptations and demonstrate many new behaviors and attitudes.

Sometimes people cannot respond to the fact of current reality with the appropriate adaptation because that response is mired in internal conflict (inhibitions, defenses, character patterns). The adaptational demand challenges them to free that response from underlying conflicts in order to be flexible enough to respond appropriately and effectively to the perceived present reality. If they succeed in resolving the conflict that caused them to be rigid, they recover a necessary function that is defined by the action they take.

Most participants (if not all) come to treatment with symptoms that are consequences of a developmental struggle triggered by an adaptational demand. Since any demand inherent in the situation calls for a piece of psychological work, we should only call those responses developmental that represent a significant piece of work involving the resolution of a conflict and structural change as an outcome. The critic who says there is no adult development but merely change in behavior responsive to changing circumstances is observing a simple, nondevelopmental pattern change in a participant who has little conflict about making that specific change. On the other end of the spectrum, therapists frequently observe immense struggles in participants responding to normal demands in the environment. The resistance to change is tied to either a nuclear neurotic belief system, or a powerful defense strategy. The attempts at change are countered by the activation of increasing doses of negative affect, the content of which is catastrophic predictions about potential adverse consequences.

When people have that much difficulty in changing a simple behavior pattern, they are often observed to be confused between the inherent demand of the *current* situation (which calls for a relatively easy change of behavior) and some *earlier* adaptational demand that required them to install or maintain the pattern they are now trying to change. They are living between two different time zones, where the past has more power to compel behavior than the present.

Given these considerations, a unit of adult developmental work encompasses three stages: (1) There is a specific demand inherent in the situation calling for a new behavior pattern. (2) The person accomplishes this behavior pattern change only after significantly sorting out the difference between current reality and past realities confused with the current situation. (3) The person arrives at a clearer and grounded understanding of current reality and from that strengthened position is more able to do the easier pieces of psychological work, which do not require sorting out past and present in the midst of a confounding, negative affect experience. We can expand our detailed knowledge of a unit of adult developmental work when we distinguish four key processes involved in completing a unit of work.

Process One: Recovery of Function. The demand of the situation unbalances the ambivalence about recovering a specific function that is inhibited. Defenses maintain and rationalize the underdeveloped function while a low-intensity, enduring, internal imperative pushes against the defenses. The demand of the situation makes the participant challenge the ambivalence.

Process Two: Intentional Action Representing a Recovered Function. The decision whether or not to act so as to recover the conflicted function represents the conscious conflict that mobilizes the internal and external conflicts. A positive answer represents an attempt to recover the function (at least temporarily) and master the pertinent confusion between past, present, and future in terms of self-doubt and the other memories mobilized in the prediction of catastrophe.

Many decisions not to act are based on realistic considerations, so the choice conflict of the present situation must be clearly distinguished from the unconscious resistance to action based on past conclusions about a past reality. When realistically wise new action is carried out, the person opts for probabilistic safety based on reality testing and gives up a cherished piece of the illusion of safety tied to the old patterns being contravened by the new action.

Process Three: Internal Conflict About Recovering Functions. Internal conflict centers our attention on the self-definition boundary as a critical clinical concept, since the threatened transgression of the boundary-controlling rule that organizes past adaptational experiences triggers the boundary-maintaining, superegolike forces. These boundary-maintaining phenomena include the catastrophe prediction (exaggeration of the possible real consequences of the intended act), memories of past painful experiences being confused with future reality, and the threatened exposure of a deeply hidden sense of a damaged or helpless self-state.

Process Four: The Resolution of an Interpersonal Conflict. The recovery of function takes place in a social context. A change in self-definition invokes a system change in that context. The current self-definition is confirmed and supported by family and fellow workers and the meaning attached to various work and social roles. An enlarged self-definition may pose a threat to others or trigger developmental envy and expose as anachronistic certain roles, values, or interactions. In order to create or find a niche that is confirming of the enlarged self-definition, the individual may have to resolve several interpersonal conflicts. The failure to resolve these conflicts threatens the viability of an expanding self-definition.

With these four key processes in mind, one can locate, describe, study, and facilitate an adult developmental unit of work and still be intimately connected to the observations and concepts about nucelar neurotic conflicts and defenses (functions are inhibited originally because of adaptations to nuclear conflicts that result in rigidification of immature defenses). The recovery of a function is a partial solution or an unraveling of a nuclear conflict and a remodeling of the defensive system in the direction of current reality responsiveness.

Steps in Short-Term Therapy
Based on Adult Development

We have defined adult development and touched on the three stages and four key processes involved in completing one unit of developmental work. The question now is, What would a short-term treatment based on this model look like? There are many ways to describe the process and content of such a therapy, but it would take a book-length presentation to do the subject justice. To cut through some of the complexity and organize this presentation to fit the constraints of this chapter, I will continue to expand the concept of psychological work.

The phenomena of psychological work are more familiar to the clinician than the concept. When we struggle with a participant to achieve clarity, we expend *therapeutic effort*. When the participant achieves clarity or when a defense is understood and relinquished in favor of a more mature behavior or when an insight is transformed from intellectual acceptance to letting go of unrealistic expectations reflected in state changes, a piece of *psychological work* has been accomplished.

We can describe the psychological work of short-term therapy based on adult development principles in the following seven steps.

Step One: Identifying and Framing the Function to Be Recovered

At times a person will open the treatment dialogue with some declaration of the developmental problem. "The trouble with me is I don't have any self-confidence," or "I'm afraid to love," or "I have talent I'm just not using in my life," or "I just can't discipline myself," or "I don't know how to have fun," or "My husband's right, I'm afraid to leave the house now that my children are grown," and so forth.

Of course, it's usually not that easy. The clinician has to expend considerable therapeutic effort separating out the function to be recovered from the drama of the presenting illness, which often involves complex and intriguing interpersonal struggles. While sorting out the problems in living from an identification of the developmental problem in the context of wellness, it is useful to keep three distingishing concepts in mind.

Stress. When people are in situations where demands that cannot be met are made upon them by others, these people are in a situation of stress. If they continue to use ineffective responses in this situation, the stress symptoms will grow more severe. A prolonged state of stress may be defined as a failure of adaptation, but the stressful situation itself should not be confused with the developmental conflict.

Developmental Conflict. A developmental conflict often starts with a stress situation. When participants begin to identify the new behavior that is required by the stress situation, they also recognize that the new behavior represents an expanded self-definition. The fear of striking down old patterns and implanting new patterns is palpable. There is also a sense of dissatisfaction with oneself for being unable to easily carry out the new behavior required, which adds another layer of stress to the total situation.

A developmental conflict may also start without any stressful situation. In fact, it is likely to surface during the tail end of a prolonged steady state when a person feels strong enough and ready to face a long-delayed developmental challenge.

Volitional Conflict. The volitional conflict is well framed when participants describe a specific action intention that addresses the stressful component of the situation and simultaneously represents the function to be recovered. When participants are in a position to say, "I know exactly what I need to do but I don't (can't) do it," then they have a painful feeling of helplessness. Within themselves, they feel that they are not in control of their own actions.

When participants are at a point where they have an acknowledged volitional conflict, the vagueness of the stress situation and the abstractness of the developmental conflict are no longer present. The focus is on the question of whether or not the participant will carry out a do-able action step that represents recovery in the face of palpable fear. This position is the outcome of the psychological work at the end of this first step.

Step Two: Clarifying the Action Intention

The intention to act is specific and concrete. It must be clear to the actor that the action in question is well thought through in the context of the immediate and specific reality situation. The act must be seen as a reasonable experiment that is likely to result in a beneficial consequence and is not likely to have a deleterious effect. After considering the overall set of costs and benefits, it must be clear to the participant that, given his or her values, the action will have a positive cost-benefit.

This clarification step intensifies the intention of acting and strengthens the participants' grounding in current reality. The responsibility as agent in their own lives is underlined and the stage is set for the next step in the process. The therapeutic effort expended by the therapist in understanding the cost-benefit analysis and the context of the participant's life is not the same as the psychological work that needs to be accomplished. The participant must not only hear and understand intellectually that the action intention is cost-benefit positive but must, in fact, come to a deep acceptance and ownership of this position, even though it temporarily intensifies the volitional conflict.

Step Three: Distinguishing Realistic Dangers from Exaggerated Fears

The third step entails looking at the fear response provoked by the intention to act and *distinguishing* realistic dangers from the exaggeration of dangers (catastrophic predictions). Some of this work will have been done in the previous step, inasmuch as one cannot make a cost-benefit decision about the action intention without also making an assessment about realistic dangers as attendant costs. When realistic dangers have been distingished from unfounded catastrophic predictions, the focus has shifted to "What is the real meaning of my fear response?" The target of therapeutic attention will have been isolated in the form of a fear response that *does not* predict real and current dangers. This piece of work requires critical self-reflexivity in the midst of pain and anxiety. Practicing self-reflexivity under these conditions in itself is a piece of developmental work.

Step Four: Isolating and Exposing the Fears as Predictions Confused with Memories

Once the catastrophic predictions have been isolated and teased out from realistic dangers, the next piece of work is for the participant to understand that the catastrophic predictions are memories that are being confused with the appraisal of current and future reality. This requires pinpointing specific errors in thinking that are the mechanisms allowing memories to prevail as action-inhibiting predictions. As each catastrophic prediction is explicated in this way, the self-reflexive capacity is strengthened because participants become more practiced in their ability to expose their self-deceptions. They enjoy the fruits of knowing exactly how they were wrong about the nature of their fears.

Step Five: Explaining the Origins of Catastrophic Predictions

Once the specific set of catastrophic predictions has been laid to rest, it is important to explain the origin of the power of the catastrophe-predicting part of the mind. Catastrophe predictions are in the service of preventing development. They function as a defense against the dread of a separation-individuation move that might expose the deeper fear of incompleteness as a not fully enfranchised adult. Growing up and taking full responsibility is associated with the complex fear of being flawed and exposed as a defective adult. When participants experiment with new behaviors that are deemed appropriate to the current reality, they are improving their reality testing and adaptational skills and increasing the likelihood of being successful in the adult enterprise. Concurrently, they are giving up a piece of the protective, magical idea that no such effort is really required of them. When learners have completed this piece of psychological work, their sense of being adults moving through time in a specific life cycle is greatly enhanced.

Step Six: Demonstrating and Diminishing
Self-Fulfilling Prophecies

In this step, learners will have exposed the illusion that they were permanently damaged in childhood, and therefore they dare not try new behavior because that damage would be exposed. The work of Step Five is to understand that damage in childhood is not irreparable. Functions can be recovered. The work of Step Six is to understand that once the conclusion of being damaged has been formed, it continues to operate like a magnet, causing distortion in reality testing so that current events seem to add evidence to the old conclusion that the damage still exists. The work of the sixth step is to demonstrate the ways in which participants engage in self-fulfilling prophecies that reinforce the illusion of being damaged or inadequate or unworthy. A common, simple example is to accept rejection or slights by others as evidence that they know about the hidden damage. This simplistic and unsatisfactory explanation usually prevails in the emotional moment unless scrupulously and exactingly examined. When this piece of work is successfully completed, participants will be able to catch themselves in the act of self-deprecation. In the moment of insight, they will make the choice between moving forward within an adult framework or remaining in a childhood framework in regard to their self-worth. It is in these instants of choice that the efficacy of the psychological work accomplished in the previous five steps is challenged and measured.

Step Seven: Consolidating New Views of Reality

The last step is consolidation. Once learners have broken through some inhibiting pattern to exercise an important part of themselves, they have also adopted new views of reality and have remodeled old values, motives, and other complex beliefs about interpersonal, intrapsychic, and intraorganizational relationships. Explicitly formulating and stating what they have learned in the form of revised beliefs is a consolidating activity that helps to put into perspective the action taken, as just another everyday, necessary activity that was temporarily enmeshed in the drama of developmental conflict. In the future, the same kind of action will not be a feat but an expected part of one's ordinary repertoire of behavior. Participants who learn to confront or to define themselves more accurately in the presence of others should come to see that activity as normal rather than extraordinary.

In a similar way, one's self-image has been rehabilitated from the point of view of eliminating belief in a specific negative label. The whole process of completing a unit of work has enhanced the sense of self-efficacy. This new experience has to be consolidated by articulation and underlining so it also becomes part of the normal, functioning self-view.

When learners have accomplished the psychological work of these seven steps, they have accomplished one unit of psychological work as defined above, inasmuch as the action taken represents the recovery of a specific function while the consolidation of worldview stimulated by these seven steps represents a structural change in the psychic organization.

Note About the Seven-Step Developmental Process

Although there is no universally accepted taxonomy of functions, it will be useful to distinguish at least two categories. We have been using the term *function* here to describe capacities or skills necessary for work and love, such as the ability to nurture or take risks or have fun or allow sexual and sensual expression, and so on. These functions are the ingredients necessary to live in the world of people and organizations.

As we described the seven steps, we also mentioned another set of functions, those involving the self-reflective capacity. These functions are closer to those commonly described as ego functions. It is useful to think of these self-reflective ego functions as sets of processing skills that are necessary to recover the love and work functions. In the seven steps defining a unit of developmental work, the focus is on the function from the first category, but we are also teaching and strengthening the processing skills of the second category that lead to generalized learning and prepare learners for the next unit of work, whenever that becomes necessary.

Each time a unit of work has been accomplished, the participants' powers of self-efficacy are enhanced. From the therapist's or counselor's point of view, the learners have developed. From the learners' point of view, they have been freed to carry out their most important intentions. They have gained free will as they moved from a divided to a unified self on some very important action issue.

The Therapeutic Learning Program (TLP)

The TLP is a computer-assisted short-term therapy program that helps learners define a specific problem, propose an action solution, and resolve any conflict about taking the action. The goal of the program is to facilitate the learning necessary to complete one unit of adult developmental work.

The program represents the condensation of years of therapeutic experience designed into a very explicit model and then translated into a computer program. The course consists of ten interactive computer sessions, each of which is an interdependent unit and cannot be taken out of order. The learner works with a counselor at the end of each session to accomplish a specific work assignment.

At each step of the way, the computer helps translate subvocal thought processes into external, visual print that participants can hold on to, talk from, think about, and carry during the time between sessions. By presenting menus for each step of the process, the computer helps individuals gain an appropriate vocabulary, make discriminations, and transform slippery feelings and thought processes into examinable pieces of information.

Learners have a controlled and private relationship directly with the program. The TLP has been designed to help them have a self-reflective experience and, in particular, to create a cleavage plane between a rational, contemporary part of the self and an irrational, past-history–dominated aspect of the self.

Users learn to think about problem resolution in a slow, step-by-step way. From their point of view, the problem focuses on three important questions: (1) What hurts, and what can you do about it that you are not already doing? (2) Would taking this action be a wise and safe thing to do? (3) What deeper fears stop you from taking the intended action? There is a building of concepts and skills necessary for the process to culminate in a decision for or against action.

Up to this point, the therapeutic learning program has been used in a medical setting, primarily in psychiatric health-maintenance organization clinics and psychiatric hospitals. We are beginning to use the program in stress centers, weight reduction clinics, wellness programs, employee assistance programs, and educational institutions. The target audience is anyone who has symptoms or an action conflict to resolve or who has some identified problem in living. Usually, people go to a mental health clinic because of psychic pain or symptoms. The therapist helps patients identify and sort out the problems that are causing the symptoms. In contrast, in educational and wellness settings, people come to learn about themselves and to enhance their positive health habits. Symptom reduction is not the primary motive, although it is often a covert motive.

The TLP has been used with all socioeconomic groups and age ranges from thirteen to eighty. The problems in living vary from simple frictions at home or at work to severe mental illness that requires hospitalization. When the TLP is used in educational programs and at the healthier end of the spectrum, it tends to be a complete treatment unto itself, with over 85 percent of the population not going on to any subsequent treatment immediately following the TLP. When the TLP is used in the hospital population, it serves as an instant treatment plan and a focusing device that enables patient and therapist to communicate more precisely with each other about those areas of concern that the patient has identified as primary. It is part of the overall treatment program.

Session Description: Overview of the TLP Content

Session One: The Personal Stress Survey. In the work of the first session, participants identify stress-related problems, self-conflict issues, and symptoms. At the beginning of the session, there is an easy tutorial that quickly familiarizes learners with the computer and the keyboard.

Once familiarized, learners collect and prioritize all the external circumstances and interactions with people that are causing stressful feelings. Then, after narrowing the selection of stressful circumstances and interactions to a maximum of six items, users select one specific adjective that best describes how they feel about each prioritized stressor. They then identify their own ineffective response to each of the stressors. By the end of this first section in Session One, the adult learner has constructed several stress-related problem statements, such as "The stress of working under excessive pressure makes me feel irritable. This is complicated by that fact that I am being pressured to be perfect. I have trouble dealing with this stress because I have difficulty expressing my feelings."

The second section looks at other self-conflict issues, such as feeling unable to take advantage of opportunities to grow and develop, lack of confidence in certain areas, and feeling out of control with respect to specific behaviors.

The last section of Session One collects any physical, behavioral, or emotional symptoms related to the stress problem. It also assesses the severity of the stress and how much it interferes with work and intimate relationships.

Session Two: Building an Action Step. In this session, participants clarify their primary developmental goal and begin focusing on action. This session takes a more proactive approach to the stress problem. Participants review all the developmental goals that they want to achieve and then focus comprehensively on the *one* that will best address the prioritized dissatisfaction.

The computer assists users in expressing the positive reasons for wanting to make this change and helps them explore potential ways of taking the appropriate action.

With the aid of a printout, participants write out an action plan that represents the first step toward resolving the stress and dissatisfaction they feel.

Session Three: Anticipated Dangers. Before participants can successfully take an action step, they need to understand and alleviate fears that may get in the way of completion. By examining possible errors in thinking, users can determine whether their fears are realistic or unfounded. In this session, participants think through the possible negative consequences to other people of taking action. They investigate how others *might* respond when the intended action is taken. After examining the predicted, undesirable consequences, participants determine whether the action step is safe and worthwhile from their current, adult perspective.

Session Four: Exploring More Fears. This session focuses on assisting participants to uncover any hidden motives and to isolate and examine their fears of failure and success that inhibit taking action. The interactive program continues to help the user recognize *errors in thinking* that are commonly made when feelings of anxiety about taking action are confused with the presence of real danger.

Session Five: Negative Feelings. In the fifth session, participants explore their angry and guilty feelings as obstacles to action and the fears associated with these feelings. The program helps users convert these explorations into useful information.

As individuals investigate the source of their feelings, they uncover more errors in thinking and rigid rules from the past that still affect them today.

Session Six: Identifying Self-Doubts. By this point in the program, participants have established that the action step is safe and do-able; from their current, adult perspective they have determined that it is the correct action to take. In Session Six, participants begin to expose the negative self-esteem labels that surface when they consider or begin to take the intended action. This session introduces the concept of self-doubts as the deepest and strongest obstacles to completing the action step.

Session Seven: The Self-Doubt System. In this session, participants examine old and detrimental patterns of behavior that sustain their negative self-image. They identify which situations cause them feelings of rejection or pain and how they react to these vulnerabilities in a habitually unproductive way that reinforces their irrational fears.

Each participant constructs three statements related to the self-doubts uncovered in Sessions Six and Seven, such as "When someone intimidates me, I feel I am weak, dependent, or helpless, and then I act like a noncompetitor."

Session Eight: Origins of Self-Doubt. By the eighth session, participants are ready to look at painful past experiences that have influenced (empowered) their current self-doubts. The goal of this session is to enhance participants' perspective regarding their negative self-esteem by showing them how their negative feelings are rooted in illogical conclusions formed earlier in life.

Session Nine: Perpetuating Self-Doubt. In this session, participants take a close look at a recent situation in which they felt their powerful self-doubt. They review how they jumped to the false conclusion that this negative label is the real truth about them. The program illustrates how participants unnecessarily perpetuate the negative label of the past and how this doubt about themselves actually distorts their interpretation of reality.

Session Ten: Review and Assessment. In this session, users evaluate the changes experienced during the course and identify the next developmental step. Participants consider all the information gathered during the course and identify the positive and negative changes. In addition, they call attention to any issues that they feel they may need further help with. They review their action step in relation to the obstacles they identified and identify attitude changes that they have made as a result of overcoming errors in thinking. The printout from Session Ten can be used as a case summary for the counselor and as a self-help guide for the participant.

The TLP and a Unit of Adult Development

We defined a unit of adult development in terms of three steps and four processes. The psychological work of completing a unit of work was described in seven steps. In addition, we described ten TLP sessions. The outline below shows the alignment of stages, processes, steps, and sessions.

Stage One: A stress situation calls for new behavior.
  Process One: The demand of the stress situation requires recovery of an underdeveloped function.
    Step One: Identifying and framing the function to be recovered.
      Session One: Personal stress survey (stress problem).
      Session Two: Building an action step (developmental goal).
Stage Two: Change happens after sorting out confusions between past and current realities.
  Process Two: Decision to act (or not) represents an acknowledgment of one's right to recover the function.

Step Two: Clarifying the action intention.

Session Two: Building an action step.

Process Three: Internal conflict resolved about recovering function.

Step Three: Distinguishing realistic dangers from exaggerated dangers.

Session Three: Anticipated dangers.

Session Four: Exploring more fears.

Step Four: Isolating and exposing the fears as predictions confused with memories.

Session Four: Exploring more fears (failure and success).

Session Five: Negative feelings (anger and guilt).

Session Six: Identifying self-doubts.

Session Seven: The self-doubt system.

Step Five: Explaining the origins of the catastrophic predictions.

Session Eight: Origins of self-doubt.

Step Six: Demonstrating and diminishing self-fulfilling prophecies.

Session Nine: Perpetuating self-doubt.

Stage Three: From strengthened position, action is taken and recovery of a particular function is completed.

Process Four: Enlarged self-definition invokes a system change and requires resolution of interpersonal conflicts.

Step Seven: Consolidating new views of reality.

Session Ten: Review and assessment.

Program Assessment

Three outcome studies of the TLP were based on data from 2,000 users in five different cities within the CIGNA Health Plan. The studies included a pilot and two-year and three-year follow-ups. The pilot involved the first 100 users who completed the TLP. Almost all users confirmed the relevance and importance of the central concepts of the program and of the therapeutic process. The pilot also found that 90 percent were comfortable with the computer and 80 percent found it easy to reveal sensitive information to the computer. Therapists rated the TLP results as follows: improved self-esteem, 80 percent; improved problem-solving ability, 79 percent; improved personal satisfaction, 83 percent; improved interpersonal satisfaction, 96 percent; and decrease in symptoms, 73 percent.

In the two-year follow-up of 278 users, over 96 percent reported an increased ability to handle their problems on their own. Even though 80 percent reported starting the TLP with high levels of stress around a specific problem, over 78 percent reported a drop in their level of distress after using the TLP. Almost all were satisfied with the program, better able to handle the specific problem and similar problems on their own, better able to handle typical "people problems" at work, and felt positive about using the computer for therapeutic learning. In fact, about 80 percent were *highly* satisfied with the program, found that it helped them think more clearly, gave them more to talk about than expected, and increased their ability to be productive at work. Most found the computer had helped them overcome their reluctance to talk about their problems to a therapist.

The three-year follow-up study involving 200 TLP users was conducted by Dr. Ronald Klein of CIGNA Health Plan. Results indicated that almost all users reported an increase in problem-solving skills during the program. About 80 percent reported reduced levels of stress, increased ability to solve problems, gains in their relationships and in their life situations as a result of the insights acquired, and continuing satisfaction with their experience with the TLP. Two-thirds credited the TLP for their enhanced ability to solve related problems, and 57 percent reported a *high* level of satisfaction with the program. Almost all the therapists working with the users rated the TLP appropriate for depressed, anxious, and psychologically unsophisticated clients, for work- and career-stressed clients, and for users recovering from substance abuse. Eighty-two percent found the TLP appropriate for users coping with stress from medical problems. Almost all the therapists disagreed that the TLP was an appropriate treatment for clients with character-personality disorders, for which many therapies are inappropriate.

Significant gains were also reported in two smaller-sample studies of students in how-to-study classes at the University of Minnesota. In a class of seventeen, assessed by the Tennessee Self-Concept Scale and subjective judgments, learning gains were found in better self-acceptance, less stress, and more control over the problem of user concern. In a comparison of TLP and group and individual counseling in the University Counseling Service, forty-six students were randomized into comparative groups involving use of the TLP and group and individual counseling. Gains were measured by the Tennessee Self-Concept, by satisfaction with problem solving, and by grade-point average before and after treatment. The TLP was found to be as effective as group and individual counseling in reducing stress and in satisfying clients and more effective than individual counseling in aiding students to earn higher grades. It was also found more efficient than the other approaches in that it freed counselors for other work while students were interacting with the computer.

The outcome studies, from pilot to three-year follow-up, are all consistent in their findings. Both therapists and users rate the program very highly for therapeutic effectiveness, broad applicability, lasting change, and generalizable learning. In these self-report studies and in the quasi-experimental studies involving university students, there is strong evidence to suggest that the TLP accomplishes what it was designed to do.

Summary and Conclusions

In this chapter, we have attempted to illustrate how the cardinal concepts of adult emancipatory education — critical self-reflexivity and transformative learning — bear upon (1) translating psychotherapy into a learning model, using adult development principles as a bridge, and (2) a specific intervention program that represents that learning model (the TLP). It is important to keep in mind the relationship of the model to the computer and the counselor.

The Computer. At each step of the way, the computer helps translate subvocal thought processes into an external, visual object — a printout that users can hold on to, talk from, think about, and carry with them during the time between sessions. By presenting menus for each step of the process, the computer program helps individuals gain an appropriate vocabulary, make discriminations, and transform slippery feelings and thought processes into examinable pieces of information.

The Model. The developmental and action-intention model underlying the program serves to convert information into knowledge by presenting a structure of meaning about a narrowly focused action intention. That is, participants who explore their anger or their guilt or their negative self-esteem do so within the framework of the question "Why am I afraid to act after I have decided the act is wise and objectively safe?" They do not learn about guilt or anger or self-esteem as it is related to *all* aspects of their lives but about those feelings as they are organized by the action question.

Because the model is explicit and because each step is instantiated in the computer program, participants learn to think about problem resolution in a slow, step-by-step way. If they are confused about any step, the counselor is present to correct the confusion.

The Counselor. If knowledge is information organized within a meaningful pattern, then wisdom is the addition of judgment to that equation. The counselor's role is to add that judgment at each step in the process and to contribute the unique human understanding that is beyond the range of the model or the computer program. The counselor keeps participants on track and helps them identify errors in thinking. The model and the computer program help users bring emotionally loaded material to the counselor. Each session is a compact and intense emotional experience for users and the counselor but is quite different from either individual or group therapy. Users feel empowered by the program and less dependent on the counselor, so that the counselor is not the target of intense positive or negative transference and is seen much more as a facilitator and guide, rather than as a guru or dispenser of scarce information. This phenomenon allows the experience to be completed easily.

The TLP is a form of mediated therapeutic communication because the medium of the computer is interposed to extend the reach of the counselor; the interposed medium affects the relationship to information and changes the relationship of the user to the counselor.

When users work with the interactive program directly, they really have a private, controlled, interpersonal relationship with the designer of the program. The program represents the condensation of years of therapeutic experience designed into a very explicit model and then translated into a computer program. The intelligence of the "counselor" designed into the computer program is instantiated in the program and is available to users. Since other consultants have contributed to the program by adding their wisdom and experience, the TLP can be said to contain over 100 years of clinical experience. In this sense, users have a phantom interpersonal conversation with a collective, clinical Other.

The program has been designed to help users have a self-reflective experience and, in particular, to create cleavage between a rational, contemporary part of the self and an irrational, past-history–dominated part of the self. Participants in the TLP report that they forget about the program and the computer very quickly because they become so intrigued with their own internal drama. Their emotions are stimulated, and they become inward, self-absorbed, and involved in a very intense, self-reflective process. In this sense, they have a private experience in which the medium is largely obliterated from emotional consciousness. The explicit wisdom of the clinical program designers has essentially vanished. To facilitate this self-reflective internal process, we use special programming techniques, particularly the use of participants' favored language patterns.

The self-generated information that users gather during the course of the interactive program concerns the multiple selves coexisting within the larger self. This information helps the person process further information necessary to complete a unit of adult developmental change as described above.

So far, we might summarize the process from the user's point of view as a phantom *interpersonal* relationship with the program designer, leading to an articulated *intrapersonal* dialogue between the facilitative and inhibitory aspects of the self over a decision about taking action that represents a new developmental behavior.

In the TLP, the interpersonal relationship between participants and counselors is different from that in individual and group therapy. Because of the program, paricipants are better prepared, less dependent, looking for a different kind of help, and more articulate than participants in the other therapies. Counselors are different also. They are face to face with a different kind of client, have less of a global resonsibility, are guided by the focus and the model, have a tool to help them perform some of the work on insight and clarification, and have an infinitely greater amount of information available to them in a recorded and usable fashion than they would otherwise have.

As a consequence of this different relationship, there is a clearer exchange of therapeutic communication between learners and counselors and a greater opportunity for learners to receive nonmediated, therapeutic communication from people in their lives besides the counselor. In addition, there is a greater emphasis on using common sense in learning and in processing information, rather than an emphasis on transference interpretation as the major avenue of insight.

In my view, the TLP is only the beginning of a whole new way to use the microcomputer for emancipatory education. The possibilities are almost limitless.

References

Erikson, E. H. *Childhood and Society.* New York: Norton, 1950.

Gould, R. *Transformation: Growth and Change in Adult Life.* New York: Simon & Schuster, 1978.

Levinson, D. J. et al. *The Seasons of a Man's Life.* New York: Knopf, 1978.

Musgrove, F. *Margins of Mind.* London: Methuen, 1977.

Valliant, G. *Adaptation to Life.* Boston: Little, Brown & Co. Inc., 1977.

Part Two

Helping Learners Become Critically Reflective: Six Key Approaches

Eight

The Reflective Judgment Model: Transforming Assumptions About Knowing

Karen S. Kitchener
Patricia M. King

For years, educators have emphasized the importance of helping children, adolescents, and young adults become critically reflective in problem solving. Mezirow, in his introduction to this book, offers a definition of critical reflection that emphasizes questioning the assumptions with which individuals typically begin problem solving. These assumptions range from beliefs about the self as an effective problem solver to beliefs about whether and when problems are solvable. Transformative learning is aimed at helping the individual become more aware and critical of assumptions in order to actively engage in changing those that are not adaptive or are inadequate for effective problem solving.

Our own writing and research has been on the development of reflective judgment. Based on the work of Dewey (1933), who identified reflective thinking as a goal of education, our

Note: The material in this chapter on developmental instruction using the reflective judgment model is based primarily on work done by Patricia M. King, Tammy M. Gocial, and Jonathan Dings at Bowling Green State University in 1987.

work defines a reflective thinker as someone who is aware that a problematic situation exists and is able to bring critical judgment to bear on the problem. In other words, a reflective thinker understands that there is real uncertainty about how a problem may best be solved, yet is still able to offer a judgment about the problem that brings some kind of closure to it. This judgment, which Dewey refers to as a "grounded" or "warranted" assertion, is based on criteria such as evaluation of evidence, consideration of expert opinion, adequacy of argument, and implications of the proposed solution.

Our research suggests that the ability to make reflective judgments is an outcome of a developmental sequence that both limits learning and can be influenced by learning. Our work has focused primarily on validating the sequence and understanding the relationship between it and other aspects of development, such as moral and ego development. As a result, the emphasis of this chapter will differ somewhat from other chapters in this book. First, we will describe the reflective judgment model. Second, we will identify several developmental parameters, based on research, that influence learning to be reflective. Third, we will suggest possible methods that educators can use to promote reflective judgment at two developmental points. Last, we will briefly describe a program that was designed to promote development.

The Reflective Judgment Model

The reflective judgment model (Kitchener and King, 1981; Kitchener and King, forthcoming) describes changes in assumptions about sources and certainty of knowledge and how decisions are justified in light of those assumptions. In other words, the model focuses on describing the development of epistemic assumptions and how these assumptions act as meaning perspectives (see Chapter One) that radically affect the way individuals understand and subsequently solve problems. Initially, the model was influenced by the work of Perry (1970) and Broughton (1975) on epistemological development.

At each step in the model, there are sets of assumptions that develop at about the same time, apparently because they are logically interrelated. As already noted, each set includes assumptions about what can be known and how certain one can be about knowing; it also includes assumptions about the role of evidence, authority, and interpretation in the formation of solutions to problems. While most often these assumptions are not explicit, they can be inferred from how individuals approach problem solving, their expectations of instructors, their beliefs about the certainty of problem solving, and so on. For example, in the following two quotations, the students imply that they expect truth to be clear and easy to decipher, that interpretation is both unnecessary and illegitimate, and that instructors ought to provide them with the "truth" about the world.

> Example A-1. "It seems as if college examinations don't test the student on the material covered in the lecture, but on whether the student can decipher a trick question. Why can't the test come right out and ask for a simple answer?"

In other words, the student asks why tests involve interpretation and why instructors can't require students simply to repeat the facts (or the "truth") on tests.

> Example A-2. "Instead of discussing all these issues, I wish you'd [the instructor] just tell us the real reasons for the Civil War."

In other words, the instructor should simply tell students the truth rather than ask them to figure it out.

Other students have given up ever finding the absolute truth and, as a consequence, they conclude that there are no ways to evaluate any conclusion as better than another. Their assumptions are reflected in comments like those in examples B-1 and B-2.

> Example B-1. "What do you mean I got a *C?* Art can be anything you want it to be and my judgment is as good as yours. I worked hard so I think I deserve an *A.*"

Without certainty, students like this one suggest that hard work is the only way to judge merit. At least it is concrete.

Example B-2. "The instructor kept trying to force her ideas about the poem on us . . . I mean, what makes her ideas any better than mine, anyway?"

In other words, this student suggests that if there are no absolute criteria for evaluation, that is, no sources of certainty, then anything goes.

The reflective judgment model regards such comments as implicit clues to students' meaning perspectives. Our research suggests that these perspectives are identifiable, that they are age related, and that they change in a predictable fashion over time. Further, our research suggests that these perspectives act as frames of reference through which students interpret learning experiences.

In the following paragraphs, each stage in the developmental sequence will be described. We refer to each step as a stage because we are describing a set of beliefs and assumptions that typically develop at about the same time. Descriptions of these stages are based on the rules for reflective judgment scoring in Kitchener and King (1985), as well as on other recent formulations of the model (Kitchener and King, forthcoming; Kitchener, King, Wood, and Davison, forthcoming). The descriptions illustrate more precisely the sets of assumptions evident at each stage.

We should note that the grade levels to which we refer throughout this next section have been drawn from interviews with more than 1,000 subjects and from several studies (Kitchener and King, forthcoming). Reflective judgment scores have consistently increased with age and education. Adult students between their mid twenties and mid fifties entering college for the first time typically score remarkably similarly to traditional-age undergraduates. In other words, the epistemic meaning perspectives of adult learners are, on the average, similar to those of a traditional-age learner at a similar educational level. The adults' scores, however, are more variable, providing a reminder of the need to acknowledge individual differences among adult learners.

Stage One. At this stage, knowing is characterized by a concrete, single-category belief system: What the person observes to be true is true. Individuals assume that knowledge is both absolute and concrete, thus, beliefs do not need to be justified. Since they need only observe to know what exists, individuals do not acknowledge that problems exist for which there are no absolutely true answers. This stage in its purest form is probably only found in young children.

Stage Two. Knowing takes on more complexity at this stage since individuals assume that, while truth is ultimately accessible, it may not be directly and immediately known to everyone. Since truth is not available to everyone, some people hold "right" beliefs while others hold "wrong" ones. Perry (1970) called this belief system *dualism.* However, since the truth may ultimately be known, individuals continue to assume that all problems are solvable. As a consequence, they assume that the knower's role is to find the right answer and that the source of this answer will be an authority, for example, a teacher, priest, or doctor. Individuals holding these assumptions often make statements like those in examples A-1 and A-2. This frame of reference is most typical of young adolescents, although some college students continue to hold these assumptions (Kitchener and King, forthcoming).

Stage Three. At this stage, individuals acknowledge that in some areas truth is temporarily inaccessible, even for those in authority. In other areas, they maintain the belief that authorities know the truth. In areas of uncertainty, they maintain the belief that absolute truth will be manifest in concrete data sometime in the future and argue that, since evidence is currently incomplete, no one can claim any authority beyond his or her own personal impressions or feelings. Beliefs can only be justified on the basis of what feels right at the moment. Consequently, like the students who made statements B-1 and B-2, individuals at this stage do not understand or acknowledge any basis for evaluation beyond those feelings. Implicitly, however, they maintain the assumption that ultimately all problems have solutions and that certainty will, in the long run, be attained. Students in their last two years of high school or first year of college typically score at about Stage Three (Kitchener & King, forthcoming).

Stage Four. The uncertainty of knowing is initially acknowledged in this stage and usually attributed to limitations of the knower. Without certainty, individuals argue that knowledge cannot be validated externally; thus, they argue that it is idiosyncratic. They often appear confused about how to make claims to knowledge in light of uncertainty and without authorities to provide them the answers. In fact, individuals at this stage frequently express skepticism about the role of authorities. Example C-1 quotes one college student who was asked about how to sort out the claims about evolution and creationism.

Example C-1. "I'd be more inclined to believe in evolution if they had proof. . . . I don't think we'll ever know because people will differ. Who are you going to ask? No one was there" [quoted in Kitchener, King, Wood, and Davison, forthcoming].

For him, uncertainty was real because people cannot go back in time to relive the event. As a result, he was at a loss to substantiate his views. Authorities were of no help because they faced similar epistemic limits.

The fact that uncertainty is clearly accepted at this stage as an intrinsic characteristic of knowing is, however, an important development. It allows individuals to distinguish between what we (Kitchener, 1983) and others (Churchman, 1971; Wood, 1983) have called well- and ill-structured problems.

Well-structured problems — for example, an arithmetic problem — can be described completely and solved with certainty. Real-world problems, such as what career path to follow or how to reduce pollution, can rarely be treated as well-structured problems since all the parameters are seldom clear or available and since it is difficult to determine when and whether an adequate solution has been identified. Therefore, we call real-world problems *ill structured.* When individuals in Stages One, Two, or Three cannot acknowledge that some problems do not have an absolutely correct solution, they cannot acknowledge the existence of real, ill-structured problems. At Stage Four, ill-structured problems are afforded legitimacy. Such reasoning is most typical of college seniors (Kitchener and King, forthcoming).

Stage Five. At this stage, individuals believe that knowledge must be placed within a context. This assumption derives from the understanding that interpretation plays a role in what a person perceives. Although these individuals move beyond the idiosyncratic justifications of Stage Four to argue that justification must be understood as involving interpretation of evidence within a particular perspective, they cannot compare and evaluate the relative merits of two alternative interpretations of the same issue. We have found that this type of reasoning is most typical of graduate students (Kitchener and King, forthcoming).

Stage Six. Individuals at this stage believe that knowing is uncertain and that knowledge must be understood in relationship to the context from which it was derived. In addition, they argue that knowing involves evaluation and that some perspectives, arguments, or points of view may be evaluated as better than others. These evaluations involve comparing evidence and opinion across contexts, which allows an initial basis for forming judgments about ill-structured problems. Such solutions are typically found among advanced graduate students (Kitchener and King, forthcoming).

Stage Seven. Although individuals at this stage believe that knowing is uncertain and subject to interpretation, they also argue that epistemically justifiable claims can be made about the better or best solution to the problem under consideration.

As with Dewey's description (1933) of reflective thinking, individuals claim that knowledge can be constructed via critical inquiry and through the synthesis of existing evidence and opinion into claims that can be evaluated as having greater "truth value" or being more "warranted" than others. Individuals argue that such views can be offered as reasonable current solutions to the problem at hand, as stated in the example that follows.

Example D-1. "[We] can argue here that one is a better argument than the other. One is more consistent with the evidence. What I am really after is a story that is . . . as intelligible as possible. . . . I don't think it's as much of a puzzle solving as it is trying to get the narrative straight" [quoted in Kitchener, King, Wood, and Davison, forthcoming].

Such reasoning is a rarity even in graduate students, although it is found in some educated adults as they mature into their thirties and beyond.

Developmental Parameters for Learning

Research on the reflective judgment model has several implications for education. First, individuals are quite consistent in their reasoning across different tasks (Kitchener and King, forthcoming; Kitchener, King, Wood, and Davison, forthcoming). Typically, when people are presented with several ill-structured problems, their assumptions about knowing and justification will best be represented by the same stage about three out of four times. On the remainder of the problems, their reasoning will seldom vary by more than one stage, even when they are tested on similar tasks drawn from disciplines as different as science and history. After identifying a student's reflective judgment stage, educators can assume that the student typically will approach most ill-structured problems with the same set of epistemic filters.

Second, recent research at the University of Denver (Lynch and Kitchener, 1989) suggests that even under conditions designed to elicit the highest stage of reasoning of which people are capable, individuals are seldom able to produce reasoning that is more than one stage above their typical response. Furthermore, the data suggest that there are age-related developmental ceilings on the highest reflective judgment stage an individual can use. These data parallel those found by Fischer and Kenny (1986) on arithmetic reasoning. The Lynch and Kitchener data and Fischer's (1980) model suggest that adolescents prior to ages nineteen to twenty are not capable of understanding the highest reflective judgment stages (Stages Six and Seven). Our own data (Kitchener, King, Wood, and Davison, forthcoming) show that even among a college-educated sample, the majority did not typically use reasoning higher than Stage Four prior to age twenty-four. In other words, educators should not assume that younger students can either understand or emulate what Dewey described as reflective thinking. On the other hand, while adult learners ordinarily reason with assumptions like those of similarly educated younger students, there may not be a ceiling on the highest reflective judgment level that adults can understand after practice and with support.

Third, our data strongly suggest that epistemic assumptions change sequentially (Kitchener, King, Wood, and Davison, forthcoming). In other words, it is not typical for individuals to move from Stage Four assumptions to Stage Seven assumptions without showing some evidence of understanding and using the assumptions of the intermediate stages. In fact, it is most typical for subjects' scores to move upward about one stage every six years. Regressions are rare.

Preliminary data from the University of Denver study (Lynch and Kitchener, 1989) also suggest that individuals have difficulty comprehending epistemic assumptions more than one or two stages higher than the stage they typically use. These data, along with the data on sequentiality, suggest that educators ought to target their interventions no more than one or two stages higher than where the student typically responds. Trying to move from *A* to *C* without attending to the meaning perspectives of *B* will probably be counterproductive.

By identifying a student's typical reasoning style and knowing the next step in the sequence, educators can identify a developmental range within which transformative learning experiences can be targeted. Learning tasks can be identified that cause critical reflection on current meaning perspectives, for example, by requiring skills more typical of the next-highest reflective judgment stage. (This point is illustrated below.)

Fourth, critical to acknowledging uncertainty is the recognition that some problems are ill structured (Davison, King, and Kitchener, forthcoming). Too often in traditional educational settings, courses are taught and textbooks are written as though they provide the absolute truth (Finster, forthcoming). By contrast, students need to struggle with ill-structured problems in many domains if they are to come to terms with the need for reflective thinking on many of life's problems.

Last, from our perspective, transformative learning that leads to developmental change does not occur without disequilibrium. Disequilibrium is frequently uncomfortable and, in some cases, can even be frightening. As Kegan (1982) has noted, giving up old frames of reference, old worldviews, or, in this case, old meaning perspectives about how and what we can know, is like losing the self. When the self is lost, individuals are often unsure that a new self or frame of reference can be found. As educators, when we accept the task of deliberately educating to promote development, we must also accept the responsibility of providing students with both an emotionally and intellectually supportive environment. In other words, we must not only challenge old perspectives but must support people in their search for new ones. Thus, we must create an educational milieu that is developmentally appropriate.

In the following section, we will describe learning objectives and the difficult learning tasks for individuals who are reasoning primarily at reflective judgment Stages Three and Five. We will then suggest the kinds of assignments that can be used to both challenge and support individuals at those stages in order to create transformative learning experiences. While these learning tasks and assignments are designed for traditional classrooms, they can be applied to nontraditional educational settings as well. It is assumed in the following examples that students are working on problems that are ill structured.

Developmental Instruction Using the
Reflective Judgment Model

Challenging and Supporting Stage Three Reasoning. As noted in an earlier section of this chapter, the following assumptions are characteristic of Stage Three reasoning: Knowledge is absolutely certain in some areas and temporarily uncertain in others; conclusions are justified via authorities in areas of certainty and via intuition in areas of uncertainty; and evidence does not play a role in reasoning to a conclusion since there is no certain way to evaluate it. It is difficult for learners who hold this view to recognize legitimate sources of authority as better qualified than themselves to make judgments or to draw conclusions about ill-structured problems. They also have difficulty distinguishing between facts and opinions and do not understand the use of evidence to justify a point of view. In addition, it remains difficult for these individuals to tolerate or value multiple evidence-based perspectives on a single issue. For many, these multiple perspectives are seen simply as adding confusion to an already confusing world or as examples of false authoritative claims in areas of temporary uncertainty.

One learning objective for individuals using Stage Three reasoning is to differentiate between evidence and opinion — for example, between the use of authority to support an argument and the evidence the authority uses. A second objective is for learners to use evidence to evaluate their intuitive beliefs about a problem. Last, they need to confront and evaluate the evidence for multiple perspectives on an issue. Some possible assignments that follow from these objectives are listed below.

1. Evaluate an argument (for or against an issue) in terms of its use of evidence, dependence upon authority, and understanding of the other view of the issue.
2. Give the best evidence you can find for a specific point of view. Identify what makes it count as evidence.
3. Identify the evidence and arguments for a view that an authority in the field is presenting. What makes the evidence for the argument strong or weak?
4. Identify two or more points of view on an issue.
5. What do you believe about an issue? Is there any evidence that supports what you believe? What is the evidence that is contrary to what you believe?

As a step in the transformation of Stage Three to Stage Four perspectives, each of these assignments is designed to help students who use Stage Three reasoning to critically reflect upon their implicit assumptions about evidence and opinion, about how arguments are validated, or about the legitimacy of different points of view. It should be noted that other naturally occurring events — for example, contact with individuals with alternative life-styles and belief systems — will also contribute to the transformation of Stage Three meaning perspectives.

Although it is important to challenge implicit epistemic assumptions, it is also important to legitimize students' struggles with their feelings of being confused and overwhelmed by alternative perspectives and with questioning what counts as evidence. Educators can acknowledge the struggle explicitly as well as help peers share their confusion with each other in discussions or written assignments. Educators can also provide support by modeling good use of evidence — for example, making explicit the justification for both sides of an argument, distinguishing inapplicable evidence from relevant evidence, or explaining the rationale behind their own use of expert or authoritative opinion.

The anxiety that comes from giving up the belief that knowledge is certain may be exacerbated by the anxiety of not knowing what an instructor expects in a class. Therefore, detailed assignments with clear expectations can provide the students at this level with an environment that allows safe exploration.

Challenging and Supporting Stage Five Reasoning. To review, Stage Five reasoning is characterized by the assumption that no knowledge is certain because interpretation is inherent in all understanding. Individuals suggest that beliefs may be justified only within a given context. Within particular contexts, however, they acknowledge that some evidence can be evaluated qualitatively as stronger or more relevant than other evidence.

It is difficult for those using Stage Five reasoning to evaluate competing evidence-based interpretations that reflect different points of view on an issue. It is hard for them to identify relationships between points of view and to act as though each were discrete. These individuals also have difficulty endorsing one view as better than another, as if doing so would deny the legitimacy of other perspectives. Consequently, the most important learning objective for those at this stage is to relate alternative points of view to each other, comparing the evidence and opinion for each in order to arrive at a conclusion that integrates the alternatives or evaluates one as better or best in a limited sense. Further, individuals must acknowledge that such conclusions need not sacrifice the appreciation for multiple perspectives that is the hallmark of Stage Five reasoning.

Possible assignments that make this goal explicit are listed below.

1. Compare and contrast two competing points of view, citing and evaluating evidence and arguments used by proponents of each. Determine which author makes the better interpretation of the evidence and which conclusion is most appropriate.
2. Select a controversial issue from those discussed in class. Explain at least two points of view from which the issue has been addressed by scholars. Indicate which point of view you believe to be most appropriate and the grounds for that decision.

As with Stage Three reasoning, the transformation of one's meaning perspective can be frustrating, confusing, and sometimes frightening. Therefore, with individuals using Stage Five reasoning, it is important to legitimize the struggle to adjudicate between competing points of view as required in the above assignments. Modeling choice making by carefully explaining the evaluation process and reasons for choices provides support for the students' own struggles. For example, instructors can give relevant interpretations of evidence from different points of view and explain the reasons for choosing one interpretation over another. Because individuals who use Stage Five constructs often equate choice making with intolerance for different points of view, legitimizing inquiry from different perspectives and valuing different points of view remains important.

A Programmatic Example

As noted earlier, our work has been primarily on developing and empirically testing the reflective judgment model. While we have applied ideas such as those discussed above to our own teaching, we have not developed or tested a program designed to help students examine their own epistemic perspectives. Kroll (forthcoming), however, has developed such a program, which we describe below.

Based on our work as well as the work of Perry (1970), Kroll designed a learning experience for a literature and composition class to help freshmen college students become more thoughtful and reflective. Based on data suggesting that many college freshmen struggle with the epistemic assumptions characteristic of Stage Three, he focused the assignments on understanding that different people in positions of authority may provide discrepant accounts of the same event, a factor that makes it difficult to know what to believe.

The content of Kroll's course was taken from accounts of the Vietnam War. Students were asked to make judgments at the beginning and at the end of the course about two different accounts of a battle. Specifically, they were asked whether one account of the battle was more believable than the other, whether one was more likely to be true, and, last, what *really* happened in this battle. In other words, Kroll asked students to identify *what* they could know and *how* they could know when they were faced with an ill-structured historical problem. The questions were designed to help the instructor understand more about the students' epistemological assumptions when they entered the class and to evaluate those assumptions again when they left the class.

At the end of the semester, most students were emphatic in claiming that the course had influenced their ability to be critical in their thinking, to be cautious about what they read, and to be more skeptical about accepting what others claim to be truth. Because many students pointed to a unit on the Hue massacre as particularly influential, it seems useful to identify the key elements of that unit.

First, Kroll had students read two quite different accounts of what happened at Hue. One presented the offical view that Communist forces had systematically massacred many South Vietnamese because of their political ties to the United States. The other account took the perspective that the Viet Cong planned to execute only a few government officials and that most of the civilians died in the ruthless counterattack of the United States forces. After reading these accounts, students read thirteen more accounts of the event and viewed a documentary that depicted several interpretations of what happened at Hue. At each step, they kept an account of their thinking about the articles in journals. Instructors' comments, both in response to journal entries and in class discussion, were focused on getting students to reflect critically on what they were reading. Instructors carefully avoided endorsing one interpretation. Instead, they asked students to identify the different positions, to articulate which claims supported each, and to begin to evaluate these claims. Later, they asked students to analyze the material they had read and to present the best case they could for what really happened in Hue in 1968.

Kroll reports that when asked at the end of the course to again interpret the two accounts of the battle on which they wrote during the first week of class, students' writing reflected some differences: Students appeared to use dogmatic approaches less often and to use what he called precritical and critical strategies more often. They also expressed skepticism more frequently about what they read. While Kroll acknowledged that there was no way to clearly prove that these changes resulted only from the course work, students attributed the changes to it. Kroll also noted that while there were some differences in students' responses at the end of the course, they did not involve major changes in what we would call epistemological orientation. He notes, and we would agree, that reflective thinking develops slowly and students need more than a single-semester course to make major changes in their meaning perspectives. However, he and we would also argue that education can make a difference in epistemological perspectives if it takes into account the developmental world through which students filter their educational experiences.

Conclusions

Research on the reflective judgment model has shown that students at different ages and educational levels enter the learning environment with markedly different assumptions about what and how something can be known and how to make judgments in light of these assumptions. Some enter believing that they can know absolutely through concrete observation. They see their learning task as discovering the truth or identifying someone, an authority, who can explicate it. Others accept that there are many problems for which there are no absolutely true answers. The task for these problem solvers is to construct a solution that is justifiable after considering alternative evidence and interpretations. In this complex world, where so many of the problems adults face involve uncertainty or are ill structured, we would argue that the latter meaning perspective is more adaptive, more essential, and more consistent with the stated mission of colleges and universities.

Our data suggest that this second meaning perspective does not develop until the adult years (that is, in the late twenties or early thirties) and that it is usually tied to participation in advanced education when individuals are involved in the creation of knowledge. Since our data also suggest that those of the same age without higher education score more similarly to younger subjects of the same educational level, we believe that education does make a difference (Kitchener and King, forthcoming).

We suspect that educational experiences, whether inside or outside the classroom, can be deliberately designed to challenge meaning perspectives and that these challenges along with appropriate environmental support will promote growth. Kroll's work on improving reflective thinking through a literature and composition course supports that position. Similarly, Welfel (1982) suggests that since career counseling involves making decisions about an ill-structured problem, it can also facilitate the transformation of epistemic meaning perspectives. Undoubtedly, many other experiences, from travel to participation in reading groups, can have similar effects. On the other hand, there may be some developmental limits to how far or how fast students at a given age level can advance. Development occurs slowly; and, in our opinion, it is unlikely that young adults, even given the best educational environment, will very often use the kind of reflective judgment that Dewey idealized.

One key to developing reflective thinking is the identification and use of ill-structured problems (Davison, King, and Kitchener, forthcoming). Kroll chose an ill-structured historical problem as the content on which to base his course in literature and writing. Ill-structured problems are not, however, limited to history and literature. They can be found in the hard sciences, the social sciences, business, humanities, and the professions because they are the problems of the real world. We believe their use as educational tools is essential if critical, reflective thinking is to be advanced.

References

Broughton, J. M. *The Development of Natural Epistemology in Years 11 to 16.* Unpublished doctoral dissertation, Harvard University, 1975.

Churchman, C. W. *The Design of Inquiring Systems: Basic Concepts of Systems and Organizations.* New York: Basic Books, 1971.

Davison, M. L., King, P. M., and Kitchener, K. S. "Developing Reflective Thinking Through Writing." In R. Beach and S. Hynds (eds.), *Becoming Readers and Writers During Adolescence and Adulthood.* Norwood, N.J.: Ablex, forthcoming.

Dewey, J. *How We Think.* Lexington, Mass.: Heath, 1933.

Finster, D. "Developmental Instruction: Part 2. Application of Perry's Model to General Chemistry." *Journal of Chemical Education,* forthcoming.

Fischer, K. W. "A Theory of Cognitive Development: The Control and Construction of Hierarchies of Skills." *Psychological Review,* 1980, *87,* 477–531.

Fischer, K. W., and Kenny, S. L. "Environmental Conditions for Discontinuities in the Development of Abstractions." In R. M. Mines and K. S. Kitchener (eds.), *Adult Cognitive Development.* New York: Praeger, 1986.

Kegan, R. *The Evolving Self.* Cambridge, Mass.: Harvard University Press, 1982.

Kitchener, K. S. "Educational Goals and Reflective Thinking." *Educational Forum,* 1983, *48,* 75–95.

Kitchener, K. S., and King, P. M. "Reflective Judgment: Concepts of Justification and Their Relationship to Age and Education." *Journal of Applied Developmental Psychology*, 1981, *2*, 89–116.

Kitchener, K. S., and King, P. M. "Reflective Judgment Scoring Manual." Bowling Green, Ohio: Bowling Green State University, 1985. (Mimeographed.)

Kitchener, K. S., and King, P. M. "The Reflective Judgment Model: Ten Years of Research." In M. L. Commons, J. D. Sinnott, F. A. Richards, and C. Armon (eds.), *Adult Development: Comparisons and Applications of Adolescent and Adult Developmental Models.* New York: Praeger, forthcoming.

Kitchener, K. S., King, P. M., Wood, P. K., and Davison, M. L. "Consistency and Sequentiality in the Development of Reflective Judgment: A Six-Year Longitudinal Study." *Journal of Applied Developmental Psychology,* forthcoming.

Kroll, B. M. "Teaching English for Reflective Thinking." In R. Beach and S. Hynds (eds.), *Becoming Readers and Writers During Adolescence and Adulthood.* Norwood, N.J.: Ablex, forthcoming.

Lynch, C. L., and Kitchener, K. S. "Environmental Conditions for Optimal Performance in Reflective Judgment." Paper presented at the annual meeting of the American Educational Research Association, San Francisco, March 1989.

Perry, W. G. *Forms of Intellectual and Ethical Development in the College Years.* New York: Holt, Rinehart & Winston, 1970.

Wood, P. K. "Inquiring Systems and Problem Structure: Implications for Cognitive Development." *Human Development,* 1983, *26*, 249–265.

Nine

Using Critical Incidents to Explore Learners' Assumptions

Stephen Brookfield

The process of critical reflection can be viewed as comprising three interrelated phases: (1) identifying the assumptions that underlie our thoughts and actions; (2) scrutinizing the accuracy and validity of these in terms of how they connect to, or are discrepant with, our experience of reality (frequently through comparing our experiences with others in similar contexts); and (3) reconstituting these assumptions to make them more inclusive and integrative. Central to the process of critical reflection, then, is the recognition and analysis of assumptions. Assumptions can be defined as comprising those taken-for-granted ideas, commonsense beliefs, and self-evident rules of thumb that inform our thoughts and actions. They are the heuristic mechanisms through which we account for events in our lives. As explanatory devices, they both confirm and shape our perceptions. How we understand what happens to us and how we create meaning and find significance in these happenings are interpretive activities that occur within the framework of our assumptive clusters. Assumptions undergird our understanding of what we judge to be "human nature." They inform our appreciation of cause-and-effect relationships and comprise our criteria for appropriate behavior in the personal and political world. They can be viewed as the interpretive glue that binds the various meaning schemes comprising our structures of understanding.

Making explicit the constituent elements of our assumptive worlds is a central task of critical education. Yet becoming aware of the assumptions underlying our thoughts and actions is enormously difficult. Attempting to identify them is like trying to catch our psychological tail. We twist and turn in a frantic attempt to grasp hold of ever more elusive suspicions about the reasons for our actions. Becoming aware of assumptions so internalized that we perceive them as "second nature," "obvious," or "common sense" is problematic precisely because of the familiarity of these ideas. Assumptions, for example, on what work we are naturally suited to, how the political world works, or what the legitimate expectations are of how to behave in relationships are etched into our mental structures. They are pivotal elements in the perceptual filters that mediate our interpretations of reality.

Questioning the assumptions on which we act and exploring alternative ideas are not only difficult but also psychologically explosive. The effect can be appreciated by visualizing an explosives expert who lays dynamite charges at the base of a building requiring demolition. When these charges ignite at key points in the structure's foundation, the whole edifice comes crashing down. Beginning to recognize and then critically question key assumptions is like laying down charges of psychological dynamite. When these assumptions explode and we realize that what we thought of as fixed ways of thinking and living are only options among a range of alternatives, the whole structure of our assumptive world crumbles. Hence, educators who foster transformative learning are rather like psychological and cultural demolition experts.

In saying this, it is important to remember that demolition is not the same as random, willful destruction. In fact, when done properly, demolition requires training and sensitivity. Demolition experts who blow up industrial chimney stacks or structurally unsound high-rise apartment buildings frequently have to bring these down in densely populated areas. The charges are laid carefully, based on the experts' judgment of how structures can collapse in on themselves without flattening the surrounding area. Similarly, when educators assist people in questioning the assumptions underlying their structures of understanding or in realizing alternatives to their habitual ways of thinking and living, they must act with care and sensitivity. They must ensure that when the foundations of these structures are shaken, the framework of the individual's self-esteem is left relatively intact. It is no good encouraging people to recognize and analyze their assumptions if their self-esteem is destroyed in the process. Assisting people to break out of their assumptive worlds without threatening or intimidating them to the point of withdrawal is highly problematic. It also raises many ethical questions and requires educators, at the very least, to point out to learners the risks and potentially harmful consequences of this activity. Engaging in critical thinking is not a continuously joyful exercise in creative self-actualization. It is psychologically and politically dangerous, involving risks to one's livelihood, social networks, and psychological stability. In some cultures, people who think critically — who question accepted assumptions — are the first to disappear, to be tortured, or to be murdered in the event of a political coup d'état.

Critical Incidents

Critical incidents are brief descriptions written by learners of significant events in their lives. They have been used widely in educational research (Killen and McKee, 1983; Wilson-Pessano, 1988), ever since Flanagan's (1954) initial formulation of the method. The educator using critical incidents gives learners a set of instructions that identifies the kind of incident to be described and asks for details of the time, place, and actors involved in the incident and the reasons why the event was so significant. Ideally, these instructions are short, clearly written, and indicate precisely what information the educator seeks to obtain. If a critical incident instruction is well written, it produces written descriptions of particular happenings so graphic that readers are able to visualize clearly the event described.

As a means of probing learners' assumptive worlds, the critical incident technique is rooted in the phenomenological research tradition and presumes that learners' general assumptions are embedded in, and can be inferred from, their specific descriptions of particular events. As with all phenomenological approaches, the purpose is to enter another's frame of reference so that that person's structures of understanding and interpretive filters can be experienced and understood by the educator, or a peer, as closely as possible to the way they are experienced and understood by the learner. As a first step in encouraging critical reflection, educators have to see the world as their learners see it. We must become phenomenological detectives, immersing ourselves in learners' worldviews and assumptive clusters, as a first step in exploring how to encourage them to move outside of their comfortable paradigms. Given the anxiety-provoking nature of asking people to analyze critically the assumptions by which they habitually live, it is crucial that educators find ways of doing this that are as accessible and nonthreatening as possible.

Underlying this phenomenological approach is the assumption that specific responses to critical incidents often have the generic embedded within them. As a technique, critical incidents are idiographic rather than nomothetic; that is, they seek to highlight particular, concrete, and contextually specific aspects of people's experiences. Their value for fostering critically transformative learning is twofold. First, because critical incidents are accounts written by people about actions in their own lives, they are incontrovertible sources of data representing learners' existential realities. Critical incident responses stand alone as primary data sources giving insights into learners' assumptive worlds in expressions that are indisputably the learners' own. Second, critical incident exercises are much less threatening to complete than asking learners to respond to general questions. The emphasis in the incidents cited in this chapter is on recalling specific situations, events, and people rather than asking learners to identify general assumptions. Indeed, a rule of thumb in assumption analysis is to use indirect rather than head-on approaches whenever possible. In assisting learners to explore their assumptive worlds, the last thing that educators should do is to ask learners directly what assumptions they operate under in various aspects of their lives. Such generalized questioning often confuses or intimidates. A far more fruitful approach is to work from the specific to the general. In this approach, learners are asked to produce richly detailed accounts of specific events and then move to collaborative, inductive analysis of general elements embedded in these particular descriptions.

My own use of critical incidents usually takes place in workshops on critical thinking, where I am often faced with groups of educators who wish to learn how to develop critical thinking in others. I believe strongly that the best way educators can help others to become critically reflective is to model this activity. Before asking others to be critically reflective of their own assumptions and meaning perspectives, educators must be able to do this for themselves while avoiding the pitfalls of their profession. There is a real danger that educators in this area of practice will present themselves as critically sophisticated gurus who have come to release learners from the chains of their distorted meaning perspectives. This approach is arrogant and alienating.

My approach is to model the kinds of critical reflection I am asking learners to explore. I state my own ideas on, say, the nature of adult learning and adult teaching and ask people to explore with me and each other the discrepancies between their own experiences and my own insights. I distribute essays, papers, and reviews that are critical of my own positions; in addition, I often take something I have written or said and analyze it publicly for its distortions, inaccuracies, oversimplifications, contradictions, and ambiguities. I do this in an attempt to encourage an atmosphere of trust. Such trust is vital, for I am asking people to make public and scrutinize critically assumptions to which they have fervently clung for much of their adult lives; this can only be accomplished if they have seen that I, as leader, am willing to live this process with them. After having done my best to exemplify the process as far as possible, I feel more comfortable asking workshop participants to analyze their own experience. I ask them to write critical incidents on aspects of their own practice and then to analyze these incidents for the generalized assumptions about teaching and learning that are embedded. I have also used the critical incident technique to help learners examine the assumptions underlying their actions in their intimate relationships and to help them become media literate. In the remainder of this chapter, I give three examples of how critical incidents can be used in workshops to explore some central domains of adult life.

Exercise One: Analyzing Assumptions About Good Practice in Education. In this exercise I give workshop participants, all of whom are educators from diverse settings with greater or lesser degrees of experience, the following instructions:

> Think back over the past year. During that time, what event made you as an educator feel a real "high" of excitement, satisfaction, and fulfillment? A time when you said to yourself, "This is what it's all about," or "This is what makes it all worthwhile"? Write a brief description of the event. Make sure you include details of when and where it happened, who was involved (roles, functions, and job titles should be used here rather than names of individuals), and what it was about the event that made you feel so good. Write these details by yourself, keeping your description to under one page.
>
> Now, find two other participants to form a group of three. In this triad, each person will take a turn reading aloud his or her description. After you have read out your description, your two colleagues will try to identify the assumptions about good educational practice that they think are embedded in your description. You, in turn, will do the same for each of your colleagues. To help you identify assumptions, it might be helpful to think of them as the rules of thumb that underlie and inform our actions. In this exercise, they are the general beliefs, commonsense ideas, or intuitions that you and your colleagues hold about teaching.
>
> Your analysis of assumptions should initially be on two levels: (1) What assumptions do you think inform your colleagues' choices of significant incidents — what do their

choices say about their value systems? (2) What assumptions underlie the specific actions they took in the incidents described? After your description has been analyzed by your two colleagues, you have the opportunity to comment on what you see as the accuracy and validity of their insights. Do you think they have gauged accurately the assumptions you hold? Were you surprised by their analyses? Or did the assumptions they identify confirm how you conceive your own practice? They, in turn, will have the chance to comment on the accuracy and validity of your assessments of their assumptions.

It is also interesting to look for commonalities and differences in the assumptions you each identify. If there are commonly held assumptions, do they represent what passes for conventional wisdom in your field of practice? If there are major differences, to what extent might these signify divergent views in the field at large? Or might the differences be the result of contextual variations?

Finally, after reading out your incident description, it is almost inevitable that your colleagues will ask you for more information about the circumstances you have just described. What do their requests for additional contextual information say about what they perceive to be valuable and significant in the incident described?

Before giving these instructions to participants, I run through the exercises once in front of the whole workshop: I ask learners to probe an incident I relate from my own experience for the assumptions they see embedded therein. In effect, I model the incident instructions outlined above by graphically describing something significant that has happened to me in the last few months. I do this verbally for reasons of time, trying as far as possible to be precise, specific, and concrete in my account. I ask participants to listen carefully to my description and then to discuss (in groups of two or three) those assumptions they see that underlie my choice of a significant event and inform my actions in the incident described. Invariably, they ask me many questions about circumstances before and after the event, about my motivations, and about the motivations I impute to others described in the incident. When this happens, I try to explore with them the assumptions embedded within their own requests for additional details. People's requests for information usually reflect concerns that are of significance to them; it helps participants engage in assumption analysis by first reflecting on the assumptions underlying their own questions.

After they have gathered all the contextual data they think important and have considered in groups of two or three the assumptions embedded within the incident I have described to them, we undertake the process of assumption analysis in a large group. Participants offer their interpretations of the assumptions they think I hold about good practice in education and I give my reactions. I will agree, disagree, ask for further clarification, ask for time to think about a point, and generally try to model the kind of discussion I hope participants will undertake in their own discussions. After about forty minutes of answering requests for contextual information and then discussing with participants their interpretations of my assumptions, I ask them to try out the critical incident exercise in small groups according to the instructions given above.

There are other ways to model this assumption analysis exercise with a large group before proceeding to small-group analysis. One can have three participants demonstrate the exercise before the whole group, with the leader being either one of the three participants or acting as an observer and commentator on the process. This takes some courage on the part of participants, which is why I generally find this approach to be too threatening for learners. Another way would be to show a video of a small group grappling with the exercise, followed by a discussion about the problems associated with this technique.

Methodologically, the small-group exercise is framed the way it is for several reasons. First, learners work from the specific to the general. Instead of asking them to identify the philosophical beliefs, criteria, or pedagogic rationales underlying their practice — a highly intimidating task that most people are hard pressed to perform — I ask them to recall a particular event. There is no pressure to appear profound, no need to espouse conventional pedagogic wisdoms whether or not one actually believes or follows them, and no requirement to speak in academically impeccable jargon. Second, the focus of the exercise is on learners' own experiences. Instead of asking them to respond to someone else's ideas (usually an expert's), I ask learners to express themselves directly in their own, authentic language. There is no pressure to frame what they say in terms of someone else's philosophy. Third, there is a strong emphasis on peer learning. It is the participants — not me, the workshop leader — who try to analyze each other's assumptions. This is, I believe, less intimidating than having me as workshop leader take on the role of assumption analyst. I do not require learners to read their incidents to the large group and then receive my public interpretation as workshop leader. My only public role is to present my incidents for their analysis in the manner already described. Learners know that their incidents will be shared only with two others during their small-group discussion. In addition to this relative privacy, learners assume the role of analyst as well as subject. This allows them to experience being the recipient of assumption analysis as well as being the analyst, which will make them more sensitive to the feelings and reactions of their learners when these same educators return to work and begin to foster critical reflection. Fourth, the analysis of commonly held assumptions that comprise the conventional wisdom in their field alerts them to the dangers of groupthink.

Groupthink represents the cozy illusion that all right-thinking people agree, so that "each member of the group feels himself to be under an injunction to avoid making penetrating criticisms that might bring on a clash and destroy the unity of the group" (Janis, 1983, p. 205). As Goleman (1985, p. 183) asserts, "the first victim of groupthink is critical thought." Hence, an important outcome of the exercise is to prompt learners to consider the possibility that their assumptions mirror the espoused groupthink of their field, rather than being accurately grounded in their own experiences.

We need to consider some other aspects of this exercise. It is frequently a good idea to pair critical incidents by asking participants to describe one successful event and one failure (or one "high" and one "low"). I always ask for descriptions of the successful event first, since to talk about one's successes is much less threatening than to talk about one's failures. However, it is my experience that a fuller picture of participants' assumptive worlds is revealed when they describe negative as well as positive incidents. Additionally, when learners do participate in analyses of highs and lows, I sometimes ask them to be a full participant in one of the exercises and then to be an observer in another. Learners benefit from playing both roles — from actively identifying and analyzing assumptions and from passively observing others perform these tasks.

Finally, I always end this exercise with a debriefing session in which learners talk about the form and focus of the exercise. This debriefing begins with my asking for reactions on the ease of the exercise. Were the instructions clear? What difficulties were there in "going public" with events from their own professional lives? How easy was it to search memory for a significant event? What problems were involved in probing colleagues' descriptions for assumptions underlying their practice? We then discuss some of the incidents described. The success of this part of debriefing is highly unpredictable. I stress that there is no pressure to talk publicly about private events — sometimes people take me at my word and there is very little comment ventured. At other times, participants explore the events and assumptions with energy and enthusiasm.

Exercise Two: Examining Assumptions About Intimate Relationships. This exercise is designed to help learners become more aware of the assumptive clusters informing their actions in one of the most significant domains of their adult existence, that is, their intimate relationships. These relationships represent one of the most crucial yet least studied settings for learning through critical reflection. The psychic arena of family life, friendships, and marriages is the focus for many people, giving deep meaning to their lives. We may present partial representations of ourselves in our work and community lives, but in intimate relationships we reveal our most private identities, allowing the emergence of that core of our being by which we define ourselves. Conversely, the private nature of this domain makes probing its assumptions particularly impenetrable. The following critical incident exercise tries to do this in as non-threatening and informal a manner as possible.

This exercise is designed to help you become aware of major assumptions informing your thoughts and actions in one of the most important domains in your lives — your intimate relationships. You will accomplish this through a form of modified, written critical incident and group analysis of responses. You can be as open or guarded as you wish in this exercise. There are no ethnomethodological tricks to knock you psychologically off balance. The purpose is simply to help you become more aware of the assumptions underlying your actions, decisions, and judgments in your intimate relationships. One consequence of this may be that you will be able to judge whether or not these assumptions make sense for your own experience and for the experience of your intimates.

The task has two stages. You must first privately write an account of a critical incident. Then you must share this with a group for analysis. As a first stage, then, think back over the last year in one of your intimate relationships, such as a marriage, parent-child relationship, love relationship, or deep friendship. Choose an event that you can point to and say (1) that was a time when the relationship was going well, and (2) that was a time when things weren't working out. Write a specific and detailed description of this event, keeping your comments to one page. Include details of where and when the event happened, who was involved, and what it was about the event that was so significant to you.

Now, find two other participants to form a group of three. In this triad, each person will take a turn reading aloud his or her description. After you have read out your description, your two colleagues will try to identify the assumptions about appropriate behavior in a relationship that they think are embedded in your description. You, in turn, will do the same for each of your colleagues. To help you identify assumptions, it might be helpful to think of them as the rules of thumb that underlie and inform our actions. In this exercise, they are the general beliefs, commonsense ideas, or intuitions that you and your colleagues hold about how to behave toward intimates.

Your analysis of assumptions should initially be on two levels: (1) What assumptions do you think inform your colleagues' choices of significant incidents — what do their choices say about their value systems? (2) What assumptions underlie the specific actions they took in the incidents described? After your description has been analyzed by your two colleagues, you have the opportunity to comment on what you see as the accuracy and validity of their insights. Do you think they have gauged accurately the assumptions you hold? Were you surprised by their analyses? Or did the assumptions they identify confirm how you conceive your own actions? They, in turn, will have the chance to comment on the accuracy and validity of your assessments of their assumptions.

It might be interesting to look for commonalities and differences in the assumptions you each identify. If there are commonly held assumptions, do they represent what passes for conventional wisdom about relationships in your culture? If there are major differences, to what extent might these represent personality differences or broader class and subcultural differences?

Finally, after reading out your incident description, it is almost inevitable that your colleagues will ask you for more information about the circumstances you have just described. What do their requests for additional contextual information say about what they perceive to be valuable and significant in the incident described?

An important note: You may currently be, or recently have been, involved in a major period of trauma in a relationship. If so, you may not wish to participate in this exercise. This is quite understandable. If you would rather be a silent observer, feel free to do so. There is no pressure to be revealing at the cost of considerable emotional upset.

Surprisingly, this exercise is a relatively popular option at critical thinking workshops I have run. One might assume that a majority of participants would resist probing such a personally significant domain of their adult lives. However, when I routinely offer learners the chance to participate in exercises to do either with examining workplace assumptions, analyzing media biases, or exploring intimate relationships, they frequently choose the last. Perhaps the fact of being with strangers (most participants do not know each other and will probably not see each other again) engenders a greater readiness to be open about intimate relationships. Participants frequently talk about domineering parents, the struggle to escape sexual stereotypes, and the pain of "letting go" when children become young adults, as well as crises of miscommunication and the open or latent conflicts present in relationships with lovers and spouses. One of the most frequent of themes to emerge is that of transformational envy. This occurs when one partner responds to a developmental imperative involving significant personal change that can alter the relationship, while the other partner wishes the relationship to remain the same.

Exercise Three: Using Critical Incidents to Analyze Political Assumptions. The power of television as an agent of political socialization in adulthood is crucial. Television shapes the form of public political discourse and develops in viewers analytical and interpretive modes by which they understand this discourse. Adults rely on television for news about political events and for the acquisition of interpretive filters through which to make sense of those events. Television does not provide political information in an objective, neutral, or detached manner. It cannot, by definition, do this. The selection of stories, the juxtaposition of image and narrative, the choice of whose voices are heard on an issue, the ways in which questions are framed to different protagonists in a dispute, the editorializing undertaken by reporters and presenters — all these factors frame the way that many adults think and talk about politics. It is not that television discovers and then reports the prevailing political agenda; rather, it creates that agenda itself in very large measure.

In workshops on critical thinking and in separate seminars on developing media literacy, I have tried to create exercises, methods, and techniques to help adults become more media literate; that is, to realize the distorting power of television, to understand that television presentations are constructed rather than objectively reported realities, and to recognize that various interpretative stances could be taken on an issue. These techniques are many and various, from content analysis and autobiographical analysis to constructing television programs. What I would like to consider here is the way in which educators can help adults scrutinize the assumptions they hold about the political world through a critical incident analysis of televised political events. The following exercise is, like the other two in this chapter, conducted in a workshop setting.

Recall the last time you became extremely angry as you watched a news report, current affairs program, press conference, or other form of political broadcast dealing with a politician's behavior. Write down a description of this broadcast, making sure you include the time it occurred, its specific content, who was involved, and what it was about the politician's actions that so incensed you.

Now, find two other participants to form a group of three. In this triad, each person will take a turn reading aloud his or her description. After you have read out your description, your two colleagues will try to identify the assumptions about appropriate political behavior that they think are embedded in your description. You, in turn, will do the same for each of your colleagues. To help you identify assumptions, it might be helpful to think of them as the rules of thumb that underlie and inform our actions. In this exercise, they are the general beliefs, commonsense ideas, or intuitions that you and your colleagues hold about how politicians should behave.

Your analysis of assumptions should initially be on two levels: (1) What assumptions do you think inform your colleagues' choices of significant incidents — what do their choices say about their value systems? (2) What assumptions underlie the specific actions they took in the incidents described? After your description has been analyzed by your two colleagues, you have the opportunity to comment on what you see as the accuracy and validity of their insights. Do you think they have gauged accurately the assumptions you hold? Were you surprised by their analyses? Or did the assumptions they identify confirm how you conceive your own actions? They, in turn, will have the chance to comment on the accuracy and validity of your assessments of their assumptions.

It might be interesting to look for commonalities and differences in the assumptions you each identify. If there are commonly held assumptions, do they represent what passes for conventional wisdom about political behavior in your culture? If there are major differences, try to explore each other's perspectives on these. Find out as much as you can about why each defines appropriate political behavior differently. Imagine yourself in the minds of your colleagues and try to see the world as they do.

Finally, after reading out your incident description, it is almost inevitable that your colleagues will ask you for more information about the circumstances you have just described. What do their requests for additional contextual information say about what they perceive to be valuable and significant in the incident described?

The analysis period of this critical incident exercise is, potentially, the most explosive of the three reported in this chapter. While learners seem able to exchange details of their intimate relationships without rancor, discussions of inappropriate political behavior become highly charged. At times, after the shouting is over, participants shut themselves off from serious consideration of others' assumptions. These episodes are sometimes inevitable, and one should not conclude that one has failed as a teacher when they happen. Displays of emotion do not betoken pedagogic failure. Rather, they can frequently be welcomed as doses of reality in the otherwise artificially bloodless arena of the classroom. However, it is wise to set ground rules for the analysis period beforehand so that entrenched prejudices do not block out the possibility of participants' taking on each other's perspectives in order to see their own views from another ideological vantage point.

Conclusion

Many critical thinking exercises found in texts on this topic focus on encouraging learners to scrutinize formal texts for the extent to which facts and opinions are mixed, the ways arguments are presented as incontrovertible when no supportive evidence has been presented, and the ways in which personal bias can masquerade as objective truth. These are useful exercises in detecting logical fallacies, but to many adults there is no connection between such activities and the realities of their daily lives. In helping people recognize and analyze their assumptions, the scrutiny of critical incidents from learners' biographies is an accessible and personalized approach. Learners are not intimidated by being asked to talk about events in their own lives, a topic about which, after all, they have more knowledge than anyone else. Focusing on biography grounds the activity of critical reflection in the context of the daily decisions and dilemmas learners face.

Admitting that our assumptions might be distorted, wrong, or contextually relative implies that the fabric of our personal and political existence might rest upon faulty foundations. Even considering this possibility is profoundly threatening; for if our past lives have been lived within faulty assumptive worlds, does that not mean that we have to jettison our current relationships, work, and political commitments in favor of some more authentic ways of living, whatever these might be? This possibility is perceived by most people when they are asked to make explicit the assumptive base on which they have built their personal and political lives. It is one reason why this activity is frequently so strongly resisted. Another is the difficulty of performing the mental gymnastics entailed in identifying and challenging assumptions. Because of the ingrained, internalized nature of assumptions, they are almost *too* obvious. Despite these challenges, helping learners explore their assumptive worlds is at the heart of critical teaching. The critical incident approach represents one point of entry into this contradictory, ambiguous, and often painful reality.

References

Flanagan, J. C. "The Critical Incident Technique." *Psychological Bulletin,* 1954, *51,* 4.

Goleman, D. *Vital Lies, Simple Truths.* New York: Simon & Schuster, 1985.

Janis, I. *Victims of Groupthink.* (Rev. ed.) Boston: Houghton Mifflin, 1983.

Killen, R., and McKee, A. *Critical Incidents in Teaching: An Approach to Teacher Decision-Making.* Newcastle, Australia: Newcastle College of Advanced Education, 1983.

Wilson-Pessano, S. R. "Defining Professional Competence: The Critical Incident Technique 40 Years Later." Invited address to Division 1 of the American Educational Research Association, New Orleans, Apr. 8, 1988.

Ten

Composing
Education Biographies:
Group Reflection
Through Life Histories

Pierre F. Dominicé

The life history approach that I slowly created and have been using for some years is an attempt to take a learning situation as a relevant context for research. Education should not be an applied field for social sciences, as it has its own epistemological foundations. The learner's learning can be an object of research; and research, for the adult learner, an opportunity for transformative learning.

Research in adult education has, up until now, been mainly concerned with the application of theoretical models to its different fields. Evaluation is a good example of a research practice captured by the need to prove the relevance of a program, instead of exploring the complex question of the different types of learning that adults experience in the educational context of this program.

What I call educational biography is a specific version of the life history approach that I use as a methodology of group reflection about learning, based on the interpretation by adults of their own reconstructed learning processes. I have developed this methodology up until now within adult students in education and adult educators working mainly in large corporations or public administration, but I believe this version of life history may be broadened to include all adult learners. The educational biography seems to be an original way to reflect critically about the knowledge, the values, and the meaning constructed by adults through their life experiences.

In this chapter, I will first describe how I have used the life history approach in the field of adult education. Then I will explain the theoretical contribution the educational biography makes to the understanding of adult learning. Finally, I will explore the potential of the educational biography for further experiments and underline its limits as well.

Life History Applied to Adult Education

The purpose of my initial research was to reconstruct with university students what they had learned in the course of their lives, in order to have a better understanding of the role continuing education could play in the process of adult learning. At the time, I did not know anything about the tradition of life history in the social sciences. I was troubled by the contradiction between the experimental design used in conventional evaluation and the theories of development that were a reference for me after reading Freud and studying with Piaget. It was difficult to explain the reasons for new professional attitudes or personal changes by data collected from evaluations of an educational activity. These difficulties caused me to probe more deeply the concept of learning and to face the emptiness of its meaning for the field of adult education. After exploring a kind of intuitive biographical approach, I systematically worked out the methodology that I have used now for some years (Dominicé, 1982). This approach greatly influenced my way of thinking because it gave me a better idea of the relationship between education and research. In order to help the reader have a clearer picture of this work, I will present briefly how I use life history in adult education.

Research as Educational Process. Originally, the life history approach was mainly used in the fields of anthropology and sociology. It belongs to a tradition of qualitative research known in social sciences as the "Chicago school." First used by Thomas and Zaniecki around 1920, this methodology was subsequently rejected in favor of the empirico-analytical model that has dominated the social sciences since World War II. In the 1980s, the French sociologist Daniel Bertaux (1982) organized an international group of sociologists that revised this approach. Life history is now considered a tool for critical reflection on empirical research. For Ferrarotti (1983), this methodology opens a new epistemological perspective because of the place given to the subject in the construction of knowledge: "If every individual is the singular reappropriation of a social and historical universality, we can come to know the social sphere on the basis of irreducible specificity of an individual practice" (p. 142). In his review of different life history approaches, Pineau (1983) also mentions psychoanalysis, psychobiography, and the work done by Erikson and others on the adult life cycle. He underlines, however, the lack of research using life history in the field of adult education, and outlines a participatory approach which will help adults become more aware of and more responsible for their learning process.

After creating my own biographical approach, and after some years of close cooperation with Gaston Pineau, I had to agree that adult education requires an original version of the life history methodology, not just an application of the work already done in the social sciences. Life history can be used in education as a tool for critical reflection, and the dynamics of this reflection can become for the researcher the real object of his research. I decided to work on this question of biographical methodology in the context of a seminar offered at the University of Geneva, Switzerland, and attended by adult students. I knew very well that the design of this research would not offer the same controls as an experimental design, but I chose it because the object of research required that the research be done where the educational activity took place. It also required that students participate actively as partners in the research process. I then had to find the right mode of cooperation with students who were more interested in the educational part of the research than in the research itself. In order that they not be used only for purposes of my own research, and once they had a good knowledge of the work already done with educational biographies, I decided to ask them to pose their own questions of research. I knew that within each student group there would necessarily be specific topics of interest, but the general question of how to identify the process of education through which we give form to our lives has remained the focus of common critical reflection.

The Practice of Educational Biography. In actual practice, university students participating in an adult education seminar are asked to present their life histories in the light of the education they have received. Students present their first narrative orally, which lasts about an hour. Seminar members then have another hour to raise questions and exchange ideas about the content of the narrative. During the following weeks, each participant is expected to work out a new written narrative. This kind of life history is not an autobiography in which the author is totally free to talk or write about his or her life. Participants have to focus on the process of how they became themselves and how they learned what they know through the various contexts, life stages, and people who were relevant to their education. Initially, I suggested a structure for them to follow. Then I realized that the structure of each narrative had to be considered as part of its meaning. Instead of trying to collect comparative biographical data on the basis of items of common structure, I let the students determine the form of their narrative. I did, however, encourage them to be attentive to the development of its content. I knew that the reconstruction of the past takes time and does not emerge suddenly upon request. Since the students were not simply filling in an anonymous series of open questions, they created a form that expressed the singularity of their life histories. This freedom of expression reinforced the quality of listening in the small groups, which were generally very intense and characterized by a sharing of experience done with a great deal of mutual respect. There was intimacy, but the participants kept a distance and did not end up in anything like group therapy. They were aware that they were doing research together, such that the public aspect of the class balanced the private dimension of the biography.

The methodology of educational biography requires different phases, which could be taken as stages of awareness about one's life. The oral narrative is a first self-interpretation of the life history of adults centered on the role of education in their process of learning and development. The discussion following each presentation enlarges this first level of interpretation, and the subsequent written version is the result of a more sophisticated and more formal interpretation of each life history. The lack of prescribed structure for the presentation of the life history became for me over the years one of the major conditions for deepening its interpretation. Participants have to be taken as the authors of their interpretations, since they are the sculptors of their own life histories. They do not have to find the right answer as they do when they are associated with research framed by a teacher in a teaching situation. They deal with their own questions and with their own resources in their own terms. This research process has to be seen in the light of emancipatory education, because it allows participants to be in charge of their lives and to become more personal and creative in their relationship to knowledge.

When adults are asked to talk about themselves in the university setting, the style of their narrative creates a kind of transformative learning situation. The theoretical framework takes the form of a language that is integrated into their daily lives. The distance that adult students very often feel from the concepts of the human sciences is not simply reduced, but the concepts themselves are understood differently. Through the educational biography, the author seems to become aware of his or her right to think in familiar terms. In one of the written narratives, the director of a children's home plays with the idea of equilibrium. She is in fact reconstructing in her own terms a concept created by Piaget and others. "I have been living for years in an unstable equilibrium which I have constantly been trying to balance. My spin is now off center, creating a 'scoliosis.'" The truth of an image, of an example, or of a poetic expression replaces the harshness of a scientific category.

As they analyze the models and values of their education and the meaningful contexts and events of their lives, the students identify their basic resources in order to understand and explain what they decided to do, what they chose to be, and how they think about the world around them. Through the educational biography, they enrich a process of critical self-reflection. This process challenges the modes of thinking they are expected to use in an academic situation. This is partly the reason why, after much debate, I decided it was fruitful to keep doing these educational biographies in an academic setting. My experience has also convinced me that the opportunity for critical reflection offered by this approach is closely related to the raison d'être of the group. This approach enriches the participants when they can share a common theme through their narratives. Almost all these adults share the same questions, doubts, and hopes concerning the academic knowledge to which they finally have access. Groups of adult educators dealing with the history of their qualifications also share the same difficulties and needs. In a formal learning situation, the educational biography plays the role of a countermodel of teaching and learning.

The Vividness of Subjectivity. The scientific model we have tried to respect in the educational sciences does not allow us to explore the vividness of subjectivity. We have had to prove the intellectual legitimacy of our questions by hiding our own interest in a specific area of research. We also have had to treat adults as anonymous subjects in the samples of our semiexperimental designs. The plurality of oral narratives, and even more of the written texts we analyzed, seemed to invalidate our data. For me, on the contrary, this subjectivity showed the complexity of adult learning when it was not related to the planning of a program but to the activity of the learner. More than anything else, the very subjectivity of the narratives made me aware that adults have multiple reasons for embarking upon a program of adult education. They will never learn the same thing in the same way. The educational biography follows the subjectivity of the author and is heard and read within the subjective categories of the hermeneutics of the researcher.

Most adult instructors mention the heterogeneity of the students as the main difficulty they encounter in teaching a class of adult students. In order to understand this heterogeneity, however, we must be willing to face the complexity of its inherent subjectivity.

An adult with a long experience of psychoanalysis will not present himself or herself in the same way as someone who has never attended a personal development workshop or therapy session. A professional who has spent many years as a teacher in a primary school or a nurse in a hospital will obviously speak a language that comes out of his or her professional socialization. Someone who has traveled a lot or worked abroad will necessarily have another view of the world than someone who has not. All these differences create the variety of languages and the plurality of meanings given to the learning experiences of a life history. The biographical approach challenges the normative, organized world of education and leads to a dialectic between the "real" world and the "disorder" of subjective human experience. It is also true that the narratives differ according to how much the writer is willing to invest and the amount of risk he or she is ready to take. Sharing does not follow a rule: What is said also depends greatly on the students' interactions with the group and with the facilitator. The richness of their subjective experience is greatly modified by the way the adult students are able to be "authentic" with each other.

Subjectivity should be considered as an epistemological foundation and does not mean revealing secrets or undergoing psychotherapy. How can a person understand how adults learn without entering into the singular dynamics of their learning process? How can a person come to any conclusions about adult learning without testing his or her own assertions through new testimony or new observation?

The Biographical Context of Learning

"Unfortunately, our personality, our religion, and our culture are not often integrated into our training or schooling . . . school was a part of my life, but my life was not part of school." Considering her life story, a young woman in her thirties has some clear memories of her school years, but does not remember much about the content of what she studied. At the end of her narrative she writes: "The idea that learning has to be taken as a whole becomes more and more obvious to me. Why do we always have to learn from slides or by compartments? How can we acquire knowledge if there is no understanding or interpretation of this knowledge on our part?"

When asked to present their educational biographies, most of the adults I have known were eager to comply; their stories were revealing. If they have succeeded or failed at school, it is very often for reasons other than their capacity to learn. Their motivation to study is primarily related to the quality of the relationship they had with a teacher or the need they felt to please their parents. Schooling as it is interpreted by adults in the context of their life history has a different meaning than when it is explained by social scientists who are specialists in the field of education. The educational biography gave me a broader view of learning and made me look at school, as well as continuing education, in a more global way.

Learning as Process. What adults learn in the context of formal education does not necessarily come from the content of a program: It often includes several other dimensions, such as social interaction outside the classroom and cultural experiences. Sometimes adults learn more about themselves by dropping out of a program than by staying in it. Therefore, to become better acquainted with adult learning, it becomes necessary to understand the processes through which adults have constructed what they know. The formation and transformation of their knowledge, culture, or value systems is, for adults, the result of the different processes that characterize their life history. The meaning of learning has been so encapsulated in the world of formal education that we tend to reduce the meaning of adult learning to a cognitive behavior related to the requirements of an educational program. For the average citizen, adult learning today refers primarily to adult education, much more than to what and how adults learn through the course of their life.

After many years of research based on oral and written narratives of adults dealing with the question of how the process of learning has contributed to the shaping of their life or, as we say in French, to their "formation," I came to the conclusion that learning in adulthood, as well as in early life, comes out of an integrated experience of different parts of oneself. If learning depends, as Piaget (1972) has stated, on the phases of "equilibration" identified in the process of cognitive development, learning in adulthood can be compared to a process of personal development characterized by different phases of equilibration. Adults learn when they can reorganize and enrich what they already know. Learning for adults takes place in the global context of their lives.

Learning as Social Interaction. All the narratives discuss the dynamics of relationships in family life. There is a clear interaction between schooling and the parent. The authors of these narratives describe how their parents, for example, had expectations of the future for their children, what one student called a "parental project." They write about the conflicts they had to resolve in their struggle for a more autonomous life. Some dropped out of school or decided to move away from home and earn their own money in order to get out from under their parents' expectations. For others, on the contrary, being a good student was a way to react against the limited views of their parents concerning the future of their professional lives. When they mention what they have done in the field of continuing education at a later date, several admit that they are still under the influence of their parents. They also describe how they became aware of that fact. They realize that by going back to school or by entering the university, they could be living out their parents' wishes. As one woman in her thirties writes: "I am certainly aware that one of the reasons I have returned to school at my age is to meet my mother's expectations. She obliged me to sacrifice other aspects of my life and to put school first."

Men in particular remember that in childhood they were always advised to take school seriously. For children of working-class parents, the idea was clear: "We do not want you to have to live through what we did. In order to have more opportunity in life, take school seriously. We will make it possible for you to study as long as you feel it necessary."

For most of the women, there is a clear link between learning and their image of their father. In a few cases, their rank in the family played an important role: They either dropped out to help an older sibling or pursued their studies to replace an older brother or sister who had failed. In the eyes of their parents, they became the last hope to have a child in the family succeed in school.

The educational biography is also an opportunity to understand learning in the context of social development. Life is, for many students, a cultural journey. As they continue their studies in a larger town or enter the social world of work, they move out of a familiar environment. They compare this old environment to a new social context to which they must adapt. They learn to respect other norms and to change their attitudes as they explore a variety of new beliefs. Sometimes they reject their families because they identify deeply with other social groups. Sometimes, on the other hand, they reject their peers whose values are too different from their own. The biographical narratives are full of examples describing the battles every adult fights in order to find his or her particular cultural identity.

In the narratives, the authors identify phases in their social development whose dynamics they interpret more in terms of a "cultural shock" or a meaningful moment that determined the course of their lives. They needed this process of socialization to learn how to reconstruct their cultural backgrounds. As one participant says:

> What I would call my life journey and its cohesiveness are slowly becoming visible. I spent nearly eighteen years building myself in accordance to others' expectations. Because I am intense, I bought into it all. I am not surprised then that when the time came, my rebellion was so violent and went through so many stages . . . . I have a clear feeling now that that phase of major turmoil is over . . . . I feel that I have got rid of the sociocultural shell that prevented

me from reaching my own self, from discovering my deepest wishes. I like to compare myself to a house whose old bricks have fallen down, and then was rebuilt, and continues to be built; my foundations, however, remain intact.

As part of this socialization process, students describe changing schools because their parents move to another part of the country. Or they move to another part of the country to attend a particular high school or college. These changes are always considered a cultural experience. The memories of the years spent in schools cannot be separated from their cultural and social environment. Learning in the classroom cannot be distinguished from learning outside the school. Some adults who have spent a long time studying feel sorry for themselves because they have missed more adventuresome experiences. There is an obvious interaction between family, school, and social life in the learning process.

Our social interactions become more complex as we grow up, but the dynamics remain the same. As the following quotation reveals, learning takes place in the global and singular context of our development:

Although I broke with my family, I still have close ties with them. The change from the culture of the farm to the culture transmitted by books, with all the doubts about my identity, all the instability and fragility, comprise two conflicting trends. These are combined with all kinds of other data, especially since I have been enriched by new experiences involving my emotional life as an adult, my professional life, my social commitments, and my motherhood, as well as my life with my husband and our shared responsibility for our four children.

Learning and the Adult Educator. In more recent research, I have used the biographical approach to identify the process through which adult educators themselves have attained their knowledge and competence. I thought that the biography would be an appropriate way to define more clearly the profile of qualifications required for this profession. From the study of the educational biographies of professional adult educators, it appears that these educators' learning processes followed patterns similar to those discussed above. What is mentioned about school is again related to the personality of the teacher or the meaning of schooling for one's parents. It also includes what was done outside of school: music, sports, or church activities.

All the adult educators participating in this research said that most of the knowledge necessary for their professional practice has to be acquired on the job. In their biographies, however, these professionals emphasize the value of social experiences more than schooling: being in charge of a group of Boy or Girl Scouts, performing in a choir or a theatrical production, discovering new cultural contexts through travel or work abroad. They also recognize what they have learned from personal experiences, such as being married or divorced. For adult educators, a university degree seems less relevant than the stimulating jobs they have had before entering the world of adult and continuing education. It shows how the process of learning extends beyond the walls of formal education, even when it comes to professional qualifications. The adult educators involved in this research were surprised themselves to realize how their life histories had shaped the style of their qualifications.

Education as an Object of Learning. Adults present their education, upbringing, and schooling as key issues in the interpretation of their life history. When they talk about education, they describe their central stuggle to know better who they are and what they want to do with their lives. School remains a crucial element not because of the content of its program but because of the critical events taking place there. Education in its formal setting provides the opportunity to experience learning. What adults mention in their narratives is their encounter with an unusual teacher or their reaction to bad grades and their tactics to obtain good ones. It is what students have done with their education that contributes to their process of learning. The same thing is true about their family and social life. Adults remember the efforts they made to create distance from the earlier models of their education: achieving more freedom as a teenager, or freeing themselves from their parents' wishes when choosing their professions or their partners. They speak positively about their early church experiences, even if they develop more critical attitudes during their adulthood. The educational biography leads adults to identify the process of learning by selecting the meaningful moments, people, and places that belong to the world of their education. It always surprises the participants to realize that learning is never quite where the models, goals, and objectives of education expect it to be.

Adult Education as Reparative Education. As they trace their education throughout their lives, people reveal that they often enter adult education classes to repair, compensate for, or fill in the gaps of the past. They dream about the university because earlier in their lives they did not have the chance to study. They embark upon personal development because they hope to overcome and to recover from wounds of the past. They decide to update and upgrade their work skills in order to move ahead. In the narratives, continuing education is always presented as a kind of further stage in the process of schooling. In other words, when adults are accepted as university students, they consider themselves as having returned to a process that was, for different reasons, interrupted (Dominicé, 1986). Women even more than men share this feeling of striving to repair the injustices of the past. Women express anger about men's monopoly of knowledge as well as fear about their own abilities to go on academically. As she entered the university, one woman in her forties wrote: "I was enthusiastic and terrified at the same time. My idea of academic life paralyzed me. I was convinced that I knew nothing, that I was not 'up to snuff' and was afraid to open my mouth . . . . Then, slowly, I became more aware of my own knowledge. This knowledge came from my life experience, from my reading, and the training courses I had attended in the past."

This opportunity to be challenged and to reconsider one's knowledge, values, and beliefs gives meaning to adult education. It is not the content of the training that counts but the opportunity to examine one's attitudes and behavior. For example, parents who attend an evening class or a workshop do not so much learn new models of education to apply to their children as they receive information that challenges or enriches what they already know. As the educational biographies show, it is what we do with our education that gives learning its meaning.

Promises and Limits of the Biographical Approach

The following general trends emerge clearly from the educational biographies I have heard and analyzed. In their narratives, most adults tell how they struggled to reconcile the expectations of their social environment with their own desire to lead a unique existence. The educational biographies are a testament to how adults have educated themselves by transforming the models, values, and knowledge of their upbringing. These adults tell of the stages of socialization they experienced in order to find their own identities, and their narratives reveal the particular learning style that came out of their different life experiences.

These general findings are in themselves already challenging for the practice of adult and continuing education. However, such generalizations should not prevent us from analyzing more thoroughly the richness of the content of these educational biographies. As I will show below, content analysis is a complex task that has to be understood as one of the learning experiences of a transformative research process.

Content Analysis, Data, and Interpretation. Content analysis of the biographies raises several problems that I will mention briefly without detailing the different quantitative and qualitative procedures I have tried in recent years. After trying to analyze a cluster of biographies selected according to sex, age, and profession, I came to the conclusion that the methodology of educational biography belongs to a mode of reflection rather than to an if-then statement and proof. The oral narratives are in many ways the first step of an interpretation that is examined more thoroughly by the written version and its various analyses. Participants become involved in the work of critical self-reflection as soon as they begin to raise questions about their first narrative. The educational biography rejects the tradition of a research design in which the phase of content analysis is planned after collecting the data. Transformative research introduces a dynamics in which new hypotheses emerge and are enriched by their continuous discussion within the group.

In my current practice of educational biography, the first analysis is prepared by a member of the group other than the author. The researcher has as much a share in the cooperative attempt to analyze the written narratives as any other member of the group. The final interpretation is closely connected to the variety of research questions posed by the entire group. The students sometimes bring new and interesting hypotheses to content analysis that contribute to the results of the research. One participant who reread all the written narratives of her group suggested, for example, that the life histories revealed a key issue or a quest for the best solution to a central and repeated conflict.

Even though I believe strongly in the participatory approach we adopted as a research team, I cannot deny that different levels of commitment do exist among participants. Students have neither the same interest in the research process nor the same qualifications as the researcher, but everyone has his or her way to contribute to a reflection that is more than the sole responsibility of a single scholar. Through this experience, research becomes a meaningful part of an educational process for the participants. It offers them an opportunity not only to read and learn about research but also to discover concretely, by actually doing it, how research can become part of a transformative learning process.

Some Ethical Questions. Who owns the written version of the narratives? Since everyone in the group has a copy, this problem exists for all members of the group, not only for the researcher. The educational biography approach, as well as other examples of participatory research, implies such ethical questions usually avoided by scientists. The researcher is witness to personal testimonies any time he or she analyzes the narratives. I found what Ferrarotti (1983, p. 230) wrote about the analysis of the biographical data to be true and profound: "When I read the biographical texts, I always have the impression that I am not sensitive or subtle enough to understand them fully, that I am not worthy of them. A kind of religious inclination, or attitude, seems essential to me as a researcher." Such a statement can be considered an ethical point of view that should be included in the methodology of content analysis dealing with life histories.

Content analysis can also be an opportunity to deepen a dialogue between the researcher and the adults involved in the research process. However, all kinds of difficulties have to be overcome. Chief among them is the lack of time available to participants. Furthermore, what is to be done with a narrative when the analysis of its content establishes the need for its further development?

The teacher-learner partnership becomes difficult when the learner persists in conferring traditional academic status upon the teacher. Some students might even expect the teacher to help them with one of the unresolved problems of their life histories. The teacher or the researcher belongs to the group, but as a facilitator, not an expert, a private tutor, or a therapist. The facilitator helps adults identify the itinerary by which they have become who they are and to reconstruct the process through which they have learned what constitutes their knowledge. This life history approach leads to critical thinking about the result of educational models, but it does not offer a direct alternative or a direct change for adult lives. The educational biography does not play the role of a magician suddenly able to transform the meaning or the pain of past experiences. It does, however, give adults the opportunity to be more in charge of their education by becoming conscious of why, what, and how they learn in the global context of their life histories.

The Myths of Educational Technology. The success of adult education in our society and the growing need to face the competitiveness of the world of work reinforces the tendency to use programmed or modulated learning. In order to be marketable today, learning has to be a visible activity. The public image of continuing education is more than ever related to audiovisual support or computer assistance. To make adult educational programs attractive requires the presence of modern technology. I do not want to deny the contribution of instrumental learning, but what comes out of the research done with educational biographies confirms the idea that adult learning is deeply rooted in the experiences of life history.

Well-structured teaching content does not guarantee efficiency in adult learning, which is a kind of self-educative process. In the formal context of teaching, adults never learn without reorganizing the content of what they have heard or hear. Adult education should, then, also be an opportunity for adult learners to be more aware of what they already know, of the way they want to continue their education, and what they hope to accomplish beyond the fantasies they have about their future.

A Variety of Biographical Approaches. My approach to life history is certainly not the only one. Some of my colleagues have lately found new ways in accordance with their own research interests. For example, Josso (1988) has examined thoroughly her own educational biography in order to identify what she calls the "process of knowing." Finger (1984) related the impact of the biographical approach to the epistemological debate of the social sciences. In a French-speaking international network, a variety of possible applications of the life history approach to the field of adult education have been explored and discussed (see also "Histoires de vie," 1984, as well as the different theoretical benefits of the biographical approach discussed in Finger and Josso, 1986).

We have mainly applied the methodology of educational biography to adult university students and adult university educators. It could also be used in many other fields, such as patient or religious education. The health care professions could use it in patient education as a therapeutic support; in chronic conditions such as diabetes or heart disease, it could be helpful to know how such patients have taken care of themselves in the course of their lives. A biographical approach centered on the relationship of these adults to their own health care would probably have a different format, but the general procedure could be similar. Patients do not change their attitudes or behaviors mechanically as a result of teaching; learning implies a reorganization of former knowledge. A biographical study could help patients identify what they need to learn by making them aware of what they already know.

The same could be true for adults who decide to join a new religious community or to renew their faith by attending study groups. A biographical approach would help adults clarify the questions they want to answer in reference to the beliefs they have consructed throughout their life history. They may discover something new that challenges the "truths" they have held through the years.

A Future for Biographical Techniques. The biographical approach could become a new fad in adult education because people love to hear and to tell stories and anecdotes. Today, it is the events of everyday life that hold people's attention. History does not refer to an ideological option but to an eclectic collection of ancient relics and sometimes even fictitious images. The success of autobiography has certainly influenced the course of modern literature. In the field of adult education, there is already a variety of different workshops or courses based on the life history approach. Any time an adult educator attempts to understand better the needs of the adult study, he or she enters into a kind of educational biography.

The idea that research is a way to preserve the kind of openness and critical reflection offered by the biographical approach has to be stressed strongly. Education biography, as I conceive it, is neither a mode nor a technique. It is a method of research centered on adult learning that brings about transformative learning among the adults involved. It is a method of cooperative learning between educator and student about the processes through which adult and continuing education can contribute to the education of adults. It is a method of critical reflection through which the theoretical questions of epistemology become an existential debate about the meaning of adulthood.

References

Bertaux, D. *Biography and Society.* London: Sage, 1982.

Dominicé, P. "La biographie éducative, instrument de recherche pour l'éducation des adultes" [The educational biography: instrument of research for adult education]. *Education et Recherche,* 1982, 3.

Dominicé, P. "La formation continue est aussi un règlement de compte avec sa scolarité" [Continuing education is also a settling of accounts with one's schooling]. *Education et Recherche,* 1986, 3.

Ferrarotti, F. "Sur l'autonomie de l'approche biographique" [On the autonomy of the biographical approach]. In J. Duvignaud (ed.), *Sociologie de la connaissance* [Sociology of knowledge]. Paris: Payot, 1979.

Ferrarotti, F. *Histoire et histoire de vie* [History and life history]. Paris: Librairie les Méridiens, 1983.

Finger, M. *Biographie et herméneutique* [Biography and hermeneutics]. Montreal: University of Montreal, 1984.

Finger, M., and Josso, C. (eds.). *Pratiques de récit de vie et théories de la formation* [The practice of the life history approach and the theories of learning]. Geneva: Department of Education Science, University of Geneva, 1986.

"Histoires de vie" [Life histories]. *Education Permanente,* 1984 (entire issue 71–72).

Josso, C. "Le sujet de la formation" [The subject of learning]. Unpublished doctoral dissertation, Subdivision of Adult Education, University of Geneva, 1988.

Piaget, J. "Intellectual Evolution from Adolescence to Adulthood." *Human Development,* 1972, 15, 1–12.

Pineau, G. *Produire sa vie: autoformation et autobiographie* [Producing one's own life: self-education and autobiography]. Montreal: Saint-Martin, 1983.

Eleven

Reflective Withdrawal
Through Journal Writing

Joseph Lukinsky

Maturing and education integrate our thinking, but this may be a mixed blessing, tied as it is to the growth of habit. Problems may be addressed through patterns of perceiving and acting that lead us to spin our wheels and avoid new responses. How important then for our lives is the search for the structures that affect the way we relate to matters great and small.

Keeping a journal may help adults break habitual modes of thinking and change life direction through reflective withdrawal and reentry. I refer to ultimate, long-range purposes but also to being able to step back from an incident, a conversation, a reading, from something heard or seen and to reflect upon it and return to it with understanding. The deeper levels of life may not be changed through decisions *in medias res* or by means of amorphous meditation. Life's particularities go on, and we may stumble upon insights—but it is hard to put insight and action together. We need to find another way to connect reflection and action.

Journal writing is a promising aid to the ongoing effort to bring together the inner and outer parts of our lives. I shall suggest some theoretical roots for current approaches to journal writing, describe its general phases, and offer some suggestions for how adult educators can use it to foster critical learning and action.

Diary writing is an old form of self-expression and reflection. Historically, diaries or journals have been places for the expression of feelings, for catharsis, for poetry, for the expression of thoughts that may not have other outlets, to preserve memories and relive them, as well as to explore themes, topics, and characters, as in a writer's workbook (Lowenstein, 1987; Elbow, 1973). A journal writer can try things out without being held responsible as in ordinary discourse. Hypothetical conjectures, half-serious and uncertain trial balloons, fantasies, and playful, tentative expressions of feeling are all valid in a journal. It is important that the journal writer feel that anything can be written there, that no one will read it without permission (a "found" diary may give a distorted or partial picture of the writer).

Ranier (1978) provides many resources to give journal writers the flexibility to make the process their own. Progoff (1975, 1980, 1983) adds an overall structure and a rationale that integrates the separate tasks. Educational journals adapt general resources to practical educational settings (Fulwiler, 1987).

In recent years, the centrality of the work of Ira Progoff has been widely recognized. Progoff has taken journal writing beyond the mere record of events or "spiritual growth" and has recreated it as a practical and accessible process in his workshops and books (Progoff, 1973a, 1973b, 1975, 1980, 1983). I shall emphasize Progoff's work while discussing these and other sources.

Journal writing as an introspective tool can be used by individuals for personal growth, by counselors as a resource for guidance and therapy, in educational applications, and in group settings.

The "new" journal, then, is a tool for connecting thought, feeling, and action — a synthesizing tool that works from the inside out and from the outside in. Implied in this is a critique of spirituality unconnected to daily life; reflection and action have to be brought together to see in a new light. When these are brought together, we can draw upon our resources without need of experts. Meaning is emergent, kinesthetically felt in the course of the writing. The writing, more than a means to an end, generates momentum and is, in a deeper sense, the *meaning*. Something happens *now*, as opposed to recording what *has happened*, and the journal becomes an objectification of the inner search, an anchor from which to make further explorations.

Some Theoretical Sources for the Model

The following are some sources for understanding the recent development of journal writing as an educational tool. It is not an exhaustive list, and the sources are not equally important or necessarily historical influences. Listing them here stresses the components of the model for discussion and research; the model is a confluence of sources that unpacks the deeper potentials of journal writing for human life.

Humanistic psychology, criticized for soft intellectual underpinnings and "touchy-feely" techniques, is a broad frame for the resurgence of journal writing. Within it, some expressions have legitimized themselves. The topic is beyond this paper's scope, but my bias is that Progoff, an exemplar of humanistic psychology, has corrected for the movement's excesses.

There have been many famous diary and journal writers, to mention at random such names as Augustine, Dostoevski, Benjamin Franklin, Ignatius of Loyola, John Wesley, and Anaïs Nin (Lowenstein, 1987). Many others, children and adults, have found the effort meaningful until they encounter frustration, boredom, or the realization that writing requires a serious discipline. In any case, the historical proclivity to reflect upon one's life, exemplified in historical diaries, is another resource.

Psychoanalysis, especially Jung's version of it stressing descent into the "collective unconscious," is another (Martin, 1976). The collective unconscious refers to universal "archetypes," rooted in the human condition and expressed in dreams, myth, symbols, and fantasy. "Constructive method" generates meaning from the associative juxtaposition of these with memories (Martin, 1976). The structured techniques of journal writing embody the constructive model. In this context, note that journal writing, therapeutic as it may be, is not therapy. It may be a *resource* for therapies of various sorts. A useful term is *introspective tool*.

Progoff is a main source for the model and the practical suggestions to be presented here. He studied with Jung and Suzuki and — influenced by, among others, Bergson's phenomenology of consciousness — developed the *intensive journal,* first as a workbook for use in his therapeutic practice and then in workshops and three main sourcebooks (1975, 1980, 1983) growing out of earlier works (1973a, 1973b) which, among others, adumbrated them. Others who currently write about journal writing use Progoff even when they are critical of him (Ranier, 1978).

Though research on the functions of the right brain and the left brain (Sacks, 1987) is not a direct influence, it has implications for the model. Distinctions between the rational, logical left brain and the intuitive, emotive right brain have led to confusion and vulgarization in research and practice, in the arts and in education (Gardner, 1978, 1983). In this regard, the moving case studies of Oliver Sacks (1987) helpfully clarify right-brain function. Progoff's insistence that journal writing be connected to life avoids the dichotomy characteristic of applications of this research (Ranier, 1978, p. 65).

The Quakers' "inner light" (Martin, 1976) is a strong, indirect influence upon modern journal writing. The search for the inner light — which connects thought, action, intention, and commitment — and the nurture of personal and collective inwardness by the group of "friends" have their resonances in journal writing practice. The classic Quaker meeting alternates verbal group experience with periods of deep reflection, but this may be an inaccessible spiritual discipline for many people. However, the stimulative effect of the physical act of writing serves as a catalyst for introspective juices in a manner *analogous* to that of the Quaker group.

In his concept of maieutic, Plato viewed learning as *re-learning*, the recalling of something already known. The teacher is the midwife who helps the student "give birth" to knowledge. Norton (1973) operationalized Plato's construct to help students understand unfamiliar ideas in philosophy in terms of their own life experiences. Similarly, journal writing substitutes for the teacher, stimulating the connection of personal material to the new and unknown.

Fulwiler (1987, p. 1) notes that "leading language scholars, including Vygotsky and others, have argued . . . that human beings find meaning in the world by exploring it through language — through their own easy, talky language, not the language of textbook or textbook and teacher." Knowledge *gained* needs to be personally meaningful and students need various kinds of entrée to the unfamiliar.

Again, these sources are mentioned to help us understand the current model in greater depth. They illuminate various facets of it that are useful for our purposes.

Journal Writing: Process and Stages

Ranier (1978) encourages writers to personalize their search by using her "diary devices" as flexible resources adapted to their individual needs. Although her open-ended suggestions seem random and without an integrating principle when compared to Progoff, they might usefully supplement it.

Ranier proposes *four basic diary devices* — catharsis, description, free-intuitive writing, and reflection — and *seven special techniques* (described later in this chapter) for use when "you can't get to a problem through the front door with one of the more traditional forms of expression" (Ranier, 1978, p. 72). She suggests areas in which basic or special devices can be applied. These include personal problems, dream work, exploring erotic feelings, overcoming writing blocks, using the diary as a time machine, and many others. She also suggests ways of using the diary in therapy and for expanding creativity (Ranier, chap. 14).

Fulwiler's (1987) anthology is a collection of essays on the uses of journal writing in education. Not all are relevant to the theme of journal writing as a transformative tool for adults, but many are, and others could be applied.

Fulwiler notes the increasing favor with which journals are looked upon in a variety of educational settings in all subject areas, to help writers experiment with language and document their progress in internships, independent study, fieldwork, and the like. In education, journals have common characteristics: *language features* (conversational, colloquial language written in the first person); *cognitive activities* (such as observation, speculation, inner questioning, self-awareness, digression, synthesis, revision, information seeking, and similar operations that demonstrate that attention is being paid to the course content); and *formal features* (frequent, long, and student-initiated entries).

Teachers' purposes for journal writing include engendering personal connections to the content, providing a place to think about the content, collecting observations and data, and providing for the practice of writing. Journals are sometimes collected and read by the teacher but not graded; they belong to the student, not the teacher. These general points are sufficient for my purposes here. Both Ranier and Fulwiler have representative extensive bibliographies for those interested in expanding their repertoires. It would be impossible to summarize the many specific suggestions in both valuable books.

Many of the articles in Fulwiler's book are oriented to teaching writing in all subjects of the curriculum and limit their discussion of journal writing to its uses for that purpose. Some of the articles in this generally useful book, along with the transformational dimensions, stress the point made above that writing something down enhances learning. Within these limitations, I suggest that the educational uses of journal writing can be viewed in the following broad rubric:

1. *Before learning something new:* Education, like religion, has been accused of answering questions that no one is asking. Journal writing enables students to think for themselves, to grasp a fading embryonic insight, and to trust their fragile, emerging sense of the problem before being squashed by the flow of others' ideas.
2. *Reflections while learning:* A pause in the learning activity allows the individual or group to reflect upon what is now being learned. This is crystallized in the journal and may be fed back into the shared learning experience.
3. *Postreflection:* Looking back upon learning completed, the student connects to it at the level of the "inner life" (Ranier, 1978; Fulwiler, 1987). It is obvious that transformation in classroom structure would be necessary when changes of this sort are introduced.

While Ranier and Fulwiler are potentially useful, the most important resource is Progoff, whose approach, in contrast to that of Ranier (1978, p. 33), I consider to be indeed flexible and amenable to making one's own. I turn now, therefore, to a brief description of his core system.

Progoff's Intensive Journal Process

The intensive journal process is embodied in Progoff's three basic workshop books (1975, 1980, 1983), which seem, in their conversational tone, to have been edited from transcriptions of several actual workshops. Working through them, minus, of course, the affective presence of the leader and the group atmosphere, gives the flavor of an actual workshop and is a good preparation for one.

As we consolidate our personalities through maturation and education, we nurture some potentials; others remain inactive, beneath the surface but "there." Active journal writing jogs the memory, brings lost potentials to the surface, and instigates retrievals. In the act of writing, connections and integrations occur to the writer; as the writing unfolds, new thoughts emerge and are written down. This process continues along paths developed by Progoff and contained in a deceptively simple format, a loose-leaf notebook with colored dividers that signify different kinds of interrelated exercises.

The Life History Section. In the first main subsection of the journal (Progoff, 1975; Halberg, 1987), life history information is entered in various ways; in another section, the life history material is confronted in dialogue formats; a third main section allows progressive deepening and integration through explorations in a "depth dimension," where dreams, meditations, metaphors, and images are worked with in their own right and as they overlap in the other sections.

The autobiographical notes, seen from the perspective of the subjective present, are entered into and reexperienced, as are dreams and meditations, the latter drawn out and extended in a "twilight" state (Progoff, 1975, chap. 6; 1980, p. 156). Meaning builds cumulatively but not through analysis or interpretation. The ongoing recording of memories, events, dreams, and images crystallizes the inner movement of the writer's life, carried forward by the structured journal exercises. This acorn that grows into an oak bounces off other memories and images and the flow of the writer's outer life. The interaction of recording life events and working with metaphors, dreams, and images in the different dimensions of the journal is a holistic process.

There are exercises that are essentially "logs," not too different from the traditional descriptive diary (Progoff, 1975, chaps. 7, 10). A daily log and one where events from a lifetime are entered as they are remembered preserve raw materials as a data bank regularly drawn upon. Dreams and meditations from a waking state become log entries, available for later use.

Two similar sections with an additional subjective quality are the *steppingstone* section and the *period log* (Progoff, 1975, chaps. 5, 8). Journal writers regularly review the formative experiences of their lives from the outlook of the present. We see them differently from the perspectives of different times, places, and circumstances; a "steppingstone" in one period may not be one in another. The steppingstones are central to Progoff's process, especially at the start of a writing period. A few steppingstones, no more than ten or twelve, are written as they arise in consciousness.

Outlining a new *period log* is a good way to begin a writing session. It is a subjective construction of the current period in the writer's life. The period is named, and then, continuing with the sentence "It is a time when I . . . ," the writer may enter a meditation about it after the date of the entry (which is written for every journal entry, adding to the sense of movement in time). After these positioning exercises, which help the writer capture the "feel" of the period, *its* steppingstones are written (again, limited in number) from the beginning of the period, listing them as they arise in the mind. The writer now feels positioned in an immediate, relevant space. The current school semester could be a significant unit for a period log entry; one could write on "since I got my degree," "since I moved from Chicago to New York," "since my father died," starting with a perceived turning point. At first the choice may seem arbitrary, but as the writing proceeds it may be reformulated and given a different name and scope.

As a period's steppingstones are listed, significant persons, events, works, achievements, issues, decisions, and dreams arise and are briefly entered, for later expansion. After the stepping-stones and their associations are sketched out, the writer has recalled the basic flow of that life period and returns to "enter" the individual steppingstones, expanding upon them in greater depth ("time-stretching" is Progoff's term [1975, chap. 11]).

The writing is not creative but from the "gut." This is one of the most compelling features of journal writing; one doesn't have to be a talented writer or worry about grammar, syntax, or punctuation; thinking "What shall I write next?" is probably a sign of overly conscious effort. The energy comes from the pen and, when it stops, the writer, given a wealth of possibilities, goes on to something else.

The log and life history sections plus the period log and steppingstone exercises create raw materials to be drawn later for use in a dialogue and a depth dimension. Though subjective, they suggest more; they draw out by association, from the perspective of the present moment in our lives, connections from the depths of the unconscious.

The Dialogue Section. The dialogue phase (Progoff, 1975) is the second major journal section. While writing in the journal, a person who played a role during the period being considered comes to mind, and the name is recorded in the dialogue section with a brief comment. Later, this entry may become the stimulus for a dialogue exercise. The steppingstones of that person's life, inasmuch as they are known, are listed, a short, empathic meditation may be framed, and then a dialogue script is written with the energy that flows from the pen until it stops.

The dialogue enables the journal writer to reengage something missed, neglected, or avoided in the past that might have provoked anxiety or embarassment, in short, to deal with un-finished business. Moreover, the person need not be a relative or friend from the writer's own life. This aspect of the dialogue section is especially interesting educationally. The dialogue may be with historical personalities or with characters from myth and literature.

In addition to writing a dialogue with a person, one may have a dialogue with an event from the journal writer's life, from history or literature, or with an ongoing, significant work or project from the past, present, or future. This has implications for literature, social studies, history, values and religious education, and even for the sciences and mathematics. One can carry on a dialogue with a part of the body (one's heart or beard or sex organ) or with a choice, personified, that is pending. In these dialogues, one writes the steppingstones of the event, project, choice, or other entity as a record of the writer's personal involvement with it. Then, again, meditation, empathy with the entity personified, inner silence, and the writing of the dialogue from the pen. This exercise was my first exposure to journal writing at a conference workshop led by Progoff, in which I was astounded to find myself writing, in the words of the "other," things that I didn't know I knew.

The dialogue dimension sets in motion a dynamic that reflects Progoff's more-than-implied critique of the view that the spiritual life is mostly a function of looking within. For Progoff, committed work and the challenge that comes from without are necessary to prevent the inward journey from degenerating into the mere contemplation of the navel. Outer works exist in tension with the inner and are connected in the journal.

The dialogue process obviously partakes of the psychological mechanism of projection. How does one know if the dialogue written in the journal is "true?" Progoff's reply seems to be that, in itself, each written dialogue is but an element in the holistic process, that the overall view comes through after many examples are included in the larger framework. For Progoff, the "self-balancing" principle of the many facets of the journal is beyond projection.

A critical and powerful use relates to *past* turning points. In life, one can't actually go back to a past choice, a "road not taken" (the name of a journal exercise, after Robert Frost; Progoff, 1975, p. 133). But there is nothing to prevent one from returning, in the journal, to the past and taking the road not taken. That choice, reexperienced emotionally, becomes tangibly part of one's life. The choice can be brought to life as, for example, in the transformation of a missed opportunity. A person regrets not having taken violin lessons as a child, goes back and moves down that path in writing. Feelings about the violin are recalled from that period and associations come to mind, including the people involved and the circumstances. The person might not decide to study the violin now but might do something else that would not have emerged without the exercise.

The Depth-Dimension Section. The depth-dimension (Progoff, 1975, p. 228) exercises are sometimes attached to those from the dialogue or life history sections and sometimes exist in their own right. They can be undertaken at any time in the process, sometimes to set the mood for exploring a steppingstone, sometimes as an entrée into a recorded dream, extending it with associations and continuing its images in a twilight meditation. Sometimes depth-dimension exercises involve metaphors and other images that occur during the course of writing in other sections. These exercises seem to be the ones that require the most practice, but Progoff's three basic workbooks provide ample opportunities to acquire this skill, as does participation in journal workshops.

Progoff's (1980) second workbook, *The Practice of Process Meditation,* expands the depth dimension with additional exercises, such as applying the steppingstones mode to moments in our spiritual histories, which then present themselves to our awareness. Peak experiences are both entered into and *take place* in the journal writing itself.

The "mantra crystal" exercise is noteworthy. A mantra is associated with a meaningful experience, and the "feel" of that experience can be recalled when the mantra is chanted or meditated upon. With a suggested seven-syllable mantra crystal like "walking on sand by the sea" associated with, say, a meaningful ocean experience, the affective and cognitive dimensions come together. By saying the mantra, one gets back into the experience, recalling it vividly and making it accessible to new levels of meaning and new exercises.

Something "Extra." Depth-dimension exercises are considerably expanded in the second workshop book. After working progressively in the various sections of the journal, something "extra" seems to happen. For Progoff, this something extra, which cannot be willed but which can be energized by committed efforts to achieve a personal "artwork," incarnates human freedom and creativity. In the depth dimension in general, work on dreams, twilight meditations, "entrance" meditations, and the like is a response to images, symbols, and metaphors that arise from the depths of the psyche. Progoff sees the process as leading to a "quality of being" akin to religious experience (Progoff, 1980). The exercises in his second-level book are structured to build a momentum that transcends the earlier first-level integrations. The ultimate meaning aspect of process meditation, however, is unachievable without the incremental buildup of the ongoing life-context work. This context is set in the first book, and the deeper level is achieved in the second.

I shall make an extreme claim. The experience of the dialogue and depth dimensions and the process meditation work that builds upon it encompass an active search for ultimate meaning that is *analogous* to the experience of revelation described by the Hebrew prophets (Norton, 1973). A "voice" speaks from outside the writer and it is "heard" in a tangible way. This experience is the something extra that emerges from the journal process as a whole, a confluence of insights that come "out of the blue." The etiology is naturalistic yet kindred to the fabulous and mystical in the history of religions. Without diminishing classical religious experience, the journal experience *does* give access to it.

Journal writing is also similar, I suggest, to the experience of hermeneutical explication of religious texts centered upon a holy writ, as well as in the exegesis of secular texts like Shakespeare's or the Constitution of the United States. When the exegete or *midrashist* is deeply absorbed in the text, it becomes a wellspring of energy that seems to "speak" as a separate entity.

The Life-Study Journal. Progoff's (1983) third practical guidebook to journal writing, *Life-Study,* has much potential for adult education. In life study, the writer becomes a "trustee" for another person's life by writing a journal *as* that person, experiencing what it would mean to look at the world as that person did, or does. What is the point of writing this type of journal? The life study journal becomes a place to go to gain new perspective by seeing through another person's eyes.

Though the regular journal exercises are adapted for life study, there are some special issues relevant to this mode. In principle, any life could be chosen as the subject for such a journal (for instance, one could choose a character from literature; Fulwiler, 1987). In practice, at least for the first time, a fairly well known person should be chosen. Since the journal writer does not have the other person's memories and therefore cannot draw on them as in the personal journal, he or she should begin with a short biography or article that presents the essential facts of the chosen person's life. Starting "outside" and moving "inside," the writer gradually is enabled through various exercises to write in the first person, using many of the journal techniques described earlier, writing from the gut and the pen. The beginning *is* about 90 percent projection. The writer encounters gaps in knowledge and therefore speculates, working within a framework of changing assumptions. Questions arise that standard biographers tend to overlook, and speculation about these (through the pen!) may lead to research for further biographical information. If the beginning of the process is highly projective, working on the border between the self and the chosen personality (Schechner, 1981), the authenticity percentage becomes greater, and, at a certain point, the writer is "inside" the subject differently than in the writing of a standard biography. Indeed, this is an excellent way to start writing a biography.

Some Exemplary Uses of Journal Writing

The previous section outlines the phases of journal writing generally but is also meant to begin to give practical guidance for its use by individuals at the personal level and in various fields. To recapitulate Progoff's approach here before moving to the application: The main points include returning to events and points of choice — roads not taken — reliving moments in life and making decisions from within them; entering dialogues with people from the past or present, from literature or history; confronting images, ideas, issues, events, projects; drawing on the unconscious to deal with problems. In the depth dimension, "something extra" happens, deriving from the integrative exploration of symbols, metaphors, dreams, and meditations. Finally, life study involves intensive empathy with another person's life, to see the world from that person's perspective.

In sum, the journal-writing techniques apply in any situation where an introspective tool could be helpful. The group experience of the Progoff workshop is very supportive, but the techniques may also be learned from the three workshop books. At a workshop, one may voluntarily share what one has written. Progoff's stress on writing from the "depths," from what comes from the pen—structured from different angles in the various journal sections—takes away the onus of deciding what one *wants* to write, this too supported in the group ambience.

Below, I shall give some examples and suggestions in the hope that professional educators can extrapolate from them, and from what has been presented so far, for their own efforts at fostering critical reflective learning (Lukinsky, 1983, 1987). Most are spinoffs of Progoff's journal-writing methods that come out of my own experiences in the field of curriculum and religious education.

Example: A Curriculum Workshop. The setting is a curriculum workshop for teachers at a Jewish elementary day school in an eastern city. The teachers, divided into two separate staffs, teach either Jewish religious subjects (from a liberal point of view) or the standard general studies of an elementary school. Philosophically, the school is committed to a unified world view and the integration of both departments. However, it is very hard to get teachers of one department to relate seriously and specifically to the other, though there is goodwill and motivation. The principle of integration is theoretically affirmed but difficult to implement.

The workshop starts with a brief introduction by the leader, who sets the boundaries of the problem and offers some practical suggestions in the field of mathematics, connecting the tension between intuition and reason in mathematics with similar tensions in religious studies. There is some polite interest but no real enthusiasm.

The leader briefly introduces Ira Progoff's "dialogue with works" (Progoff, 1975, pp. 178–193) and has the teachers write on the following subjects: a spontaneous list of personal steppingstones that represent the development of interest and involvement in the teacher's field of study and teaching; books and toys received as a child; parents' and friends' influence; teachers who were role models; experiences that led to new interests; early formal courses and then more advanced work as part of training for a career; related employment; hobbies; current classroom efforts — training, exciting ideas, conflicts, discouragements, what the teacher is trying to accomplish with students. After writing this list, the leader asks the teachers to read it over twice in silence and then react to it in writing, with associations, feelings, and anything else that comes to mind. Those in the group are told that what they write is private, that all sharing will be voluntary. They then expand by association one or two of the points on the list. If other incidents come to mind, they are listed and enlarged upon, too. At least one steppingstone is developed in some depth. One more question at this preliminary stage: What would the teachers, as adults interested in the field, still like to do in it for themselves?

Sitting in silence, this life interest and work project is "personified"; that is, a dialogue-script is written by each teacher with it as if the project were a person.

The leader then asks one of the teachers in general studies and one in Jewish studies to each present a list of themes dealt with in the official curriculum of their respective subjects at each grade level.

After a silence, the teachers in the group are asked to write connections between their own fields and the themes addressed by their curriculum. The teachers read their connections to the group.

In this case, the connection between the teachers' personal relationships and their own work enabled them to connect with the deep structure of the various disciplines. "Integration became a felt process rather than an abstract concept."

Example: A Training Seminar. The setting is a summer training session for principals of a Jewish day school, during which the principals study the Bible and develop curricular projects for their schools. The course content is the Book of Deuteronomy, the last address of Moses before the Israelites cross the Jordan to the Promised Land. The method of the text study is academic and educational. At the end of the course, students are introduced to the dialogue technique and then write a dialogue with Moses. Based upon the earlier academic study of the historical background and their analysis of the text, they write steppingstones for Moses's life and then a dialogue between themselves and Moses, using the procedures described above. This connects the academic study of the text with the personal lives of the writers — a personal connection between each student and the central Biblical character of Jewish tradition; it becomes a rich resource for creating a meaningful curriculum for their own students.

Suggestions for Curriculum Workshops. A staple of curriculum theory is that there are four "commonplaces" that a curriculum must address: the subject matter, the students, the milieu, and the teacher (Schwab, 1978). In a workshop on curriculum for principals and teachers, the work may falter because, with no children present, the deliberation is of children "in general." Another problem is that the workshop participants often work with a wide range of ages and social milieus. To lend reality to the curricular discussion, the leader teaches them the dialogue technique. Workshop participants then write dialogues with specific children in their schools: First, they establish the personal relationship and the child's presence, and then they turn to the particular issues of the new curriculum material worked on in the workshop. The tendency of educators to work out of preconceptions about children is challenged by the simulated presence of "real" children in the journal writing. This lends a reality to the deliberations that would otherwise be lacking.

This technique has also been used in workshops to engage in dialogues with parents, between teachers and principals, and the like.

Suggestions for Students. In graduate-level professional training programs (teachers, clergy, social workers), students can use journal writing to trace the development of their interest in a particular field, writing the steppingstones of the growth of their involvement and their points of choice. This can be followed by the dialogue mode. It can also be made at different stages of the program, with the possibility of comparisons and deepening self-awareness as the program continues.

Suggestions for Life-Study Methodology. A full course and several shorter (one-day or even three-hour) workshops on the life of a historical figure. I have done this several times with the lives of Abraham Joshua Heschel, a philosopher and theologian who joined Martin Luther King in the civil rights struggle, and David Ben-Gurion, first prime minister of Israel, using Progoff's life-study method. In the shorter workshops, steppingstones are provided by the leader in order to conserve time — not an ideal adaptation, but a workable one. The rest proceeds according to Progoff's basic journal-writing approach.

A problem in using journals in a course is that the teacher cannot read students' journals in the form in which they are originally written unless students allow it. Students can provide the teacher with edited versions, from which they have removed personal elements they do not wish to share. Such a version is more like a standard course paper but still preserves many of the dynamic qualities that emerge in the writing. (See Halberg, 1987, for discussion of ethical issues in using this approach in eduation; there are many examples in Fulwiler, 1987. See also Brown and Walter, 1983, for some parallel issues in a somewhat different context.)

Other Journal-Writing Methodologies

The more resources the adult educator brings to the work, the better. I have dealt at length with Progoff because I find his methodology more rational and integrated and less random than others; and one that, once mastered, can be self-generating. Nevertheless, I think a brief summary of other methodologies — specifically those of Ranier and Fulwiler — is in order here. Once the overall possibilities, anchored in Progoff, are understood, other special techniques might prove useful. A description of some of Ranier's techniques follows.

1. *Lists* are clusters of ideas on a topic — "the things that irritate me, beliefs I have discarded," a table of contents for an "autobiography of the person you are at this moment" (Ranier, 1978, p. 76). (The latter is similar to Progoff's steppingstones.) "A list will help you focus, tame and comprehend wayward parts of your experience" (p. 79).

2. *Portraits* are descriptions of people that start with "fascination" and focus on what one learns about oneself in the developing portrait (p. 80). One identifies with specific qualities of the subject or builds a confidential and harmless weapon against him or her. The sketches may become resources for conventional literary efforts, as do writers' sketchbooks.

3. *Maps of consciousness* are drawings in which the writer captures a state of mind and "floats" (p. 84). Spontaneous images can be drawn. The diary can be *all* drawing, to serve as an entrée to the dynamics of the writer-artist's personality (p. 86).

4. *Guided imagery* techniques claim to tap the right side of the brain (Ranier, 1978, p. 87) and include the recording of daydreams. This is similar to Progoff's twilight meditation (Progoff, 1975, p. 77). The writer (or, in a group, the leader) may stipulate or suggest a context: "Imagine yourself in a forest." The journal writer "goes" to that place, looking for an experience of "wonder" like that which myth and ritual once gave people. Dream images may be continued in the waking state (also like Progoff) and then transmuted into a poem, drawing, or story. There is also, in this mode, the possibility of "behavior rehearsal," which involves imagining onself behaving in a potential situation in alternative, desirable ways. Athletes and artists have used similar imaging techniques. The approach can also be used as a warmup before writing in other modes.

5. *An altered point of view* is gained by writing about oneself in the third person or about someone else in the first person (again, like Progoff's dialogue), the purpose being to gain empathy or objectivity, to write about something painful, to imagine oneself in a different place or in a different time, as in, for example, writing from the standpoint of oneself as a child (Ranier, 1978, p. 115).

6. With *unsent letters,* the writer expresses thoughts impossible to say in reality, as, for example, a hostile word to a loved one or speaking to a stranger or to someone dead (p. 100).

7. In *dialogues,* the journal writer composes both sides of a dialogue with conviction. Ranier is most like Progoff here and, in fact, has a long section on him (p. 112).

I will now briefly present some techniques from Fulwiler that fit the overall purposes of this essay. A useful starting point is in Macrorie's foreword, where he discusses the ideal "classroom where everyone including the teacher is keeping a journal and revealing parts of it" (Fulwiler, 1987, p. 100). For Macrorie, journals "counter the tendency to freeze the mind, to incapacitate it from ranging and connecting as is its physiological wont" (p. 112). A description of some of Fulwiler's techniques follows.

1. The *dialectical notebook,* in which writing as a way of knowing lets us represent ideas so that we can return to them and assess what is written, is an overarching technique that relates to many suggestions in Fulwiler's book. The idea is that entries — of observations, memoranda, notions of all sorts, before and after learning — lead to looking carefully at it and a dialectic of "feedback" and "feedforward," to identifying and tolerating ambiguity, to moving from meaning to writing and from writing to meaning, to a sense of "allatonceness."

2. In some cases, the teacher responds by *writing directly in* the students' dialogue journals, clarifying what students do not understand — both for the teacher and the student — and helping the teacher identify when students are falling behind or losing interest (pp. 7, 9). The student's learning to document an ongoing, progressive understanding of a text could be most useful both for the teacher and the student.

3. Journals can be used as a place to *sketch drafts* for future papers.

4. In a literature class, students can write *letters* in their journals from one fictional character to another or *monologues* for one of the characters.

5. In response to a reading of a text, students can write, on facing pages, substantive explanations of the reading on one page and personal comments on their explanations on the other (pp. 11–12).

6. Journal writing is especially significant in *history,* which requires interpretation and judgment in addition to a grasp of the facts. History provides a good opportunity for thinking, wondering, and speculating. Although formal papers and exams have their place in the study of history, they are not necessarily the best place for *learning* history (p. 22).

7. A *music journal* written while listening to music stimulates musical associations and fantasy (p. 26).

8. Journals can be used in the classroom study of *philosophy* for a dialogue between teacher and student as an analogue to the Socratic method (p. 28).

9. Journal writing has implications for *therapy:* Journals can be written as homework for the patient or written during the actual session, in conjunction with more traditional therapeutic approaches (p. 31).

10. In a *team journal,* every team member writes regularly in the same journal and reads what other members have written. The teacher may read it, as well (p. 32).

Conclusion

E. L. Doctorow, interviewed in connection with a review of his recent novel, *Billy Bathgate,* reports that the novel "has its origins in an image lurking in the [author's] imagination: men in tuxedos on a tugboat . . . I just kept thinking about what it meant and what it could possibly mean, and that's how the book got started" (Freitag, 1989, p. 46). Most of us are not world-class novelists; we have not learned to pay heed to the images that press for our attention and could pique our curiosity in a similar manner. But our lives do have a message. They "speak" to us on many levels. I have presented some materials here on how journal writing can help us, as persons, learn to listen and, as educators, to help others do so.

References

Abbs, P. "Education and the Living Image: Reflections on Imagery, Fantasy, and the Art of Recognition." *Teachers College Record,* 1981, *82* (3), 475–496.

Brown, S. I., and Walter, M. I. *The Art of Problem Posing.* Philadelphia: Franklin Institute Press, 1983.

Elbow, P. *Writing Without Teachers.* London: Oxford University Press, 1973.

Freitag, M. Interview with E. L. Doctorow. *New York Times Book Review,* Feb. 26, 1989, p. 46.

Fulwiler, T. (ed.) *The Journal Book.* Portsmouth, N.H.: Boynton/Cook, 1987.

Gardner, H. "What We Know (and Don't Know) About the Two Halves of the Brain." *Harvard Magazine,* 1978, *80* (4), 24–27.

Gardner, H. *Frames of Mind: The Theory of Multiple Intelligences.* New York: Basic Books, 1983.

Halberg, F. "Journal Writing as Person Making." In T. Fulwiler (ed.), *The Journal Book.* Portsmouth, N.H.: Boynton/Cook, 1987.

Lowenstein, S. "A Brief History of Journal Keeping." In T. Fulwiler (ed.), *The Journal Book.* Portsmouth, N.H.: Boynton/Cook, 1987.

Lukinsky, J. "Making the Seder a Personal Experience: A Workshop." Melton Journal, 1983, *15,* 7.

Lukinsky, J. "Scholarship and Jewish Education: Maybe the Lies We Tell Are Really True." In N. Cardin and D. Silverman (eds.), *The Seminary at 100.* New York: Rabbinical Assembly and Jewish Theological Seminary of America, 1987.

Martin, P. W. *Experiment in Depth: A Study of the Work of Jung, Eliot, and Toynbee.* Boston: Routledge & Kegan Paul, 1976.

Norton, D. L. "On Teaching What Students Already Know." *School Review,* 1973, *82* (1), 45–56.

Progoff, I. *Jung, Synchronicity and Human Destiny*. New York: Dell, 1973a.

Progoff, I. *The Symbolic and the Real*. New York: McGraw-Hill, 1973b.

Progoff, I. *At a Journal Workshop*. New York: Dialogue House Library, 1975.

Progoff, I. *The Practice of Process Meditation*. New York: Dialogue House Library, 1980.

Progoff, I. *Life-Study: Experiencing Creative Lives by the Intensive Journal Method*. New York: Dialogue House Library, 1983.

Ranier, T. *The New Diary*. Los Angeles: Jeremy P. Tarcher, 1978.

Sacks, O. *The Man Who Mistook His Wife for a Hat*. New York: Harper & Row, 1987.

Schechner, R. "Performers and Spectators: Transported and Transformed." *Kenyon Review,* 1981, *3* (4), 83–113.

Schwab, J. J. "The Practical: Translation into Curriculum." In J. J. Schwab, *Science, Curriculum, and Liberal Education: Selected Essays*. Chicago: University of Chicago Press, 1978.

Twelve

Analyzing the Influence of Media on Learners' Perspectives

Stephen Brookfield

Central to the process of emancipatory education is the effort to encourage in learners a critical awareness of the sources from which their meaning perspectives are acquired. Some of the most potent of these sources are the mass media, particularly television. If we are trying to help adults understand how they have developed their value frameworks, belief systems, and habitual behaviors, then we must pay careful attention to the media. In all realms of contemporary experience — from depictions of family and other intimate relationships to the creation of agendas for political discourse — the mass media have a powerful role in creating the interpretive frameworks through which we make sense of many events in our lives. Television, in particular, is less a river of messages, symbols, and images into which we occasionally dip than an ocean in which we perpetually swim. For example, in its depiction of family life in situation comedies from "Ozzie and Harriet" to "Family Ties" to "The Cosby Show," television has a potent symbolic force. It creates mythical images of an idealized, "typical" family existence against which we measure our own pluralistic, ambiguous, and contradictory experiences.

Television also encourages viewers to incorporate epistemic distortions into their meaning perspectives. Epistemic distortions, as discussed by Mezirow in Chapter One, are distortions concerning the nature and use of knowledge. Examples of these are believing that every problem has a single correct solution; reifying a source of authority as the sole purveyor of "objective" truth; or thinking concretely when abstract thought is necessary. In the case of family sitcoms, television fosters in viewers the first of these epistemic distortions — that family crises, disruptions, and problems have neat solutions. In thirty-minute episodes (which end up as eighteen to twenty-two minutes of action between commercials), familial problems are recognized, defined, and solved, frequently by a "cute," younger member of the family showing that all one needs is love. Situations are always resolved to the satisfaction of all. There is no suggestion that problems often have, at best, partial or contextual solutions; that participants can have radically differing perspectives on a situation, which are all, in their own terms, correct; that alternative interpretations might be made of a single action; that emotionally distressing situations do not improve overnight; that the reality of family relationships is in any sense messy, haphazard, and inchoate.

In the political realm television fosters the second and third of the epistemic distortions mentioned by Mezirow above. The second distortion — reifying a source of authority as the sole purveyor of "objective" truth — is endemic to the medium itself. Masterman (1985, p. 6) writes that "those who control and work in the media do not simply have the power to set agendas, provide explanations and construct their own versions of events. They have the much more significant power to project these things as natural and authentic — simply part of the way things are." Television presents itself as a seamlessly authentic "window on the world" in which unfiltered, objective depictions of reality are conveyed. Furthermore, this reality, as represented on television, appears impenetrable. A report on adults' perceptions of the political world (Ridley, 1983), largely shaped through television viewing, notes a widespread belief that the formation of public policy occurs in a zone of such remoteness and non-interference as to be regarded in much the same way as the weather — governed by uncontrollable forces completely outside people's spheres of influence. The political world is portrayed as a separate dimension, a twilight zone of unreality into which individual citizens cannot enter. Learning about events of this world through a technology that most cannot comprehend only serves to encourage a sense of disconnectedness between the happenings of one's own life and those in the political realm. It fosters in viewers a predisposition to passive observation. We tune in nightly between game shows and situation comedy reruns to learn how the world has been reshaped for us by inaccessible political superiors. This is why, as Masterman (1985, p. 21) argues, "the first principle of media education from which all else flows, and to which teachers and students will continually return, is that *the media are symbolic (or sign) systems which need to be actively read, and not unproblematic, self-explanatory reflections of external reality.*"

The third example of an epistemic distortion mentioned above — that concrete thought adequately equips us to understand the complex nature of reality — is also fostered in television's depictions of political events. Events, issues, and conflicts are invariably presented in a highly personalized manner. Complex policy questions are reduced to personality conflicts. Ideological schisms or strategic differences are recast as personal disputes. Nowhere is this more evident than in presidential campaigns, where the focus of attention is almost wholly on the candidate's image or "character." In the reporting of superpower summits, this tendency to focus on personality to the exclusion of political complexities has meant that the success of such summits becomes defined by the length of handshakes between heads of states, by how close the leaders stand to each other at summit photo shoots, and by the nature of their postmeeting smiles (whether they are closed-lipped half-smiles or full, teeth-bared grins).

For all the reasons outlined above, educators seeking to foster critical reflection in adults must have as a central concern the development of media literacy. Any exercise that prompts viewers to realize the constructed nature of television reality is not merely an end in itself. Through such exercises, adults realize that television is not an objective depictor of political life "out there," but that its representations of political realities are often culture specific, framed within dominant meaning perspectives, and influenced by the wishes of vested interests who own the media. In terms of fostering critical reflection, this is crucially important. When we become aware that televisual depictions of what were taken-for-granted realities are contextually constructed and fit only one of several possible frames of reference, then we are jolted into an awareness of the contextual nature of our own assumptions. For example, viewers watching a thirty-minute situation comedy in which problems are raised, identified, and then neatly and comfortably solved to the satisfaction of all involved may feel a vague sense of dissatisfaction or unease considering their own abilities to do the same thing in their own lives. They may feel that they are poor mothers if they cannot balance their work and childrearing activities in the seamlessly perfect ways exemplified by the women in "Family Ties" and "Kate and Allie." Admittedly, mother-child problems do arise in such shows, often dealing with "contemporary" issues such as drug abuse, teenage pregnancy, or suicide. But these problems are usually solved within the allotted thirty minutes by expressions of love accompanied by selected, one-line wisecracks.

If learners in a media literacy program are helped to realize that the story lines in such shows are created to attract advertising revenue, they have achieved a powerful insight. The show then becomes analyzed in terms of how its story is designed to attract the largest numbers of viewers (by titillating them with contemporary social problems) and to keep them watching (by suggesting that such problems can be simply resolved by calling on capacities—love and humor—that most of us feel we possess). Analyzing the show as a commercially created artifact, rather than as a depiction of reality, means that learners come increasingly to trust the validity of their own feelings, instincts, and insights when compared to the events portrayed on the screen. They realize that their own experiences of slowly coming to a painful awareness of problems within their family after many episodes of denial are at least as valid a reality as the quick and easy diagnosis evident on television. They realize that the (at best) partial and multiple solutions they have evolved do not represent failures to exemplify the problem-solving capacities of "superparents" in sitcoms. Rather, they are left with a sense of the massive discrepancy between television's portrayal of family life and its reality and with an enhanced sense of the worth of their actions. The periods of reflection and experimentation involved in understanding and responding to problems that on television would be excluded as too complex or unsettling for viewers are seen as the reality that must be trusted. Television family sitcoms come to be seen as creating and perpetuating the epistemic distortion that familial and other interpersonal problems are easily and quickly solved by neat and unequivocal remedies, usually focusing on displays of love by those involved. The private suspicion that this might not be the case is undoubtedly held by many viewers, but when the suspicion is publicly confirmed in a learning group that meets to analyze critically the distorting powers of television, this can engender an exponential leap forward in learners' abilities to trust their own judgments and intuitions.

This willingness to trust one's own experiences helps learners resist concluding that simply because what they feel is not in tune with dominant cultural values or widely held meaning perspectives, it is therefore inaccurate or invalid. This readiness to trust the credibility of one's own experiences is crucial to fostering critical reflection. Myles Horton, the founder of the Highlander Folk School, says that the most important thing that Highlander does is to help people know that their experiences have credibility and validity, that they are worth something (Horton, 1988). By affirming that individuals' perceptions of reality have an innate validity and are not wrong simply because they do not fit the dominant, typical meaning perspectives encoded in television programs, media educators encourage in learners a sense that their ideas mean something important. This sense of having the validity of one's perceptions confirmed, and of coming to trust the rightness of one's own instincts, is cumulative and powerful. People are exhilarated by being free to point out that the media emperor has no clothes, that television does not reflect objective reality. This is an emancipatory realization in the fullest meaning of that term, and it engenders the habit of watching television through critical filters. Once people realize that television family sitcoms are products designed to attract the greatest viewing audience in order to encourage advertisers to buy commercial time during these programs, they become reflectively skeptical of all television programs.

Analyzing television in this way is addictive. When people notice discrepancies between their own experiences of family life and television's portrayal of these, and when they find that their perceptions of these discrepancies are reinforced by the confirmation of other learners, the way is open to viewing other aspects of television coverage critically. Learners may ask themselves the question "If family life on television is portrayed in the safest, most anodyne way so as to keep the largest number of people watching in order to attract advertising, aren't political events likely to be reported in the same safe, unobjectionable way?" This is a powerful and empowering question to ask. It means that television portrayals of the political world are decoded instead of being taken as objectively truthful. We begin to wonder about the biases, assumptions, and meanings encoded in the choice of images shown, leaders interviewed, and topics chosen as "lead" stories. We also start to ask whether all possible interpretations of events have been given, whether the questions being asked about issues represent the only ways of treating them, and whether some explanations and viewpoints are being excluded as too uncomfortable. When we realize that there are epistemic distortions in the ways family problems are dealt with on television, we begin to look for the same kinds of distortions in the ways political problems are neatly packaged by producers, editors, reporters, and anchorpersons. We may ask ourselves, "If some truths that we know to be true about family life are too uncomfortable, divergent, and unsafe to be aired in sitcoms, are there some political truths that aren't being broadcast for fear of turning viewers off?"

Asking such questions is at the heart of education for media literacy. It is also central to fostering critical reflection. As Masterman (1985, pp. 28–29) writes, "The teacher's task is to help everyone concerned make problematic what they think they know, and to develop the ability to question underlying assumptions. . . . The practice of media education, [then] is one in which all participants share what they think and question why they think as they do." When we question the accuracy of sit-coms or news broadcasts, and when we hear others raise similar doubts, we not only focus on the distorted and oversimplified nature of television, we also critically reassess the validity of our own assumptions. Given that television is such a shaper of consciousness throughout life, to ask awkward questions about the accuracy of its depiction of reality is to raise those same awkward questions about the kinds of schemas, habits of expectation, assumptions, and meaning perspectives that we have uncritically assimilated from the medium. From realizing that television encodes and transmits meaning perspectives in which dominant cultural values are enshrined, it is but a short step to realizing that those same meaning perspectives, with all the epistemic and political distortions they involve, have been embedded in our consciousness for years. In questioning the accuracy of the truths, givens, and commonsense wisdoms built into television's coverage of familial and political life, we are also prompted to question the source and the accuracy of our own assumptions.

Fostering Critical Reflection

Four general approaches to fostering critical reflection about the media, each of which involves more specific techniques, are relevant to our discussion. One of these — autobiographical analysis — has already been described in Chapter Nine. The other three include decoding exercises, content analysis, and program construction. For reasons of space, the focus of these approaches will be on encouraging critical reflection regarding television's treatment of the political world. For further examples of how these techniques can be used, see Handron (1988) and Brookfield (1986).

Decoding Exercises. Television programs can be read as texts; that is, as collections of signs, symbols, images, and narrative in which certain preferred meanings intended by the producers, editors, and reporters are enshrined. The process by which programs are intentionally invested with preferred meanings is called *encoding* (Hall, 1980). The activity of "reading" these same television texts (or programs) for their encoded meanings is usually referred to as *decoding*. When learners decode programs, they critically analyze the preferred meanings enshrined in these collections of signs, symbols, images, and narrative. They analyze broadcasts for the ways in which certain dominant values, interpretations, and meanings are implicit in the juxtaposition of image and narrative. Williamson (1978) has shown very effectively the encoding process in television commercials and how viewers can decode the values and meanings implicit in these. Berger (1983) discusses how television programs can be decoded through semiological, Marxist, psychoanalytic, or sociological analysis. Some interesting examples of encoding are also given by Morino (1985) in her analysis of how advocacy commercials (those that sell a company's image rather than its specific services) embed certain preferred meanings. In one commercial she discusses, wolves are shown in an idyllic woodland setting while a narrative compares wolves' ability to stop short of fighting by their use of a complex system of snarls, howls, and grimaces with governments' ability to preserve world peace. The building of arms stockpiles and the deterrent effect this induces is said to be similar to the natural deterrence practiced by wolves. The commercial portrays a positive relationship between peace and the building of nuclear weapons, in which the latter secures the former. As Morino observes, "The menacing aspect of the arms race is put into a natural process, thereby turning a social process into a 'natural' one" (p. 13). Strong arguments can be made for the use of force in the defense of social systems that citizens consider democratic and humane. Indeed, peace activists frequently debate those last-resort instances when the use of force can be morally justified. In decoding the commercial described above, however, Morino points out the exclusion of such ethical and moral concerns. Deterrence is equated with, and implicitly presented as, a natural, evolutionary process. Hence, debate about such a "natural" process can be seen as illogical and unnecessary; for what is there to question if deterrence is natural and therefore inevitable? Media educators, however, would raise questions with learners about the alternative interpretations that might be made of nuclear politics. Has there ever been a time when a state that has invested in weapons has not eventually used them? Did not the Allies, in fact, drop two nuclear bombs within the last fifty years? What about the dangers of technological accidents, such as computer malfunctions triggering a nuclear war?

Encoding is perhaps most readily detectable in reportage of contentious social issues, such as strikes. For example, it is easy to encode the strong message that nurses' or teachers' strikes are fundamentally antisocial acts, threats to public health and welfare. Through the kinds of questions asked of participants in the strike and the ways these questions are asked, an apparently neutral reporting of facts can contain within it a cluster of highly partisan, preferred meanings. A phrase that might appear to be objective reporting in a news broadcasts, such as "Today workers again rejected the pleas of management," contains within it a number of implicit assumptions: that workers are persistently unreasonable (the use of *again*), that workers are unnecessarily strident (the use of *reject*), and that management is quietly con- ciliatory but helpless in the face of workers' mindless resistance (the use of *pleas*). By juxtaposing narrative reporting on the prog- ress of negotiations with provocative images of pickets fighting with police, patients facing the locked doors of hospitals, or pupils being turned away from classrooms, some preferred meanings regarding the violent unreasonableness of strikers are, after critical analysis, clearly evident.

With regard to programs reporting political events and issues — including news broadcasts and current affairs shows such as "60 Minutes," "Nightline," or "The MacNeil-Lehrer Report" — several decoding techniques have been suggested by Master- man (1980, 1985), Brookfield (1986), and Handron (1988). One of these is *information mediation analysis,* which focuses on the ways in which anchorpersons, news reporters, and chairpersons of discussions or debates function as mediators of information and framers of discussion. Learners can be encouraged to focus on several variables regarding how interviewers mediate discussion:

the kinds of styles the interviewer uses and with whom (gladiatorial with "deviant" opinion holders, neutral or deferential with politicians, devil's advocate); the kind and tone of language the interviewer adopts with different interviewees (technical, colloquial, serious, sarcastic, condescending, respectful); whether interviewers rephrase, edit, and interpret for the audience the contributions of interviewees and discussion participants, and whether the interviewer encourages spontaneous interruptions or controls the flow of discussion. An example of this kind of decoding is Handron's (1985) study of six Donahue shows in which the host, Phil Donahue, served both as the focal point and conduit of questioning. By the ways he directed questions and selectively involved guests and audience members, he functioned as both gatekeeper and prompter, sanctioning which approaches were to be explored further while ensuring that a diversity of opinions was expressed.

A second decoding technique is *setting analysis*. In setting analysis, viewers read the television text to see how the physical setting of an interview or discussion has embedded certain messages concerning the symbolic status of the participants. The location and "set" of an interview is an important element in how much credibility the articulation of a certain viewpoint implicitly receives. For example, in undertaking a setting analysis of British television coverage of industrial disputes, the Glasgow University Media Group (1976, p. 26) concluded, "All those things which enhance a speaker's status and authority are denied to the mass of working people. This means that the quiet of studios, the plain backing, the full use of names and status are often absent." When interviews with managers take place in quiet, well-lit boardrooms with one company spokesman calmly answering the interviewer's questions, while interviews with strikers take place on a noisy factory floor or on picket lines with extraneous noise and activity, then the viewpoint of one side implicitly receives preferential treatment.

Viewers can also undertake *question analysis,* in which the questions put to the protagonists in a political event are scrutinized for the embedded preferred meanings. They can study whether one side receives strongly critical questioning, while the other is allowed a more or less unedited expression of opinion. To continue with the example of a strike, viewers can study what kinds of questions are put to management and what kinds to workers. For example, asking a union leader, "Aren't your members only bringing pain on themselves and others by this action?" or "What do your members feel about the children who aren't being taught/the sick who aren't being treated?" implicitly conveys the assumption that strikes are not only antisocial but also wholly harmful with no beneficial consequences to anyone. Conversely, asking a management representative, "What harm is this strike doing to the company/to the country's economy?" or "What are the prospects for firings as a result of this strike?" encodes the same messages. Taken out of context, these questions may seem entirely reasonable. But when the interview focuses solely on one line of inquiry, the cumulative effect is to frame interpretations of the strike in a highly partisan manner. In its studies of strikes, for example, the Glasgow University Media Group (1976, 1980, 1982) notes that when news reporters interview those involved, "questions put to management tend either to be an open invitation to give their views or to lead directly to these. As a result such interviews are fairly harmonious: the 'devil's advocate' and the 'difficult' questions are reserved largely for shop stewards" (1982, p. 37).

Content Analysis. A technique familiar to students of popular culture, content analysis of newspapers, advertisements, and magazines has been a common exercise in school and adult education settings. The low price of video cassette recorders (VCRs) now means that this technique can be applied within adult learning groups. For example, a media study group could divide among its members the responsibility for monitoring a week's news broadcasts on the major networks, in order to examine how much time each network devoted to a particular news story. Or a group could focus on a particular issue (for example, a strike or accusations of governmental corruption), with different learners recording how much prominence various newscasts and current affairs programs gave to the views of different parties involved in the issue. It would also be simple to chart how news stories rose to prominence during various days or weeks and then how they receded as other items were given attention. Learners in a content analysis group could compare news bulletins on different networks during the breakfast show, at lunchtime, and on the evening news, to study changes in tone and content that reflected how any one story was treated on the same day.

Logan (1979), Handron (1988), and the Glasgow University Media Group (1982) provide many examples of how content analyses might be undertaken. For over a decade, the Glasgow group has monitored British television news coverage of strikes, wars, political infighting, and peace campaigns. Exercises as simple as counting the number of interviews granted to the protagonists in a dispute indicated "whose views were deemed to be legitimate and authoritative voices in terms of the dominant view" (1982, p. 120). The group concludes that "the kinds of information and explanation that appear in the news essentially flow from the dominant view. Alternative facts and explanations, where they appear at all, appear in fragmentary and sometimes contradictory form" (p. 116). Again, viewers might simply clock the amount of time provided for the participants in disputes to air their views in an unedited form on television. Or they may count the number of questions put to these different participants and reflect on what it means to ask more questions of a particular actor in an event.

Another interesting variant of these approaches is *context analysis,* in which learners study whether or not news stories focus on the microlevel, with strong emphasis on the personality-specific elements of a dispute or issue, or whether they deal with the macrolevel, with the societal or community context within which the dispute or issue occurs. Learners may raise questions about the extent to which news stories give preliminary context-setting explanations of the events and issues they feature. In reporting strikes or demonstrations, for example, do newscasters discuss the causes and history of these events, or do they simply mention the times, places, and numbers involved before cutting to provocative visual footage of pickets fighting with police, demonstrators burning the flag, and so on?

Program Construction. The final approach to developing critical reflection through media analysis focuses not so much on the scrutiny of programs prepared by others but on learners constructing their own programs. It is a learning-by-doing approach, in which the inevitable realities of selection and editing in the construction of television programs are brought powerfully home. For example, as learners put programs together, they experience how items of information must be left out for reasons of limited time, and they reflect on the decision-making processes informing their choices as to which items were to be included and which rejected. If people have to put together news reports, documentaries, or dramatizations of current events, they live the same kinds of processes experienced on the broader level of network television. Examples of this kind of approach are found in Heaney's account of the Rockford Interactive Media Project, in which inhabitants of Rockford, Illinois, used VCRs "to create materials that would enhance critical reflection on day-to-day life" (1983, p. 41). In Handron's "Expand the Story" exercise, learners were asked to construct questions about facets of a news story that were not dealt which in actual television coverage, but that, if raised, might have altered markedly viewers' perceptions of the story (Handron, 1988). Jarvis (1985) describes how British Open University students were given photographs of a strike and were then asked to create a news broadcast covering this strike as if they were producers, editors, and reporters in British, American, and Russian television stations. Through a judicious selection of photographs, accompanied by ideologically appropriate narrative commentary, participants were able to present the same event in vastly different (and frequently opposing) ways. Because these students constructed news reports in which values, assumptions, and ideologies were deliberately encoded, they became more aware of the fact that preferred meanings are inevitably encoded in national news broadcasts, and they learned to watch for these.

Conclusion

How do these exercises in media analysis prompt critical reflection of one's own assumptions? As I see it, they help us undertake this process in four ways. First, they encourage us to become more aware of the epistemic distortions embedded in the media and, by implication, in their own meaning perspectives. We realize that when sitcom families neatly resolve difficult problems in thirty-minute episodes, or when newscasters portray one side in an event as wholly moral and the other as wholly immoral, or when ideological disputes are represented as personality conflicts, these are distortions having to do with processes of reasoning and knowing. Realizing this, we are more likely to study our own reasoning processes for such distortions. Second, these exercises make us more aware of the sources of our own meaning perspectives. We realize that the habits of expectations we have about, for example, what a normal or healthy family looks like may in part be derived from television's depictions of these. Third, these exercises make us more aware of the constructed, contextual nature of meaning perspectives. We realize that how television families are portrayed or how news events are reported is affected by a network's desire to keep as many people watching for as long as possible so as to be able to justify charging advertisers the highest rates for commercials. Knowing this, we begin to scrutinize our own meaning perspectives for the ways in which they have been constructed in order to win the approval not of advertisers but of those significant other authority figures whose approval we desire. Fourth, these exercises give credibility to our private misgivings about the supposedly objective nature of television reality. They alert us to the dangers of groupthink (Janis, 1983); that is, to consensual interpretations of events and issues that no one wishes to challenge for fear of appearing deviant, divergent, or unsound. We come to know that alternative, nonconsensual interpretations of political events and issues or divergent images of family life are not likely to be shown because producers believe this will upset viewers, causing them to switch channels to find something with which they are comfortable (whether this has to do with the myth of happy families or with an affirmation that the government always behaves in the interests of its citizens). Knowing this, we are aware of how it is much easier to subscribe to dominant myths than to challenge them. This may mean that we are readier to listen to those inner voices that tell us that although everybody on television seems to think or act in a particular way, it makes no sense for us. Acknowledging the validity of such apparently deviant, divergent, or unsound internal misgivings is frequently the first step on the journey of critical reflection.

References

Berger, A. A. *Media Analysis Techniques.* Newbury Park, Calif.: Sage, 1983.

Brookfield, S. D. "Media Power and the Development of Media Literacy: An Adult Educational Interpretation." *Harvard Educational Review,* 1986, *56* (2), 151–170.

Glasgow University Media Group. *Bad News.* London: Routledge & Kegan Paul, 1976.

Glasgow University Media Group. *More Bad News.* London: Routledge & Kegan Paul, 1980.

Glasgow University Media Group. *Really Bad News.* London: Writers and Readers Cooperative, 1982.

Hall, S. "Encoding/Decoding." In S. Hall, D. Hobson, A. Lowe, and P. Willis (eds.), *Culture, Media, Language.* London: Hutchinson, 1980.

Handron, D. "Critical Reflectivity in Action: An Observational Analysis of the Donahue Show." Unpublished paper, Department of Higher and Adult Education, Teachers College, Columbia University, 1985.

Handron, D. "Developing Methods and Techniques for Fostering Media Literacy in Adults." Unpublished doctoral dissertation, Department of Higher and Adult Education, Teachers College, Columbia University, 1988.

Heaney, T. "Materials for Learning and Acting." In J. P. Wilson (ed.), *Materials for Teaching Adults: Selection, Development, and Use.* New Directions for Continuing Education, no. 17. San Francisco: Jossey-Bass, 1983.

Horton, M. Talk given to adult education doctoral students, Department of Higher and Adult Education, Teachers College, Columbia University, June 22, 1988.

Janis, I. *Victims of Groupthink.* Boston: Houghton Mifflin, 1983.

Jarvis, P. "Thinking Critically in an Information Society." *Lifelong Learning: An Omnibus of Practice and Research,* 1985, *8* (6), 11–14.

Logan, B. (ed.). *Television Awareness Training.* Nashville, Tenn.: Abingdon, 1979.

Masterman, L. *Teaching About Television.* London: Macmillan, 1980.

Masterman, L. *Teaching the Media.* London: Comedia Publishing Group, 1985.

Morino, D. "Re-framing: Hegemony and Adult Education Practice." Paper presented at the Standing Conference on University Teaching and Research in the Education of Adults (SCUTREA), Sheffield University, England, July 1985.

Ridley, F. F. "What Adults, What Politics?" In Advisory Council for Adult and Continuing Education, *Political Education for Adults.* Leicester, England: Advisory Council for Adult and Continuing Education, 1983.

Williamson, J. *Decoding Advertisements: Ideology and Meaning in Advertising.* London: Marion Boyars, 1978.

Thirteen

Realizing Literature's Emancipatory Potential

Maxine Greene

When novels and short stories are read outside academic or literary contexts, they are read largely for entertainment or distraction. Competing with television, film, and countless magazines and journals, they are used to fill up otherwise empty hours — in waiting rooms, on bus rides, in planes. Practitioners in fields other than the humanities seldom think of imaginative texts as occasions for emancipation or the gaining of critical consciousness. If they become involved in them as disclosures of alternative or imaginary realities, they feel faintly embarrassed, as if a professional assignment obligates an individual to keep both eyes on what is unarguably and objectively "real."

Certain adult educators have used works of imaginative literature as data bases (Merriam, 1983). Others have used them as fictional renderings of classroom encounters, the kinds of renderings that have highlighted motivations and perhaps the dynamics of learning itself (Ohliger, 1988; Quigley, 1988). Still others have viewed them as modes of humanizing or illustrating familiar discursive accounts. When insights associated with "conscientization" (Freire, 1970) are sought, educators quite naturally encourage critical reflection on the themes of learners' own lived lives. Or they turn to the writings of Freire himself, or of Herbert Marcuse, Jürgen Habermas, Theodor Adorno, so-called "radical" educators like Henry Giroux, feminist writers like Carol Gilligan, Barbara Ehrenreich, and Sara Ruddick. Now and then black writers like James Baldwin, Ralph Ellison, Amiri Baraka, or Henry Louis Gates, Jr., are consulted. Seldom is the emancipatory potential in literary art explored.

One reason for this may be the way in which the reading of literature has been tainted for many people by a "school knowledge" imposed in English classes early in life. They cannot but remember the insistence on learning and reporting on "great" and irrelevant texts like *Silas Marner.* If it were a work offering somewhat more pleasure, like *A Tale of Two Cities,* there always seemed to be an emphasis on a "correct" reading, one in accord with some authoritative interpretation. Plots, themes, character development, narrative point of view — all these had to be properly identified for the sake of an acceptable reading. Even the figurative language or the symbolism studied seemed to have fixed referents. Little was done to help students mediate between the assigned narratives and the actualities of their own life stories. In some classrooms, there was so much stress on authors' biographies or on the social phenomena that gave rise to their works, little attention could be given in the long run to the works themselves. In more formalist classrooms where the "new criticism" came to be dominant, attention was rigorously focused on the structures of works that were treated as hermetic little universes referring only to themselves. Any references to ordinary existence were simply out of line; any speculation about an author's intention was criticized as an "intentional fallacy"; the only values to be considered were esthetic ones.

For the fortunate young, there were reading experiences in odd corners or by flashlight in bed. These were the exciting and significant ones, despite all. It was then, not in school, that images of Parisian cafés or Spanish battlefields and anti-Nazi underground cells disclosed themselves as experiential possibilities. It was then that perceptions of friendship and love and adventure were filled out, then that imagination really took flight. Boundaries would be broken through at moments like these. Visions would be discovered, perspectives on alternative ways of being human in an unsettled world: Captain Ahab's and Ishmael's (Melville, [1851] 1981); Huck's and Jim's (Mark Twain, 1959); Edna Pontellier's and Adèle Ratignolle's (Chopin,

1972); Nick Carraway's and Jay Gatsby's (Fitzgerald, 1953); Sula Peace's and Shadrack's (Morrison, 1975). Those moments, studded with forbidden insights, were extraordinary in most people's lives; they broke, in other words, from the ordinary, the taken-for-granted. They estranged those who chose themselves as readers from the normal and the endlessly normalized; and often they revealed things in the normal that were usually never seen. What with the pressure to set aside childish things, many adults set those moments aside as playful and therefore unrelated to "real" life. But, it seems to me, those are precisely the moments that hold emancipatory potential; and this is what may still be realized in adult education.

Literature and Consciousness

We have reached a period in the teaching of literature that is full of open, provocative questions. We have certainly come to recognize the insufficiencies of pure estheticism, as we once recognized the insufficiency of mere "talk" about literature in the place of direct encounters. We have stopped blandly assuming (thinking of Auden) that literature "makes nothing happen" (1979, p. 32). We have come to recognize that aware engagements with literary art — that the use of imagination those engagements make possible — make a great deal happen in human consciousness. How else explain the passionate insistence that attention be paid to neglected works by black writers, women writers, Hispanics, and Orientals? How else account for the impact of the recognition that prevalent conceptions of "English" or "great books" or even what constitutes "literature" have been defined in centers of power, usually held by Eurocentric white males? The very notion of "constructed" definitions has made problematic beliefs about the transcendent (and untouchable) status of literary art. Traditional "canons" and standards are therefore being questioned, often to the alarm of those preoccupied with the importance of a cultural "core" or a unified conception of "cultural literacy" (Hirsch, 1987). The connection between conceptualizations of literature and the power of certain elites, and the reinterpretations of books long considered neutral or gender free or color blind, indicate that imaginative texts can no longer be confined in enclaves. They are, it is said increasingly, of extreme potential consequence for diversely lived lives; and the pulses of those lived lives must be allowed to throb in what is selected as "literature" (Eagleton, 1983; Gilbert and Gubar, 1979; Jameson, 1982; Lentricchia, 1985). Narrative, as Jameson (1982) has said, has to be viewed today as to some degree "socially symbolic"; literary criticism, as Lentricchia sees it, has in certain of its dimensions to be linked to social change.

This does not mean that the only worthwhile literature is that informed by social or political themes, nor that relevant literature has to be didactic or "message" literature. Nor does it suggest that esthetic considerations can now be ignored. Louise Rosenblatt (1978) has written significantly in *The Reader, the Text, the Poem* that two sorts of experience can be created in transactions with any work, regardless of its intentions. *The Adventures of Huckleberry Finn*, for instance, or *Middlemarch*, or *The Grapes of Wrath*, or *The Stranger*, or *The Unbearable Lightness of Being* can allow for an esthetic transaction in which the work is read for its esthetic values: its shapes, levels, rhythms, voices, images, metaphors, atmospheres. But it can also allow for an "efferent" transaction, meaning one that carries over some insight or illumination or disclosure into lived experience. There probably ought, of course, to be original attention paid to the "art" in art. This suggests that some time ought always to be spent on the esthetic dimension, at least to the degree that readers recognize the difference between a novel or a short story and a document, newspaper article, or case history. Equally important is the realization that it takes imagination to release readers into the created "unreal" worlds brought into being by the language of the text.

Yes, that means a suspension of disbelief, as it entails a deliberate break with the habitual, the routine, the ordinary. At once it requires the deliberate establishment of a relationship by an act of imagination, allowing for the positing of a literary work as an esthetic object and "unreal." The work exists in relation to the consciousness or experience of its readers, who must have lent it some of their life (Sartre, 1963). Dorothy

Walsh (1965, p. 610) has written of "imaginative vistas out of the actual" and of how important it can be to "pass through the context of the actual to the appreciation of a unique, discontinuous possibility." For Vitorino Tejera, imagination must be thought of as "the imaging, probing, relating, and sympathetic power . . . which creates the 'realm' of possibility" (1965, p. 215). For Sartre (1949, pp. 45–46), the reader has to become consciously involved: "disclosing in creating . . . creating by disclosing" under the guidance of a writer, but always going beyond what is written, what is given, and enabling the text to come to be. The reader cannot be passive, wrote Sartre; since reading is not a mechanical operation, "if he is inattentive, tired, stupid, or thoughtless, most of the relations will escape him," and the object will remain mute, unrealized. It is the reader, after all, who has to traverse the realm of possibility.

Imagination and Agency

The activity of readers and their awareness of a sense of agency are crucial to hold in mind. Experiences of bringing texts alive are experiences in interpretation; and, with each, comes the recognition that the meanings of things and their significance are contingent on a certain way of attending from the ground of intersubjectively lived life. Indeed, it is the stuff of lived life — stored images, memories, feelings, perceptions, understandings — that is shaped and ordered in the imaginative encounter. Working in collaboration with the writer, the reader creates patterns in her or his experience, discovers meanings scarcely suspected before. Among the many theories of criticism that have developed in the recent past, the one that sheds most light on what can happen to the reader is the theory called *reader reception theory*. It posits the presence of an active reader ready to *achieve* a text as meaningful, not to uncover predefined meanings presumably buried in the work (Fish, 1980; Iser, 1980; Rosenblatt, 1978; Suleiman and Crossman, 1980).

According to this approach, the reader is enabled to understand at the start that the text to be opened exists *between* the book — the esthetic object on the desk or table — and the reader's subjectivity. It is now up to particular human beings, ready to decide what it means to be readers of fiction, to actualize the work, to render it meaningful, to give it life. For Iser (1980, pp. 108–134), since there is no way of grasping an entire text at once, there must be a moving or a wandering viewpoint traveling along *inside* what the reader is striving to gasp. That may mean looking through the various perspectives established by any text: the perspective of the narrator, of the diverse characters, of the reader, of the "social reality" behind and around the text, even of the style or the tradition to which the text belongs. As the reader looks through these perspectives, she or he cannot but try to synthesize them, to establish some wholly coherent order at the end. It will soon be discovered, however, that the perspectives do not all mesh, that gaps appear between and among them, gaps to be filled through the reader's own imaginative ingenuity.

   In *The Adventures of Huckleberry Finn,* for instance, there are the viewpoints — frequently contesting, sometimes overlapping, sometimes merging — of the ardent, innocent, restless adolescent Huck Finn and those of his cruel, game-playing friend Tom; there are the perspectives of the slave society's representatives, ranging from the Widow Douglas to the murderous Colonel Sherburn, from Pap to the virtuous Phelps family; there are the competing views inherent in life on the open river and in life on the hypocritical, violent riverbank. There is the fearful indifference of the steamboat captain; there is the clowning treachery of the Duke and the Dauphin; there is Jim's growing wisdom, his articulations of love for Huck and for his own children. Moving forward and backward among these perspectives, filling in gaps by creative acts of her or his own, eventually engaging in dialogue with others about what has been disclosed, the reader does in fact bring into being an imaginary world. In the course of the reading, as Dewey pointed out, familiar, stored materials interact with the new experiences provided by the encounter with the text. The junction of the new and old leads to a "re-creation in which the present impulse gets form and solidity while the old, the 'stored' material is literally revived, given new life and soul through having to meet a new situation" (1958, p. 60).

Achieving Meaning

We may assume that the stored materials have to do with memories of adolescence, with ambivalent rebellions against village or family pieties, with childish games, with moments of shock in the face of mindlessness or pointless cruelty, with struggles to escape and desires to go home. In interaction with a narrative in an invented childish vernacular, a narrative given unexpected solidity by referring to materials summoned up from the reader's past, what has been comfortable and familiar may suddenly be defamiliarized. Certain aspects of the reader's lived biography will emerge as figures against a ground — aspects never heeded before: childhood racism and superstitions, perhaps; powerlessness in a dehumanized world; the ambiguities of the "natural man" and of nature itself; the distortions in a womanless space. Perhaps more significantly, the clash between the "cash nexus" of an emergent capitalism and the values of a person-to-person community may come clear, as may the ineradicable scars left by the treatment of human beings as possessions, as mere "things." How are simple beings to stand up and affirm themselves against the plunging steamboat? How, in a corrupt and manipulative society, can conscience develop? Is it always necessary to "pray a lie"? If readers can remain aware of what they are doing, if they can watch themselves being involved even as they are involved, they cannot but feel the critical questions arise. Moreover, confronting the questions against the landscapes of *The Adventures of Huckleberry Finn,* they cannot but feel the incompletion, the lack of resolution. At the end, slavery is not abolished, for all the fact that Jim has been freed; the villages are still desperate to "sivilize" Huck Finn; and, although he says he is going to "light out," every informed reader knows by now that there *is* no "territory ahead." If the indeterminacy and the incompletion stimulate the imagination to reach beyond, to project, to seek some transformation, we might guess that something emancipatory has taken place.

Freedom and Relationship

For Sartre, a work of literature is an act of confidence in human freedom (1949, p. 51). He meant that it moves people to break with the given, to arouse themselves from immersion in the familiar, to see afresh. And because it activates the imagination, it may well urge people to act, to transform, to repair in some fashion to their own inhabited space. This is especially so if a novel, instead of confirming what readers know all too well, appeals to their indignation or, as Sartre put it, discloses a social world animated by indignation. Toni Morrison's *Beloved* offers an example of this. It deals with slavery and with the humiliations associated with the brutalities of slavery in a fashion even Mark Twain could not conceive. Even though, for instance, few women who have been mothers can see themselves remaining indifferent to the loss of a child, something startling and fundamentally unfamiliar is revealed through the reading of this text.

In the course of the telling, Baby Suggs, once a slave, remembers aloud what it was to have her children sold away from her:

> The last of her children, whom she barely glanced at when he was born because it wasn't worth the trouble to try to learn features you would never see change into adulthood anyway. Seven times she had done that: held a little foot; examined the fat fingertips with her own—fingers she never saw become the male or female hands a mother would recognize anywhere. She didn't know to this day what their permanent teeth looked like; or how they held their heads when they walked. Did Patty lose her lisp? What color did Famous' skin finally take? Was that a cleft in Johnny's chin or just a dimple that would disappear soon's his jawbone changed? Four girls, and the last time she saw them there was no hair under their arms. Does Ardelia still love the burned bottom of bread? All seven were gone or dead [1987, p. 139].

The concrete details are not difficult to summon to the surface. Anyone who has raised children or had anything to do with babies responds to "fat fingertips," permanent teeth, a lisp, a cleft, a dimple. But, in conjunction with Morrison's rendering of Baby Suggs's horrendous loss, the remembered experiences with the children are profoundly changed. Aspects of mothering, of mother loving never seen before, are likely to become visible. The meaning of loss — through sale or adoption or death or breakup of some sort — is abruptly highlighted, perhaps along with the persistent fear of loss. The context may expand to include "disappeared" children in other countries, starving children, homeless children. Outrage may flood in with regard to lost children, violated or abused children. That is when, with images of the lost and violated imbued with indignation, readers may see themselves acting to stop such things, to mend a wound in human existence that never seems to heal.

It is hard not to recall Dostoevski's *The Brothers Karamazov* in this connection, if only to suggest how varied are the sources of an "efferent" transaction. Ivan, the rational brother in the novel, is talking to young Alyosha about how hard it is to love one's neighbors when one considers the widespread suffering of children. "There was a little girl of five," Ivan says, "who was hated by her father and mother, 'most worthy and respectable people, of good education and breeding.' You see . . . it is a peculiar characteristic of many people, this love of torturing children and children only. To all other types of humanity these torturers behave mildly and benevolently, like cultivated and humane Europeans; but they are very fond of tormenting children" (Dostoevski, [1880] 1945, p. 286). Ivan wants justice, it will be recalled, here on earth. He does not want to see forgiveness; he does not want harmony at the cost of unavenged suffering. Those reading it cannot but experience a rupture and a demand. At once, they may experience a particular unease at the mention of "justice" in such a frame.

The recent recognition of what have been called "women's ways of knowing" (Belenky, Clinchy, Goldberger, and Tarule, 1986) may expand the context even further when we recognize a certain lack in Karamazov's thinking, desperately humane as it seems to be. It is based upon his own despair; *he* is the one who is going "to give my ticket back"; *he* is the one agitated by the thought of cosmic harmony bought at the cost of children's suffering. Belenky and her colleagues, like many other women scholars today, speak of "connected knowing" and of using the self as a way of knowing, of the kind of passion that informs Morrison's work and might move a Dostoevski to render an empathic knowledge of the "little girl of five" whose feelings (in his context) are left out. When Sara Ruddick writes of "maternal thinking," she puts her stress on preserving the lives of children and says it is "the central constitutive, invariant aim of maternal practice" (1989, p. 19). Surely, Toni Morrison's power has something to do with her empathic passion, as does the emancipatory power of writers like Tillie Olsen and Maya Angelou and (earlier on) Kate Chopin and Zora Neale Hurston, whose voices were silenced for so long.

It may be that, after the moment of re-vision, readers comprehend what Sartre meant when he wrote about the importance of projects and of the human characteristic of going *beyond* situations in efforts to transcend determinism. The idea of finding out how to read situations is of great educational relevance. For Sartre, the meaning of the past depends greatly on present projects. What I am today gives whatever meaning my past can have for me and others. And "the fundamental project which I am decides absolutely the meaning which the past which I have can have for me and for others. I alone in fact can decide at each moment the *bearing* of the past" (1956, p. 498). He wrote also about surpassing an unendurable, unacceptable reality — one involving, we might say, lost children, voiceless poverty, staring despair — by taking "a leap ahead, at once a refusal and a realization" (1963, p. 92). The point was to refuse the unendurable by taking the kind of action that in some way remedied it. Knowing, he believed, was a moment of praxis; like Paulo Freire, Sartre was linking knowing and critical reflection to action, to effecting (along with others) some kind of change.

Were it not, however, for a sense of something resistant, something "up against" the person, there would be no refusal and no consciousness of freedom. The "knowing" made possible by a Morrison, say, or a Dostoevski, or a Tillie Olsen, may well become a moment of praxis depending on the way the reader understands his or her situation. If the selling of slave children, the abuse of children, and the institutional subjection of children were accepted as normal or natural, they would not be conceived as barriers, interruptions, or resistances. Unperturbed, passively regretful, a person would scarcely feel provoked to action. If literature has the capacity, however, to engage readers in such a manner as now and then to appeal to their indignation (because of the impact of the discourse, the language, or the enactments), those readers' lives might well be changed. They might at least be able to see, to attend, to notice what was hidden until then. Attending, they might discern faultlines, deviations, gaps that might call upon them to reject withdrawal and choose some sort of action, to surpass.

Quite obviously, the reading of a demanding book can never guarantee the taking of transformative action. Practical judgments always have to be made in particular situations; connections have to be found between the interpretation — the "seeing" or the naming — and what Sartre and others speak of as praxis. Hans-Georg Gadamer (1975, p. 316), who has been especially interested in the ways in which interpretation can enhance vision and provoke self-reflection, emphasizes the way in which the ability to interpret "vindicates the task of decision-making according to ordinary individuals' own responsibility. No longer are they so driven to hand over the task to the expert." It is at least conceivable that a reflective and responsible involvement with a novel, a created world, may enhance the sense of hermeneutic agency Gadamer describes. It may even provoke the kinds of judgment he believes can be found in all understanding: *phronesis* or practical judgment, a process at the furthest remove from scientistic thinking or simple contemplation.

Such a sense of agency is required if people are to grasp the ways in which works of art stand "against established reality," as Herbert Marcuse put it (1978, p. 58). Certain novels estrange their readers from the normal or the taken-for-granted, sometimes for years of their lives. (I think of Herman Melville's *Moby Dick*, Gabriel Garcia Márquez's *One Hundred Years of Solitude*, Albert Camus's *The Plague*, Margaret Atwood's *Surfacing*, John Irving's *The Cider House Rules*, Alice Walker's *The Color Purple*, Milan Kundera's *The Unbearable Lightness of Being*, George Konrad's *The Caseworker*, Lawrence Thornton's *Imagining Argentina*, and then I think of how important it would be for every reader and, if we are lucky, every educator to make her or his own authentic list.) Marcuse, in any event, suggests what can happen when the "established" is refused. "Art breaks open a dimension inaccessible to other experience, a dimension in which human beings, nature, and things no longer stand under the law of the established reality principle. . . . The encounter with the truth of art happens in the estranging language and images which make perceptible, visible, and audible that which is no longer or not yet perceived, said, and heard in everyday life" (p. 72).

Marcuse knew well that, although the arts might not themselves change the world, they could contribute to changing the consciousness of the men and women who could change the world. Others, like Theodor Adorno, wrote that committed art was intended "to work at the level of fundamental attitudes" and not to pass legislation, reform jails, or cure venereal disease (1986, p. 180). But he also made a point like Sartre's: that the task of art may well be to awaken free choice and overcome the neutrality that marks the indifferent one. In the presence of art, perspectives may open in unpredictable directions; they may disclose the unthought, the unacted upon, (again) the territory that lies beyond. Those who teach may ponder what can be done to provoke those who read to invent forms of praxis as they return to the mundane, or devise projects for situations that sometimes do not yet exist.

Emancipatory Moments

Jürgen Habermas, among others, views emancipation as a release from dependence upon seemingly natural constraints and mystifications; and it seems evident that literature, if read self-consciously, has roles to play in such release. An emancipatory cognitive interest, for Habermas, oriented to the pursuit of reflection for its own sake, may often allow for self-reflection (1971, p. 310). Engaging in it, human beings can recover the course of their own self-formation. Brought into contact with their own stories and vantage points, they may be enabled to overcome predilections to divide themselves as "subjects" from what they have considered "object," to acquiesce in the "for-itself," a finished and presumably normal reality, which is supposedly the same for everyone.

Encounters with fiction can and do acquaint people with alternative ways of seeing, feeling, and understanding, as has been suggested, just so long as readers can view the works at hand as something other than pseudohistories or mirrors held up to nature or representations of something self-existent outside. Those who realize the significance of using their imaginations and negating the commonplace may be released from the dependence Habermas describes. What is to substitute for that dependence? When persons respond in their imaginative freedom, do they actually evolve toward the "autonomy and responsibility" Habermas linked to self-reflection (p. 315)? If they do, can they at some time be provoked to reach beyond autonomy toward connectedness with others, toward rationality and active social concern?

I have talked to some degree about the concern of certain literary critics for the socially emancipatory, especially when they are faced with what they think of as the sterile and canonical. They argue about the separating of novels and tales from their affiliations with the world; they challenge psychic distancing, the excessive separations between the esthetical and the ethical (Booth, 1988). Many works are still treated as locked structures, dependent on more or less esoteric mastery of "establishment" codes and ways of speaking. A number of these codes are rooted, Terry Eagleton says, in ideology, by which he means "the ways in which what we say and believe connects with the power-structure and power-relations of the society we live in" (1983, p. 14). Like a number of others, from different locations in the world of literature, Eagleton is working to overcome the passive acceptances that have been encouraged and, at once, to expose the connections between such acceptances and the maintenance and reproduction of social power.

Frank Lentricchia, in often similar tone, talks about literary intellectuals trying to contribute "to the formation of a community different from the one we now live in; 'society' as the function of many things, one of them being 'education.'

Not all social power is literary power, but all literary power is social power. . . . The literary act is a social act" (Lentricchia, 1985, p. 9). He goes on to pursue the issue of literary criticism as a social force; and, if it is the case that the teaching of literature is a mode of critical communication, this too has implications for the classroom. Edward Said clearly agrees with that when he recalls the way in which advocacy of "close reading" entailed a hostility to outsiders who could not grasp its importance. He speaks about exclusiveness and about "savants" as a separate caste and about the secular realm he would like to see. It would be the kind of realm that requires a more open sense of community "as something to be won and of audiences as human beings to be addressed" (1983, p. 152). A problem central to emancipation would appear to be how esoteric intellectualism can indeed be reduced in the name of community, and how members of the wider pluralistic community can in the long run be empowered to crack the codes of difficult, demanding, and (yes) potentially emancipatory works. To repeat: Works are only likely to appeal to readers' freedom or indignation if readers can become present to them, personally present, as individuals and participants at once.

For Raymond Williams, "so important an activity and experience as literature is equally both individual *and* social" (1977, p. 24). He saw the practice of literature as both "the practice of a collective mode and the practice of what are in effect innumerable individual projects" (p. 36). Like a number of his contemporaries, he wanted to find ways of reading or responding that would recognize the collective and the individual without reducing any individual project "to a collective mode, or seeing literature as an endless series of individual projects without recognition of anything but the more *abstract* collective modes" (p. 37). This concern for the communal and the public, often in a kind of tension with the personal, ought to be a crucial one for the adult educator. Needing to avoid elitism, the educator must keep an eye on the "collective mode"; needing to avoid submergence in the crowd, he or she must keep an eye on the individual project. But, at the same time, the educator has to remain aware of the need to recognize and resist the forces that work for subservience and fetishization in the culture, even where the arts are concerned. That means a continual attentiveness to self-directed learning as well as engagement in dialogue.

There must be an ongoing intentional activity if literature is to be realized as emancipatory. The fixed and arbitrary must be acknowledged and refused; there must be a consciousness of differing modes of discourse, of changing voices in the dialogue. Mikhail Bakhtin reminded us that "reality as we have it in the novel is only one of the many possible realities; it is not inevitable, not arbitrary, it bears within itself other possibilities" (Bakhtin, 1981, p. 37). Along with this and the heteroglossia he described (the multiplicity of voices in any culture, any world), he emphasized the importance of the "carnivalesque," the culture of laughter he found outside of hierarchies in the public space: "free, full of ambivalent laughter, sacrileges, profanations of all things sacred, disparagement . . . familiar contact with everybody and everything" (Bakhtin, 1984, p. 173). If we recall Umberto Eco's *The Name of the Rose* and the ways in which laughter threatened the hidden knowledge in the labyrinthine library and the very structures of a hierarchical faith, we may add the idea of laughter to our notion of the emancipatory. It may be still another way to combat elitism and to open pathways to community.

None of what I have been describing and asking for are empirical or measurable events. I have been talking about what occurs in the feeling structure, mind, imagination, and sensibility of a living social being empowered for dialogical relations with texts. Total coherence will never be attained; the gulfs and discrepancies will never be fully closed. Each time a reader engages with a novel, it will change; she or he can neither exhaust nor completely realize it. But this is in tune with the perspectival nature of knowing and, yes, with the enticing incompleteness of the world. Readers should be left with indignation aroused, with their lived worlds more problematic than before, with a praxis still to be devised.

There are and will be multiple modes of relating to the world. The adult educator working toward "reflection-in-action" (Schön, 1983) certainly must grasp what it signifies to turn attention to the shared and the everyday from a social-scientific and even a natural-scientific point of view. Sociology, ethnography, psychology, biology: All provide potential perspectives on what it means to teach and what it means to transform. As with other arts, literature offers occasions to attend from the center of a consciousness thrusting into the intersubjective world. Provoking moves beyond the actual, the commonplace; involvements with imaginative works make possible visions of what might be, what ought to be; and it is often the vision of a better order of things that allows persons to identify what is unendurable.

To make works of literature present, to affirm the uses of imagination: Both offer a sense of open possibility. The realm of possibility that must be traversed, as we have seen, demands that new initiatives be continually taken, multiple voices tapped. Martha Nussbaum, exploring the discontent with the normal that writing can arouse, talks about how it might "displace both writer and reader from a loving acceptance of the world" (1988, p. 253). Acceptance can too easily become subservience and thoughtlessness. The adult educator's concern (indeed, her or his *loving* concern) can still be to provoke an unease that leads to wonder and to inquiries, that awakens passion, that provokes desires to choose and to transform. It is again a matter of confidence in human freedom. That, where literature is involved, is where emancipation might begin.

References

Adorno, T. *Aesthetic Theory*. New York: Routledge & Kegan Paul, 1986.

Auden, W. H. "In Memory of W. B. Yeats." In E. Mendelson (ed.), *Selected Poetry of W. H. Auden*. New York: Vintage Books, 1979.

Bakhtin, M. *The Dialogical Imagination*. Austin: University of Texas Press, 1981.

Bakhtin, M. *Problems of Dostoevsky's Poetics*. Minneapolis: University of Minnesota Press, 1984.

Belenky, M. F., Clinchy, B. M., Goldberger, N. R., and Tarule, J. M. *Women's Ways of Knowing*. New York: Basic Books, 1986.

Booth, W. C. *The Company We Keep: An Ethics of Fiction.* Berkeley: University of California Press, 1988.

Chopin, K. *The Awakening.* New York: Avon Books, 1972.

Dewey, J. *Art as Experience.* New York: Vintage Books, 1958.

Dostoevski, F. *The Brothers Karamozov.* New York: Modern Library, 1945. (Originally published 1880.)

Eagleton, T. *Literary Theory: An Introduction.* Minneapolis: University of Minnesota Press, 1983.

Eco, U. *The Name of the Rose.* San Diego, Calif.: Harcourt Brace Jovanovich, 1983.

Fish, S. *Is There a Text in This Class? The Authority of Interpretive Communities.* Cambridge, Mass.: Harvard University Press, 1980.

Fitzgerald, F. S. *The Great Gatsby.* New York: Scribner's, 1953.

Freire, P. *Pedagogy of the Oppressed.* New York: Herder and Herder, 1970.

Gadamer, H.-G. "Hermeneutics and Social Science." *Cultural Hermeneutics,* 1975, *19,* 310–318.

Gilbert, S., and Gubar, S. *The Madwoman in the Attic.* London: University Press, 1979.

Habermas, J. *Knowledge and Human Interests.* Boston: Beacon Press, 1971.

Hirsch, E. D., Jr. *Cultural Literacy.* New York: Houghton Mifflin, 1987.

Iser, W. *The Act of Reading.* Baltimore, Md.: Johns Hopkins University Press, 1980.

Jameson, F. *The Political Unconscious: Narrative as a Socially Symbolic Act.* Ithaca, N.Y.: Cornell University Press, 1982.

Lentricchia, F. *Criticism and Society.* Chicago: University of Chicago Press, 1985.

Marcuse, H. *The Aesthetic Dimension.* Boston: Beacon Press, 1978.

Melville, H. *Moby Dick.* Berkeley: University of California Press, 1981. (Originally published 1851.)

Merriam, S. B. (ed.). *Themes of Adulthood Through Literature.* New York: Teachers College Press, 1983.

Morrison, T. *Sula.* New York: Bantam Books, 1975.

Morrison, T. *Beloved.* New York: Knopf, 1987.

Nussbaum, M. "Narrative Emotions: Beckett's Genealogy of Love." *Ethics,* 1988, *98* (2), 225–254.

Ohliger, J. *The Fictional Adult Education.* Madison, Wis.: Basic Choices, 1988.

Quigley, B. A. "Systematizing Fiction and Non-Fiction as Sources of Data for Adult Education Research." In M. Zukas (ed.), *Papers from the Transatlantic Dialogue.* Leeds, England: University of Leeds, 1988.

Rosenblatt, L. *The Reader, the Text, the Poem.* Carbondale: University of Southern Illinois, 1978.

Ruddick, S. *Maternal Thinking.* Boston: Beacon Press, 1989.

Said, E. W. "Opponents, Audiences, Constituencies and Community." In H. Foster (ed.), *The Anti-Aesthetic: Essays on Postmodern Culture.* Port Townsend, Wash.: Bay Press, 1983.

Sartre, J.-P. *What Is Literature?* New York: Citadel Press, 1949.

Sartre, J.-P. *Being and Nothingness.* New York: Philosophical Library, 1956.

Sartre, J.-P. *Search for a Method.* New York: Knopf, 1963.

Schön, D. A. *The Reflective Practitioner.* New York: Basic Books, 1983.

Suleiman, S. R., and Crossman, I. (eds.). *The Reader in the Text.* Princeton, N.J.: Princeton University Press, 1980.

Tejera, V. *Art and Human Intelligence.* East Norwalk, Conn.: Appleton-Century-Crofts, 1965.

Twain, M. *The Adventures of Huckleberry Finn.* New York: New American Library, 1959.

Walsh, D. "The Cognitive Content of Art." In E. Vivas and M. Krieger (eds.)., *The Problems of Aesthetics.* New York: Holt, Rinehart & Winston, 1965.

Williams, R. "Literature in Society." In H. Schiff (ed.), *Contemporary Approaches to English Studies.* New York: Harper & Row, 1977.

Part Three

Uncovering and Mapping the Personal Perspectives of Learners

Fourteen

———— ✺ ————

Repertory Grids:
Playing Verbal Chess

Philip C. Candy

In recent years, athletes have been able to achieve feats of strength, speed, agility, and endurance once thought impossible. There are many reasons for this: controlled diets; carefully constructed training schedules; improved knowledge of both sports psychology and physiology; and more "professional" or "scientific" approaches to coaching. Technology, too, has had a role to play, and this includes the use of video to capture and record details of competitors' movements and actions.

At first, this may seem simply one of the many tools in the coach's bulging kit of training aids, but it is fundamentally different from others. Not only does it provide the *coach* with more information about the trainee's performance, but it allows the *competitor,* perhaps for the first time, to see his or her own performance as others see it. With the aid of a video, athletes can examine their own performance at leisure and in minute detail; slowing down, speeding up, zooming in, freezing, replaying, analyzing, and comparing a particular action in a way that is simply not possible while actually engaged in the sport itself.

This example deals with behavior — the outward and visible manifestation of what we are thinking about or striving for. But the act of thinking (or for that matter of valuing, expecting, or judging) is not simply something that occurs inside a mysterious black box; it too can be the subject of intentional reflection and review and, accordingly, of change.

271

Since time immemorial, philosophers and others of a reflective disposition have attempted to look in on their own thoughts and values with the aim of better understanding themselves and people in general. This tradition of introspection has given rise to some of our most moving poetry; it has resulted in personal insights of great depth and significance (Paffard, 1973); and it has undoubtedly contributed to our store of knowledge about the human spirit and the human intellect.

There are limits, however, especially from the point of view of the individual, to what introspection can achieve. It may not allow us to unravel our intricately intertwined attitudes, habits, values, beliefs, and thought patterns for the very reason that we lack "a place to stand." It is like the athlete who, in the absence of an external record of his or her performance, cannot be objectively self-critical. Mindful of this, psychologists, educators, and therapists have developed a range of tasks, exercises, questionnaires, and inventories that seek to help people in their quest for improved self-understanding. However, although they are widely used and extensively discussed in the literature on therapy and learning, many of these approaches suffer from a number of drawbacks.

Some, such as the Rorschach or Thematic Apperception Tests, are artificial and present the respondents with imaginary or hypothetical situations for which they must *invent* rather than recall responses. Others have a tendency to "put words into the respondents' mouths," seeking reactions or responses that are not natural to the person. Because of their structure, they become both a conceptual straitjacket and a guessing game in which the respondent has to figure out the meaning that the person who framed the questions and answers had in mind. In addition, many such instruments and activities require a high degree of inference about the significance of the findings; they are designed for use by clinicians, therapists, or educators, who interpret the meaning for the respondent. Linked to this is the fact that characteristically they do not reveal alternative ways in which the respondent *could* view or value the test items; they do not, in themselves, suggest "pathways or channels along which the respondent is free to move" (Bannister and Mair, 1968, p. 39).

In view of these criticisms of many psychological tests, the late George Kelly set out to develop an approach to understanding how people think and feel about aspects of their world. The device he came up with was the Role Construct Repertory Test or, more simply, the Repertory Grid.

The Repertory Grid is a conversational strategy that seeks to externalize and, to a degree, to objectify salient aspects of a respondent's personal construct system; that is, his or her thinking and feeling about a set of objects, ideas, people, or events. As far as possible, the Repertory Grid draws on real-life experience; it allows the respondent to express his or her point of view in personally meaningful terms; it is "user-friendly" in the sense of providing insights both to the respondent and to his or her adviser or helper; and, perhaps most important, it embodies dimensions rather than mere descriptions and hence allows for the identification of different ways in which the respondent *could* view the situation if he or she chose to do so.

In this chapter, I will describe the process of eliciting a Repertory Grid and of analyzing its meaning. I will introduce the basic tenets of personal construct psychology, from which the grid is derived, and explore the potential of the grid as an aid to transformative learning. It will be argued, however, that knowledge of one's meaning perspective in itself is not sufficient to bring about a perspective transformation, and that the opportunity to experiment with alternatives is also required. The chapter therefore concludes with some observations about the nature of personal meaning perspectives or, as they are called here, personal construct systems, and the need for a person to entertain alternate ways of thinking about his or her world in order to undergo a transformation in meaning perspective.

The Repertory Grid in Action

As an aid to understanding and envisaging how the grid is used, I have decided to present a hypothetical situation in which an adult educator seeks to help a respondent who has decided that she wants to know more about how she relates to other colleagues in her workplace. The grid also has applications in classroom settings and, as discussed later, with groups; however, it is easier to get a "feeling" for its use in a one-to-one, counseling situation.

The interview begins with the interviewer (Ian) and the respondent (Robyn) sitting together in comfortable lounge chairs in the respondent's home. There is a low coffee table between them, and the interviewer has a clipboard with a preprinted grid form on it and a number of small, blank cards. After some preliminaries, Ian asks Robyn to note down, each on a separate card, the name, initials, or some distinguishing feature of each person with whom she regularly comes into contact in her workplace. Ian also asks Robyn to prepare a card with the name of the "best colleague I have ever worked with" and another for "the worst colleague I have ever worked with" and a third with Robyn's own name or initials on it. Ian writes the same names or initials at the head of each column across the top of the prepared form; it is not necessary for him to know who the people are; in fact, their anonymity may be a positive advantage.

Ian starts by shuffling the cards and placing three of them in front of Robyn. He says to her, "In what way are two of these people similar and thereby different from the third person?" Robyn thinks for a moment, then places two of the cards together.

"These two are both helpful to me," she says.

"And this one?" asks Ian.

"That person really tries to make things difficult for me," replies Robyn.

"Give me a word or a phrase to describe the similar people," says Ian, and Robyn immediately replies, "Helpful."

"What word would you use for this third person?" asks Ian. Robyn hesitates before saying, "Obstructive."

This brief exchange allows Ian to write on his prepared grid form the word *helpful* in the left-hand margin and opposite it, in the right-hand margin, *obstructive.* Several points are important at this stage: first, it is not relevant whether Robyn's judgment is objectively true or not — it is true for her; second, it does not matter whether Ian agrees or disagrees — it is Robyn's personal constructs we are interested in; and third, the two ends or "poles" of the construct do not have to be dictionary opposites — they can be simply opposites in the respondent's mind.

The next step involves Robyn in some very careful thinking, because Ian places all the named cards — perhaps as many as twelve of them, including Robyn's — on the table. "I want you to arrange these people along an imaginary continuum from 'helpful' to 'obstructive,'" Ian says. "If you can't separate several people, put them at the same point along the line." After a period of shuffling and reorganizing, Robyn completes the task, and she and Ian together allocate a score from 1 to 7 to each person, where 1 represents "very helpful," 7 stands for "very obstructive," and other numbers indicate shades of difference between the extremes. It is important to note that Robyn has to give herself a score out of 7 on the scale "helpful/obstructive." Ian notes these scores on the grid sheet and, when he is finished, presents Robyn with another set of three cards, again asking, "How are two of these people alike, in a way that distinguishes them from the third person?"

This time, Robyn identifies the similarity as "highly specialized" (the emergent pole of the construct) and its opposite as "not at all specialized" (the submerged pole of the construct). Ian notes these on his prepared grid, and again asks Robyn to assign a score from 1 to 7 to every person (element) on the grid, including to herself. This process continues for an hour: Ian presenting Robyn with different combinations of three people (triads) each time, helping her to elicit a bipolar construct, and then assisting (but not shaping her responses) as she gives a score to every person in the array on each of the scales. As they proceed, they chat informally about relationships, about experiences, about personalities. As Robyn becomes less self-conscious about the task, constructs start to "bubble up" spontaneously. Sometimes she does not even wait for Ian to present a triad of three names before she has identified another pair of descriptors: experienced-inexperienced; sociable-antisocial; tidy office-messy office; up-to-date–out-of-date; writes well–writes poorly; good communicator–poor communicator; and so on.

All the time, Ian notes her responses on his grid form, building up a matrix of numbers and a set of bipolar constructs.

Name: Robyn

Date: 15 Oct

Topic: Work Relationships

Figure 14.1. Repertory Grid Form.

PAIR 1	Geoff	Peter	Zelda	Ryan	Nathan	Shirley	Alison	Robyn (myself)	Bob	Elsie	Helen	Jack	SINGLETON 7
Helpful	6	2	2	7	3	2	7	2	6	3	2	2	Obstructive
Highly specialized	1	6	4	4	2	4	4	3	3	2	3	2	Not at all specialized
Experienced	2	1	5	2	1	5	4	6	1	3	6	1	Inexperienced
Sociable	3	2	1	6	2	1	7	1	5	2	1	3	Antisocial
Has tidy office	6	2	2	7	3	2	7	7	6	3	2	2	Has messy office
Up-to-date	2	5	3	1	2	3	7	1	2	2	2	3	Out-of-date
Writes well	3	4	4	3	5	4	7	5	5	1	4	2	Writes poorly
Good communicator	6	3	4	6	4	4	7	1	3	1	1	4	Poor communicator
Initiator	2	4	1	5	2	1	6	3	2	4	3	2	Follower
Spreads gossip	5	7	6	3	6	6	1	6	1	3	6	6	Keeps quiet
Plans ahead	2	6	3	2	2	3	2	2	2	4	2	2	Reacts to events
Has outside contacts	4	1	1	5	2	1	2	4	5	2	4	3	Has limited outside contact

Italicized items above indicate handwritten insertions.

Unlike on a conventional test, the respondent has provided all the names (the elements), all the criteria to distinguish people (the constructs), and all the scores. Ian has simply helped her to identify and articulate aspects of her personal construct system with reference to relationships. He has not prompted, and he certainly has not provided either the construct labels or the scores, but that does not mean that he has been completely passive. He has probed her answers and encouraged Robyn: "Be more specific," "Give an example," "Tell me why you feel that way," "What do you think could have made you react that way?" "Can you imagine a different way you could have viewed that situation?" The repertory grid is a dynamic aid to counseling and self-awareness: It yields some useful data, but the act of completing it is a learning experience in its own right.

By the end of the session, Ian and Robyn have produced a completed grid form, which is now ready for the second phase — interpretation and analysis (see Figure 14.1).

The completed Repertory Grid form, although it looks somewhat daunting at first, is a mine of information. At its simplest, it identifies the criteria that Robyn actually and habitually uses in everyday situations to distinguish colleagues at work. These constructs are unique and idiosyncratic; it is unlikely that anyone else would use precisely the same words to refer to the underlying qualities that she has in mind — and even if they did, it is unlikely that they would rank or rate people in precisely the same way she has. The constructs show that Robyn regards both Zelda and Shirley as fairly helpful, not too specialized, sociable, and as initiators with lots of outside contacts. Alison, on the other hand, is clearly not her favorite person: obstructive, antisocial, messy, and a rumormonger who communicates poorly. It is possible to infer that Robyn likes Peter, whom she judges to be a very experienced person in the office, helpful and sociable with lots of outside contacts. However, he is not very specialized, tends to be out-of-date, and rarely plans ahead, preferring instead to react to events as they arise — perhaps because he has had so much experience.

In analyzing the grid, however, probably the most telling column is that which relates to Robyn herself. Glancing down the column headed *Robyn,* we can see that she believes herself to be fairly helpful and sociable, she keeps up-to-date with changes in the field, thinks she communicates well with others, and she plans for the future. She classifies herself, however, as fairly inexperienced and is prepared to admit that she has a "messy office." Interestingly, she regards herself as very similar, on almost every dimension, to her friend Helen, except that Helen has a "tidy office" — this is an area of her working life that, along with the quality of her written reports, Robyn would like to improve.

When the grid is read in rows — that is, across the constructs instead of down the elements — perhaps the most striking finding is the strong relationship between having a "tidy office" and Robyn's judgment about people's helpfulness. There is almost complete agreement between the scores on these two dimensions. The implication of this is that if Robyn's experience has taught her that people with tidy offices are helpful and conversely that people with messy offices are obstructive, then knowing about one of these aspects will lead her to *anticipate* the other aspect. Thus, if she walks into someone's office and it is tidy, this will lead her to expect that person to be helpful as well. This anticipation, in turn, will influence in subtle ways how she approaches and interacts with that person and, in the light of what we know about the notion of "self-fullfilling prophecies," may well result either in the person behaving helpfully, or rather in Robyn construing his or her behavior as helpful. Unfortunately, as demonstrated in Rosenthal and Jacobson's classic work (1968), the converse is also true. If, for Robyn, a messy office is synonymous with obstructiveness, her encounter with someone with a messy office is likely to lead her to anticipate obstructiveness; this then places her on guard and will probably lead to negative interactions with that person.

Unlike many other forms of test or questionnaire, the process of eliciting a grid is a learning experience in its own right. It is virtually impossible for a respondent to generate construct labels or to assign meaningful rankings or ratings to the elements in an array without critical reflection. The result is that a person will often have reconstrued some part of his or her universe in the process of completing a grid; if it were to be administered again, a slightly different but no less valid result is perfectly possible.

Moreover, once a grid is completed, it has captured a great deal of information that the respondent may never have thought about consciously or have articulated before. Because the grid helps the respondent to systematize his or her thinking about (and attitudes toward) aspects of life, it can highlight inconsistencies, show up dominant and at times dysfunctional patterns of thinking, reveal implications of construing things in particular ways, and demonstrate alternative and perhaps preferable ways of understanding the world and relating to it.

The Grid and Its Relationship to Personal Construct Theory

The Repertory Grid is indeed a useful and versatile instrument. It can be used successfully by interviewers with a minimum of training, although there are dangers in this; and it does not require elaborate, expensive, or complex equipment or instruments. The way I have introduced and illustrated it in this chapter, it may appear rather like a cross between *Q* sort and Semantic Differential, and indeed many researchers and clinicians have used the Repertory Grid, or modifications of it, as a stand-alone device, incorporating it into their repertoire of counseling, teaching, or research tools. But the Repertory Grid is a methodological outgrowth of a comprehensive, innovative, and sophisticated theoretical perspective — the psychology of personal constructs — and users miss a great deal if they concentrate on the technique without regard for its parent theory:

Psychologists often behave as if all that is needed for effective research or applied work is a single idea and an instrument. They ignore the fact that behind any single idea are whole series of assumptions and underlying any instrument yet a further series of assumptions. The assumptions underlying the "instrument" may well contradict the assumptions implicit in the "idea." Thus grid method is frequently brought into play, quite without relation to its parent theory. It has often been looked on as some sort of measure of "attitudes" or "meaning" or "personality" or "concepts" and it has achieved a status as a sort of rich man's semantic differential.

Yet psychologists who use the grid thoughtfully will find themselves assuming the truth of many of the assumptions of personal construct theory even when they are ignorant of the theory as such [Fransella and Bannister, 1977, p. 4].

In 1955, after more than twenty years as a counseling psychologist and academic, George Kelly published his two-volume *Psychology of Personal Constructs*. It was, and still is, quintessentially a theory of role occupancy, and "the concept of role is equally central to the methodology (Role Construct Repertory Test and Grid) and the therapeutic technique (Fixed-Role Therapy) associated with the theory" (Bannister and Mair, 1968, p. 25). In many respects, it was ahead of its time, and Kelly's work lay comparatively unrecognized for a further twenty-one years until 1976, when it became the focal point of the Nebraska Symposium on Motivation. Since then, there have been a series of international conferences and a number of national conferences, workshops, and seminars focusing on his work; an international clearinghouse has been established with regional representatives and over 400 members in various parts of the world; there has been a steady volume of research throughout the world based on his work; and there is a burgeoning literature of books, articles, and research papers reported in an annual reading list compiled by the clearinghouse.

Apart from the elegance and completeness of his theory, one of the factors that has led to this spectacular increase in interest in personal construct psychology is its congruence with recent trends in phenomenological and constructivist research paradigms. The psychology of personal constructs is a formally stated theorem, comprising three basic assumptions, a fundamental postulate, and eleven corollaries, each of which is elaborated in turn by Kelly. It is explicitly based on explaining the *real* attitudes, thoughts, and behaviors of *real* people in *real* situations and is derived from extensive counseling and teaching experience, rather than from laboratory experimentation. In the decades since it was first published, however, every aspect of the theory has been exhaustively and minutely examined, with the consequent development of an impressive research literature.

Essentially, Kelly argues that *people's psychological processes are channelized by the ways in which they anticipate events.* He holds that personal systems of meaning comprise an elaborate and complexly interlinked hierarchical structure consisting of dichotomized pathways or constructs. These constructs derive from our past experience and cause us to anticipate events and to construe experiences as they befall us in predictable and regular ways. A person's system of personal constructs, however, is "not a collection of treasured and guarded hallucinations, it is the person's guide to living. It is the repository of what one has learned, a statement of one's intents, the values whereby one lives and the banner under which one fights. A personal construct system is a [personal] theory being put to perpetual test" (Bannister and Fransella, 1971, p. 27).

According to Kelly, no two people have exactly the same construct systems, since they cannot have had identical bases of experience; and, accordingly, no two people construe (or make sense of) reality in precisely the same way. However, accepting this point of view, we do not need to embrace what Lakoff and Johnson (1980) call the "myth of subjectivism" entirely; we do have sufficient experience in common to be able to share at least some meanings, and our systems of personal constructs are what permit us to communicate with one another, to create cultural systems, languages, and so on. This is as true of large groups, such as tribes, communities, and nations, as it is of smaller groups, such as families and work teams.

When Kelly first articulated his theory of personal constructs, he was confronted with the very real difficulties of assessing or measuring them. By his own admission, each person's construct system is unique and idiosyncratic, and this leads to the logical difficulty of trying to enter into such private universes using the crude tools of language and common experience. To get around this perplexity, Kelly devised the Role Construct Repertory Grid Technique, which was used to assist clients to construe their social relationships. In the original version, Kelly generated a list of nineteen "significant others" in terms of whom the client might be expected to judge or value himself or herself. As Kelly mentioned, and others have since reiterated, the inclusion of "self" as an element in this process is a powerful means of identifying how a respondent views himself or herself on personally meaningful criteria and has the potential at least to point the way to significant personal change in desired directions.

Kelly operationally defined a construct as the way in which two things were similar and thereby different from a third or more things, and this definition provided the basis of his elicitation procedure. As in the example in this chapter, he would simply confront the client with three of the descriptors chosen from the array and ask them to nominate the similarity and difference. These became the two poles or ends of the personal construct, and it was then a comparatively simple matter to have the client rate or rank *all* the people in the array along that and other (similarly elicited) dimensions. This process, known as the *triadic elicitation procedure,* yields a matrix that embodies a good deal of information about how the respondent views himself or herself and significant others on construct dimensions that are generated by each client independently. The Repertory Grid is also susceptible to a variety of statistical manipulations including "principal components analysis, multidimensional scaling, hierarchical cluster analysis and non-parametric factor analysis, among others" (Adams-Webber, 1984, p. 225).

In the case of factor analysis, it is possible to calculate which constructs or groups of constructs account for the largest share of variance in the total grid. It is not uncommon to find that a person's thinking about some aspect of his or her world is dominated by one or two higher-order constructs and that the many apparently separate constructs generated by the elicitation process are really just slightly different ways of expressing the same underlying dimension. If, in the example given earlier, it could be shown that Robyn's thinking about her colleagues was disproportionately influenced by whether their offices were tidy or messy, such information could be fed back to her, along with the observation that others have found this a relatively trivial or unreliable indicator of the trustworthiness or competence of one's colleagues.

Another common approach to interpreting the data in repertory grids is cluster analysis, in which constructs are re-ordered so that each is placed next to the one to which it is mathematically most similar. Likewise, the elements (in this case, the names of the co-workers) are reordered so that they are also next to the ones to which they are most similar. Computer programs can calculate the percentage degree of match between adjacent rows and columns and produce dendrograms, or tree diagrams, that show the progressive collapsing of constructs and elements into a smaller and smaller number of clusters.

Whereas principal components analysis and factor analysis can be very informative for research purposes, they tend to involve certain transformations of the grid that render it unrecognizable to the respondent. The two-way cluster diagram, however, is useful in feeding back the analysis of the grid to the subject without displaying any mathematical "magic [or] complex computer printout" (Shaw, 1978, p. 62). It retains all the labels supplied by the respondents and merely reorganizes them in a form that is recognizable and can be the basis for further discussion of the grid with the respondent: "The ensuing conversation is an exploration of the personal meaning attached to these groupings by the elicitee. The validity of the analysis is measured only in terms of the subjective feeling of personal significance assessed by the occurrence or otherwise of what has been called the 'aha' experience, or 'the creative flash'" (Shaw, 1980, p. 33).

This is an extremely valuable point. Some users of the Repertory Grid have tended to place disproportionate emphasis on the statistical elegance of techniques used to analyze and transform the grid (see, for example, Beck, 1986; Bell, 1983; Cliffe, 1986; Rathod, 1981; Slater, 1976, 1977) and have been "inclined to see grids as a scientific procedure not because of their value in helping us understand another's outlook, but simply because of the reams of paper output" they generate (Fransella and

Bannister, 1977, p. 81). The grid, however, is only as good as the information that is placed in it, and it is important not to lose sight of the value of conversation in eliciting it in the first place (Thomas and Harri-Augstein, 1985).

> "Are you Pablo?" I asked.
> "I am not anybody," he replied amiably. "We have no names here. . . . I am a chess player. Do you wish instructions in the build-up of the personality?"
> "Yes, please."
> "Then be so kind as to place a few dozen of your pieces at my disposal."
> "My pieces?"
> "Of the pieces, into which you saw your so-called personality broken up. I can't play without pieces." [The chess player then magically transforms the pieces into characters in successive scenes where they enact their own world.] "This is the art of life," he said dreamily. "You may yourself as an artist develop the game of your life and lend it animation. You may complicate and enrich it as you please. It lies in your hands" [Hesse, 1929, pp. 213, 215].

The Potential of the Repertory Grid for Transformative Learning

The potential of repertory grids to help people to gain enhanced self-understanding is virtually unlimited and, for all practical purposes, the range of topics that might be explored using a repertory grid is restricted only by our imaginations (Thomas and Harri-Augstein, 1985). In the educational context, domains such as learning situations, instructional methods, or teaching styles suggest themselves as possible elements to be construed. But a person wishing to explore aspects of his or her own value system might choose friends, colleagues, poems, books, works of art, cities, or virtually anything else where there is a qualitative similarity in the range of elements. Even three-dimensional objects such as flower arrangements or sculpture and tactile or sense objects such as wines, cheeses, or textiles can be presented to a respondent in a triadic procedure to elicit the constructs used by the person to differentiate between them. Grids, too, need not even be written down. It might be possible to present a person with an array of, say, pieces of sculpture and ask him or her to arrange these items along an imaginary continuum, without necessarily naming or specifying the two poles of the construct (Neimeyer, 1979).

There is an almost limitless variety of ways in which grids can be used, too. At the simplest level, as I have already shown, the completion of a single repertory grid on an area of personal interest or concern can be valuable. A variation on this is to complete more than one grid on the same topic — for instance, before and after a learning experience — as a way of reflecting changes in one's construing. If more than one person is involved, a variety of alternative strategies is possible. For instance, respondents can "exchange constructs" and try to rate or rank elements on each other's criteria; the ensuing discussion gives rise to much animated debate about personal systems of meaning and attempts to clarify both the underlying distinction that was envisaged and the verbal labels chosen to identify the construct poles. An alternative approach is to invite a group of people to construe the same array of elements (for instance, a group of learners might construe a range of different threats to the environment), and then to calculate and discuss the extent of their shared construing. Identification of points of difference as well as similarity can become the basis for collective action and even social transformation. A computer program, SOCIOGRIDS, can assist in this process (Shaw, 1980, chap. 7).

One of the purposes of emancipatory education at the personal level is to reduce people's dependence on meaning perspectives that are derived and uncritically internalized from other people. This is not to imply that emancipatory education will necessarily lead people in the direction of complete autonomy and social isolation; but critical self-reflection, without the filter of someone else's perceptions, can be a truly liberating experience. Perhaps one of the most congruent applications of the Repertory Grid, therefore, is the emergence of interactive computer programs that allow respondents to explore dimensions of their construct systems privately, at leisure, and in terms that are exclusively personal (Boot and Boxer, 1979; Chambers and Grice, 1986; Jankowicz, 1986; Shaw, 1978, 1980, 1981; Shaw and Gaines, 1979; Shaw and Thomas, 1978; Stones, 1982).

The computer has the capacity to store, retrieve, and transform information impersonally, and once a respondent has overcome the initial reservation about "talking" to a computer and the fear that the data will somehow be manipulated or corrupted by the machine, it is possible to use a microcomputer as a sort of "cognitive mirror" in which one's attitudes, habits, beliefs, and understandings may be externalized and reflected upon. Shaw and Thomas (1978), for instance, produced the widely used PEGASUS program (an acronym standing for Program Elicits Grid And Sorts Using Similarities). PEGASUS interrogates the respondent, asking him or her to enter the subject of the grid (for instance, learning situations), the names of the elements to be construed (a range of different settings in which learning takes place), and presenting him or her with randomly generated triads to elicit relevant personal constructs. As the respondent enters the numerical scores for each element, the computer constantly compares these against previously entered responses and makes occasional comments, such as "Every time you say an element is exciting, you also say it is threatening. Can you think of a new element that is exciting but not threatening?" Or, alternatively, "You have given 'Lectures' and 'Reading' an identical score on every construct. Can you think of an important way in which they differ?" This sort of interactive dialogue allows the user to add new constructs or new elements and challenges the respondent to go beyond simple stereotypes and to probe the values and thoughts implicit in his or her answers.

Along with the development of the PEGASUS program, several other sets of computer programs have been devised to do everything from comparing a respondent's grid on one occasion to a previous grid on the same subject and calculating the degree of change; comparing one or more respondents' grids with those generated by others, such as subject matter experts; examining the extent to which constructs are shared by members of a group; and performing a variety of statistical manipulations intended to reveal the underlying structure of the respondent's construct system (Shaw, 1980, 1981; Slater, 1976, 1977; Thomas and Harri-Augstein, 1985).

In discussion grids, in this way, there is the danger that I might create the impression that the Repertory Grid is no more than a highly abstract, technical, sophisticated, and remote technique, which denies people's humanity and overintellectualizes their meaning perspective. To avoid giving any such impression, let me hasten to quote from its originator:

> What has already happened in our experience may seem obvious enough, now that we have been through it. But literally it is something that will never happen again. It can't, for time refuses to run around in circles. If, then, as we live our lives, we do no more than erect a row of historical markers on the spots where we have had our experiences, we shall soon find ourselves surrounded by a cemetery of monuments, and overburdened with biographical mementos.

> But . . . we can do more than point realistically to what has happened in the past; we can actually set the stage for what may happen in the future — something, perhaps in some respects, very different . . . .

> It is precisely because we may venture to look ahead only by construing never-to-be-repeated events, rather than merely recording or duplicating them, that we must continually and adventurously hold all matters open to the possibility of fresh reconstruction. No one knows yet what all the alternative constructions are, except that, if the history of human thought offers us any clue, there must still be an awful lot of them [Kelly, 1977, pp. 4–5).

The Repertory Grid is much more than a "cemetery of monuments." As Kelly says, although it may derive from and to an extent represent "what has already happened in our experience," it is also a guide to how we might potentially construe events that have not yet transpired. The repertory grid is an elegant, versatile, and powerful device that can "dissolve the boundary between cognition and affect" (Kelly, 1970b, p. 29), and can provide a window into the psyche and the soul. As such, it is an invaluable aid to identifying our taken-for-granted assumptions and assisting in critical self-reflection.

There are, however, some reservations concerning repertory grids. Although the Repertory Grid is a useful and theoretically defensible method for "tapping in to" a person's construct system, it would be unrealistic to pretend that simply completing a grid would inevitably lead to significant personal learning. It is widely recognized that "learning which involves a change in self-organization — in the perception of oneself — is threatening and tends to be resisted" (Rogers, 1969, p. 159); and, accordingly, if a person perceives that aspects of his or her personal construct system are mutually incompatible or logically indefensible, this may lead to a tendency to disown the results and to seek to discredit the methodology. As Nutting (1988, p. 171) puts it: "Denial is sometimes experienced by those undertaking the grid exercise, followed by later acceptance and finally a change in behavior. In the words of one student, the repertory grid exercises 'lay it on the line.'"

Reservations about the grid are not limited to this sort of denial or resistance, however, and it is necessary to acknowledge that over the years, both repertory grid technique and its parent theory, the psychology of personal constructs, have been brought into question on both practical and theoretical grounds. It has been suggested, for instance, that constructs need not be bipolar and that one end, the emergent pole, is all that is required for effective learning and counseling to take place; that the triadic elicitation procedure is not essential and that people can generate constructs from a smaller or greater number of elements; that respondents "create" constructs to meet the demands of the elicitation procedure; that supplied constructs may be just as good as elicited constructs in mapping at least certain aspects of people's cognitive domains; that constructs may in fact be kinked or bent in the middle rather than being strictly linear; that modifications to the technique are required to account for the inherently subjective and "fuzzy" nature of construing; that various forms of grid analysis are more appropriate than others to portraying the multidimensional nature of a personal construct system; and, perhaps most significant of all, that grids are inadequate to the task of capturing and representing the dynamic and constantly shifting nature of people's constructs.

A full consideration of these and other debates in the literature lies well outside the scope of this chapter, but the interested reader would be well advised to look at the section headed "The Crisis of Methodology" in Chapter Eight of Neimeyer (1985) and at the papers by Adams-Webber (1970), Morrison (1982), Shaw (1980), and Yorke (1978, 1983, 1985) in particular.

Conclusion

When Kelly first offered his metaphor of "person-as-scientist" or, as he put it, "man-as-scientist" (Kelly, 1955, p. 5), he was provocatively suggesting that "behavior is an experiment" (Kelly, 1970a) and that people in their everyday lives do the same things as scientists do: observe, construe relationships, articulate theories, generate hypotheses, venture predictions, experiment under controlled conditions, and take account of outcomes (Kelly, 1970b, p. 7). He writes, "Scientists are people, and, while it does not follow that all people are scientists, it is quite appropriate to ask if it is not their human character that makes scientists what they are" (Kelly, 1970b, p. 8).

If we take this proposition as a working notion and seek to understand people as indulging in a form of scientific behavior as they live out their lives, one possible corollary is to go the next step and imagine the progress of individual development as analogous to the progress of scientific development (Candy, 1982; Vander Goot, 1981). Doing this, we could think of a personal construct system as similar to a paradigm in science. We could regard the normal processes of learning as having their parallel in the "mopping-up" operation of "normal science" that Kuhn (1970) claims "engage[s] most scientists throughout their careers" (p. 24). And, perhaps most significantly, we could see a parallel between the profound, dramatic, and far-reaching changes that at the disciplinary level are called *paradigm shifts* and at the personal level *transformative learning*. In fact, this parallel is explicit in Kelly's writings when he discusses how scientists themselves transform their understandings:

> Science is often understood by students as a way of avoiding subjective judgments and getting down to the hard facts of reality. But I am suggesting that the avoidance of subjectivity is not the way to get down to hard realities. Subjective thinking is, rather, an essential step in the process the scientist must follow in grasping the nature of the universe. Let me see if I can make this point clear.

> When we know something, or think we do, we make up sentences about it, using verbs cast in the indicative mood. We talk about it in a way that appears to be objective. But science tends to make its progress by entertaining propositions which appear initially to be preposterous. Quite often this is done secretly, the scientist being careful not to let people know what he is imagining until after he has accumulated some evidence to support his position. After he has a foothold in evidence he can, of course, claim that he was simply a careful observer and that, being a careful observer, he "discovered" something. But unless he has been willing, at some point in the sequence, to open his mind to possibilities contrary to what was regarded as perfectly obvious, he would have been unable to come up with anything new [Kelly, 1964, p. 140].

In the same way that the scientist must be "willing . . . to open his mind to possibilities contrary to what was regarded as perfectly obvious," the Repertory Grid can help to emancipate people by raising to a level of conscious awareness presuppositions and premises that are rarely examined or thought through. In this way, when the grid is used in a sensitive, thoughtful, and reflective way by people interested in enhancing their self-understanding, it can be a powerful aid to transformative learning.

In the field of adult and continuing education, grids can be applied in a variety of different areas (Thomas and Harri-Augstein, 1985, pp. 344–352). For instance, learners might be asked to construe physical entities (such as geological specimens, photographs, or learning resources); people (colleagues, learners, teachers, subordinates); temporal events (learning experiences, interview situations, events in a family relationship); social entities (departments or units, political parties, roles in an institution); behaviors and activities (learning strategies, hobbies, activities for the unemployed); abstractions and evaluations (personal beliefs about learning, personal relationships, metaphors); or emotions and sensations (drug experiences, pieces of poetry, awareness-raising techniques).

Whenever and however grids are used, two things in particular must be borne in mind. The first is that the constructs elicited are highly personal statements of people's beliefs and values that have implications for action. They are not mere abstractions or items of curiosity for a researcher and must accordingly be treated with respect. The second is that emancipatory education is inevitably predicated on some vision of a "better world" (Jarvis, 1987, p. 307). Although the dominant focus of the Repertory Grid is with individuals transforming their own perspectives and worldviews, the end result is a community where reflective self-awareness is the norm, and where, both individually and collectively, people are free to become "masters of their own destiny" (Armstrong, 1977).

References

Adams-Webber, J. R. "Elicited Versus Provided Constructs in Repertory Grid Technique: A Review." *British Journal of Medical Psychology*, 1970, *43*, 349–354.

Adams-Webber, J. R. "Repertory Grid Technique." In R. J. Corsini (ed.), *Encyclopedia of Psychology*. Vol. 3. New York: Wiley-Interscience, 1984.

Armstrong, A. K. *Masters of Their Own Destiny: A Comparison of the Thought of Coady and Freire*. Occasional Papers in Continuing Education, no. 13. Vancouver: Centre for Continuing Education, University of British Columbia, 1977.

Bannister, D., and Fransella, F. *Inquiring Man: The Theory of Personal Constructs.* Harmondsworth, England: Penguin, 1971.

Bannister, D., and Mair, J. M. M. *The Evaluation of Personal Constructs.* London: Academic Press, 1968.

Beck, D. "The SYMLOG Three-Dimensional Space as a Frame of Reference for the Comparison of Individual Construct Systems." *International Journal of Small-Group Research,* 1986, *3,* 21–25.

Bell, R. "The Spatial Interpretation of Repertory Grids." In L. L. Viney (ed.), *Selected Papers of the First Australasian Conference on Personal Construct Psychology, University of Wollongong, August 1983.* Wollongong, N.S.W., Australia: University of Wollongong, 1983.

Boot, R. L., and Boxer, P. "Reflective Learning." Paper presented at the conference on advances in management education, Institute of Science and Technology, University of Manchester, England, Apr. 1979.

Candy, P. C. "Personal Constructs and Personal Paradigms: Elaboration, Modification and Transformation." *Interchange: A Journal of Education Policy,* 1982, *13* (4), 56–69.

Chambers, W. V., and Grice, J. W. "Circumgrids: A Repertory Grid Package for Personal Computers." *Behavior Research Methods, Instruments, and Computers,* 1986, *18* (5), 468.

Cliffe, M. J. "Three-Dimensional Representation of Repertory Grid Data." *British Journal of Clinical Psychology,* 1986, *25* (3), 227–229.

Fransella, F., and Bannister, D. *A Manual for Repertory Grid Technique.* London: Academic Press, 1977.

Hesse, H. *Steppenwolf.* (B. Creighton, trans.) New York: Holt, Rinehart & Winston, 1929.

Jankowicz, A. D. *Gridmap: A Manual and Software for Personal Decision-Making with Repertory Grid Techniques.* Shannon Software, 1986.

Jarvis, P. (ed.). *Twentieth Century Thinkers in Adult Education.* London: Croom-Helm, 1987.

Kelly, G. A. *The Psychology of Personal Constructs.* 2 vols. New York: Norton, 1955.

Kelly, G. A. "The Language of Hypothesis: Man's Chief Psychological Instrument." *Journal of Individual Psychology,* 1964, *20* (2), 137–152.

Kelly, G. A. "Behavior Is an Experiment." In D. Bannister (ed.), *Perspectives in Personal Construct Theory.* London: Academic Press, 1970a.

Kelly, G. A. "A Brief Introduction to Personal Construct Theory." In D. Bannister (ed.), *Perspectives in Personal Construct Theory.* London: Academic Press, 1970b.

Kelly, G. A. "The Psychology of the Unknown." In D. Bannister (ed.), *New Perspectives in Personal Construct Theory.* London: Academic Press, 1977.

Kuhn, T. S. *The Structure of Scientific Revolutions.* (2nd ed.) Chicago: University of Chicago Press, 1970.

Lakoff, G., and Johnson, M. *Metaphors We Live By.* Chicago: University of Chicago Press, 1980.

Morrison, T. R. "The Soft Underbelly of Personal Construct Theorists: A Critique." *Interchange: A Journal of Educational Policy,* 1982, *13* (4), 76–81.

Neimeyer, R. A. "The Structure and Meaningfulness of Tacit Construing." Paper presented at the Third International Congress on Personal Construct Psychology, Breukelen, Netherlands, July 1979.

Neimeyer, R. A. *The Development of Personal Construct Psychology.* Lincoln: University of Nebraska Press, 1985.

Nutting, R. "Report on Learning-to-Learn Techniques Based on PCP." In F. Fransella and L. F. Thomas (eds.), *Experimenting with Personal Construct Psychology.* London: Routledge & Kegan Paul, 1988.

Paffard, M. G. *Inglorious Wordsworths.* London: Hodder and Stoughton, 1973.

Rathod, P. "Methods for the Analysis of Repertory Grid Data." In H. C. J. Bonarius, R. Holland, and S. Rosenberg (eds.), *Personal Construct Psychology: Recent Advances in Theory and Practice.* New York: St Martin's Press, 1981.

Rogers, C. R. *Freedom to Learn: A View of What Education Might Become.* Westerville, Ohio: Merrill, 1969.

Rosenthal, R., and Jacobson, L. *Pygmalion in the Classroom:*

Teacher Expectations and Pupil's Intellectual Development. New York: Holt, Rinehart & Winston, 1968.

Shaw, M. L. G. "Interactive Computer Programmes for Eliciting Personal Models of the World." In F. Fransella (ed.), *Personal Construct Psychology — 1977: Papers Presented at the Second International Congress on Personal Construct Psychology, Oxford, July 1977.* London: Academic Press, 1978.

Shaw, M. L. G. *On Becoming a Personal Scientist: Interactive Computer Elicitation of Personal Models of the World.* London: Academic Press, 1980.

Shaw, M. L. G. (ed.). *Recent Advances in Personal Construct Technology.* London: Academic Press, 1981.

Shaw, M. L. G., and Gaines, B. R. "Externalizing the Personal World: Computer Aids to Epistemology." Paper presented to the Society for General Systems Research, London, Aug. 1979.

Shaw, M. L. G., and McKnight, D. "ARGUS: A Program to Explore Intrapersonal Personalities." *International Journal of Man-Machine Studies,* 1980, *13,* 59–68.

Shaw, M. L. G., and Thomas, L. F. "FOCUS on Education: An Interactive Computer System for the Development and Analysis of Repertory Grids." *International Journal of Man-Machine Studies,* 1978, *10,* 139–173.

Slater, P. (ed.). *The Measurement of Intrapersonal Space by Grid Technique.* Vol. 1. Chichester, England: Wiley, 1976.

Slater, P. (ed.). *The Measurement of Intrapersonal Space by Grid Technique.* Vol. 2. Chichester, England: Wiley, 1977.

Stones, M. J. "The Microgrid: A Computer Version of the Rep Grid." *Canadian Psychology,* 1982, *23,* 102–104.

Thomas, L. F., and Harri-Augstein, E. S. *Self-Organised Learning: Foundations for a Conversational Science of Psychology.* London: Routledge & Kegan Paul, 1985.

Vander Goot, M. "Paradigm Shifts: A Playful Application of Personal Construct Theory." Paper presented at the Fourth International Congress on Personal Construct Psychology, Brock University, St Catherine's, Ontario, Aug. 1981.

Yorke, D. M. "Repertory Grids in Educational Research: Some

Methodological Considerations." *British Educational Research Journal,* 1978, *4* (2), 63–74.

Yorke, D. M. "Straight or Bent? An Inquiry into Rating Scales in Repertory Grids." *British Educational Research Journal,* 1983, *9* (2), 141–151.

Yorke, D. M. "Administration Analysis and Assumptions: Some Aspects of Validity." In N. Beail (ed.), *Repertory Grid Technique and Personal Constructs: Applications in Clinical and Educational Settings.* London: Croom-Helm, 1985.

Fifteen

———*———

Metaphor Analysis: Exorcising Social Ghosts

David Deshler

What this chapter is about is how the recognition, identification, and creation of metaphors by adult learners can be the occasion for critical reflection and transformative learning. Through metaphors, we can examine and exorcize the "ghosts" of our socialization so that we can freely choose meanings out of which we want to live our lives and express them through metaphors. Although important to scholars of literature and philosophy, this chapter is *not* about the history of the use of metaphor in literature, the analysis or place of metaphor in language, or the many different types of metaphors. Our purpose is to explore the way analysis of meaning through metaphors can assist us in reflecting on our personal, popular cultural, and organizational socialization, and, through "unpacking" meaning associated with these domains, uncover frames of reference or structures of assumptions that have influenced the way we perceive, think, decide, feel, and act upon our experience. The process of metaphor analysis described in this chapter is designed to facilitate emancipatory education with educators who are committed to helping learners recognize major unexamined influences over their lives and who want to be skillful in helping learners validate freely chosen metaphoric meanings for their future.

Metaphor Defined

Many complicated distinctions regarding definitions of metaphor are advocated by semantic scholars. However, let us settle on a broad popular definition, "any comparison that cannot be taken literally" (Bartel, 1983, p. 3). Another important feature of metaphors is that they have two subjects: a primary subject and a secondary or metaphorical subject (Black, 1962). The meaning of a metaphor is found in the interaction between these two subjects. According to Black, both subjects are better regarded as systems of belief than as individual things. One interprets a metaphor by constructing a set of beliefs about the primary subject that parallels the set about the secondary subject. The two subjects interact, the secondary subject highlighting some features of the primary subject and suppressing others that are not relevant to the primary subject. In this interaction, two ideas merge. The subjects in juxtaposition are both similar and dissimilar, but it is the bundle of shared features that the communicator intends and the receiver must attribute. To interpret any metaphor, an intuitive leap to connect aspects of two distinct semantic realms is required. Metaphors are concrete images that require us to find the threads of continuity and congruence between the metaphor and the primary subject. A metaphor is a "deliberate conjunction of disparate items" (Dickey, 1968). Using parts of the given world, a correspondence is established between qualities of that given world and the primary subject under consideration.

The Focus of Analysis

Our everyday language is saturated with metaphor. Metaphors abound in advertising, in vocal music, in classic and popular literature, in business and industry, in religious writing, and in political speech. However, metaphor analysis in this chapter is limited to only those metaphors that learners select for reflection, that is, metaphors associated with learners' specific primary subjects that can be the focus of critical reflective thought. Further, metaphor analysis is limited to only those metaphors recognized in popular use by learners or created by them as expressions of their past experience or their commitment to meaning in the present or future. Metaphor content is not to be introduced by the facilitator or adult educator except as starter examples; rather, the learners are to supply their own metaphorical content for analysis in response to specific suggested primary subjects in three domains that can be the focus of critical reflection. Those primary subjects in the *personal domain* include family life-styles, parents and parenting, careers, gender and human sexuality, financial resources, sports and leisure activities, and friends or reference groups. Primary subjects in the *popular culture domain* include products, vehicles, art and architecture, popular music, and literature. Primary subjects in the *organization domain* include educational institutions, places of employment including business and industry, religious institutions, voluntary associations, government, social movements, and public policy issues. These lists are obviously limited and are not intended to include all the many possible subjects that can be the starting point or primary subject for metaphor analysis. However, they do provide a few major "power points" for identifying how the meaning of our lives has been shaped and how we might shape meanings for ourselves.

Although the personal, popular culture, and organization domains are acknowledged to be interrelated, they are conceptually divided in this process as a device to make sure that metaphor analysis is not limited to primary subjects found in only one of the domains.

This technique can be used in conjunction with almost any formal or nonformal continuing education activity when the purpose includes reflection on meaning perspectives in the personal, popular culture, or organization domains. Classroom settings, small informal groups, and one-on-one counseling sessions can provide occasions for this method. I have personally used the method in church groups, graduate courses, organization-development feedback sessions, volunteer youth worker training, and counseling with individuals. It is best used when dialogue in dyads and triads is possible and when learners understand its purpose. Otherwise, they will see it as a diversion from learning new subject matter, rather than learning from examining the way metaphors connected with the focus of their primary subject have exerted unexamined influences over them.

Metaphor Analysis as a Method

Steps for Facilitating Metaphor Analysis. Examples of facilitating metaphor analysis will follow a brief description of the eight steps that provide the basic structure for metaphor analysis. The educator asks the learners to:

1. Select a primary subject from the three domains described above (personal, popular culture, and organization domains).
2. Scan their memories associated with the primary subject and try to recognize several metaphors that were or are in use with that primary subject. If they cannot think of any easily, then ask them to create metaphors that describe their past experience with that primary subject. (A few people may have difficulty at first. Without trying to influence their memory or their selection or creation, several metaphors that others have used may be provided as examples.)
3. Select one of the metaphors they have recognized or created. Ask them to take that metaphor and unpack it by describing in detail on paper its meaning in reference to the primary subject. (If this is being done in a large group, learners could be encouraged to share their metaphors and unpacked meanings with others in groups of two or three people. When unpacking the meaning perspective of a metaphor, learners can ask themselves what characteristics of the metaphor correspond to each of the unexamined realities under consideration and what examples from memory illustrate each characteristic.)
4. Reflect on the values, beliefs, and assumptions that are embedded in the meanings of the metaphors.
5. Question the validity of each metaphor's meanings by comparing these with their own life experience, knowledge, information, and values or belief systems that confirm or deny the meanings derived from the metaphors. Ask themselves

if they *now* affirm these same assumptions, beliefs, values, or understandings.

6. Create new metaphors that express meanings that they now want to emphasize regarding the primary subject under discussion. Share those meanings with others and listen to what others are creating and expressing.

7. Consider implications for action that derive from the newly created metaphor.

8. Repeat the process with additional metaphors for the same primary subject or go on to new primary subjects in the personal, popular culture, or organization domains.

Although this process can be undertaken through internal self-directed reflection, it is best undertaken as dialogue so that we can (1) assist one another in the analysis and interpretation of meanings of unexamined influences unpacked from our metaphors; (2) collaborate in the creation of new metaphors; and (3) in some cases, take collective action out of the meaning of newly created metaphors.

Examples of Personal-Domain Metaphor Analysis. You will recall that the primary subjects in the personal domain include family life-styles, parents and parenting, careers, gender and human sexuality, financial resources, sports and leisure activities, and friends or reference groups. For example, learners can be asked to think of a metaphor that was either in use to describe their childhood family life-style or one that to them now best describes their family life-style as a child. Metaphors such as *cafeteria, nest, baseball game, circus,* or *prison* have been suggested by learners. Even types of architecture can be metaphoric. For instance, one person at a workshop stated that his family life was *Victorian farmhouse.* Activities such as *cruises* or *adventures* also can be used as metaphors. Even historical groups can be used as metaphors. Another learner at a professional conference stated that the dominant metaphor for her family life and of her present work values and personal expectations is that of a Puritan. When asked to unpack the Puritan metaphor, she referred particularly to her attitudes toward conscientious work, along with feeling guilty about play and leisure. After being encouraged to compare this Puritan metaphoric life-style with her present values, she described what, for her, were the assets and limitations of the meaning of her childhood family. When asked to name a metaphor that she would choose consciously for herself now to replace or supplement the influence of the Puritan metaphor for family life-style, she said, "Life is a beach." When encouraged to unpack this meaning, she referred to an appreciation of fun and leisure that makes her aware that she is part of the beauty, mystery, and eternal restlessness of nature. Family life-style for her, she says, should include less guilt about leisure and more vacation activities.

Another person during counseling said that her family life-style was a *safe haven*. When asked to unpack the meaning of this metaphor, she mentioned the economic severity of the Depression, the presence of danger out on the streets, and the meaning of safety among her family in the midst of scarcity. When asked how this meaning has influenced her life, she replied that it had made her cautious, fearful, and lacking adventure. In addition, her family did not entertain friends. She was asked the question "Is this consistent with what you now believe family life should be?" She described many characteristics of family life she wanted now to confirm or deny. When asked to create a metaphor for family life-style now, she replied that the metaphor *"hotel"* would best describe what she wants her family life to be now. This led to dialogue about possible decisions regarding activities that would move her toward living the meaning of family life-style as *hotel*.

This same process of recognition, reflection, comparison, creation, and decision making evoked by metaphor analysis can be undertaken in relationship to other primary subjects in the personal domain. It can help learners to become aware of distorted expectations and then assess the grounds of their beliefs and values. Creating new metaphors can move learners to take reflective action out of new integrated commitments.

Examples of Popular-Culture Metaphor Analysis. Our socialization through popular culture has been pervasive and quite often unacknowledged. Metaphors influence our social understanding, particularly through advertising, entertainment, and the mass media. Those who market products or attempt to shape cultural values through music, art, literature, and the mass media use metaphor extensively. Critical reflection on these deliberate attempts to shape culture and also on the artifacts of popular imagery expressed by working people in their neighborhoods can help us to unpack unexamined popular culture meanings, invalidate or validate them, and express our own meanings through creating new metaphors. Suggested primary subjects in the popular culture domain include products, vehicles, art and architecture, popular music, and literature.

A starter list of products that have significant cultural meaning would probably include, but would not be limited to, food and drugs, fashion, clothing, furniture, appliances, and electronics. What cultural meanings are attached to *grub, TV dinners, fast food, junk food,* and *organic food?* We drink *firewater* and *Gatorade.* The metaphors associated with alcohol and illegal drugs are quite plentiful, as are those for prescription and over-the-counter remedies advertised in magazines and on television. What does *drug culture* mean? What do the metaphors associated with it promise? Have we purchased toothpaste that provides an *invisible shield* against tooth decay? What did a *Tupperware* social relationship mean in suburbia during the 1950s? What was the meaning of *populux* fashion that was represented by Barbie and Ken dolls, and how did it change with the *hippie* fashion of the late 1960s? Can you remember the importance of the label that was attached to your jeans when you were teenagers? Listen to the metaphors associated with today's footwear and their importance to peer acceptance among today's youth. What does *fast forward, heavy metal,* or *punk* fashion mean? What meanings are embedded in *early American* furniture, *flying saucer* lamps, *Stonehenge* office furniture? Electronic products suggest a whole different range of metaphors. Through AT&T, we can *reach out and touch someone.* Computers have *memory* and *intelligence.* They *talk* to us, and they *bomb out.*

These illustrations only begin to show that bundles of cultural meanings are being communicated through metaphors associated with products. Critical reflection on metaphors attached to products can be the occasion for extrapolating the values and meanings that products had for us during specific periods of our lives and the meanings that such products have for us today. In addition, we may describe our positive or negative reactions to the cultural values that these metaphors represent. By comparing the meaning of product purchases then and now, we can become less vulnerable to manipulation from advertising and the images of popular culture associated with our purchases. We also can consider how we felt about not purchasing some of these products. In turn, we may want to assign new metaphors that embody our current value system toward these products.

Let us consider metaphors attached to automobiles. When we purchased cars in the 1960s with *fin tails* that were supposed to *rocket us* into space, or cars with names like *Mustang, Jaguar,* or *Cougar,* what meanings did ownership have for us then and what meanings does it have for us today? Needless to say, automobiles are more than transportation. Even driving a *junker* or *renting a wreck* has specific symbolic and metaphoric meaning. Some cars, we are told now, are the *heartbeat of America.* To what extent are many Americans' identities enhanced by the cars they drive? Would we have purchased these cars if manufacturers had not given them these metaphoric qualities?

Metaphors bear considerable meaning when we critically reflect on the popular culture of architecture. For instance, although surburban houses have standardized floor plans and are mass produced, they are sold with metaphors that bring the romance of *ranch, colonial, Cape Cod, early American, contemporary, Victorian, Gothic, English Tudor, Spanish, Italianate,* and *Greek revival* with respective prestige, identity, and expected life-styles attached. The meaning is not limited to specific architectural decor but extends to the meaning of living in suburbia in *little boxes* with fences and walls. Houses have *picture* windows, *split* levels, and *cathedral* ceilings. In urban areas, metaphors describe the way people decorate their flats. The culture of the homeless also has its images and metaphors. The middle class are supposed to provide *safety nets* for these poor as part of the welfare state.

Our public buildings are *cities* within cities. What metaphors can you think of for shopping malls, insurance and bank buildings, or convention centers and factories?

Consider also the metaphors in popular music on the radio or the music video channels on television along with the sales of recordings and compact discs. Each successive type of popular music brings forth a new set of metaphors. The names of performing groups are typically expressed in metaphor. The metaphors in the lyrics are often expressing the values of a counterculture.

Popular literature includes not only newspapers and novels but also magazines that appeal to specialized readers. Newspapers typically use metaphors in headlines and particularly on their sports pages. Novels as a whole are often metaphors. Magazines contain many metaphors, especially in their extensive advertisement pages.

The influence of popular culture expressed through products, vehicles, art and architecture, popular music, and literature is extensive. The validity of that influence on us can be examined through reflection on metaphors attributed to these expressions of culture. By unpacking these metaphors, we can engage in transformative learning.

For example, my son gave me a book titled *Populuxe* by Thomas Hine, an architect and design critic. It contains over 250 photographs of products that were popular during the decade 1954–1964. The *1950 suburban dream* was the metaphor that my wife and I recognized—we had bought into that life-style during the early years of our marriage. We began to unpack that metaphor by describing the objects that we purchased and their meaning to us at the time. Looking back, we could easily see the way the metaphor had been sold to us and how its meaning had had implications for our consumer budget, our gender roles, our assumptions about how to raise children, and our social aspirations in suburbia. Upon reflecting on our present values in contrast to those of the *1950 suburban dream,* we became quite aware of how that dream promoted an environmentally wasteful culture in which we had fully participated, a socially segregated society, and a materialistic consumer culture. The model homes in suburbia along with the social pressure of neighbors provided us with strong, unexamined consumer introjections. The values embedded in the metaphor and our current value system belied most of the commitments we had made that were associated with the *1950 suburban dream* metaphor. This led to a discussion about creating a metaphor for our current life-style commitment. The metaphor *tree house* came to mind. It represents a commitment to live inside of nature as much as possible. This had led to further reflection regarding our consumer practices as they affect the environment, including energy conservation, biodegradable packaging, and solid-waste reduction through recycling. This metaphor now consciously comes to mind when considering consumer choices.

The metaphors of popular culture are so subtle and pervasive that we are not likely to become aware of their power over us unless we deliberately make opportunities to reflect on our past and our present consumer commitments to popular dreams. Continuing educators have many opportunities to assist learners in reflecting on popular culture through metaphor analysis to understand their values better and to make better, conscious cultural choices.

Examples of Organization-Domain Metaphor Analysis. Organization-domain metaphor analysis is best undertaken with persons who have experience with a common organization so that dialogue can occur in the process of reflection and the creation of new metaphors. At the outset, learners should be reminded that organizations create their own cultures and that these cultures have profound effects on us. Metaphors used in organizations or metaphors attributed to these organizations can be thought of as linguistic artifacts that reflect the value systems of organization cultures. Our lives have been shaped by the primary organizations we have experienced, including educational institutions, places of employment including business and industry, religious institutions, voluntary associations, government, social movements, and public policy issues.

Let us take, for example, schools as organizations. We would begin our organizational metaphor analysis by asking learners to recall or select metaphors for their schooling in general or to recall or select metaphors for subjects associated with school, such as teachers, buildings, classrooms, assignments, grades, playgrounds, clubs, athletics, and academic achievement. After sharing these metaphors (often in pairs and in small groups), learners are encouraged to unpack them for meanings and to compare these meanings with information, values, and beliefs that they now hold. Learners are then encouraged to create new metaphors to emphasize current meanings and desired changes for schools and to consider any action that they as individuals or groups would like to take to strengthen the values and meanings embedded in the newly created metaphors.

Another example of a primary subject for school organizational analysis is the university. When selecting metaphors for a university, one woman, without hesitation, said that the dominant metaphor that described everything was *"the military."* She went on at great length to describe the effect of the university's hierarchical decision making and its philosophy of treating individuals as replaceable *manpower.* People became *target populations.* The university did *strategic planning.*

When metaphors were collected from faculty members, administrators, and secretaries at one large university, it was found that the metaphors reflected a hunger for appreciation and recognition, professional survival, a sense of community, empathy, compassion for others, active participation in governance, and academic responsibility (Deshler, 1985). These metaphors describing life in the university were most often expressed in negative form. The metaphors *slave labor, shophands, cattle, industrial labor force, plumbers,* and *homebred boys and girls* referred to ways some faculty members felt that they were treated by some administrators. Some administrators, referring to students, used metaphors such as *warm body counts.* Referring to the budget process, they had to learn the art of *robbing Peter to pay Paul* in order to cope with *retrenchment* while running *tight ships.* Students *fell through cracks, were lost in the shuffle,* or *were forced to jump through hoops.* Faculty members were *blitzed* by student course evaluations. Metaphors reflect emotional intensity about life in organizations. They can be used as catalysts to encourage critical reflection and discussion about the values that organization members want to strengthen. Learners, undertaking the method of organization metaphor analysis, should be encouraged to create new metaphors for positive organization identity that can, in turn, shape the direction and renewal of organization life. These metaphors can then be used to suggest specific action that would be consistent with new meanings and understandings in the organization.

Metaphors describing employment in the workplace should provide a rich source of material for critical reflection. The culture of the workplace can be pervasive, emotionally seductive, and persuasive due to our dependency upon the workplace for survival. The workplace can be a *machine*, a *family*, a *Monopoly game*, a *cave*, a *rat race*, a *disaster area*, or a *computer*, to name a few examples. More specific metaphors regarding management, decision making, human relations, productivity, rewards, and communication also make additional primary subjects to explore through the selection or creation of metaphors. The corporate culture of business and industry has recently been given attention by organization researchers who consider metaphorical language important to the understanding of organization behavior (Bolman and Deal, 1984).

Metaphor analysis of religious organizations is especially challenging since a large proportion of religious language is metaphoric. For example, consider these common religious metaphors: *spiritual battles, sacred covenants, divine mother, sunrise, sunshine, light, flame of sacrifice, righteousness as a mighty stream, cleansing rivers and sacred waters, washed as white as snow, born again, shepherds and lost sheep, souls in the dark of night, resurrection, kingdom of heaven, sacred meal, king of the universe, members of one body, mother church, spiritual pilgrimage,* and *the last judgment.* Scriptures of major world religions abound with metaphor, as do sermons, poetry, and hymns. Metaphors for the church, the temple, the mosque, and other holy places provide rich, complex sources of beliefs and assumptions to be validated from observations, experience, and knowledge. Most adults have not critically reflected on their socialization process in religious organizations. Metaphor analysis, as part of religious adult education, provides that opportunity. However, analysis of religious metaphors should not be limited to persons who have active relationships with religious organizations, since the existential human condition that gives rise to religion is universal, and all persons to varying degrees have been exposed to religious culture.

Government, as a primary subject for organization metaphor analysis, is especially significant, since local, state, and federal government influence on all of us as citizens has been pervasive, largely unexamined, and confused by political rhetoric abundant with metaphors. Identifying and selecting metaphors for government in general can reveal to us many of our underlying assumptions. Identifying and selecting metaphors for specific functions of government can make the task more specific and uncover inconsistencies between our overall assumptions and those that relate to specific benefits and limitations that we experience from government services, controls, and regulations. Government functions that merit consideration as primary subjects for metaphor analysis include welfare, criminal justice, defense, taxation, commerce, transportation, emigration, waste disposal, energy, natural resources, agriculture, Native American affairs, tariffs, land use, and civil rights.

Voluntary associations including clubs, youth-serving agencies, recreation groups, self-help groups, cultural societies, and health organizations also have influenced our socialization, values, beliefs, and assumptions. Metaphors that describe these types of organizations also can provide the starting point for critical reflectivity.

Social movements and public policy issues provide significant primary subjects for metaphor analysis. Those who are active in social movements often face public policy issues embedded in metaphoric political rhetoric, especially during presidential election years. Political speeches are saturated with metaphors that mislead, distort, and seduce as well as clarify and express differences over values and assumptions about what are potential consequences of government action. For example, the use of the metaphor *Star Wars,* referring to the Strategic Defense Initiative (SDI), reflects a battle over assumptions about the adequacy of technology as well as a battle over the need for arms control. The peace movement, if it is to have a following, must find ways to engage potential constituents in transformative learning over metaphors like the *evil empire*. The Beatles metaphor "We all live in a yellow submarine" is an example of the creation of a metaphor that supports the perspective of both the peace movement and the environmental movement. The *spaceship earth* metaphor is another example of a countermetaphor to the *evil empire*.

Political metaphors are cultural artifacts reflecting the values, beliefs, and assumptions of various historical periods. Most of us have forgotten the persuasive power of the *falling domino* metaphor, which referred to the belief that if the United States did not participate in the Vietnam War, all Southeast Asia would go Communist. At the time, this prevailing metaphor of pro–Vietnam War rhetoric failed to receive critical analysis on the part of many politicians and millions of citizens. The foreign policy it advocated was very costly, and history proved its view of reality wrong, so most informed citizens no longer are persuaded by the *domino* metaphor for U.S. foreign policy. The metaphor now is a cultural and linguistic artifact. Worn-out or trite metaphors become so because they no longer can bear the burden of new insights, attitudes, and knowledge. The history of politics is, to some extent, a history of dominant metaphors that prevailed until they were unpacked and invalidated. Politicians and leaders of social movements are usually in search of metaphors that can capture the loyalty of a constituency. It is incumbent upon citizens to obtain the capacity to reflect critically upon the dominant metaphors that generate support for public policy lest we become manipulated by demagogues.

Metaphor analysis is a technique that can easily be inserted into almost any formal or informal continuing education activity. The identification of metaphors provides an occasion for reflection on meaning perspectives in the personal, popular culture, or organization domains. Self-help groups, study circles, religious education, and counseling provide obvious opportunities for considering metaphors from the personal domain. Consumer education, classes in science, the humanities, and music and art, and continuing education in the professions provide many opportunities for considering metaphors from the domain of popular culture. Organization development in business, industry, human services, and government also provides opportunities to conduct metaphor analysis from the organization domain. Facilitators of social action groups, popular education, people's education, and community-based education concerned with gender, poverty, social justice, environmental conservation, and peace issues also will find metaphor analysis essential to consciousness raising and praxis.

Toward a Metaphor Analysis Model

Why analyze metaphors for transformative learning? Metaphors are important because they exert forceful, immediate, unobtrusive influence over our lives. Embler (1966, p. ix) states: "Cultural beliefs, ideas, causal assumptions are embedded in figurative language about the human condition." As a form of language, metaphors are without doubt the most powerful form of persuasive rhetoric. Embler goes on to say that these figurative forms of language, which developed out of social conditions, influence us in our socialization and shape our social behaviors. Our metaphors "use us as much as we use them" (p. iv). Metaphors exert social control. In fact, the study of metaphor until modern times was considered by academics to be a subcategory of the art of rhetoric, or persuasion. Metaphors provide perspectives that define how we construe meaning. Their power comes through the way they frame meaning and reinforce perspectives through bundling visual and other sensory characteristics attributed to a primary subject. Because of their capacity to persuade, seduce, and socialize us to their selected perspectives, metaphors deserve primary consideration in any learning process that attempts to assist us in critical reflection of our presuppositions regarding meaningful primary subjects. Through the analysis of metaphors that were in use in our personal socialization, that are present in our popular culture, and are prevalent in our organizational participation, we can examine and validate those perspectives that have had the most influence on our personal meanings.

Metaphors also are important for transformative learning because they provide us with the capacity as agents to make sense of the universe, sort out perceptions, make evaluations, create an adventure in meaning, and guide our purposes. They have the capacity to empower and emancipate as well as to seduce. Humans are the only animals to create metaphors. Creating metaphors is an act of naming the world and thus is an act of power. When we accept without critical reflection others' definitions of the world, we have not exerted our own power. Sometimes we have to emancipate ourselves from others' naming of the world before we can exert our own power to do so. Dickey (1968, p. 5) states that the use of metaphor "is not so much a way of understanding the world, but a way of creating it from its own parts." He goes on to say that in creating metaphors "we are absolutely free, in the sense of the definition of creativity as the capacity to act to laws of one's own devising. When one grasps this, the feeling of liberation and the attendant devotion to one's own vision are so exciting that the dedication of life to follow these things wherever they may lead seems a small enough endeavor, the least that one can do" (pp. 8-9). In creating metaphors, we also participate in the thrill of ingenuity and puzzlemaking. It encourages the mind to be daring and to think freely and with novelty. We can engage in our own personal science. We can conduct experiments with meaning while having control over the subjects. Metaphor analysis provides us with the means for owning our own language and personhood as well as exerting our collective power in social transformation through the creation of counterhegemony.

Transformative learning is enhanced through dialogue and active participation. Metaphors are important to that process because they require active involvement and special effort on the part of the hearer to participate in the search for meaning. Metaphors assume dialogue and discourse. Both the speaker and the listener must actively participate in selecting meanings. The speaker of a metaphor issues a concealed invitation to the hearer to make sense out of the implied meaning. Metaphors are surprisingly like jokes. You have to bring your knowledge to the joke in order to "get it." A paraphrase of a metaphor fails in the same way that an explanation of a joke fails to replace the joke. Communication is facilitated through the selection of metaphors that define by appealing to imagery that is common to both speaker and listener. If the listener is not familiar with the metaphoric subject, the meaning fails.

Metaphor analysis also can contribute to transformative learning through the historical comparison of metaphors. Sometimes metaphor analysis assists us in our own personal historical pilgrimage of meaning. At other times, the analysis of the same primary subject for different periods of history may provoke comparisons of different metaphors. *Witches' pronouncements* and *statistical probability* are metaphors from two different historical periods referring to the same primary subject, "fate." The metaphor of a *pinball machine,* used to refer to contemporary urban life, is soon replaced by the metaphor *computer game* when the marketplace makes pinball machines antiques. The next generation may not find any meaning in *pinball machine* as a metaphor for urban life. However, the two metaphors are similar in that both are games with small degrees of freedom for the players who are represented by *balls* or *icons* that get bounced around, shot at, or gobbled up during the game. The metaphor implies that the game player tries to beat the odds but has no power to change the rules or structure of the game itself.

The procedures for metaphor analysis that have been suggested in this chapter are based on the following assumptions:

- It is necessary to analyze metaphors for transformative learning because they exert influence on our socialization.
- Critical reflection on metaphors that have influenced us gives us the opportunity to become critical about possible distortions of perspectives or undue influence.
- Creating our own metaphors contributes to our emancipation not only in our pilgrimage for personal meaning but also collectively in the interpretation of popular culture and the creation of counterhegemonies against social forces that oppress, maintain social injustice, or prevent global sustainability of life.
- Metaphor analysis leads to action based on new meaning perspectives.

The popular folk singer Pete Seeger, referring to the self-destructive tendencies of human beings to misuse science and thus contribute to global pollution and nuclear war, sang the hymn "Amazing Grace," written by John Newton, who was once the captain of a slaving vessel bringing a load of slaves to the United States. Seeger said that John Newton, as a result of his reflection during the voyage, turned the slave ship around and took the slaves back to Africa. Seeger said that he liked to sing the song because it gave him hope that we could still *turn the ship around* after reflecting upon our own *slaving voyages*. Reflecting on our own and collective socialization through metaphor analysis provides us with another opportunity to work toward the exercise of our proactive wisdom as an alternative to unreflective participation in the *slave trade* of our own time.

References

Bartel, R. *Metaphors and Symbols: Forays into Language.* Urbana, Ill.: National Council of Teachers of English, 1983.

Black, M. *Models and Metaphors.* Ithaca, N.Y.: Cornell University Press, 1962.

Bolman, L. G., and Deal, T. E. *Modern Approaches to Understanding and Managing Organizations.* San Francisco: Jossey-Bass, 1984.

Deshler, D. "Metaphors and Values in Higher Education." *Academe,* 1985, *71* (6), 22–29.

Dickey, J. *Metaphor as Pure Adventure.* Washington, D.C.: Library of Congress, 1968.

Embler, W. *Metaphor and Meaning.* De Land, Fla.: Everett/Edwards, 1966.

Hine, T. *Populuxe.* New York: Knopf, 1986.

Ricoeur, P. *The Rule of Metaphor: Multi-disciplinary Studies of the Creation of Meaning in Language.* Toronto, Canada: University of Toronto Press, 1975.

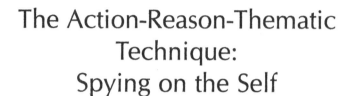

Sixteen

The Action-Reason-Thematic Technique: Spying on the Self

John Peters

Harre and Secord (1973, p. 9) proposed that an explanation of social behavior should concern "self-directed and self-monitored behavior . . . the prototype of behavior in ordinary living." Self-directed behavior is self-reflective behavior. These authors claim that an explanation of reflective behavior lies in the identification of "generative mechanisms," which "drive behavior via a self-direction according to the meaning ascribed to the situation" (p. 6). What is referred to here is the network of assumptions each person forms for himself or herself as a result of a continuous adaptation to varying situations in life. If the generative mechanisms are a function of the meaning of a situation for a person, it follows that one very direct way of assessing these meanings is by gathering first-person accounts of that person's behavior in specific situations. An analysis of such accounts ought to put us in a position to discover the structure and composition of the person's beliefs, wants, norms, and factual knowledge that comprise the person's underlying network of assumptions. The method described in this chapter, called the Action-Reason-Thematic Technique (ARTT), is a way of uncovering and describing these assumptions.

The basic structure of the technique is an interview-analyze-interview cycle. The interview component is an open-ended, probing yet structured procedure designed to identify the actions and the reasons for actions taken by a person engaged in an actual problem-solving event. The identification of actions and reasons is strictly from the problem solver's point of view and is accomplished by asking the person what they did to solve a problem and why each action step was taken. It is from this account that assumptions guiding the interviewee's problem-solving experiences can be identified and described. Uncovered by the analysis component of the technique, these assumptions become the focus of critically reflective learning.

ARTT was developed in a research project on adult problem solving and learning in the early 1980s (Peters, 1983; Lazzara, 1985). It has since been used in the following ways:

1. As a research tool, it is used to extract information from one or more persons, with the intention of using the data to understand adult behavior in problem situations.
2. As a personal tool, Interviewers can use ARTT to extract information primarily for their own use. An example of this would be its use by a supervisor as part of an employee's performance appraisal.
3. Interviewers can use ARTT to give interviewees the benefit of the interviewers' interpretation of information provided by the interviewees. A therapist might do this, in an effort to help the client better understand himself or herself.
4. The ARTT process itself can be a learning experience, in the sense that interviewees benefit from accounting for their problem-solving activities. In this use of the technique, interviewees stand to gain from the process of reflecting upon their experiences and possibly from reflecting upon the process of reflecting, and so on.

This chapter is concerned with the third and especially the fourth use of the technique. It will discuss how the person whose actions and reasons are explored can benefit from the educator's use of the technique.

A Phenomenological Framework

The roots of ARTT are in phenomenology. Phenomenalists use the phenomenological method to describe the nature of an individual's life-world structure in the form of meaning. They also assume that the structure of meaning between the person and his or her world is initially "prereflective" and that prereflective experiences are brought to the level of reflective awareness through the description of relevant experiences (Valle and King, 1978). A phenomenological description captures the meaning of central themes across situations in the individual's life. Themes are recurring ideas, actions, and ways of thinking that characterize the individual's relationship with his or her world.

The phenomenalist who seeks to identify themes and understand an individual's characteristic ways of living through certain relationships and situations obtains descriptions directly from that individual. These descriptions are then "reduced" to their essential psychological meaning (Fischer, 1978). The interview is a favorite tool used by the phenomenalist to gather such information about individual experiences. This choice is grounded in the high value placed on verbal accounts of personal experiences. According to Kvale (1983, p. 161), "The only way to know what certain events mean to persons is to have them express something about them, even if only in terms of language. . . . The data are those aspects of the situation that are consciously thematized by the subject . . . meanings are those aspects of events that the subject consciously thematizes."

Even though the focus may be on the person's thinking in particular situations, it is not the person's interpretation of their own thinking process that is described; rather, it is the phenomenalist's interpretation of the person's account of actual experiences that is finally reported. Moreover, the phenomenalist "seeks to describe specific situations and action sequences in the world of the interviewee. It is not general opinions which are investigated" (Fisher, 1978, p. 176).

The phenomenological interview is thus guided by technical rules of description, amounting to what Valle and King (1978, p. 7) call "description through disciplined reflection." The interview itself exists on a continuum between description and interpretation, according to Kvale (1983). On the description end of the continuum, interviewees describe their life-worlds as precisely as possible, in terms of specific situations, action sequences, and feelings. During this time, the interviewers remain sensitive to and critically reflective of their own presuppositions and hypotheses regarding the interview topic and the status of interviewees relative to the topic. As Kvale (p. 253) puts it, "In order to understand the subject's intentional world of lived experience, one must first arrive at it by a suspension, or bracketing, of all presumptive constructs about it." Further along the continuum, the experience of accounting for actions and feelings may result in the interviewees' discovery of new features of their own thinking and acting. Interviewees can therefore expect some degree of change through reflection, simply as a result of the interview experience itself. At the other end of the continuum, interviewers condense and interpret the meanings expressed by the interviewees. Interviewers may draw upon their own theory, common sense, formal or informal logic, as well as the social context for interpretation of interviewees' meanings. This use of the "existential baseline" helps the interviewer to make a psychologically relevant interpretation of the interviewee's meaning structure.

In summary, phenomenalists who use the interview as a means of obtaining descriptions of individual life-worlds strive to make *explicit* the *implicit* dialectic of the person and situation. The description of the interviewee's meaning structure is then subjected to interpretation by both participants in the interview. In order to provide a description of his or her experiences, the interviewee must at some level reflect upon those experiences. To the extent that these experiences and related meaning structures are "prereflective," the act of reflection is a step toward better understanding of these experiences and meaning structures. In the meantime, the interviewer draws in increasingly broader contexts to aid in his or her interpretation of the description. This reflected subjectivity is a specific mode of understanding and one that requires reflective thinking by both the interviewees and the interviewer. ARTT is a particular application of this process; the remainder of this chapter describes and illustrates how it works.

The Technique of Interviewing and Analysis

As discussed earlier, the structure of ARTT is an interview-analyze-interview cycle. Its focus is on the actions taken by interviewees to solve some problem in their lives and on the reasons they give for taking these actions. Accounts of actions and reasons serve as a basis for identifying assumptions that guide the interviewees' problem-solving efforts.

The ARTT interview must take place in a climate of mutual trust and respect. It is especially important that the interviewer convey genuine interest in what interviewees have to say, that the event be centered on the interviewees' own descriptions of their problems and solutions, and that the interviewer ask questions in a way that demonstrates such a focus. Otherwise, the interview procedure itself will be invalidated.

ARTT involves five steps. Specific guidelines for these steps are presented later in this chapter. The steps are:

1. Identification of the interviewee's problem
2. Establishment of the time frame of the problem
3. Identification and description of specific actions taken to solve the problem
4. Identification and description of reasons for each action taken
5. Reduction of actions and reasons to argument themes

The first step is to identify the interviewee's problem, as defined by the interviewee. Few problems in daily life are "well defined," wherein the problem and solution are fixed. The nature of a particular "ill-defined" problem is actually determined by the solver, not by some objective, outside reality. Therefore, it is imperative that the interviewer accept the interviewee's own definition and begin a discussion of the steps taken toward solution of the problem based on that definition.

There are at least two limitations on this step, however. One is that the problem must be directly related to the life of the interviewee, and the interviewee must have actually attempted to solve the problem by taking one or more specific actions toward reaching a solution. This would usually eliminate from consideration such "problems" as a concern for world peace, an anxiety about our failing national economy, and the like. An example of a problem that fits the technique is a person's difficulty in dealing with the demands of a particular job and of his or her family and the person's attempts to reconcile the competing demands. This is also the kind of problem that could fit the theme of this book, insofar as the person also may have related difficulties, dealing with conflicting beliefs about his or her role as a parent and spouse vis-à-vis a role in the workplace. A second limitation is that the technique works best in cases in which the problem is "fresh" on the minds of the problem solvers and least well when they are asked to recall events earlier in their lives. In practice, interviewees have experienced some difficulty in recalling actions and reasoning that occurred over a year prior to the interview; most successful interviews concern problem-solving actions that are less than six months old.

The second step establishes the beginning and end of the problem and its solution. All problems have a beginning and end, or at least a perceived end. The objective of ARTT is to uncover the actions taken to solve the problem and to identify the reasoning that supported the actions. This step is a memory aid for the interviewee who, when asked about past actions, may otherwise begin at almost any point in the history of the problem-solving event and omit important details. The beginning-end schema is thus an organizing framework for the interview and helps ensure that a complete picture of the problem-solving process is obtained.

Actions are the focus of the third step. One action at a time is identified by the basic question "What did you do?" This procedure is followed in the identification of each subsequent action (that is, "What did you do next?", "And then what did you do?"), until all actions are described. If the end of a problem in a particular case has not yet occurred, the initial interview ends with the most recent action taken by the problem solver. The third step is based on the assumption that the problem solver is in the best position to determine what should count as a solution to the problem, even as the situations and situational meanings for the interviewee necessarily change as the end of the problem approaches. The challenge of ARTT is to represent the actions as closely as possible to the way in which the interviewee sees them. One action at a time is identified, and each is described as it actually happened. For example, an action might be described as "I talked to a specialist about my problem," but not as "I generally talk to people who are specialists in the field."

In the fourth step, the interviewee gives an account of the actions identified in the third step. Here the interviewer probes for elements of the learner's reasoning structure that underlie his or her actions. Questions are of the "why" type, in search of the reasons for actions as perceived by the interviewee. As in the first three steps, the interviewee is expected to respond in the way he or she intends to be understood. Thus, the interviewee does not sit in judgment of the worthiness of the interviewee's responses, but instead assumes that the way the interviewee conceptualizes and communicates the actions and a justification for the actions represents the meaning that these elements of the problem have for the interviewee.

The final step of the technique is a thematic reduction. As the interviewer notes actions and reasons described by the interviewee, he or she searches the "text" of the interview for themes. The important thematic level of a problem-solving event is that of the reasoned explanations a person gives for what they are doing or did while solving a problem. At this level, such themes consist of the *underlying assumptions* that guide behavior. They are expressed in the form of arguments for taking particular actions.

The ideas intended by the interviewee are not always stated in a manner that is self-explanatory. People use speech not only to communicate but also to formulate their ideas as they go along. Because they do not generally speak in well-formed sentences, it is often difficult to decide exactly where one idea starts and another stops in a spoken conversation. The analyst is therefore faced with the problem of identifying the interpretation intended by the interviewee.

The intended interpretation of an utterance is derived from a contextual analysis of the surface structure of the interviewee's problem-solving account. This means that the interviewer must use the general information contained in the account (the context) to decide what a person means by some statement when that statement is not altogether clear or when it has more than one possible interpretation. If a statement does not literally convey the intended idea, it is paraphrased by the interviewer so that it does. However, any paraphrase necessarily alters the wording of an utterance and must be supportable by evidence of the interviewee's intentions derived from the overall context. Most of the changes that are made in such statements will be structural, such as (1) conjunctive statements are divided into separate statements; (2) incomplete ideas are completed on the basis of contextual references; (3) false starts are eliminated; and (4) embedded sentences are extracted from their context and paraphrased as separate statements. At this level of description, a statement that is a paraphrase is just as valid as a literal transcription.

When interviewees are asked to provide an account of actions and reasons, they are likely to express that account in terms of such natural language categories as beliefs, wants, norms, intentions, and facts. In other words, they will speak in terms of what they believe, what they want, the norms they follow, and what they intend to do, and will cite factual information as well (Von Wright, 1963; Coulter, 1980; Dennett, 1983). These elements of ordinary language are examined for natural and logical connections that form a practical argument or justification for some action (Lazzara, 1985).

Practical arguments have various threads (such as reasons and intentions) dispersed throughout the fabric of the interview in which they are presented. The interviewer's task is to bring these threads together without violating the interviewee's intended meaning. The procedure involves identifying both verbally expressed reasons and hidden premises, which are unspoken reasons for actions. In any analysis of arguments, it is necessary to make explicit any part that has been left unstated. After the interview is completely analyzed, the process can be repeated, using the hidden premises as probes for further and more detailed reasoning about background assumptions.

Whereas at one level the ordinary language elements give

us a picture of the *content* of reasons associated with an action, it is helpful to also examine the *structure* of the argument. There should be one diagrammed argument for each action step recorded in the interviewer's notes. While there is no upper limit to the number of reasons contained in each argument, as a general rule there must be more than one reason supporting an action. As discussed earlier, reasons may be made explicit by the interviewee or they may be hidden, requiring the interviewer to deduce what the reasons must be in order to make the argument complete. Essentially, the interviewer will add reasons to the interviewee's argument only if he or she believes that the interviewee would have intended the reasons to be taken for granted and if the added premises strengthen the reasoning.

The Questioning Technique. While each of the components of ARTT is distinguishable in terms of steps or stages, in actual practice the components are inseparable. After an initial set of questions, subsequent questions asked by the interviewer hinge on his or her analysis of interviewee answers to previous questions. The questioning technique itself therefore is the key to an accurate analysis of the interviewee's assumptions. This involves both the type of questions asked and the ways in which they are asked. The following are ten guidelines for asking ARTT questions:

1.   There are two broad types of questions to be asked of the interviewee: What did you do? and Why did you do it? Admittedly, these questions may sound as if they are the language of the police interrogator, but variations in wording are usually employed by the interviewer to soften the impact. For example, instead of asking, "Why did you do (the action)," the interviewer may instead say, "Please tell me more about that (action)." The point is, the "what" question is needed to identify the problem solver's actions and the "why" question is needed to uncover reasons.

2.   Questions should be open-ended to allow the interviewee room to describe his or her experiences and reasoning. It is safe to say that the more the interviewee is allowed

to talk (and the less the interviewer talks), the greater will be the amount of information available for analysis.

3. The interviewer should be prepared to ask probing questions, in order to reach as deeply into the structure of the interviewee's reasoning as possible. Questions that require a simple yes or no answer rarely accomplish this objective.

4. Only one question at a time should be asked by the interviewer. Multiple questions, or questions not well thought out, can confuse the interviewee and may result in partial answers. A useful practice is for the interviewer to pause before asking each question, reflect on the answers up to that point, and frame the next question in the context of the overall interview results.

5. Leading questions should be avoided. It is the interviewee's own description that is needed, not a predetermined answer provided by the interviewer.

6. Answers given by the interviewee should be mirrored by the interviewer. This not only enhances the interviewer's understanding but also indicates interest to the interviewee.

7. The interviewer should postpone judgment of interviewees' answers and let the interviewees continue to explain the problem and its solution without interruption.

8. The interview questions should be stated in a conversational tone, thus avoiding the appearance of an interrogation.

9. The interviewer should avoid giving opinions, instructions, or other forms of help until a complete analysis of the assumptions is made.

10. The focus of the questions should always be on the interviewee and his or her problem. Interviewer-centered questions only reflect the thinking of the interviewer.

An Illustration of the Method. To illustrate how ARTT is used, the following excerpts are taken from an actual interview conducted by the author. The person being interviewed is a mother, age thirty-three, who is unable to read and write and whose nine-year-old child suffers from a vision problem. The beginning of the interview established the mother's problem as "I thought my child had a problem seeing, and I didn't know what to do about it." The mother's name is Lillie and the daughter's name is Tora.

Interviewer: What did you first do when you thought Tora had a problem seeing?

Lillie: I talked with Tora about it.

Interviewer: Tell me more about that.

Lillie: Well, I watch Tora when she does things, and I knew that it wasn't right that she was holding things she reads close to her face. Tora would say, "Look, mama, I can't see" when she held her book away from her face.

Interviewer: What did you do then?

Lillie: I talked to her father about it.

Interviewer: Why did you talk to her father, Lillie?

Lillie: I ask my husband about things I don't understand. I wanted to know what he thought was wrong.

Interviewer: What did you do next?

Lillie: I decided that Tora didn't need glasses.

Interviewer: Can you tell me why you decided that?

Lillie: Well, her father said she didn't need glasses . . .

Interviewer: And . . . ?

Lillie: Well, I thought maybe she was pretending. Sometimes children pretend, you know, they pretend they need something when they really don't. I thought she wanted glasses because some of her friends have them. She talked about wanting glasses and false teeth when she was real little.

Interviewer: Anything else?

Lillie: No . . . except I wanted her to be well.

Interviewer: What did you do then, Lillie?

Lillie: I talked with Tora's teacher about her schoolwork. She wasn't doing well in school, and her teacher asked to see me about that. Tora's teacher said she wasn't doing enough homework. I was worried that it might be her eyes. Tora asked me to ask her teacher to move her closer to the front. She said she couldn't see things on the board.

Interviewer: I see, you talked with Tora's teacher because (paraphrase of reasons above). What did you do next?

Lillie: I talked with my sister.

Interviewer: Tell me about that.

Lillie: I talk with my sister about things. Besides, one of her daughters has bad eyes so she ought to know what is going on. She told me earlier something was wrong with Tora's eyes. I thought she would know what to do.

Interviewer: And then?

Lillie: Well, I talked with a nurse about Tora.

Interviewer: A nurse . . . ?

Lillie: I was at the doctor's office with Tora. She had the flu. The nurse knew Tora and me. She knew Tora wasn't acting right.

Interviewer: Please go on.

Lillie: Well, then I took her to an eye doctor.

Interviewer: Tell me about why you did that.

Lillie: The nurse told me to do that. So did the doctor who saw her for the flu. I still wanted to know if something was really wrong with her eyes.

Interviewer: The nurse told you to take Tora to an eye doctor. You wanted to know what was really wrong. What did you do next?

Lillie: I became very upset about what the eye doctor said and ran out of his office crying.

Interviewer: Why?

Lillie: The doctor told me Tora was almost blind in her right eye. If only I had her checked earlier, she wouldn't have gone blind. I felt awful. Really terrible.

Interviewer: What happened after that, Lillie?

Lillie: Well, I made an appointment to get Tora glasses.

The above is only the first portion of the actual interview. The remainder of the interview includes a discussion of Lillie's attempt to buy affordable glasses, obtain new frames, and so on. A follow-up interview is also planned, but first an analysis of the first interview is necessary.

Analysis of the Interview. In his notes, the interviewer should have a list of Lillie's actions taken in her problem situation. From the above interview, it can be assumed that Lillie meant to describe the following actions:

1.   I talked with Tora.
2.   I talked with Tora's father.
3.   I decided Tora didn't need glasses.
4.   I talked with Tora's teacher.
5.   I talked with my sister.
6.   I talked with a nurse.
7.   I took Tora to an eye doctor.
8.   I became very upset.
9.   I made an appointment to get Tora glasses.

These actions were described in response to "what" questions asked by the interviewer. But the interviewer also asked "why" questions. Lillie responded by describing her reasons for each action. The interview had systematically asked for reasons following each of Lillie's action descriptions, so Lillie's statements of reasons are easily identifiable from notes organized around each action step. For example, the statements that describe reasons associated with action two are the following:

1. I ask my husband about things I don't understand.
2. I wanted to know what he thought was wrong (with Tora's eyes).

Reasons associated with action five are the following:

1. I (make it a practice to) talk to my sister about things (that concern me).
2. One of her daughters has (a vision problem).
3. She ought to know what is going on (in Tora's case).
4. She told me earlier that something was wrong with Tora's eyes.
5. I thought she would know what to do (about solving Tora's vision problem).

Note that some phrases or words are placed in parentheses in the above list of reasons. These are additions that, in the opinion of the analyst, are needed to make intended ideas clear or complete. They are also hypothetical in nature, so that they must be validated by subsequent questions; that is, did the interviewee really mean to say those things? More critical, however, are hidden premises or apparent omissions of entire reasons. This feature of the analysis will be taken up later.

The result of this part of the analysis is a better understanding of the nature of Lillie's assumptions. She has cited at least two norms that she used in taking actions, both of which involved her relationship with significant others in her life (her husband and her sister). Lillie also expressed beliefs that these two persons would know what to do about her problem. Believing that, and given the actual experience of her sister, it must have seemed reasonable to Lillie that she could receive some help from her sister. Interestingly, Lillie also must have believed that she could receive help from her husband, although she did not make that belief explicit. The next stage of the analysis deals with this.

To identify themes in Lillie's argument, we look for actions and reason statements that together form connections that are practically logical. We look for arguments cited by Lillie in support of specific actions and in the context of all other actions and supporting arguments. For example, an examination of action three reveals the peculiar decision that "Tora didn't need glasses." In the context of the previous two actions and the statement of her problem, Lillie's decision seems inconsistent and unreasonable. However, when the supporting arguments are considered, the action itself becomes "reasonable." But what about these arguments? How can they support such a decision? We will now examine the specifics of the arguments.

The (action three) decision was supported by the claims "Her father said she didn't need glasses" and "I thought she was pretending." A diagram of this argument reveals the following:

Action 3: I decided Tora didn't need glasses.

Reason 1:   Her father said she didn't need glasses.
Reason 2:   I thought she was pretending.
Reason 2a: Children sometimes   Tora had pretended
             pretend they need   to need glasses (when
             something when   younger).
             they don't.

             She might have   Her friends have
             wanted glasses   glasses.
             because her friends
             have them.

             When children   Tora would change
             change their minds   her mind when her
             under threat of   father said he would
             unpleasant conse-   take her to the eye
             quences, they are   doctor.
             probably pretending.

So, Lillie had several reasons to suspect Tora was not suffering from a vision problem, but were they convincing? Apparently, Lillie's doubts surfaced some time later, when the teacher pointed out Tora's problems with her school assignments. And what about the statement that "her father said she didn't need glasses"? No description of that reason was offered by Lillie, yet it was one of two initially offered for her decision and would therefore seem worthy of further discussion. The need to clarify this reason and to verify others led to a second interview with Lillie.

When asked about her discussion with her husband, Lillie said this: "Her father said she didn't need glasses because her eyes weren't crossed." Now the argument presented above must be changed, to reflect the addition of another reason — a reason that changes the meaning of the argument altogether. Diagrammed, the argument now reads:

Action 3: I decided Tora didn't need glasses.

Reason 1: Her father said she didn't need glasses because her eyes weren't crossed.

Tora's eyes weren't crossed.

(Reason 2 and supportive reasons remain the same.)

Perfectly reasonable? It is easy to see that the premise stated by Lillie's husband was false, since not all eye problems are associated with crossed eyes; but if that premise were acceptable, the argument would certainly seem reasonable enough. However, the critical factor here is Lillie's apparent dependency on her husband "about things I don't understand." Her dependency seems to extend beyond those matters strictly a function of her inability to read. Moreover, she seems dependent on others in a more general sense, as evidenced by her discussion with her sister, the teacher, the nurse, and, later, the doctor who treated Tora's vision problem. Lillie was doubtful of the validity of her own observations, as she deferred to significant others in her life.

It should be pointed out here that this stage of analysis is approaching the interviewer's end of the descriptive continuum cited by Kvale and discussed earlier in this chapter. That is, the description increasingly is stated in the interviewer's language and informed by an interpretation of the context in which it occurs. Hence, terms like "dependency" and "significant others" enter the description. It is assumed, of course, that these thematic items are firmly anchored in the interviewee's own life-world.

Asked in the second interview about her propensity to "ask my husband," "usually discuss things with my sister," and "do what the doctor says to do," Lillie offered the following reasons:

1. "If someone is not very smart, it pays to ask someone who is. I don't have an education."
2. "Someone in the family has to be in charge. I think my husband is [in charge] in this family."
3. "My sister was always the smart one when we were growing up. I've always looked up to her."
4. "Doctors are supposed to know. Don't they?"

Lillie's assumptions and characterization of these significant people in her life suggest some more basic assumptions about authority and the protector roles that others play in her life. In the case of Tora's vision problems, she relied on some sense of authority that she assigned to these people, even to the point of rejecting the meaning of her own direct experience with the problem. These assumptions and perhaps others lie at a deeper structure in Lillie's thinking and seem worthy of further discussion. Unfortunately, the interviews with Lillie ended here, and no further follow-up was conducted. However, the results of the interviews were shared with Lillie, and some discussion of her beliefs and premises took place. The need for further action in a case like this is discussed later in the chapter.

The value of ARTT lies at the level of the recognition and understanding of assumptions that guide actions. The depth of understanding depends on how deeply the probes are sent into the interviewee's meaning structure. While ARTT does uncover premises that support intentional actions relative to a specific problem such as Lillie's, it only indirectly implicates deeper, underlying assumptions that may have been formed over a lifetime of experiences. However, in keeping with Mezirow's claim (in Chapter One) that "reflection on one's own premises can lead to transformative learning," a first step toward understanding any deeper assumptions made by an adult is to reveal the beliefs, wants, norms, and factual information associated with particular problem-solving actions. As noted earlier, the interview itself requires the interviewee to reflect upon premises that supported specific actions.

Problems exist at different levels, and an ill-defined problem is what the problem solver says it is. In Lillie's case, one interpretation of the problem would be that her daughter needed glasses; moreover, in this sense, the problem was solved when glasses were obtained. Another perspective would be that Lillie had a problem with her husband's role in the decision; once she circumvented his immediate influence, the problem was solved. But, consistent with the theme of this book, a useful, third perspective would be that Lillie is trapped in dependent, structured, and passive roles of parent and spouse, and that her problem is accordingly deeply rooted in her past experiences. On this view, the interview event would seem only to "intellectualize" the problem, and it probably would not go away by that means alone. No claim is made that understanding, per se, would solve such a problem, but as noted above, it is a necessary first step toward transformative learning.

In Lillie's case, a logical next step would be for a helping agent to explore with Lillie how she came to form her assumptions and how she might view them in a different light. They would explore further the reasons for and consequences of Lillie's assumptions about her roles as a parent and spouse and about how she learned to play those roles. Lillie, of course, would need to go beyond understanding and "mental modification" of her assumptions and take some action consistent with changes in her thinking. Further reflection and action and reflection, as discussed by Mezirow in Chapter One, would help ensure authentic change in her meaning perspective. Lillie's problem may be rooted in both epistemic and psychological distortions, but if Mezirow's assumptions about the power of emancipatory education are correct, and if this problem is indeed solvable, Lillie might be helped to overcome these distortions with the help of a skilled adult counselor. Insofar as ARTT is concerned, the counselor would probably benefit from its use in the initial contact with Lillie and, for that matter, from the application of its active listening features during subsequent interactions with Lillie.

Applying the Method

The illustration used in this chapter has been used in more than a dozen workshops involving social workers, parent educators, and adult educators who work in a variety of organizations. Someone familiar with the case (usually the workshop leader) plays the role of Lillie, and a workshop participant plays the role of social worker or another "helping agent" who could reasonably expect to encounter a situation like Lillie's. In every workshop experience to date, the helping agent who "interviewed" Lillie was unable to complete the interview along the lines discussed in this chapter. In almost all cases, the interviewer, upon learning of the child's plight, insisted that Lillie immediately "take Tora to a doctor." Many went so far as to offer transportation and other forms of direct assistance to ensure that Lillie did exactly what they demanded of her. No one went beyond the immediate impression of a medical problem and the appearance of the mother's inability or unwillingness to properly handle the problem. No one went on to uncover the particular relationship that Lillie had with her husband nor did anyone uncover any other information about Lillie's characteristic way of involving others in her decisions. The interviewers' "existential baseline" was limited to their trained responses to similar situations, and they did not make themselves aware of other elements of the problem context, simply because they did not ask for them.

The approach taken by workshop participants clearly illustrates the mode of understanding and educative approach taken by the majority of adult educators. This approach evinces a technical interest in knowing and is one that usually results in some form of direct instruction in what to do in particular circumstances. Lillie's response to such an interest is also typical, illustrating the power of implicit background assumptions to block "logical" recourse in the face of an "obvious problem." It seems reasonable to argue that ARTT can be used in situations calling for a "slowing down" of the oral communication between an educator and a learner, and that the qualities of listening implicit in the technique are potentially useful to any educator who would base help on the implicit or explicit needs of a learner.

The technique places constraints on the educator as listener, such that he or she must remain without presuppositions in the early stages of a communication and remain open to the speaker's point of view. While this constraint would seem to be a commonsense notion and unworthy of mention, actual experiences with educators who have attempted operating within it refute this assumption. It is one of the most difficult elements of communication to learn, yet it is one of the most vital to effective dialogue with others. The step-by-step ARTT was designed as a subjectively rigorous way of ensuring that facilitators of critical thinking include such essential elements of communication in their interactions with adult learners.

There is a sense in which ARTT is an implicit instruction in the process of critical thinking. The focus of ARTT is on the interviewee's account of actual experiences and related reasoning. Minimally, any purposive action or decision requires some level of reflection upon one's own capacity to carry out actions, some assessment of the role of others in the actions, and some reflection about goals, plans, and possible outcomes. When a person is asked to recall and account for intentional actions taken toward some goal, he or she must reflect upon those actions and reasons at some level. It is entirely possible that the interview situation presents the first opportunity the interviewee has had to reflect on a particular set of experiences. In any event, when the adult articulates, or "languages," the experience, he or she engages in reflective thinking and therefore learns.

Conclusion

As noted at the beginning of this chapter, ARTT has multiple uses, including both research applications and applications in educational settings. In keeping with the focus of this book, a "practical" application was illustrated here, one that should relate to the concerns of counselors, tutors, and others who would facilitate learning by undereducated adults. ARTT should be of use to educators who want to help learners to recognize and better understand their own assumptions that influence what and why they learn. It also should be of interest to educators who choose to organize learning experiences that focus on learners' assumptions and not directly on their behaviors, even though behavioral changes may be the educational goal. From this starting point, applications of ARTT may be appropriate in such diverse adult education settings as training in business and professional organizations, adult basic and functional education, parent education by social workers and other helping professionals, job counseling, personal counseling, marriage counseling, reentry education programs, and other settings where transformative learning for the individual adult learner might occur.

References

Coulter, J. *The Social Construction of Mind.* Totowa, N.J.: Rowman and Littlefield, 1979.

Dennett, D. *Intentional Systems in Cognitive Ethology: The "Panglossian" Paradigm Defended.* New York: Cambridge University Press, 1983.

Fischer, W. F. "An Empirical-Phenomenological Investigation of Being-Anxious: An Example of the Meanings of Being-Emotional." In R. S. Valle and M. King (eds.), *Existential-Phenomenological Alternatives for Psychology.* New York: Oxford University Press, 1978.

Harre, R., and Secord, P. F. *The Explanation of Social Behavior.* Oxford, England: Blackwell, 1973.

Kvale, S. "The Qualitative Research Interview: A Phenomenological and a Hermeneutical Mode of Understanding." *Journal of Phenomenological Psychology,* 1983, *14* (1), 171–196.

Lazzara, P. J. "Foundations for a Method for Knowledge Analysis." Unpublished doctoral dissertation, Department of Psychology, University of Tennessee, 1985.

Peters, J. *Problem Solving by Adults in Nonformal Settings: A Research Report.* Grant Number NIE-6-79-0180. Washington, D.C.: National Institute of Education, 1983.

Valle, R. S., and King, M. "An Introduction to Existential-Phenomenological Thought in Psychology." In R. S. Valle and M. King (eds), *Existential-Phenomenological Alternatives for Psychology*. New York: Oxford University Press, 1978.

Von Wright, G. H. *Norm and Action*. New York: Humanities Press, 1963.

Seventeen

Conceptual Mapping: Drawing Charts of the Mind

David Deshler

The purpose of this chapter is to describe conceptual mapping as a practical technique that can be used to reflect critically upon our concepts, their relationship to each other, and our underlying assumptions and values about matters under consideration. This technique can be applied to a broad range of subject matter to assist in making explicit to ourselves as learners our taken-for-granted frameworks, propositions, and structures of assumptions that influence the way we perceive, feel, and act upon our experience. Concept maps provide a summary of what we say we believe, think, feel, or value at a particular point in time. Our critical reflections on these maps reveal new pathways we may take to connect meanings among concepts in propositions. Also revealed to us may be omissions and missing links, inconsistencies, false assumptions, and previously unrecognized relationships. In addition, concept maps can provide the basis for negotiating shared meaning and social communicative validation through dialogue.

Conceptual mapping can be used in classroom settings as well as in nonformal education settings, including counseling. Chalkboard, newsprint, or paper and pencil are the only supplies necessary.

Origins of Conceptual Mapping

The application of conceptual mapping to transformative learning and emancipatory adult education is an extension of the creative work of Novak and Gowin (1984), who have introduced the method to elementary, secondary, and higher education as a means to increase what they call "meaningful learning." More than a dozen master's and doctoral theses at Cornell University have described the technique for curriculum development and instruction in elementary schools (Novak and Symington, 1982; Rowell, 1978; Stewart, Van Kirk and Rowell, 1979); in secondary schools (Kinigstein, 1981; Melby-Robb, 1982; Novak, Gowin, and Johansen, 1983); and in higher education (Cardemone, 1975; Minemier, 1983). Deshler and Sock (1985) used conceptual mapping to review, compare, and synthesize documents drawn from the international literature on popular participation in community development.

Conceptual Mapping as a Method

Conceptual Mapping Defined. A concept map is a schematic device for representing sets of concept meanings embedded in a framework of propositions (Novak and Gowin, 1984, p. 15). It is one type of representational depiction. Flow charts or organizational charts with their administrative units or positions are representational depictions but are not really concept maps because their key words usually are not concepts with meanings. Semantic networks and predictability trees likewise are not concept maps. Concept maps are holistic, spatial, hierarchically constructed representations of the relationships among essential concepts. Any subject matter or discipline can be organized according to a conceptual hierarchy in which minor elements of knowledge are associated with or subsumed under larger, more general concepts. Hence, there is no limit to the degree of inclusiveness, breadth, or detail that can be incorporated when organizing the component parts. Whereas road maps help us to check our assumptions regarding where we are now and where we want to go, concept maps help us check our assumptions regarding relationships among our ideas, problems with our thinking, and what we think will happen.

Concept maps can be read as compound sentences that visually depict the branching of subordinate concepts and operations. Thus, complex multiple relationships can be displayed. Written or spoken concepts usually come to us in the form of linear propositions. Conceptual thinking, on the other hand, is more hierarchical or holographic (Novak and Gowin, 1984, p. 53). Concept maps assist us in transforming linear material into more holistic visual imagery and therefore help us to evaluate, synthesize, and perceive in new ways.

The process of creating concept maps, critically reflecting upon them, and reconstructing and validating them can contribute to transformative learning and emancipatory education.

Examples of Simple Concept Maps. Two examples will provide an introduction to the process. The first is an overly simple concept map from my own personal, day-to-day frustrating and dissonant experience. The second example is a bit more complex, illustrating an important decision about future retirement of concern to an adult learner.

The first example concerns my bird feeder, which also attracts squirrels and thereby provokes my annoyance and anger. A simple concept map of this experience is shown in Figure 17.1.

This simple map reveals my major assumptions as well as my frustration in dealing with squirrels. My initial response was to consider a technological solution. However, technological solutions are all too often quickly embraced without addressing our underlying linguistic, esthetic, social, and moral assumptions, particularly about relationships between us as humans and our place within nature. Setting technological solutions aside, I began reflecting about why this bothered me so much. Although I think of myself as a person who appreciates nature, I asked myself, with some embarrassment, why I excluded squirrels from my appreciation of nature. My initial answer was that the squirrels were eating out of a bird feeder. I then noticed that it was I who had named the seed container a *bird feeder* and

Figure 17.1. A Concept Map of Enjoyment and Anger for a Bird-Watcher.

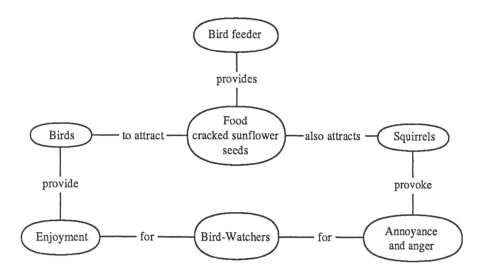

that from the perspective of both birds and squirrels the container was a place for food that was attractive to both. My simple concept map revealed that I held a cognitive contradiction between my appreciation for nature and my appreciation for squirrels. This insight led me to rename the seed container to include my being both a bird- and a squirrel-watcher. Figure 17.2 provides an alternative way of viewing the event.

After renaming the food container, my anger toward squirrels began to subside as I began enjoying my new identity as a squirrel-watcher as well as a bird-watcher. I noticed many enjoyable characteristics about squirrels that I had previously overlooked. Squirrel feeding did not discourage birds since they alternated in their feeding. By reflecting on my experience and renaming the world, I now am experiencing the world of nature differently. My transformative learning concerning bird-squirrel feeders did result in some changed behavior toward squirrels. I no longer shouted and threw things at them. A praxis, the joining of thought and action, had occurred. In addition, my relationship to nature as a whole had improved somewhat.

Now let us consider an example drawn from a preretirement

Figure 17.2. A Concept Map of Enjoyment
for a Bird-Watcher and a Squirrel-Watcher.

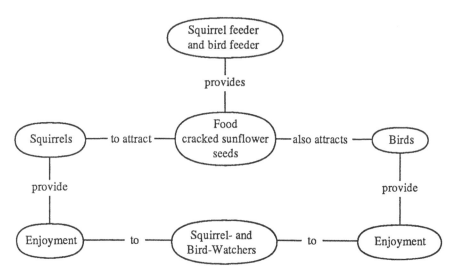

course for educators. One important issue facing one participant was where to retire. After talking out his concern, he made
a list of concepts and from these drew an initial concept map
upon which he critically reflected. His initial list of concepts included weather, income, cost of housing, freedom and independence, recreation including tennis and fishing, and rural
life-style. His initial concept map is shown in Figure 17.3.

While drawing the map, other concepts emerged and additional values were acknowledged. A new list of concepts was
drawn up to include income, freedom and independence, friendship, family ties, weather, service opportunities, geography of
relatives, church membership, transportation, rural life-style,
costs of housing, nearness to grandchildren, and health concerns.
The second concept map (Figure 17.4.) depicts a shift in values.
The first map contained popular cultural assumptions of retirement that emphasized the images of recreational leisure and the
importance of climate. The second map acknowledged values
of friendship, family ties, health concerns, and service, all of
which expanded the criteria for choice and raised new criteria
for what would constitute a wise decision.

Figure 17.3. Concept Map on Choice of Retirement Location.

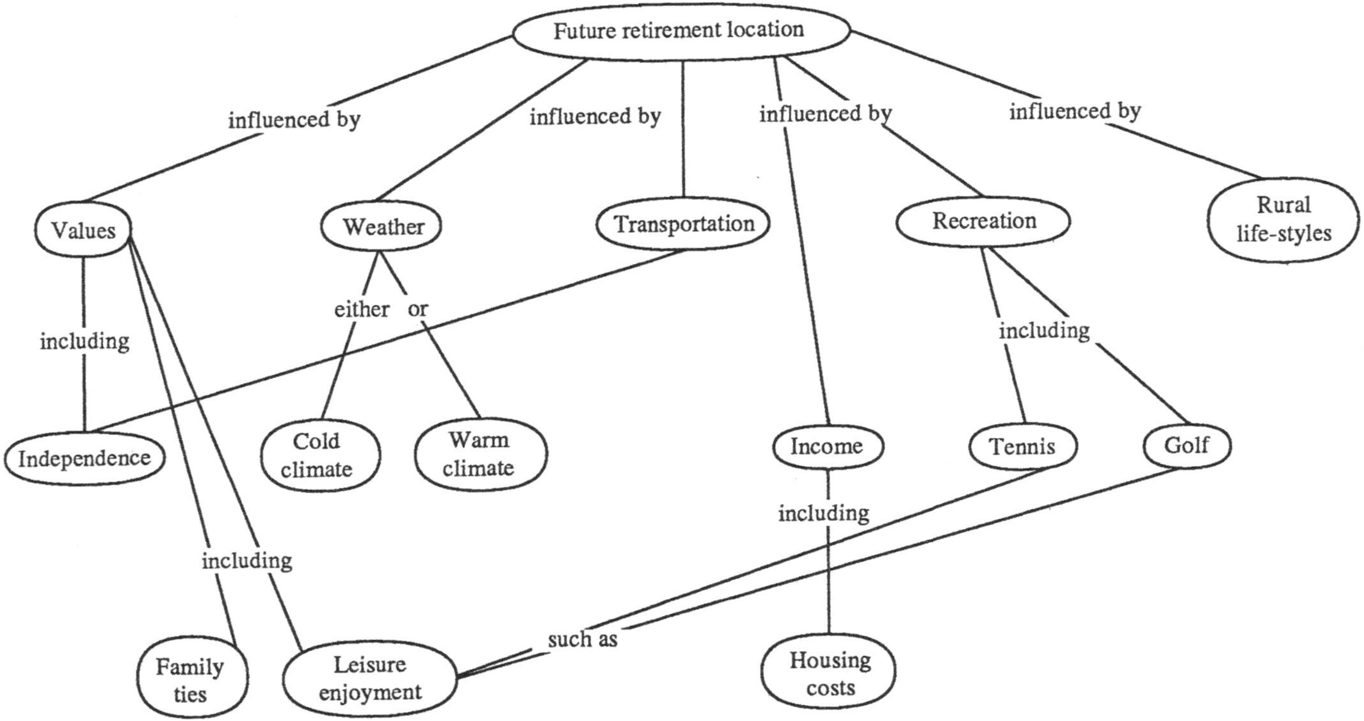

Figure 17.4. Reconstructed Concept Map on Choice of Retirement Location.

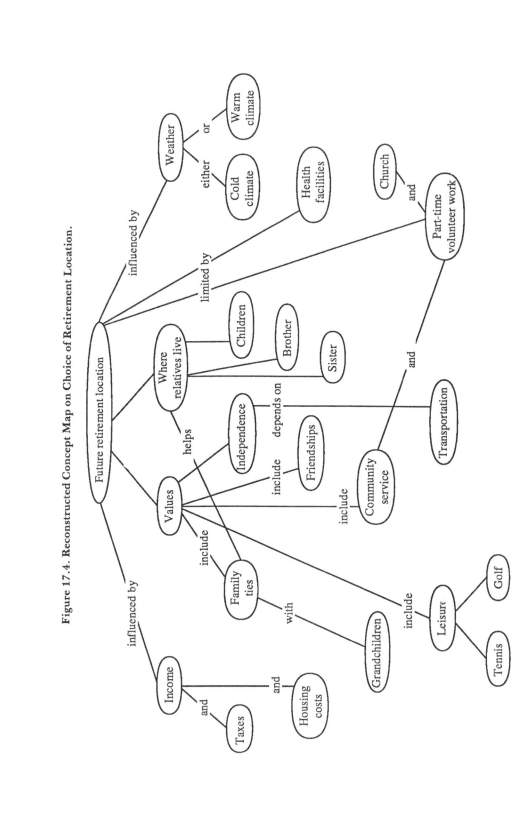

Creating Initial Concept Maps. Although we as adult educators can didactically dispense to our learners concept maps created by us or others, their use in this way will not produce transformative learning. What is recommended here is the use of the maps to help learners tap in to their own existing cognitive structures, or what Ausubel, Novak, and Hanesian (1978) call "prior knowledge." These conceptual starting places are the bases for critical reflective thinking. For learning to be transformative, a change in the cognitive meaning of experience must occur. That change can occur when learners critically reflect on their existing cognitive meanings of experience.

The purpose of an initial concept map is to confront ourselves with what the current structure of our knowledge is about the subject at hand. It is not, at this point, an attempt to be critical about what we know, but to describe our ideas and assumptions as they are — with all their inconsistencies, omissions, and gaps in understanding. Conducting a critique comes later. The process of mapping begins with explicating what we currently think about our experience or knowledge for a specific concern or decision.

To introduce conceptual mapping, educators should begin with content of concern to learners: (1) concerns with which learners are personally struggling; (2) concerns from popular culture that have considerable but unrecognized influence on us; (3) concerns drawn from organizational or group life; or (4) concerns that are part of public decision making and about which we can engage in social action. Educators also can introduce current dilemmas that will provoke a need to reflect critically through the creation of concept maps. Transformative learning is most likely to occur through concept mapping when the focus is on concerns that we as learners recognize as:

- *Important,* so that learning central to our future situations, environmental conditions, life-style, or ethical behavior can occur
- *Puzzling, or cognitively dissonant,* so that learning can result in new synthesis of knowledge, ideas, or feelings
- *Constraining,* so that learning can result in the expansion and emancipation of choice.

After the focus of concern has been identified, the procedures for creating initial concept maps include the following steps:

- Write or talk out the substance of concern.
- Understand the difference between concepts, names, and linking words.
- Make lists of the key concepts.
- Select the one concept that is most general.
- Arrange the other concepts underneath that general concept.
- Draw linking lines between concepts and write linking words.
- Consider the maps as temporary, pliable, in-process, and never finished.

The examples of the squirrel and bird feeder and of the choice of retirement location both showed evidence of transformative learning resulting from critical reflection on the initial maps, which leads to a more specific explanation of the steps for critical reflection.

Critical Reflection on Concept Maps. After a map has been constructed, we have the opportunity to reflect critically on its adequacy. Reflective operations that facilitate transformative learning from our own initial concept maps include the following:

- View the map as a whole to discover whether the most general concepts are at the top and not obscured among subordinate concepts.
- Observe whether concepts are subsumed to our satisfaction; whether we have confused what goes under what.
- Scan for duplication.
- Ask ourselves what is missing on the map that relates two or more concepts or should be added to make better sense of the experience or subject.
- Consider the possibility that our map contains contradictions that we can identify and remedy.
- Scan for inadequate linkages and new cross ties.
- Ask ourselves whether our values and feelings are adequately represented.

- Ask ourselves whether or not the meanings of the concepts on our maps are consistent with other beliefs, assumptions, values, and knowledge that we hold to be true.
- Ask ourselves what assumptions underlie the relationships depicted and, if needed, make adjustments.
- Consider the possibility that we are holding false conclusions or misconceptions.
- Ask ourselves if there are other possibilities of relationships other than those we have described.
- See what happens when we push some concepts together or separate them.
- Consider whether assumptions about cause and effect are more than one way, that is, reciprocal (for example: roads wear out cars, and cars wear out roads).
- Consider substitution of alternative terms or insertion of new concepts and see what happens to the overall meaning.

The task of the educator during this phase is to assist learners in raising these questions and making lists of concepts and of their implications and connections, which can then be included in reconstructed concept maps.

Reconstruction of Concept Maps. The redrawing of maps is recommended because it not only makes the maps more esthetically pleasing but also reduces flaws and increases clarity. In some cases, it may be desirable to show the direction of relationships through the use of arrows. The reconstructed maps can then incorporate neatness, clarity, and — above all — through critical reflection, the solving of conceptual gaps, contradictions, inconsistencies, circular thinking, unattached concepts, and invalid conclusions. It is through reflection on the initial maps and the reconstruction of them that transformative learning occurs. While reconstructing the map, new insights and relationships often are recognized. Careful attention to the words selected to link concepts will improve the quality of thinking about the nature of relationships. To aid this process, we can use a chalkboard and experiment with different spatial arrangements, or we can take the key concepts and transfer them to small rectangular pieces of paper and rearrange them on the top of a table. Sometimes important changes occur when we reconstruct our concept maps around a different general concept.

Validation of Concept Maps. Sometimes we can validate our concept maps as self-directed learners through critical reflection by asking ourselves some of the questions listed above as part of the process of reconstructing our maps. However, many times we find ourselves trapped in circular thinking, unable to unveil our false consciousness, faulty assumptions, or misconceptions on our own. We need to test the validity of our concept maps through dialogue and through comparisons with the thinking and concept maps of others. Dialogue forces us to make explicit to others what seems clear to us but may, at the same time, be flawed. It is the process by which we can validate our thinking through comparisons with what others think. Challenges to our misconceptions are more likely to occur in dialogue than when we are by ourselves. Dialogue also makes possible the creation of mutually negotiated shared meanings. The following suggestions apply to a dialogical use of concept maps:

- Explain our concept maps orally and notice whether we change our minds while explaining.
- Listen actively to others explain their concept maps and enter into dialogue about relationships we do not understand.
- Compare with other learners' concept maps on similar subjects to stimulate alternative ways of interpreting or changing our maps.
- Ask others to study our maps and have a dialogue with us, soliciting their feedback and alternative interpretations.
- Come back to the map after a short lapse of time (several hours or days) and view it afresh to see if we have changed toward it.
- Use the questions suggested for reconstruction of the maps during dialogue.
- Reconstruct maps, taking into consideration the validation that dialogue usually brings.

Let us now consider an example of the potential validation of concept maps. Suppose that a group of women were to engage in creating concept maps explicating their experiences in returning to higher education for a degree. After making their initial concept maps, reflecting upon them, and then reconstructing them, they engage in dialogue with each other over their reconstructed maps. Figures 17.5 and 17.6 provide examples of maps that can be used as the basis for a dialogue of validation. Because of limitations, the examples have been reduced and simplified. Nevertheless, we can note the potential dialogical opportunity that a dozen or more such maps could produce, as the women confirm what they have in common and what is unique about the way they conceptualize their experiences. Following their dialogue, they again reconstruct their maps to take into account the transformations they have experienced.

Shared Social Communicative Validation. Collective or corporate concept maps also can be constructed by groups of people seeking to engage in transformative organizational or group learning. The same steps for the creation of individual concept maps are used. However, instead of individuals creating their own maps, the group or organization works toward consensus in the conceptualization of its own group or organizational life history and culture. Aditjondro (1988) has described the process and the product of conceptual mapping with twelve staff persons of an environmental development organization in Southeast Asia. Staff members participated actively in the process, even though some of the work was done by mail and tape recording because of scattered work locations. The organization focused on creating a concept map of the agency's espoused community development theory. Dialogue and reflection over a four-month period resulted in the creation of a map that has contributed not only to shared, socially validated assumptions but to greater clarity in the organization's philosophy, values, and ethics.

Assumptions for Conceptual Mapping

Conceptual Mapping as Explicative Discourse. Conceptual mapping can be viewed as an instrument of what Habermas (1984, 1987) calls explicative discourse, a mode of communicative action directed toward language itself. Although conceptual

Figure 17.5. A's Concept Map on Reentry to Higher Education.

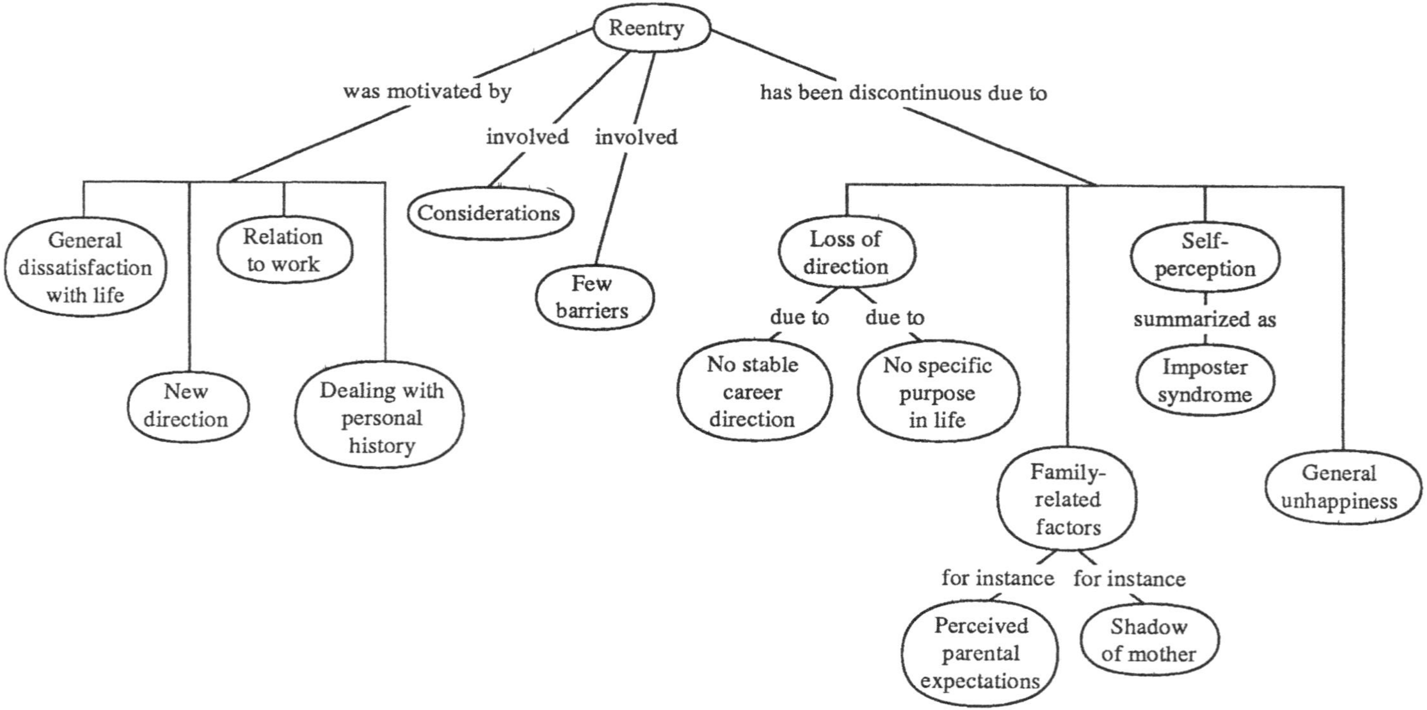

Figure 17.6. B's Concept Map on Reentry to Higher Education.

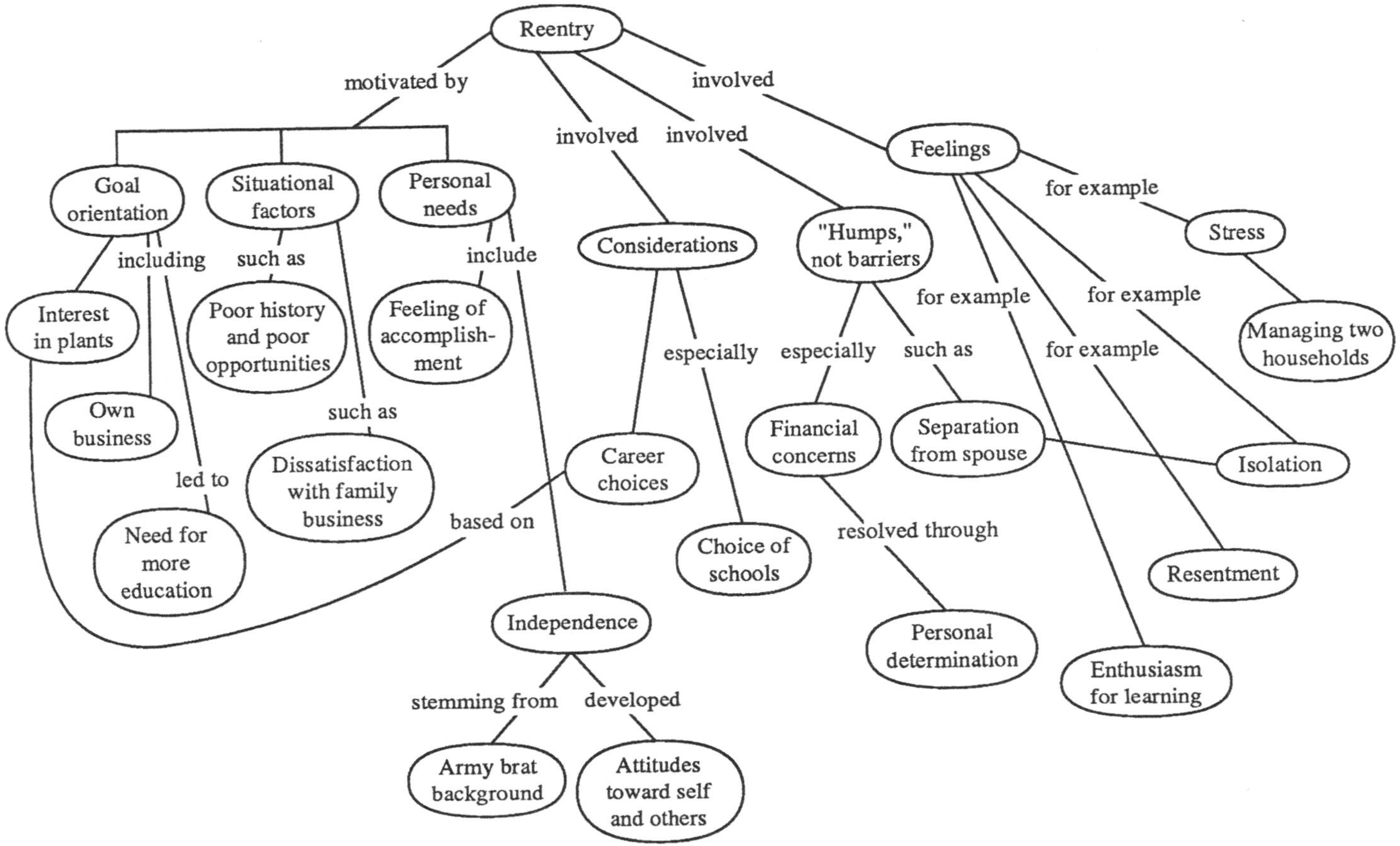

mapping can be a tool of instrumental rationality, particularly when used as a descriptive device for teaching or research, its use as advocated in this chapter is in the service of explicating propositional knowledge assertions that attempt to unify the objective world and the intersubjectivity of our life-world within that of society. Habermas (1987) holds that communicative understanding — essential to providing the counterbalance to our current overdependence upon rational, purposive discourse — includes our moral-interpretive, esthetic-expressive, and explicative capabilities to unshackle ourselves from self-incurred immaturity. The explicative capability refers to our paying direct attention to language itself in an attempt to clarify the validity claims offered to us through our external sphere (natural events and facts), our social sphere (rightness of the rules governing relations between social actors), and our inner sphere (personal desires, wishes, and needs); and to reflect on, question, and reconstruct the language that we use to constitute reality. In this chapter, the focus is on the explication and critique of concepts that are central to language. In Chapter Fifteen, on metaphor analysis, the focus also is on explicative discourse. Concepts, metaphors, myths, symbols, language structure, rules of thought, all can provide the focus for explicative discourse.

Procedural Principles. The procedures for creating concept maps incorporate three major principles: hierarchical structure, progressive differentiation, and integrative reconciliation. According to Ausubel, Novak, and Hanesian (1978), meaningful learning or knowledge construction is enhanced when learners recognize that (1) new information is related to and subsumable under more general or more inclusive concepts (*principle of hierarchical structure*); (2) new concepts are continuously acquired and differentiated (*principle of progressive differentiation*); and (3) new relationships between related sets of concepts or propositions are linked (*principle of integrative reconciliation*). With these three principles in mind, creators of concept maps first discern or nominate a list of essential concepts that are associated with the event, object, or phenomenon under consideration. Concepts on this list are then ranked, with those most inclusive at the top of the list. Using this ranked list as a guide, a concept map is then constructed along a vertical axis according to the breadth or degree of inclusiveness, the broadest concept being at the top hierarchical structure. The organization of the map then unfolds as clusters of concepts are grouped and differentiated (progressive differentiation). Concepts are usually circled or placed in boxes. Lines are then drawn between concepts (integrative reconciliation) with words placed on the lines to indicate the nature of the relationship (caused by, supported by, affected by, reciprocally related to, can be, cannot be, leads to, depends on, examples of, such as, and so on). All three of the principles are used when learners reflect critically on their initial concept maps and then engage in reconstructing them. The principle of integrative reconciliation is the primary principle used during the reflection and validation stage, when the major propositions of the concept map are critiqued, first by ourselves and then through shared dialogue with others. Concept maps often embody assumptions and value judgments that can be validated through appeals to facts and value tests. Claims of fact can be validated through appeals to evidence, others' experience, research findings, or respected authority. Metcalf (1971) has suggested the following reconciliation tests for validating our value claims: (1) the appeal to *new cases* (Are the value claims consistent when applied to other cases to which they are logically relevant?); (2) the appeal to *subsumption* (Are the value claims consistent with a more general value principle that we accept?); (3) the appeal to a *role exchange* (Do the value claims hold if you trade places with persons who are in different roles?); and (4) the appeal to *universal consequences* (Could we accept the value claim if everyone in similar circumstances held it or acted upon it?).

Applications of Conceptual Mapping. Concept maps have been used as instructional tools and as means to assess the cognitive needs of learners. Concept maps can be extrapolated by researchers from curriculum sources, documents, research reports, purpose statements, case studies, legislation, philosophical essays, novels, poems, personal documents, and qualitative interview transcripts (any data source that is rich in concepts and coherent meaning). Creating maps from these sources enables researchers to accomplish a synthesis of concepts that contributes to making judgments through comparative analysis of the various maps that have been created. These comparisons can reveal similarities and differences, omissions, alternative assumptions, conflicting claims, and competing paradigms. Composite maps using the most common concepts can be created. These have usefulness in summarizing the conceptual "state of the art" for the population of documents under consideration. However, what is being recommended in this chapter is the use of conceptual maps produced by learners for the purpose of transformative learning through (1) reflection on possible lack of clarity or misconceptions; (2) reconstruction of concept relationships; and (3) the validation of assumptions through critical thought and dialogue with others.

References

Aditjondro, G. J. "Irian Jaya — Rural Community Development Foundation." Unpublished organizational material, Cornell University, 1988.

Ausubel, D. P., Novak, J. D., and Hanesian, H. *Educational Psychology: A Cognitive View.* (2nd ed.) New York: Holt, Rinehart & Winston, 1978.

Cardemone, P. F. "Concept Mapping: A Technique of Analyzing a Discipline and Its Use in the Curriculum and Instruction in a Portion of a College Level Mathematics Skills Course." Unpublished master's thesis, Cornell University, 1975.

Deshler, D, and Sock, D. "Community Development Participation: A Concept Review of the International Literature." Paper presented at the International League for Social Commitment in Adult Education, Ljingskile, Sweden, 1985.

Habermas, J. *The Theory of Communicative Action.* Vol. 1. (T. McCarthy, trans.) Boston: Beacon Press, 1984.

Habermas, J. *The Theory of Communicative Action.* Vol. 2. (T. McCarthy, trans.) Boston: Beacon Press, 1987.

Kinigstein, J. B. "A Conceptual Approach to Planning an Environmental Education Curriculum." Unpublished master's thesis, Cornell University, 1981.

Melby-Robb, S. J. "An Exploration of the Uses of Concept Mapping with Science Students Labeled Low Achievers." Unpublished master's thesis, Cornell University, 1982.

Metcalf, L. (ed.). *Values Education: Rationale, Strategies, and Procedures.* Washington, D.C.: National Council for the Social Studies, 1971.

Minemier, L. "Concept Mapping: An Educational Tool and Its Use in a College Level Mathematics Skills Course." Unpublished master's thesis, Cornell University, 1983.

Novak, J. D., and Gowin, D. B. *Learning How to Learn.* New York: Cambridge University Press, 1984.

Novak, J. D., Gowin, D. B., and Johansen, G. T. "The Use of Concept Mapping and Knowledge Vee Mapping with Junior High School Science Students." *Science Education,* 1983, *67* (5), 625–645.

Novak, J. D., and Symington, D. "Concept Mapping for Curriculum Development." *Victoria Institute for Educational Research Bulletin,* 1982, *48,* 3–11.

Rowell, R. M. "Concept Mapping: Evaluation of Children's Science Concepts Following Audio-Tutorial Instruction." Unpublished doctoral dissertation, Cornell University, 1978.

Stewart, J., Van Kirk, J., and Rowell, R. "Concept Maps: A Tool for Use in Biology Teaching." *American Biology Teacher,* 1979, *41* (3), 171–175.

Eighteen

Conclusion: Toward Transformative Learning and Emancipatory Education

Jack Mezirow

If critical self-reflection is central to the nature of adult learning in modern cultures (Bowers, 1984), other characteristics of adult learning are clearly discernible to guide educators. Because critical reflection is a process of testing the justification or validity of taken-for-granted premises, the role of dialogue becomes salient. It is through dialogue that we attempt to understand—to learn—what is valid in the assertions made by others and attempt to achieve consensual validation for our own assertions.

Consequently, education for adults may be understood as centrally involved in creating and facilitating dialogic communities to enable learners to engage in rational discourse and action. From this vantage point, adult education becomes the process of assisting those who are fulfilling adult roles to understand the meaning of their experience by participating more fully and freely in rational discourse to validate expressed ideas and to take action upon the resulting insights. Rationality means assessing the validity of expressed ideas through reflective and critically reflective discourse. Rational thought and action are the cardinal goals of adult education.

However, reflective discourse and its resulting insight alone do not make for transformative learning. Acting upon these emancipatory insights, a praxis, is also necessary. Here, we enter into the conative dimension of transformative learning. The learner must have the will to act upon his or her new convictions. Making a decision to act or not to act is itself an action, but a decision not to act must not be based on a rationalization or self-deception.

As explained in Chapter One, praxis can pertain to action resulting from critical reflection regarding premises that distort the way we interpret experience. These distortions may be epistemic, sociocultural, or psychological in nature. Sociocultural ideologies are often institutionalized and require social action in some form to change them, as Hart in Chapter Three and Heaney and Horton in Chapter Four suggest. However, the form that such social action takes clearly depends upon context. It can be direct, collective political action in the community (Heaney and Horton); it can be movement from a consciousness-raising group to effect change in family, interpersonal, and career relationships (Hart) or, through action learning, to effect change in the workplace (Marsick, Chapter Two). Social action can mean resisting from within organizations or within the political and economic system to change oppressive practices, norms, and structures. As Heaney and Horton observe, even within hegemonic institutions can be found "open spaces" wherein one can play upon the system's embedded contradictions and align oneself with movements for change.

The nature of the action required to deal with epistemic distortions (Roth, Chapter Six; Kitchener and King, Chapter Eight) and psychic distortions (Gould, Chapter Seven) is likely to be different but will also involve changes in social behavior—in ways of judging and dealing with others and their ideas as a consequence of the new insights gained. In these cases, social action will probably not be collective in the sense of collective political action, since what are transformed are meaning perspectives or habits of expectation. What is enhanced through transformative learning is what Habermas has called "communicative competence," defined by Bowers (1984) as "the individual's ability to negotiate meanings and purposes instead of passively accepting the social realities defined by others" (p. 2).

Of course, these three areas of distortion are interrelated.

Not taking collective social action may be a function of either or both epistemic or psychic hang-ups. Such hang-ups are often the direct or indirect result of sociocultural distortions. The learning process involving sociocultural distortions may or may not lead to social transformation; it can stall or fail. A learner may not be able to act because he or she lacks the emotional stamina to do so, because of misdirection caused by epistemic distortions or tunnel vision, because of situational factors or inopportune timing, or because of lack of information or skills required to take collective action.

It is important to remember that there are different kinds of learning transformations and different kinds of social action. Learners who share a transformative learning experience can effect social change in a variety of ways, by affiliating with like-minded persons who are devoted to change within an organization, by changing interpersonal relationships, or by collective political action.

In the transformation of sociocultural distortions, it is an artificial dichotomy to present as competing polarities learning that occurs in relatively risk-free settings in which individual empowerment is a goal and learning that occurs within the struggle of collective action to change institutional structures or practices. These are different moments in the process of transformation and involve different kinds of transformative learning experiences. Learners come into workshops, courses, or other secure settings at different junctures within their learning process. This process may be precipitated by or fostered in an educational environment, but it is incomplete without the learner taking action and subsequently reflectively assessing the action, possibly in a secure educational setting, before taking further action. The transformative learning process does not end in the classroom. Praxis is a requisite condition of transformative learning. It is not inherently a question of personal development versus social development or aborting social action by emphasizing individual development, although this too frequently happens. There is a major difference between learning to negotiate meanings and purposes, realizing values for oneself, and validating one's personal beliefs through reflective dialogue and the task of learning to successfully overcome oppressing power in one's external world through social action. Both are components in transformative learning involving distortions in sociocultural presuppositions; individual and social development interact dialectically. As Hart writes in Chapter Three, "Relevant questions originate in the world of individual experience, but neither individual experience nor society as a whole can be understood by remaining within its scope."

Because of professional or institutional constraints, an educator may be unable to provide emancipatory education across the entire process of transformational learning involving sociocultural distortions. However, every adult educator has a responsibility for fostering critical self-reflection and helping learners plan to take action. Ideally, learners will meet as a group over an extended period of time to assess action steps taken throughout the transformative learning process. Social action educators who work to foster collective social action will be able to accompany learners into the collective struggle to change the system through action learning (Pedler, 1985) and participative or action research (Argyris, Putnam, and Smith, 1985). Still other adult educators who administer programs for the public have a professional obligation to foster transformative learning by offering challenging programs designed to encourage learners to critically examine internalized social norms and cultural codes in courses, workshops, and conferences dealing with public issues, consumer education, understanding the media, self-understanding, and with political controversy involving dissent and alternative meaning perspectives. They also have an obligation to select instructors skilled in transformative learning approaches or to teach them skills through faculty development programs. These obligations are grounded in the nature of adult learning and what educators must do to skillfully facilitate it.

Transformative learning for emancipatory education is the business of all adult educators. We know that we must respond to initial learner interests and self-defined needs, but we do so with the intent to move the learner to an awareness of the *reasons* for these needs and how the learners' meaning perspectives may have limited the way they customarily perceive, think, feel, and act in defining and attempting to satisfy their needs. This is what being a professional adult educator means, a quite different role from that of a group process technician or a subject matter specialist. Of course, these educators may also be educators of adults, and many professional adult educators may also be subject matter or group process specialists.

It should be clear, then, that every adult educator has a central responsibility for fostering critical reflection and transformative learning. Transformative learning includes learners making informed decisions of how and when to act upon their new perspectives. We have an obligation to assist them to learn how to take the action found necessary by the new perspective. As we have seen, this may involve new ways of understanding and using knowledge or new ways of understanding oneself and acting in interpersonal relationships. It may also involve taking individual social action (writing your congressman, financially supporting a cause, changing your vote, changing relationships within a family or a workplace) or group political action.

While not every adult educator is able to leave the classroom, workshop, or other educational setting to accompany every learner who decides to join a group to take collective political action, we do all have a professional obligation to become skilled in the strategies and tactics of social action education and to share this expertise where we can with those with whom we have a sense of solidarity. We do share a rich body of experience and a proud professional legacy from community development and social action education. These are areas of specialization within adult education, and we have much to learn from social action educators like Heaney and Horton, who devote themselves to working within oppressed groups throughout the entire process of transformation, including taking collective political action themselves.

The authors in this volume raise many other provocative points. Kitchener and King remind us that ill-defined problems require a different learning dynamic and that learners who must overcome distortions in epistemic assumptions are limited by age and education. Reflective judgment may be found in mature adults but is much less likely to be encountered in children, youth, or even young adults. It appears that there is great variation in meaning perspective among adults (and among children as well) who are at different stages of development. Recognition of these individual differences is crucial for educators. Each stage in the development of reflective judgment (or any other dimension of adult development — moral, ethical, ego, and others) involves a developmentally advanced and progressively more functional meaning perspective. The axiom in adult education to "begin where the learner is" takes on a whole new dimension from these findings. The learners may be functioning at several different developmental stages. Educators may have to group learners at one stage with those at the next-higher so that they may better learn from each other. This diversity in ways of knowing also complicates but does not preclude learners arriving at a validating consensus through critical discourse.

It is not that some adults are inherently incapable of thinking abstractly, becoming critically reflective, or making reflective judgments. It is only that they have not learned how to think in these ways. Many are socialized in subcultures — including those of schools — that place little or no value on such ways of knowing. The dependency role of the child inherent in the primary socialization process militates against critical reflection. While it may be true that children have to learn the rules before they can become critically reflective of them, Bowers (1984) argues that schooling can be reconceptualized to foster communicative competence. Reclaiming this stunted function of critical reflection for transformative learning is what emancipatory adult education is all about.

Many of the contributors to this book have noted the threat to psychological security that transformative learning imposes: the challenge to comfortably established beliefs and values — including those that may be central to self-concept — and the changes in long-established and cherished relationships. Recurring themes included role modeling; uncritical group support and solidarity; helping learners to link self-insights with internalized social norms and to understand that others share their dilemma; and providing a secure environment that fosters the trust necessary for critical self-examination and the expression of feelings. In these and other ways, adult educators provide the needed emotional support to help learners over the difficult terrain of transformative learning.

Implicit throughout this book is the finding that theory building may derive from encounter and challenge in either the context of social action or in an educational setting with significant learning experiences as points of departure. When, in response to a dilemma, analysis of incidents from different perspectives leads to critical assessment, this leads to interpretation, which, in turn, leads to explanation and the formulation of theory, which is subsequently modified by reflection of feedback on action undertaken. Comparative approaches to perspective analysis now familiar to the reader include understanding how we have learned and the consequences of our espoused theories; contextualizing problems; opening oneself to alternative perspectives; validating beliefs through rational dialogue; and recognizing implicit assumptions by analyzing metaphors, constructs, concept maps, incidents, life-history intepretations, perceptual lenses, psychic mechanisms, and reasons for beliefs that structure our meaning perspectives.

The ways to identify meaning perspectives and the approaches to transforming them described in this book should not be understood as a set of techniques for use by educators so they may act upon, treat, or direct the actions of their "students" or "clients" when they are seen as objects to be acted upon. Precipitating and fostering critically self-reflective learning means a deliberate effort to foster resistance to just such technicist assumptions, to thoughtlessness, to conformity, to impermeable meaning perspectives, to fear of change, to ethnocentric and class bias, and to egocentric values.

To be an educator in this context means to be an empathic provocateur; it also means to serve as a role model for critical reflection and the ethical idea of caring and to serve as a committed co-learner and occasional guide in the exciting journey of transformative learning. Our tasks as educators are to encourage the multiple readings of "texts," to make a wider range of symbol systems or meaning perspectives available to learners, and to create reflective dialogic communities in which learners are free to challenge assumptions and premises, thereby breaking through the one-dimensionality of uncritically assimilated learning. Our function is to help learners to critically examine the sources and consequences of their own meaning perspectives and the interpretations they have made of their own lives. We must develop skill and sensitivity in the role of "teacher as stranger" (Greene, 1973), the outsider who helps learners to question why things must be as presented by others and to learn about the sources of these assumptions and their consequences in the lives of those whom they affect.

Ethical Issues

Educators are understandably concerned with the ethical implications of efforts to assist learners in challenging and transforming their meaning perspectives, especially when collective social action is a logical outcome. Here the risk of indoctrination becomes apparent. There is an obvious dilemma in that even the "neutral" educator, who deliberately avoids the potential for controversy inherent in alternative perspectives, is taking a stand that favors maintenance of the status quo. Moreover, the essence of adult education consists of helping adults construe experience in a way in which they will more clearly understand the reasons for their problems and the options open to them, so that they may assume responsibility for decision making.

Perhaps the most significant kind of adult learning involves bringing psychocultural assumptions into critical consciousness to help learners understand how they have come into possession of conceptual categories, rules, tactics, and criteria for judging that are implicit in their habits of perception, thought, and behavior. Such transformative learning enhances our crucial sense of agency over ourselves and our lives.

Emancipatory education, which helps learners become aware and critical of the presuppositions that shape their beliefs, is not the same thing as prescribing a preferred action to be taken. Nor does the transformed meaning perspective itself prescribe the action to be taken; instead, it presents a set of rules, tactics, and criteria for judging. The decision to act upon a new perspective is an essential part of the transformative learning process, but even when this leads to a decision to take collective social action, doing so will depend upon situational factors, the knowledge and skills for taking this kind of action, and the personality variables discussed earlier.

Education becomes indoctrination only when educators try to influence specific actions as extensions of their will, or perhaps when they blindly help learners to blindly follow the dictates of an unexamined set of culturally assimilated assumptions that determine how learners perceive, think, and feel about themselves, their relationships, and their world. To show learners a new set of rules, tactics, and criteria that allows them to judge situations in which they must act is significantly different from trying to engineer learner consent to take the action favored by the educator.

This argument does not mean to imply that educators are value free. It is only natural to assume that educators' own meaning perspectives will be included among the alternative perspectives opened up for learners. But no educators who take themselves seriously as educators would permit their own perspectives to be either the only ones made available to learners or would attempt to "sell" their own beliefs or to consciously foster dependency upon themselves. Adults, at least in our own culture, are apt to be educated to think for themselves. The educator can be influential, but the adult learner is often quite appropriately skeptical of authority and able to differentiate between education and efforts to indoctrinate.

Even educators working in collective social action, like Heaney and Horton, limit their role to fostering critical awareness; to helping learners understand the dynamics of their dependency upon an oppressive system; to helping them discover action options and to anticipate their consequences, drawing upon prior experience by others in taking action; to helping learners develop the ability to take collective action; to helping them learn how to interpret the feedback on their own efforts; to helping them learn how to deal with adversity or setbacks; and to helping them learn direct-action tactics for dealing with the system.

The social action educator *never* "takes charge" or becomes a formal leader or spokesperson for learners. The educator's function is to foster leadership and effective participation in others, not to usurp the leadership role. Of course, social action educators would not choose to assist groups with whom they did not feel a strong sense of solidarity. Other emancipatory educators do not have this option. Like all other educators, social action educators succeed to the degree that they become less and less necessary to the self-directed learning process. Social action educators in Scandinavia and England inspired pioneers in the United States who established adult education as a professional field. Today it is a seriously neglected but highly respected field of practice among professional adult educators.

Other Themes and Issues

Adult educators have differing views on whether individual or social transformations are the ultimate goals of adult education. What emerges as common ground is that we must begin with individual perspective transformations before social transformations can succeed. It is also clear that the individual perspective transformation process includes taking action, which often means some form of social action — which in turn can sometimes mean collective political action. Few adult educators may be able to follow up every learner's experience with collective political action. Those who can, do make such commitments to groups of learners with whom they have feelings of solidarity.

A related question pertains to whether an adult educator should be understood as a professional or nonprofessional role. References made above to professionalism in adult education refer to a higher order of understanding, skills, and competence pertaining to fostering transformative learning, as distinct from the implied exclusivity of a specialized education, degrees, credentials, or peer responsibility for quality assurance. However, adult educators do share two things: a distinctive meaning perspective in which the importance of learner-centeredness, critical discourse, and self-directedness are central theoretical assumptions; and a body of knowledge and skills pertaining to facilitating adult learning in individuals, groups, and communities. There is also a clear trend toward practitioners learning these things in the context of graduate programs in adult education.

Among the contributors to this book, other common themes are found. One is a recognition that adult learning takes place in both a social context and in the context of a meaning perspective. One's personal, private, subjective outlook is a function of social learning, for the most part culturally assimilated in the process of socialization. A perspective is transformed by the resolution of a dilemma through exposure to alternative perspectives and participation in critical discourse with others to verify one's new reality. Transformative learning is not a private affair involving information processing; it is interactive and intersubjective from start to finish.

This book suggests several specific procedures for obtaining information about one's meaning perspectives. The approaches to mapping and to effecting changes in perspectives are amenable for use in classrooms, workshops, counseling settings, schools and colleges, workplaces, unions, social service agencies, civic and religious organizations, government, the military, and wherever adult education is to be found.

Which of the approaches are appropriate and the proper order in which they may be used in combination will depend on situational constraints, such as the time available, levels of learner expectation and readiness, the nature and scope of the educational encounter, already-recognized dilemmas, and the homogeniety of the learners. Different learners may be at different points in the process of transformative learning and will require different kinds of educational interventions.

Another theme concerns the timing and nature of intervention by educators in the process of transformative learning. When learners are going through the transformative learning process, they often do so without fully recognizing that they are engaged in such a process. Their equilibrium has been upset by the advent of a dilemma, and they are in a state of readiness to learn anything that will ease their distress. They are looking for help, and the help that educators give may include assisting them to learn more about their own meaning perspectives and alternative meaning perspectives for interpreting their situation; providing emotional support for such an inquiry; giving information about alternatives, such as other careers or life-styles or ways to take social action; or giving the emotional support for taking such action. Here the role of the educator in meeting expressed learner needs is self-evident.

The adult educator actively *precipitates* transformative learning when, in the process of helping learners address their expressed needs, he or she seeks to move the learners' interest beyond their articulated needs to understanding the reasons for them and the way that psychocultural forces have shaped the learners' interpretation of the worlds of others, and of themselves. Here, the role of the educator calls for a higher degree of creative effort, to conceptualize ways of drawing learners into critical self-reflection about their own ideas and assumptions. As this process of transformative learning begins, its initiative and control reside in the learner; increasingly, the role of the educator is to provide a sounding board for testing new learner realities.

Individuals who encounter dilemmas that force them to challenge established ways of seeing and thinking and are able to move developmentally toward more inclusive, discriminating, and integrative meaning perspectives may do so as self-directed learners. Although they may need some help in the course of this developmental process, other learners have not begun to feel the need for transformative development. For these learners, the resources in Parts One and Two of this book should be especially relevant in helping them to recognize their own unexamined presuppositions. Part Three can provide additional techniques for examining the various dimensions of how one's meaning perspective affects the way one sees, thinks, or feels. In this book, we show the educator how he or she can, through Socratic questioning, help learners come face to face with contradictions in the way they deal with their reality, which reveals the necessity of critically analyzing presuppositions through study of critical incidents, personal ideologies, habits of expectation, life histories, journal writing, literature, or through Gould's therapeutic learning program (TLP). The ideas, approaches, and techniques suggested here may be used to design whole programs; to develop a course, unit, or module devoted to perspective assessment in a more comprehensive educational program; or to help individuals in a counseling setting deal with existential dilemmas.

The Adult Education Guided Independent Study (AEGIS) at Teachers College, Columbia University, is an example of an entire doctoral program in adult education in which fostering self-directed critical reflection by participants of themselves as learners or educators has been made a central focus. Courses by Marsick, Brookfield, Greene, Kennedy, this writer, and others elaborate on the approaches described in this book. Participants in the program take a course in life histories, introduced by Marsick, and have access to Gould's TLP as well, individually or in small groups. This writer introduces new participants to the concept of critical reflection by demonstrating how assumptions behind a published statement detailing principles of continuing education may be analyzed. Participants then analyze a case study of a training program, identify the assumptions implicit in their criteria for making these judgments, and, through critical discourse, assess the validity of these assumptions as a collective statement of their beliefs about adult education.

In adult education, the educator sets democratic norms to govern critical discourse and fosters participation in dialogue. He or she does not simply act as a passive "facilitator" of learning but as an empathic provocateur, gently creating dilemmas by encouraging learners to face up to contradictions between what they believe and what they do, disjunctures between espoused theory and actual practice, and discrepancies between a specific way of seeing, thinking, feeling, and acting and other perspectives that may prove more inclusive, differentiating, and integrative of experience.

The Emancipatory Educator

In this section, I would like to review the experience of a few other educators who have attempted to facilitate emancipatory education, that is, to encourage critical reflection in order to precipitate or facilitate transformative learning by adults.

Boud, Keogh, and Walker (1985) have suggested that reflective learning has three stages. First is return to the experience to recapture as much detail as possible. They have found it helpful for learners to share this in writing or with others. The educator's role in this stage is to prompt the learner to describe as objectively as possible what has happened without interpreting or analyzing. The second stage is to attend to feelings attached to the experience and to review them. Again, these are frequently written and shared. The third stage is to reevaluate the experience. This often parallels the first two stages. Components include association, integration, validation, and appropriation. *Association* refers to connecting the ideas and feelings about the original experience and those that occurred during reflection with existing knowledge and attitudes. Free association, brainstorming, and other techniques by which the group collects ideas without evaluating them are useful. *Integration* involves an examination of the meaning and utility of the associations by grouping them, drawing simple maps of linkages, and relating the ideas of others. *Validation* involves examing ideas and feelings that are in process of being between new appreciations and existing knowledge and beliefs. It can also involve integrating these and parallel data from others or trying out new perceptions in new situations. Role play may be most useful here. *Appropriation* refers to making the new knowledge a part of how we act and feel.

Shor and Freire (1987) describe a "dialogic method of teaching" for fostering critical reflection and transformation in classroom settings. The educational experience begins with an identification of the learners' real-life problems as they define them in their own idiom. The educator helps them place these and the subject matter of the course in a historical and cultural context through an examination of how social norms and cultural codes affect learners' perception and judgment. For Shor and Freire, transformation means social transformation and the transformation of sociocultural perspectives. I have suggested in Chapter One that learning may include epistemic and psychic transformations as well.

The dialogic method approximates the ideal conditions

of critical discourse of free, full participation by all. The situa-tion separates learners from their assumptions. The classroom or counselor's consulting room is a reality separate in time and space from other dimensions of knowing. It allows adults a tem-porary respite from the pressures of action and convention to experiment with reflection on all aspects of their lives. The time involved has been allocated to new ways of thinking: The learner and educator have a contract to help the learner become a bet-ter learner. The learner's expectations are a crucially impor-tant condition for an effective educational or therapeutic intervention. With careful attention to fostering a supportive and democratic social climate, the classroom can become the place to experiment with long-held values and beliefs without penalty or humiliation for exposing one's ignorance or taking risks and making mistakes. This separation from mass culture is highly desirable for fostering transformative change. Of course, its implementation means an often stressful return engagement with the outside world. Even groups involved in collective social action need time to regroup, assess action efforts, and reinforce their commitments.

The educator may know more than the learners about the subject of instruction at the outset, but he or she relearns what is known in the context of the learners' efforts to interpret these insights in terms of their own lives. This is what adult educators mean when they write of collaborative learning.

Shor and Freire suggest that educators must begin by building confidence in the learner and being sensitive to estab-lished meaning perspectives. As collaborative learners, educators communicate that they respect what students know and look for ways to enable them to show what they know: "I must be clear that I need to reknow what I think I know, to the extent that the educatees know with me and among themselves. I have also to be clear that the starting point for them to experience some knowable object which I propose cannot be my understand-ing of the object and the reality" (Shor and Freire, 1987, p. 180).

The educator actively seeks to know learners' expectations and aspirations to enable the educator to understand learners' levels of perception, their language, and the difficulties they may have understanding the academic language or the nature of instruction. For Shor and Freire, the educator must be critical of how society works to be able to understand the social functions that education fulfills. He or she must reinvent the abstract academic idiom to permit easy communication with the uninitiated. The authors urge the reading of texts with different perspectives from the learners' as another way of assisting them to "read the world." The teacher's function is to diminish the distance between the learner reading words and the learner reading the world (Shor and Freire, 1987, p. 182).

"Transsituational learning" is identified by Cell (1984) as any change in our ability to interpret a situation. Its most important form is "the development of our capacity to examine an interpretation — especially one of our own — and to develop alternatives to it" (p. 204). The key to transsituational learning is contrast. "The more we learn to think in terms of contrasts, to direct our attention to them as they occur and to generate them for ourselves, the more creative we can be in working with the meaning of a situation" (p. 204). Cell identifies the skills involved in transsituational learning as including evaluation (developing new criteria for assessing situations) and divergence (developing new perspectives on a situation) and the ability to find alternatives in a given situation — new ways of seeing, new questions to ask, new ways to use things. "When we search for the meaning of an event rather than reacting concretely to the event itself, when we treat a problem-statement as if it were a symptom rather than a basic ill, when we inquire into the meaning of our differences with someone else, we use these thought processes" (Samuel Culbert, quoted in Cell, p. 204).

Opening ourselves up to the ideas of others, especially when these provide a new angle of vision, can improve skill in divergence. Talking or reading about viewpoints in other academic disciplines or fields of activity can generate contrasting ideas as can contact with another culture. Any contrasting idea can result in what Cell refers to as a "productive tension" with the original idea. Practice in taking the perspective of the Other can enhance the skill of divergence significantly. Cell refers to the development of these skills as *transcendent learning,* learning through which we change the concepts we use to interpret a situation. Transcendent learning is learning through critical reflection.

The theories we have for designing our interaction with one another are referred to as theories of action by Argyris and Schön (Schön, 1987). These include the values, strategies, and underlying assumptions that inform our patterns of interpersonal relationships. Theories of action may operate as *espoused theories,* which are used to explain or justify behavior, or as tacit *theories-in-use,* which are implicit in our patterns of spontaneous interaction with others. Theories-in-use are similar to introjected meaning perspectives; espoused theories are similar to reflective meaning perspectives. Theories-in-use are often incongruent with the theories of espoused action.

Argyris and Schön have developed their theory in the context of professional development, especially of managers at Harvard and the Massachusetts Institute of Technology. They have developed two models of theories-in-use. Model I reflects the following values: "Achieve the objective as I see it," "Strive to win and avoid losing," "Avoid negative feelings," and "Be rational (stay cool)." Strategies include unilateral control of the task environment and of protection of self and others. This meaning perspective sees interpersonal relations as a win-lose game. It is a closed and defensive orientation. Learning tends to be "single loop," that is, instrumental learning about strategies or tactics for achieving one's own objectives. There is little, if any, critically reflective, "double loop" learning about the values and assumptions that generate one's own or another's behavior.

The governing variables of Model II are valid information, internal commitment, and free and informed choice. "Model II aims at creating a behavioral work situation in which people can exchange valid information, even about sensitive matters, subject private dilemmas to shared inquiry, and make public tests of negative attributions that Model I keeps private and undiscussable" (p. 259). A Model II behavioral world makes room for double-loop learning.

For their graduate students, Argyris and Schön have developed a series of seminars designed to foster Model II skills.

These "reflective practica" involve a series of case studies through which learners inquire into the nature of interpersonal theories-in-use, factors that facilitate and impede movement from Model I to Model II and the kinds of help most useful in making this transformation. Students are asked to describe the meaning of the situation, the strategy they devised to deal with it, and what they would actually say or do. Argyris and Schön call this method "decomposition." By applying their analyses of the case studies, through role-playing interventions of their own, and through issues raised in subsequent discussion, students are made to understand that often the way they interpret the situation (Model I tactics) would itself further contribute to the problem they have identified. This was so despite the fact that they understood both theories at the outset and had agreed with the Model II theory. Although they were able to detect and reject Model I features in their colleagues' responses, they found it less easy to identify such responses to their own difficult interpersonal relationships. Argyris and Schön (p. 264) have devised the following Model II heuristics:

- Couple advocacy of your position with inquiry into the other's beliefs.
- State the attribution you are making, tell how you got to it, and ask for the others' confirmation or disconfirmation.
- If you experience a dilemma, express it publicly.

Argyris and Schön recognize that interventions predicated upon Model II involve an artistry that is not part of the model itself; thus, they can relearn what they know in the context of each student attempting to learn how to use what has been learned. This collaborative learning is a leitmotiv of an emancipatory education which would foster transformative learning. Argyris and Schön provided the conceptual models, criticized student interpretations, and demonstrated the sort of behavior they and their students would like to produce.

The educator does not follow a fixed program but brings a repertoire of ways of framing and responding to situations that arise as a result of student interventions. Schön writes, "Having access to a repertoire, rather than a program, allowed him the freedom to listen to the client's back talk and to construct new strategies in response to the meanings he found in the client's utterances" (p. 271).

To help students learn about the internalized inhibitions that kept them from moving to a Model II orientation, the educators had the students write and share papers about the fears and difficulties they experienced when they tried to function in the Model II mode. In another approach, the students designed their own learning experiments, focusing on the particular Model II skills with which they were having trouble and writing a report on their experiments. Each student read his or her paper to the class, who then identified common patterns.

The educators also played out a dialogue reflecting a Model II orientation and converted it to a script. A pair of students would read the script and act it out in their own words. The class would then reflect on this experience and construct a schema of the dialogue, which could be supplemented and adapted to other role-playing situations. Argyris and Schön found it useful to differentiate reflection on discovery, invention, and production to help students manage the complexities of analysis. Until late in the process, reflection on group process was limited to situations in which the group climate seemed to them to have become a critical impediment to learning (p. 292). The educators tried to be explicit about their reasoning behind their experimental approaches and to encourage their students to actively participate as both designers and subjects in their experimentation.

The educators identified three approaches to coaching. The first, joint experimentation, helps the student to formulate the qualities he or she wants to achieve and by demonstration or description to explore ways to produce them. This is the process of collaborative inquiry. The coach may generate a variety of solutions to the problem being addressed, leaving the student free to choose and produce new possibilities in action.

A second approach to coaching is what the educators call "Follow me!" In this approach the coach improvises a whole performance within which there are identifiable units of reflection-in-action. The relations between a whole performance and its parts become central to the students' learning by mimicry.

The third approach to coaching is called "the hall of mirrors," in which the coach and the student continually shift perspective. "They see their interaction at one moment as a reenactment of some aspect of the student's practice; at another, as a dialogue about it; and, at still another, as a modeling to its design" (p. 297). The coach must be forthcoming about his own failures and misgivings.

This hall-of-mirrors approach is appropriate when coaching resembles the interpersonal practice to be learned, when there is a re-creation by students of patterns of practice in interaction with the coach and each other, or when the mode of inquiry established in the learning experience resembles the mode of inquiry the students want to exemplify in practice. In the Argyris and Schön practica, both the coach and the student act as researchers inquiring into their own and the other's changing understandings. There is a premium placed upon making ideas explicit to someone else. "When inquiry into learning remains private, it is also likely to remain tacit. Free of the need to make our ideas explicit to someone else, we are less likely to make them explicit to ourselves" (p. 300). Another book by Schön, *The Reflective Practitioner* (1983), is an invaluable resource to any educator concerned with understanding or fostering reflective thought in the context of professional development.

Brookfield (1987) describes other effective strategies for facilitating critical thinking. Educators can create a supportive social climate; listen attentively to verbal and nonverbal cues so as to be able to frame critical questions in terms learners understand; sensitively balance the provision of unqualified support with a challenge to old modes of thinking; mirror the learners' attitudes, rationalizations, and habitual ways of thinking and acting to enable them to see themselves from a different perspective; encourage learners to believe that the realization of emancipatory ideas is possible and to act upon these ideas based on a realistic assessment of risk; provide opportunity for reflective evaluation or taking stock of the process of critical thinking; help learners form networks and support groups of fellow learners; and help learners become aware of their preferred learning styles.

Brookfield synthesizes the roles of the teacher of critical thinking proposed in the literature, placing emphasis on assumptions, focusing upon learners' perceptions of their own experiences, encouraging group analysis of relevant issues, and presenting alternative meaning perspectives. "Teachers function sometimes as catalysts of discussion and inquiry, sometimes as contributory group members. They perform such diverse roles as being advocates for missing perspectives, adversaries to propaganda, recorders of sessions, mediators of divisive tendencies and resource persons" (p. 80).

Critical questioning — questioning designed to elicit assumptions rather than to elicit information — involves a set of facilitator skills that usually requires training. One must be able to frame evocative questions that are readily understood by learners, that explore highly personal matters with sensitivity, and that raise intimidating issues in a nonthreatening way. These are skills more familiar to therapists and ethnographic and other qualitative researchers than to adult educators. Brookfield's guidelines include *be specific* (avoid general questions, focus on specific events or particular people, ask about qualities needed for specific roles and accomplishments, and ask how the learner knows he or she has done well); *work from the particular to the general* (ground responses addressing general themes in a specific activity or occurrence); and *be conversational* (avoid appearing to follow a standard, formal, and therefore threatening, interview protocol) (pp. 93-97).

In addition to critical incident exercises as described in this book in Chapter Nine for helping others examine their assumptions, Brookfield recommends criteria analysis (analysis of one's standards for attributing worth and merit), role play and critical debate (defending a position you oppose), and crisis decision simulations (deciding among distasteful choices, such as Whom do you save from drowning, a mother or her infant, if only one can be saved?). Techniques for imagining alternatives include brainstorming, envisioning alternative futures, developing preferred scenarios, inventing futures, and esthetic triggers (poetry, fantasy, art, songwriting, drama).

Closing Note

As adult educators, we are committed to encourage the opening of public spheres of discourse and to actively oppose social and cultural constraints that impede free, full participation in discursive learning. Such constraints include impediments to freedom, equality, justice, democratic participation, civil and human rights, education, health, safety, shelter, and rewarding employment. A society in which free, full participation in discursive learning is assured every adult learner is an educator's guiding, utopian social vision. Learners and educators become justifiably radicalized when societies preclude the redress of grievances, enforce unjust laws, or become oppressive in response to efforts to make institutions more responsive to the fundamental needs of learners.

While it is appropriate and important for educators to attempt to infer a philosophical orientation of how things should be from a theory that describes the nature of learning, the two should not be confused. Learning is not a desirable outcome or a goal; it is the activity of making an interpretation that subsequently guides decision and action. Learning is grounded in the very nature of human communication. Becoming reflective of the content, process, and especially the premises of one's prior learning is central to cognition for survival in modern societies. It is the way we control our experiences rather than be controlled by them, and it is an indispensable prerequisite to individual, group, and collective transformations, both perspective and social. Especially in modern societies where authority is relative and adults increasingly tend to transform themselves through critical self-reflection, educators seek ways to understand and enhance this vital, natural learning function.

References

Argyris, C., Putnam, R., and Smith, D. M. *Action Science: Concepts, Methods, and Skills for Research and Intervention.* San Francisco: Jossey-Bass, 1985.

Boud, D., and Griffin, V. (eds.). *Appreciating Adults Learning: From the Learners' Perspective.* London: Kogan Page, 1987.

Boud, D., Keogh, R., and Walker, D. (eds.). *Reflection: Turning Experience into Learning.* London: Kogan Page, 1985.

Bowers, C. A. *The Promise of Theory: Education and the Politics of Cultural Change.* New York: Longman, Green, 1984.

Brookfield, S. D. *Developing Critical Thinkers: Challenging Adults to Explore Alternative Ways of Thinking and Acting.* San Francisco: Jossey-Bass, 1987.

Cell, E. *Learning to Learn from Experience.* Albany: State University of New York Press, 1984.

Greene, M. *The Teacher as Stranger.* Belmont, Calif.: Wadsworth, 1973.

Habermas, J. *The Theory of Communicative Action.* Vol. 1: *Lifeworld and System: A Critique of Functionalist Reason.* (T. McCarthy, trans.) Boston: Beacon Press, 1978.

Pedler, M. (ed.). *Action Learning in Practice.* Aldershot, England: Gower, 1985.

Schön, D. A. *The Reflective Practitioner: How Professionals Think in Action.* New York: Basic Books, 1983.

Schön, D. A. *Educating the Reflective Practitioner: Toward a New Design for Teaching and Learning in the Professions.* San Francisco: Jossey-Bass, 1987.

Shor, I., and Freire, P. *A Pedagogy for Liberation: Dialogues on Transforming Education.* South Hadley, Mass.: Bergin & Garvey, 1987.

Name Index

Subject Index

Lightning Source UK Ltd.
Milton Keynes UK
UKOW06n1336100615

253269UK00002B/39/P